D0124312

THE THEATRE AT EPIDAURUS

Showing seats, orchestra, and rear building and a plan of the theatre

TEN GREEK PLAYS

TRANSLATED INTO ENGLISH BY

GILBERT MURRAY
AND OTHERS

With an Introduction by
LANE COOPER

And a Preface by
H. B. DENSMORE

NEW YORK
OXFORD UNIVERSITY PRESS
1929

CONTENTS

PREFACE

A brief survey of the tendencies of thought in higher education today reveals that there is a growing interest in the ancient world, its civilization and its literature, and a realization that modern civilization must inevitably turn back to the culture of the Greeks for its study of man as the measure of the universe. There may be fewer in these days who have the training or the inclination to read Sophocles in the orginal, but there are increasingly large numbers of students eager to read the masterpieces of Greek literature in translation, and who bring to the study of the New Hellenism the intellectual independence and scientific openmindedness of contemporary thinking.

It is fortunate, therefore, that Greek literature has been translated more adequately and more sympathetically than any of the other literatures, except the Bible, that have come to form a part of our cultural tradition. And if it has been fortunate in its translators, it has been equally blessed in its critics. Much of the finest scholarship of modern times has been spent in furnishing us with interpretative materials, throwing light and ever fresh light upon every phase of Greek thought, stating, restating, exemplifying, comparing, enforcing, amplifying all the values that challenge, sometimes destructively but always helpfully, the standards of our own civilization.

To furnish student and general reader with outstanding translations of some of the finest pieces of Greek literature, and to give ready access to the results of the finest classical scholarship, this volume of dramas is presented.

HARVEY BRUCE DENSMORE.

University of Washington

INTRODUCTION

THE air is pure and cool; it is a sunbright morning near the end of March, at Athens, and the year, let us say, 429 B. C. Three days ago began the great annual feast of the City Dionysia, most impressive of the festivals of Bacchus; an ancient image of the god, patron of the tragic and comic drama, was taken from his shrine, escorted in a grand and colorful procession to a grove in the country, and, after a day of feasting and merriment for young and old, brought back by torch-light to Athens to be set up in the orchestra of his theatre, there to witness the dithyrambic choral contests which ended yesterday, and the dramatic contests of to-day, to-morrow, and the day thereafter. Over one hundred years ago (535 B. C.) Thespis took part in the earliest competition of tragic poets that was authorized by the State. Seventy years ago (499) Aeschylus began competing; fifty-five years ago (484), at the age of forty-nine, he first won the coveted prize, an honor that fell to him thirteen times, all told, before he died. In 484 Sophocles was thirteen years old, Euripides an infant of one year; when he was a child of four, the Greeks overthrew the Persians in the sea-fight at Salamis. Thirty-nine years ago (468) Aeschylus lost the prize to Sophocles, who then began to compete. Ten years later (458) Aeschylus, on his last appearance, won with the Orestean trilogy; he died in 456, the year before Euripides first had plays accepted for presentation. In the year 429, therefore, Euripides and Sophocles have been rival tragic poets for a quarter of a century. They will be rivals for a quarter of a century more with the watchful eye of Aristophanes upon them; we may suppose that he is in the audience to-day, a stripling sixteen years of age. Sophocles is now sixty-eight years old, still at the height of his powers; and this morning we may imagine that among the four plays he will present will be *Oedipus the King*. As a rule, on each of three successive mornings there are a satyr-drama and three tragedies; on the first two afternoons corresponding there will be two comedies, on the third, but one. In the days of Aeschylus, a group of three plays, a trilogy, might deal with phases of the same tragic story, and if the fourth play, the satyr-drama which then followed, dealt with that theme in a humorous way, we should have a tetralogy proper. Sophocles does not thus link his plays together; at times, following ancient custom, he does act in them, though taking but some minor part. In the dramatic competitions, then, three tragic poets have been, and are, engaged, as authors, trainers, and actors; and, similarly, five comic poets, each presenting one comedy. This will not, we predict, be one of the twenty occasions on which Sophocles is victor in tragedy, for the group of plays including *Oedipus the King* will be adjudged second to the group exhibited by Philocles, nephew of Aeschylus. Two years ago the *Medea* of Euripides fared even worse. There may be five judges for tragedy, as there are five for comedy; the selection of them is an elaborate affair, partly by lot.

Open to the sky, the great theatre of Dionysus lies in his precinct and near his shrine, on the southern slope of the Acropolis, below the Parthenon. The wooden seats, arranged as a vast amphitheatre, will accommodate thousands of spectators, or a good share of the voting population of the city, with a number of boys, probably some women, some of the better-educated slaves, and many of the visitors who throng to Athens at this season. At the winter festival of the Lenaea, when the seas are inclement, fewer alien faces would be seen, and a comic poet would feel freer than he will to-day to ridicule the foibles of the city. The audience is brilliant and lively, and critical; it will audibly reveal its pleasure or displeasure in the action or the actors. It is equally sensitive to false cadence and to expressions of impiety, and is suspicious of improbabilities in the sequence of incident. Though capable of misjudging a play, and of attributing to an author the sentiment he utters as an actor in the imagined scene, it is the most intelligent audience a poet could hope for; or it will be such after Aristophanes and his fellows have shown on the comic stage what is out of proportion in Greek tragedy. For three generations this audience has been tutored by Aeschylus, Sophocles, Euripides, and their rivals. Many of the spectators have sung in a dithyrambic contest; many, in fact, have been members of a dramatic chorus, so that some actually have been trained by Aeschylus and Sophocles in the recitation and music of their plays. The influence of music and the drama has permeated the domestic and communal life of Athens.

Far beneath the topmost row of seats lies the orchestra, a circle 88 feet in diameter, where the actors and chorus jointly perform the play. Nearest to this circle, and to the statue of Dionysus, is the seat of his priest; in neighboring seats are the judges, other civic worthies, and notable visitors from other city-states. In the middle of the orchestra is an altar; at the rear, a long, low, wooden structure which serves for background, for entrance and exit, and for other ends of stage-presentation.

A Greek tragedy or comedy, we perceive, is in the nature of a civic religious rite, celebrated in a building that is devoted to a god. True, if the impulse from Dionysiac worship was strong in the beginnings of the drama, the natural human impulse to imitate was stronger in the end. Yet the choral Attic drama seems never wholly to have lost its original character; herein, therefore, it differs from the modern secular drama, which soon enough forgot its mediaeval origins in the Mass, in the service for Easter. Aeschylus took tragedy from the market-place to the precinct and theatre of Dionysus, and comedy later followed thither. The modern drama left the cathedral for the market-place; ultimately, it found abode in a type of building that descended through Rome from the Greek theatre. Greek tragedy took origin, it seems, from the improvising leaders of the early Bacchic dithyramb; it seems that the leader split off from the chorus to become an actor, the protagonist. In the chorus he was replaced by a new leader, who in turn was withdrawn by Aeschylus, and converted into a second actor. In various ways Aeschylus diminished the part taken by the chorus. The dithyrambic chorus was large, later numbering fifty; his dramatic chorus numbered twelve. And he drew plots not only from the tales of Dionysus, the satyrs, and Thebes, but from the entire epic cycle, taking 'slices,' as he said, 'from the great banquet of Homer.' Sophocles added a third to the complement of actors, an innovation that was adopted by Aeschylus, as in his *Agamemnon*, where indeed, for the last episode, one of the chorus may be temporarily a fourth actor; ordinarily three actors could fill a half-dozen or more parts. Sophocles, then, has subtracted a third person from the chorus, but, by a kind of restoration, has increased the tragic chorus from twelve to fifteen members. Moreover, in the time of Aeschylus, he developed scene-painting, and Aeschylus seems to have learned to do something for himself with that, too. Both these masters of a very complex art have taught the age much even about the affair of spectacle and outward presentation. Sophocles' weak voice will not let him take a leading part, as did Aeschylus at first, in his own plays; but, like Shakespeare and Molière of later days, he is his own stage-manager. He has trained his chorus and actors, and, with the help of a costumer, attended to their garb, masks, padding, and foot-wear. In the great theatre, his persons must be of heroic mould and stature. They have been carefully drilled in declamation, for they must be heard by an immense, and sometimes noisy, audience. Apart, however, from the noise and bustle in the seats, the acoustic function of this outdoor theatre is well-nigh perfect. Careful modulation of spoken words and choral song need not be lost. The note of tragedy is not too often strident; more often its voices are tense, its tones are dreary. When the audience is quiet with pity and fear, a sigh in the orchestra may be heard in the topmost seats.

The meaning of the words will not be concealed by the music, for, in this art, poetry, music, and rhythmical action unite to assist the understanding, as they combine to produce one emotional effect. If the dithyramb proper, as it developed side by side with tragedy, came to be something like a modern oratorio, then tragedy itself, say *Oedipus the King*, has its nearest counterpart in the best modern opera. There is this difference, however, that in Greek tragedy music in the stricter sense was intermittent, being supplied by the chorus and one flutist. The actors spoke most of their lines, yet delivered some others in an intoned chant, and sang the more lyrical passages as solos, or in duets or trios; or, again, they joined with the chorus in a song, for example, of lamentation. Since we know very little about Greek music, we can only infer its beauty in the drama from the verbal and metrical beauty of the choral odes and other songs in the extant works of the tragic poets and Aristophanes; these dramatists were, in truth, the greatest of the ancient lyrical poets. And we can but partly conceive the effect of a play in which the chorus was a group of finished dancers. Their statuesque poses and measured evolutions had the greatest share in producing the whole amazing spectacle of an Attic drama. The orchestra, or place of dancing, was the centre of the entire wheel.

The dramatist, then, had to be poet, musician, and expert in pantomimic dancing as well, a Molière and a Mozart in one. Sophocles was all these things, and more; we have seen that he was also a painter. He and Aeschylus were the chief developers of this inclusive poetic art from a choral dance into a form more comprehensive than is drama or opera in our modern sense; in modern opera the poetic art is feeble. And in modern times this art receives virtually no support from the State. In the age of Pericles all the arts received public encouragement. Painting, sculpture, architecture, music, flourished with all the rest, but drama above all others. The efforts of the poets were directly favored by the government, and by wealthy citizens. In particular, the cost of staging the play, and of supplying and training the chorus, was borne by a private citizen who, unless he volunteered for the service, was chosen by lot, and obliged to serve as 'choregus.' Perhaps the choregus for *Oedipus the King* was unwilling, and a niggard, and the group of plays failed through his parsimony. The rich choregus Antisthenes, who knew nothing about the arts, was always successful in his contests because he never shirked any expense in the preparations.

A poet is often thought to be a man with a singular gift of diction, with a flow of metaphor, and with a knack of composing in metre. The diction and metres of the Greek drama need not be discussed at length in a volume of translations. Aeschylus, apparently more than any one else, elevated the style of tragedy above the level of the old dithyrambic plays. The language of Sophocles is clearer than his, with no loss of dignity or beauty; witness the ode on mankind sung by the Theban Elders in *Antigone*. The diction of Euripides is closer to the language of conversation. But perhaps most natural and beautiful of all is the utterance, clear and bright, of Aristophanes, when he is not distorting his medium for comic ends; he was also the most versatile metrist of antiquity.

But a poet is more than an adept in figures of speech and metrical composition. In a drama, from beginning to end he is framing speeches, which must be suited to the persons of his story, and must fit and promote the march of the action. The Greek dramatists learned much about the art of eloquence and dialogue, and of characterization, from the narrative poems of Homer with their speakers impassioned or subtle. Further, if Aeschylus did not know the Sicilian art of rhetoric at first hand, Sophocles would know it when it came to Athens. As for Athenian eloquence, all four of the great dramatists could have heard Pericles; and all but Aeschylus could have talked with Socrates as a man; all must have known some of the leading Sophists. All seem expert, too, in forensic speaking; Euripides certainly had to defend himself in court, and Sophocles and Aeschylus are said to have done the like. The great trial-scene in the *Eumenides* may have started the tradition about Aeschylus. But of course the dramatic contests themselves fostered the rhetoric of poetry. Actor-managers learned how to weave speeches through declamation, through training their players, and, as did Aeschylus and Sophocles, from each other. Euripides was self-centred, but could deliberately adapt and improve a line from Aeschylus; he was also infected with sophistical rhetoric. It is easy to find fault with him, yet it has always been hard to escape his hold upon our emotions. Aristotle praised his tragic quality, referring, however, not to the speeches, but to the unhappy ending of plays like *Medea*. The same critic thinks extremely well of *Iphigenia in Tauris* for its construction and emotional effect, and withal because the deed of horror is avoided.

It is Euripides rather than Aeschylus who should pass for the type of enthusiastic poet, giving utterance to his own thoughts and emotions. Aeschylus, according to Sophocles, did right as an artist without knowing why; but Aeschylus, after forty years of practice on the stage, is, in *Agamemnon*, for example, more adroit than is Euripides in *Medea*. With Greek reticence, he yet depicts the cold, hard, verbal sparring between unfaithful husband and faithless, murderous wife when they meet after a long separation. In this scene there is an element of that dramatic irony of which Sophocles is thought to be the first and great master, and Euripides master at times. Aeschylus is adroit also in making Clytemnestra a wily deceiver; a difficulty in the play is solved if we interpret her account of the fire-signals as a calculated lie. Euripides is the framer of poignant speeches, and of tragic fantasy; his own personality is not unified, and hence, though it intrudes itself into his plays, it is baffling to study. Sophocles, in devising speeches, as in other points of art, did right, knowing why. Although antiquity found some of his plays to be very inferior, to us his art at its best seems infallible. His heart and head operated in conjunction. The result has the outward finish of sculpture in marble; within, it lives and moves and glows. He seems to have had from nature what Aeschylus must labor for, the plastic ability to enter into one personality after another—an Oedipus, an Ajax, Creon, Antigone—for the ends of artistic representation. Aeschylus gave us men and women of colossal stature. Euripides depicted human nature as it is? So said Sophocles, while affirming that he himself drew men as they should be drawn in tragedy. With acts of will that are distinct and intelligible, the characters of Sophocles are true to type, true to life, and self-consistent; whoever thinks him inferior to Shakespeare in the life-like delineation of personality should read both poets in the original or both in translation. In spite of the flaws which his personages must reveal if there is to be tragedy, we are struck with their nobility and their desire for justice. Antigone appeals to the higher law; Oedipus and Creon speak like statesmen. Low, petty, and ridiculous motives, bare egoism, pure malignity, are banished from the Sophoclean stage; thus the poet hits the mark at which his two great rivals generally aimed, and is typical of his age and race. The debasement of humanity, noticeable in recent American novels and dramas, will not be learned from Attic tragedy or comedy. Of course we have to reckon with comic foible as well as tragic error. But there is nothing painful or corrupting about the ludicrous characters in the *Frogs*; while the errors of Antigone and Oedipus are often to the modern reader concealed by their virtues. Note, however, that Antigone perishes, not because she buries her brother the first time, or even the second; she taunts her uncle who has power of life and death over her, and finally she is a suicide. Meanwhile, if the virtues of Creon are often overlooked, so also is the fact that his errors are tragic. Oedipus, again, is often considered the generous victim of fate. There is not a word about fate in Aristotle's remarks on tragedy, and hardly as much fatalism in Euripides as in Shakespeare. The characters of Aeschylus will and perform acts which they attribute to ancestral curses. It is Roman tragedy, with its modern offspring, that is fatalistic. In Sophocles' work, one should examine, at each point, which moves first, the hero or his fate. Young Oedipus kills an old man, whom he should have revered, in a dispute over the right of way, and thus unknowingly slays his own father. Unpremeditated murder, under provocation, was done in hot blood. Upon this act, which is anterior to the play, more light is thrown by the repeated bursts of anger from Oedipus in the play, and particularly by his violence to old men, of whom this tragedy has a large share.

Out of the choices of the agents grow dramatic actions. Creon decides that his nephew Polynices, dead foe of the State, shall lie unburied; Antigone, self-appointed instrument of the 'higher law,' resolves to bury the corpse of her brother. The situation is the more piteous because the clash of wills is between members of a family; and the results are deeds of horror. Of seven tragedies by Sophocles, four begin with words like, 'Sister, mine own dear sister!' and, 'Son of him who led our hosts at Troy!' In *Agamemnon* the husband with great effrontery brings home as concubine Cassandra, poor fatalist, now in love with him; here is the ultimate exasperation to guilty Clytemnestra, who would justify her slaughter of Agamemnon by dwelling on his part, ten years before, in the death of their child Iphigenia, at Aulis. By keeping the hateful paramour Aegisthus in the background, Aeschylus makes an ugly domestic situation, of four persons, less ugly. Scholars who do not observe these facts of life, idealized, miss the pity of it, and wonder why the dramatist brings in Cassandra at all. Some think that love has small place in Greek tragedy; oddly enough, they mean the wholesome romantic love that belongs to comedy, and forget the tragic love awry in Clytemnestra and Medea.

That the families concerned are of high estate, while a matter of less importance than is inward nobility, was important enough to the democratic Athenian audience. The stories are about ancient houses, the members of which associate with the gods, and have birth, wealth, power, and physical excellences, so that their tragic humiliation is impressive. In general they have imagination and eloquence with which to signify their glory and bewail its loss; how many of the tragic heroes seem like poets who have gone to wreck! The ever happy and fortunate Sophocles had a genius for representing this type of hero, winning prizes with his ruin.

One may divide the stories into those which deal with Dionysus and those which do not. Perhaps the essential first step in Greek tragedy was taken when its themes widened out from Dionysiac associations with goat-like and equine satyrs so as to include all the story of Thebes and the whole body of Greek myth. At an early date, says Aristotle, the tragic poets took any subjects that came to hand. If so, they had an ample range of selection in the richest mythology any race has possessed. Later, he says, they narrowed down to the legends of a few houses. And that is the effect the surviving tragedies have upon us; the themes seem limited. We have seven plays of Aeschylus, out of ninety; seven of Sophocles, out of one hundred and twenty; eighteen or nineteen of Euripides, out of ninety-two. Of these surviving thirty-three plays, sixteen deal with aspects of the Trojan cycle, and six with the story of Thebes. But this preponderance is accidental; the choice of plays from Sophocles, for example, three on Thebes, three from the Trojan cycle, and one about Heracles, was made by grammarians at Alexandria for study in the schools. The fragments and titles of lost plays indicate a wider range than that of Elizabethan and classical French tragedy. There were themes from the other two great centres of Grecian story, the Calydonian Hunt and the tale of the Argonauts. To this last cycle belongs the *Medea* of Euripides. If other poets were as prolific and varied as he and Aeschylus, the tragedies of the great age must have numbered perhaps fifteen hundred or two thousand, drawn from many sources besides the four main ones we have noted. The comedies were not quite equally numerous. The eleven we have from Aristophanes, added to thirty-two tragedies plus Euripides' satyric *Cyclops*, give us forty-four surviving plays in all, or, with the fragments from Sophocles' *Trackers*, another satyr-drama, say forty-five that can be studied in some detail. The ten in this volume will fairly introduce the reader to the rest.

Turning to the comedies here included, we see that they

throw light upon tragedy, which influenced them, and can be studied in that influence. Of primitive comedy we know little. The comic drama had developed far in Sicily before it made much progress at Athens. Here it first received support from the State in the year 486 B. C. The 'Old Comedy' began to flourish about the year 450, reached maturity with Aristophanes, and in his hands was turning into something else when he closed his career. Aristophanes, born about 444, first exhibited, at the Lenaea, in 427; produced the *Frogs* in 405 soon after the death of Sophocles, hardly a year after that of Euripides; and himself died some time after the *Plutus* was exhibited in 388, perhaps after 375. Before he was born, the use of three comic actors had been taken over from tragedy, possibly by Cratinus from Sophocles; and Crates had improved and universalized comic plots. But Aristophanes was the great developer of the Old Comedy, in the *Clouds* (423), *Birds* (414), and *Frogs* (405); his *Women in Council* (392) and *Plutus* (388) set a standard for the Middle Comedy; thereafter, in two plays now lost, or in the last of them, he struck out the type which ultimately matured in the New Comedy of Philemon and Menander. The variety and opulence of Aristophanes, his deep intuitions, and the strange, vivid beauty with which he invests comic ideas, make it difficult to speak of him in brief. Some knowledge of external nature belonged to the Old Comedy in relation to the Dionysiac cult of fertility, but in his amazing knowledge of it Aristophanes doubtless surpassed his rivals. The *Birds* gathers up all the poetry of its subject, and more than we have on birds from Chaucer, Shakespeare, and Wordsworth conjoined. Plays like the *Birds* and the *Frogs*, again, gave rare opportunities for elaborate and fantastic spectacle; an imperfect notion of the feathered Chorus may be had from certain remains of vase-painting. But doubtless what we chiefly now miss in the plays of Aristophanes is the music—in the *Frogs*, the music of both flute and harp. All told, the poet had many means of embellishment, and a genius not only for comic distortion. Moreover, an orderly element in the composition of his dramas atones for any seeming lawlessness in them. The metrical scheme, and the elaboration of parts like the *parabasis* and *agon*, offered special difficulties to the poets of the Old Comedy. These and other difficulties the good sense and good taste of Aristophanes turned to the advantage of his art. He takes credit to himself for diminishing the traditional element of phallic worship in comedy, and for limiting the indecency of the comic dance. In *Plutus*, jokes at the expense of well-known individuals have virtually disappeared. Indeed, in the *Frogs* the poet attacks no one; in a literary comedy he makes two great tragic poets attack each other. His choice of contestants for this *agon* marks his good sense. Even in more improbable situations he has an eye to probability. He laughingly draws attention to what is important and real. Like Molière, once having attained artistic maturity, Aristophanes virtually never makes a mistake in the comic art. His sure skill may be noted in his avoidance of actual pain as a comic motive, and in his way of leading us from familiar circumstance into the world of imagination.

His hold upon reality and his power of imagination make Aristophanes a great political economist and a great literary critic. Ruskin admits a heavy debt in his concepts of poverty and wealth to the *Plutus*; and the other comedies likewise have their subject-matter in the realm of political ideas. It is this, as much as anything else, that distinguishes even the *Plutus* from the later domestic comedy of Greece and Rome. And these political concepts are sound; by skilfully throwing things out of proportion Aristophanes reveals their true proportions. The *Birds* is his comic Utopia, the State as a whole. In the *Frogs* he anticipates a problem of the Platonic Utopia, the function of the poet in the State; this problem he displays in an action that travesties an entire Dionysiac festival.

In the *Persians* (472 B. C.) Aeschylus had celebrated the crushing defeat (480) by the Greeks of their Asiatic foe. The *Frogs* appeared when Athens was exhausted by her last effort in the Peloponnesian war, a few months before her overthrow at Aegospotami; within a year starvation forced the surrender of the city (404), and ended the war. The comedy, however, looks like an expensive one to produce; at all events the poet had an elaborate object to travesty if he was minded at the Lenaea to offer a mock City Dionysia. The parts of the festival are present, adapted to the scheme of a comedy. The wanderer Dionysus becomes the wanderer Heracles for a new harrowing of hell; his labor is to bring back a tragic poet to Athens, for the great age of tragedy has ended. On the way he first has a dithyrambic contest with the Frogs. Then comes the procession, by torch-light, of the initiated, and then the contest of tragic poets, duly closed by an official decision. With unerring intuition Aristophanes anticipates the judgment of all time respecting the three leaders. The *agon* of a comedy, however, is a contest between two opponents; for this he chooses Aeschylus and Euripides. They are extremes in a proportion, where Sophocles doubtless is the golden mean. The comic contrasts between Aeschylus and Euripides betray a profound literary criticism in which Aristophanes is a worthy precursor of Aristotle.

Plutus (388) is (save perhaps the undatable *Rhesus*) the latest extant play of the great Greek drama. In it the difficult features of the Old Comedy are hardly discernible. The structure is simplified, political satire is absent, local allusions are few, and the theme, completely generalized, is intelligible to all. *Plutus* was long the most popular of Aristophanes' works in England. This comedy of Wealth was given when Athens was poor, and depends less than the *Frogs* upon spectacular effect. In time, however, stage and theatre recovered their well-being. In the latter half of the fourth century the old theatre was rebuilt, with Pentelic marble. In this theatre, before an audience of perhaps 17,000 persons, the successors of Euripides and Aristophanes exhibited their tragedies and comedies; in it Aristotle (died 322 B. C.) doubtless studied the emotions of pity and fear, and mirth, in the spectators; and here the comedies of Menander (342-291) and his fellows were presented. Meanwhile theatres of the Attic type had begun to spread; the Romans built the like, even an additional one in Athens; and first and last such buildings have been erected in various parts of the world from the shores of the Black Sea to a sunlit spot in Berkeley, California. They are monuments to the effect of the Attic drama upon the mind of the civilized world.

LANE COOPER

Cornell University

SOPHOCLES
OEDIPUS, KING OF THEBES

※»※«※

TRANSLATED
By
GILBERT MURRAY

CHARACTERS IN THE PLAY

OEDIPUS, *supposed son of Polybus, King of Corinth; now elected King of Thebes.*

JOCASTA, *Queen of Thebes; widow of Laïus, the late King, and now wife to Oedipus.*

CREON, *a Prince of Thebes, brother to Jocasta.*

TIRESIAS, *an old blind seer.*

PRIEST OF ZEUS.

A STRANGER *from Corinth.*

A SHEPHERD *of King Laïus.*

A MESSENGER *from the Palace.*

CHORUS of the Elders of Thebes.

A Crowd of Suppliants, men, women, and children.

ARGUMENT

While Thebes was under the rule of LAïUS and JOCASTA there appeared a strange and monstrous creature, "the riddling Sphinx," "the She-Wolf of the woven song," who in some unexplained way sang riddles of death and slew the people of Thebes. LAïUS went to ask aid of the oracle of Delphi, but was slain mysteriously on the road. Soon afterwards there came to Thebes a young Prince of Corinth, OEDIPUS, who had left his home and was wandering. He faced the Sphinx and read her riddle, whereupon she flung herself from her rock and died. The throne being vacant was offered to OEDIPUS, and with it the hand of the Queen JOCASTA.

Some ten or twelve years afterwards a pestilence has fallen on Thebes. At this point the play begins.

The date of the first production of the play is not known, but was probably about the year 429 B.C.

OEDIPUS, KING OF THEBES

SCENE.—*Before the Palace of* OEDIPUS *at Thebes. A crowd of suppliants of all ages are waiting by the altar in front and on the steps of the Palace; among them the* PRIEST OF ZEUS. *As the Palace door opens and* OEDIPUS *comes out all the suppliants with a cry move towards him in attitudes of prayer, holding out their olive branches, and then become still again as he speaks.*

Oedipus. My children, fruit of Cadmus' ancient tree
New springing, wherefore thus with bended knee
Press ye upon us, laden all with wreaths
And suppliant branches? And the city breathes
Heavy with incense, heavy with dim prayer
And shrieks to affright the Slayer.—Children, care
For this so moves me, I have scorned withal
Message or writing: seeing 'tis I ye call,
'Tis I am come, world-honoured Oedipus.

Old Man, do thou declare—the rest have thus
Their champion—in what mood stand ye so still,
In dread or sure hope? Know ye not, my will
Is yours for aid 'gainst all? Stern were indeed
The heart that felt not for so dire a need.

Priest. O Oedipus, who holdest in thy hand
My city, thou canst see what ages stand
At these thine altars; some whose little wing
Scarce flieth yet, and some with long living
O'erburdened; priests, as I of Zeus am priest,
And chosen youths: and wailing hath not ceased
Of thousands in the market-place, and by
Athena's two-fold temples and the dry
Ash[1] of Ismênus' portent-breathing shore.

For all our ship, thou see'st, is weak and sore
Shaken with storms, and no more lighteneth
Her head above the waves whose trough is death.
She wasteth in the fruitless buds of earth,
In parchèd herds and travail without birth
Of dying women: yea, and midst of it

[3]

A burning and a loathly god hath lit
Sudden, and sweeps our land, this Plague of power;
Till Cadmus' house grows empty, hour by hour,
And Hell's house rich with steam of tears and blood.

   O King, not God indeed nor peer to God
We deem thee, that we kneel before thine hearth,
Children and old men, praying; but of earth
A thing consummate by thy star confessed
Thou walkest and by converse with the blest;
Who came to Thebes so swift, and swept away
The Sphinx's song, the tribute of dismay,
That all were bowed beneath, and made us free.
A stranger, thou, naught knowing more than we,
Nor taught of any man, but by God's breath
Filled, thou didst raise our life. So the world saith;
So we say.

            Therefore now, O Lord and Chief,
We come to thee again; we lay our grief
On thy head, if thou find us not some aid.
Perchance thou hast heard Gods talking in the shade
Of night, or eke some man: to him that knows,
Men say, each chance that falls, each wind that blows
Hath life, when he seeks counsel. Up, O chief
Of men, and lift thy city from its grief;
Face thine own peril! All our land doth hold
Thee still our saviour, for that help of old:
Shall they that tell of thee hereafter tell
"By him was Thebes raised up, and after fell!"
Nay, lift us till we slip no more. Oh, let
That bird of old that made us fortunate
Wing back; be thou our Oedipus again.
And let thy kingdom be a land of men,
Not emptiness. Walls, towers, and ships, they all
Are nothing with no men to keep the wall.

  Oedipus. My poor, poor children! Surely long ago
I have read your trouble. Stricken, well I know,
Ye all are, stricken sore: yet verily
Not one so stricken to the heart as I.
Your grief, it cometh to each man apart
For his own loss, none other's; but this heart

For thee and me and all of us doth weep.
Wherefore it is not to one sunk in sleep
Ye come with waking. Many tears these days
For your sake I have wept, and many ways
Have wandered on the beating wings of thought.
And, finding but one hope, that I have sought
And followed. I have sent Menoikeus' son,
Creon, my own wife's brother, forth alone
To Apollo's House in Delphi, there to ask
What word, what deed of mine, what bitter task,
May save my city.

                    And the lapse of days
Reckoned, I can but marvel what delays
His journey. 'Tis beyond all thought that thus
He comes not, beyond need. But when he does,
Then call me false and traitor, if I flee
Back from whatever task God sheweth me.

Priest. At point of time thou speakest. Mark the cheer
Yonder. Is that not Creon drawing near?

> [*They all crowd to gaze where* CREON *is
> approaching in the distance.*

Oedipus. O Lord Apollo, help! And be the star
That guides him joyous as his seemings are!

Priest. Oh! surely joyous! How else should he bear
That fruited laurel wreathed about his hair?

Oedipus. We soon shall know.—'Tis not too far for one
Clear-voiced.

(*Shouting*) Ho, brother! Prince! Menoikeus' son,
What message from the God?

Creon (*from a distance*). Message of joy!

> [*Enter Creon.*

I tell thee, what is now our worst annoy,
If the right deed be done, shall turn to good.

> [*The crowd, which has been full of excited
> hope, falls to doubt and disappointment.*

Oedipus. Nay, but what is the message? For my blood
Runs neither hot nor cold for words like those.

Creon. Shall I speak now, with all these pressing close,
Or pass within?—To me both ways are fair.

Oedipus. Speak forth to all! The grief that these men bear
Is more than any fear for mine own death.

Creon. I speak then what I heard from God.—Thus saith
Phoebus, our Lord and Seer, in clear command.
An unclean thing there is, hid in our land,
Eating the soil thereof: this ye shall cast
Out, and not foster till all help be past.

Oedipus. How cast it out? What was the evil deed?

Creon. Hunt the men out from Thebes, or make them bleed
Who slew. For blood it is that stirs to-day.

Oedipus. Who was the man they killed? Doth Phoebus say?

Creon. O King, there was of old King Laïus
In Thebes, ere thou didst come to pilot us.

Oedipus. I know: not that I ever saw his face.

Creon. 'Twas he. And Loxias now bids us trace
And smite the unknown workers of his fall.

Oedipus. Where in God's earth are they? Or how withal
Find the blurred trail of such an ancient stain?

Creon. In Thebes, he said.—That which men seek amain
They find. 'Tis things forgotten that go by.

Oedipus. And where did Laïus meet them? Did he die
In Thebes, or in the hills, or some far land?

Creon. To ask God's will in Delphi he had planned
His journey. Started and returned no more.

Oedipus. And came there nothing back? No message, nor
None of his company, that ye might hear?

Creon. They all were slain, save one man; blind with fear
He came, remembering naught—or almost naught.

Oedipus. And what was that? One thing has often brought
Others, could we but catch one little clue.

Creon. 'Twas not one man, 'twas robbers—that he knew—
Who barred the road and slew him: a great band.

Oedipus. Robbers? What robber, save the work was planned
By treason here, would dare a risk so plain?

Creon. So some men thought. But Laïus lay slain,
And none to avenge him in his evil day.

Oedipus. And what strange mischief, when your master lay
Thus fallen, held you back from search and deed?

Creon. The dark-songed Sphinx was here. We had no heed
Of distant sorrows, having death so near.

Oedipus. It falls on me then. I will search and clear
This darkness.—Well hath Phoebus done, and thou
Too, to recall that dead king, even now,
And with you for the right I also stand,
To obey the God and succour this dear land.
Nor is it as for one that touches me
Far off; 'tis for mine own sake I must see
This sin cast out. Whoe'er it was that slew
Laïus, the same wild hand may seek me too:
And caring thus for Laïus, is but care
For mine own blood.—Up! Leave this altar-stair,
Children. Take from it every suppliant bough.
Then call the folk of Thebes. Say, 'tis my vow
To uphold them to the end. So God shall crown
Our greatness, or for ever cast us down.

> [*He goes in to the Palace.*

Priest. My children, rise.—The King most lovingly
Hath promised all we came for. And may He
Who sent this answer, Phoebus, come confessed
Helper to Thebes, and strong to stay the pest.

> [*The suppliants gather up their boughs and
> stand at the side. The chorus of Theban
> elders enter.*

Chorus.

*(They speak of the Oracle which they have not yet
heard, and cry to* APOLLO *by his special cry "I-ê.")*

A Voice, a Voice, that is borne on the Holy Way!
What art thou, O Heavenly One, O Word of the Houses
of Gold?
Thebes is bright with thee, and my heart it leapeth;
yet is it cold,
And my spirit faints as I pray.
I-ê! I-ê!
What task, O Affrighter of Evil, what task shall thy people
essay?
One new as our new-come affliction,
Or an old toil returned with the years?
Unveil thee, thou dread benediction,
Hope's daughter and Fear's.

[7]

(They pray to ATHENA, ARTEMIS, *and* APOLLO.)
Zeus-Child that knowest not death, to thee I pray,
O Pallas; next to thy Sister, who calleth Thebes her own,
Artemis, named of Fair Voices, who sitteth her orbèd throne
    In the throng of the market way:
            And I-ê! I-ê!
Apollo, the Pure, the Far-smiter; O Three that keep evil away,
  If of old for our city's desire,
    When the death-cloud hung close to her brow,
  Ye have banished the wound and the fire,
    Oh! come to us now!

(They tell of the Pestilence.)
Wounds beyond telling; my people sick unto death;
  And where is the counsellor, where is the sword of thought?
And Holy Earth in her increase perisheth:
  The child dies and the mother awaketh not.
          I-ê! I-ê!
We have seen them, one on another, gone as a bird is gone,
  Souls that are flame; yea, higher,
  Swifter they pass than fire,
    To the rocks of the dying Sun.

(They end by a prayer to ATHENA.)
Their city wasteth unnumbered; their children lie
  Where death hath cast them, unpitied, unwept upon.
The altars stand, as in seas of storm a high
  Rock standeth, and wives and mothers grey thereon
        Weep, weep and pray.
Lo, joy-cries to fright the Destroyer; a flash in the dark they
    rise,
  Then die by the sobs overladen.
  Send help, O heaven-born Maiden,
    Let us look on the light of her eyes!

(To ZEUS, *that he drive out the Slayer.)*
  And Ares, the abhorred
  Slayer, who bears no sword,
But shrieking, wrapped in fire, stands over me,
  Make that he turn, yea, fly

      Broken, wind-wasted, high
  Down the vexed hollow of the Vaster Sea;
      Or back to his own Thrace,
      To harbour shelterless.
  Where Night hath spared, he bringeth end by day.
      Him, Him, O thou whose hand
      Beareth the lightning brand,
O Father Zeus, now with thy thunder, slay and slay!

      (*To* APOLLO, ARTEMIS, *and* DIONYSUS.)

      Where is thy gold-strung bow,
       O Wolf-god, where the flow
  Of living shafts unconquered, from all ills
      Our helpers? Where the white
      Spears of thy Sister's light,
  Far-flashing as she walks the wolf-wild hills?
      And thou, O Golden-crown,
      Theban and named our own,
  O Wine-gleam, Voice of Joy, for ever more
    Ringed with thy Maenads white,
      Bacchus, draw near and smite,
Smite with thy glad-eyed flame the God whom Gods abhor.

    [*During the last lines* OEDIPUS *has come
      out from the Palace.*

Oedipus. Thou prayest: but my words if thou wilt hear
And bow thee to their judgement, strength is near
For help, and a great lightening of ill.
Thereof I come to speak, a stranger still
To all this tale, a stranger to the deed:
(Else, save that I were clueless, little need
Had I to cast my net so wide and far:)
Howbeit, I, being now as all ye are,
A Theban, to all Thebans high and low
Do make proclaim: if any here doth know
By what man's hand died Laïus, your King,
Labdacus' son, I charge him that he bring
To me his knowledge. Let him feel no fear
If on a townsman's body he must clear

Our guilt: the man shall suffer no great ill,
But pass from Thebes, and live where else he will.

[No answer.

Is it some alien from an alien shore
Ye know to have done the deed, screen him no more!
Good guerdon waits you now and a King's love
Hereafter.
Ha! If still ye will not move
But, fearing for yourselves or some near friend,
Reject my charge, then hearken to what end
Ye drive me.—If in this place men there be
Who know and speak not, lo, I make decree
That, while in Thebes I bear the diadem,
No man shall greet, no man shall shelter them,
Nor give them water in their thirst, nor share
In sacrifice nor shrift nor dying prayer,
But thrust them from our doors, the thing they hide
Being this land's curse. Thus hath the God replied
This day to me from Delphi, and my sword
I draw thus for the dead and for God's word.

And lastly for the murderer, be it one
Hiding alone or more in unison,
I speak on him this curse: even as his soul
Is foul within him let his days be foul,
And life unfriended grind him till he die.
More: if he ever tread my hearth and I
Know it, be every curse upon my head
That I have spoke this day.
All I have said
I charge ye strictly to fulfil and make
Perfect, for my sake, for Apollo's sake,
And this land's sake, deserted of her fruit
And cast out from her gods. Nay, were all mute
At Delphi, still 'twere strange to leave the thing
Unfollowed, when a true man and a King
Lay murdered. All should search. But I, as now
Our fortunes fall—his crown is on my brow,
His wife lies in my arms, and common fate,
Had but his issue been more fortunate,
Might well have joined our children—since this red

[10]

Chance hath so stamped its heel on Laïus' head,
I am his champion left, and, as I would
For mine own father, choose for ill or good
This quest, to find the man who slew of yore
Labdacus' son, the son of Polydore,
Son of great Cadmus whom Agenor old
Begat, of Thebes first master. And, behold,
For them that aid me not, I pray no root
Nor seed in earth may bear them corn nor fruit,
No wife bear children, but this present curse
Cleave to them close and other woes yet worse.

   Enough: ye other people of the land,
Whose will is one with mine, may Justice stand
Your helper, and all gods for evermore.

                              [*The crowd disperses.*
   Leader. O King, even while thy curse yet hovers o'er
My head, I answer thee. I slew him not,
Nor can I shew the slayer. But, God wot,
If Phoebus sends this charge, let Phoebus read
Its meaning and reveal who did the deed.
   Oedipus. Aye, that were just, if of his grace he would
Reveal it. How shall man compel his God?
   Leader. Second to that, methinks, 'twould help us most . . .
   Oedipus. Though it be third, speak! Nothing should be lost.
   Leader. To our High Seer on earth vision is given
Most like to that High Phoebus hath in heaven.
Ask of Tiresias: he could tell thee true.
   Oedipus. That also have I thought for. Aye, and two
Heralds have sent ere now. 'Twas Creon set
Me on.—I marvel that he comes not yet.
   Leader. Our other clues are weak, old signs and far.
   Oedipus. What signs? I needs must question all that are.
   Leader. Some travellers slew him, the tale used to be.
   Oedipus. The tale, yes: but the witness, where is he?
   Leader. The man hath heard thy curses. If he knows
The taste of fear, he will not long stay close.
   Oedipus. He fear my words, who never feared the deed?
   Leader. Well, there is one shall find him.—See, they lead
Hither our Lord Tiresias, in whose mind
All truth is born, alone of human kind.

[*Enter* TIRESIAS *led by a young disciple. He is an old
blind man in a prophet's robe, dark, unkempt and
sinister in appearance.*

Oedipus. Tiresias, thou whose mind divineth well
All Truth, the spoken and the unspeakable,
The things of heaven and them that walk the earth;
Our city . . . thou canst see, for all thy dearth
Of outward eyes, what clouds are over her.
In which, O gracious Lord, no minister
Of help, no champion, can we find at all
Save thee. For Phoebus—thou hast heard withal
His message—to our envoy hath decreed
One only way of help in this great need:
To find and smite with death or banishing,
Him who smote Laïus, our ancient King.
Oh, grudge us nothing! Question every cry
Of birds, and all roads else of prophecy
Thou knowest. Save our city: save thine own
Greatness: save me; save all that yet doth groan
Under the dead man's wrong! Lo, in thy hand
We lay us. And methinks, no work so grand
Hath man yet compassed, as, with all he can
Of chance or power, to help his fellow man.

Tiresias (to himself). Ah me!
A fearful thing is knowledge, when to know
Helpeth no end. I knew this long ago,
But crushed it dead. Else had I never come.

Oedipus. What means this? Comest thou so deep in gloom?

Tiresias. Let me go back! Thy work shall weigh on thee
The less, if thou consent, and mine on me.

Oedipus. Prophet, this is not lawful; nay, nor kind
To Thebes, who feeds thee, thus to veil thy mind.

Tiresias. 'Tis that I like not thy mind, nor the way
It goeth. Therefore, lest I also stray . . .

[*He moves to go off.* OEDIPUS *bars his road.*

Oedipus. Thou shalt not, knowing, turn and leave us! See,
We all implore thee, all, on bended knee.

Tiresias. Ye have no knowledge. What is mine I hold
For ever dumb, lest what is thine be told.

Oedipus. What wilt thou? Know and speak not? In my need

[12]

Be false to me, and let thy city bleed?

Tiresias. I will not wound myself nor thee. Why seek
To trap and question me? I will not speak.

Oedipus. Thou devil!

[Movement of LEADER to check him.

Nay; the wrath of any stone
Would rise at him. It lies with thee to have done
And speak. Is there no melting in thine eyes!

Tiresias. Naught lies with me! With thee, with thee there lies,
I warrant, what thou ne'er hast seen nor guessed.

Oedipus (*to* LEADER, *who tries to calm him*). How can I hear
such talk?—he maketh jest
Of the land's woe—and keep mine anger dumb?

Tiresias. Howe'er I hold it back, 'twill come, 'twill come.

Oedipus. The more shouldst thou declare it to thy King.

Tiresias. I speak no more. For thee, if passioning
Doth comfort thee, on, passion to thy fill!

[He moves to go.

Oedipus. 'Fore God, I am in wrath; and speak I will,
Nor stint what I see clear. 'Twas thou, 'twas thou,
Didst plan this murder; aye, and, save the blow,
Wrought it.—I know thou art blind; else I could swear
Thou, and thou only, art the murderer.

Tiresias (*returning*). So?—I command thee by thine own
word's power,
To stand accurst, and never from this hour
Speak word to me, nor yet to these who ring
Thy throne. Thou art thyself the unclean thing.

Oedipus. Thou front of brass, to fling out injury
So wild! Dost think to bate me and go free?

Tiresias. I am free. The strong truth is in this heart.

Oedipus. What prompted thee? I swear 'twas not thine art.

Tiresias. 'Twas thou. I spoke not, save for thy command.

Oedipus. Spoke what? What was it? Let me understand.

Tiresias. Dost tempt me? Were my words before not plain!

Oedipus. Scarce thy full meaning. Speak the words again.

Tiresias. Thou seek'st this man of blood: Thyself art he.

Oedipus. 'Twill cost thee dear, twice to have stabbed at me!

Tiresias. Shall I say more, to see thee rage again?

Oedipus. Oh, take thy fill of speech: 'twill all be vain.

[13]

Tiresias. Thou livest with those near to thee in shame
Most deadly, seeing not thyself nor them.

    Oedipus. Thou think'st 'twill help thee, thus to speak and
       speak?

    Tiresias. Surely, until the strength of Truth be weak.

    Oedipus. 'Tis weak to none save thee. Thou hast no part
In truth, thou blind man, blind eyes, ears and heart.

    Tiresias. More blind, more sad thy words of scorn, which
       none
Who hears but shall cast back on thee: soon, soon.

    Oedipus. Thou spawn of Night, not I nor any free
And seeing man would hurt a thing like thee.

    Tiresias. God is enough.—'Tis not my doom to fall
By thee. He knows and shall accomplish all.

    Oedipus (*with a flash of discovery*). Ha! Creon!—Is it his
       or thine, this plot?

    Tiresias. 'Tis thyself hates thee. Creon hates thee not.

    Oedipus. O wealth and majesty, O skill all strife
Surpassing on the fevered roads of life,
What is your heart but bitterness, if now
For this poor crown Thebes bound upon my brow,
A gift, a thing I sought not—for this crown
Creon the stern and true, Creon mine own
Comrade, comes creeping in the dark to ban
And slay me; sending first this magic-man
And schemer, this false beggar-priest, whose eye
Is bright for gold and blind for prophecy.
Speak, thou. When hast thou ever shown thee strong
For aid? The She-Wolf of the woven song
Came, and thy art could find no word, no breath,
To save thy people from her riddling death.
'Twas scarce a secret, that, for common men
To unravel. There was need of Seer-craft then.
And thou hadst none to show. No fowl, no flame,
No God revealed it thee. 'Twas I that came,
Rude Oedipus, unlearned in wizard's lore,
And read her secret, and she spoke no more.
Whom now thou thinkest to hunt out, and stand
Foremost in honour at King Creon's hand.
I think ye will be sorry, thou and he

That shares thy sin-hunt. Thou dost look to me
An old man; else, I swear this day should bring
On thee the death thou plottest for thy King.

 Leader. Lord Oedipus, these be but words of wrath,
All thou hast spoke and all the Prophet hath.
Which skills not. We must join, for ill or well,
In search how best to obey God's oracle.

 Tiresias. King though thou art, thou needs must bear the
   right
Of equal answer. Even in me is might
For thus much, seeing I live no thrall of thine,
But Lord Apollo's; neither do I sign
Where Creon bids me.

          I am blind, and thou
Hast mocked my blindness. Yea, I will speak now.
Eyes hast thou, but thy deeds thou canst not see
Nor where thou art, nor what things dwell with thee.
Whence art thou born? Thou know'st not; and unknown,
On quick and dead, on all that were thine own,
Thou hast wrought hate. For that across thy path
Rising, a mother's and a father's wrath,
Two-handed, shod with fire, from the haunts of men
Shall scourge thee, in thine eyes now light, but then
Darkness. Aye, shriek! What harbour of the sea,
What wild Kithairon shall not cry to thee
In answer, when thou hear'st what bridal song,
What wind among the torches, bore thy strong
Sail to its haven, not of peace but blood.
Yea, ill things multitude on multitude
Thou seest not, which so soon shall lay thee low,
Low as thyself, low as thy children.—Go,
Heap scorn on Creon and my lips withal:
For this I tell thee, never was there fall
Of pride, nor shall be, like to thine this day.

 Oedipus. To brook such words from this thing? Out, I say!
Out to perdition! Aye, and quick, before . . .

          [The LEADER *restrains him.*
Enough then!—Turn and get thee from my door.

 Tiresias. I had not come hadst thou not called me here.

 Oedipus. I knew thee not so dark a fool. I swear

[15]

'Twere long before I called thee, had I known.

Tiresias. Fool, say'st thou? Am I truly such an one?
The two who gave thee birth, they held me wise.

Oedipus. Birth? . . . Stop! Who were they?[2] Speak thy
prophecies.

Tiresias. This day shall give thee birth and blot thee out.

Oedipus. Oh, riddles everywhere and words of doubt!

Tiresias. Aye. Thou wast their best leader long ago.

Oedipus. Laugh on. I swear thou still shalt find me so.

Tiresias. That makes thy pride and thy calamity.

Oedipus. I have saved this land, and care not if I die.

Tiresias. Then I will go.—Give me thine arm, my child.

Oedipus. Aye, help him quick.—To see him there makes wild
My heart. Once gone, he will not vex me more.

Tiresias (*turning again as he goes*). I fear thee not; nor will
    I go before
That word be spoken which I came to speak.
How canst thou ever touch me?—Thou dost seek
With threats and loud proclaim the man whose hand
Slew Laïus. Lo, I tell thee, he doth stand
Here. He is called a stranger, but these days
Shall prove him Theban true, nor shall he praise
His birthright. Blind, who once had seeing eyes,
Beggared, who once had riches, in strange guise,
His staff groping before him, he shall crawl
O'er unknown earth, and voices round him call:
"Behold the brother-father of his own
Children, the seed, the sower and the sown,
Shame to his mother's blood, and to his sire
Son, murderer, incest-worker."
                                    Cool thine ire
With thought of these, and if thou find that aught
Faileth, then hold my craft a thing of naught.

> [*He goes out.* OEDIPUS *returns to the Palace.*
> *Chorus.*
> (*They sing of the unknown murderer.*)

What man, what man is he whom the voice of Delphi's cell
Hath named of the bloody hand, of the deed no tongue may tell?
    Let him fly, fly, for his need
    Hath found him; oh, where is the speed

That flew with the winds of old, the team of North-Wind's spell?
   For feet there be that follow. Yea, thunder-shod
   And girt with fire he cometh, the Child of God;
And with him are they that fail not, the Sin-Hounds risen from
      Hell.

For the mountain hath spoken, a voice hath flashed from amid
   the snows,
That the wrath of the world go seek for the man whom no man
   knows.
        Is he fled to the wild forest,
        To caves where the eagles nest?
O angry bull of the rocks, cast out from thy herd-fellows!
   Rage in his heart, and rage across his way,
   He toileth ever to beat from his ears away
The word that floateth about him, living, where'er he goes.

     (*And of the Prophet's strange accusation.*)
Yet strange, passing strange, the wise augur and his lore;
   And my heart it cannot speak; I deny not nor assent,
But float, float in wonder at things after and before;
   Did there lie between their houses some old wrath unspent,
That Corinth against Cadmus should do murder by the way?
   No tale thereof they tell, nor no sign thereof they show;
Who dares to rise for vengeance and cast Oedipus away
     For a dark, dark death long ago!

Ah, Zeus knows, and Apollo, what is dark to mortal eyes;
   They are Gods. But a prophet, hath he vision more than
     mine?
Who hath seen? Who can answer? There be wise men and
   unwise.
   I will wait, I will wait, for the proving of the sign.
But I list not nor hearken when they speak Oedipus ill.
   We saw his face of yore, when the riddling singer passed;
And we knew him that he loved us, and we saw him great in skill.
     Oh, my heart shall uphold him to the last!
                      [*Enter* CREON.

   Creon. Good brother citizens, a frantic word
I hear is spoken by our chosen Lord
Oedipus against me, and here am come
Indignant. If he dreams, 'mid all this doom

That weighs upon us, he hath had from me
Or deed or lightest thought of injury, . . .
'Fore God, I have no care to see the sun
Longer with such a groaning name. Not one
Wound is it, but a multitude, if now
All Thebes must hold me guilty,—aye, and thou
And all who loved me—of a deed so foul.

   Leader. If words were spoken, it was scarce the soul
That spoke them: 'twas some sudden burst of wrath.

   Creon. The charge was made, then, that Tiresias hath
Made answer false, and that I bribed him, I?

   Leader. It was—perchance for jest. I know not why.

   Creon. His heart beat true, his eyes looked steadily
And fell not, laying such a charge on me?

   Leader. I know not. I have no eyes for the thing
My masters do.—But see, here comes the King.

              [*Enter* OEDIPUS *from the Palace.*

   Oedipus. How now, assassin? Walking at my gate
With eye undimmed, thou plotter demonstrate
Against this life, and robber of my crown?
God help thee! Me! What was it set me down
Thy butt? So dull a brain hast found in me
Aforetime, such a faint heart, not to see
Thy work betimes, or seeing not to smite?
Art thou not rash, this once! It needeth might
Of friends, it needeth gold, to make a throne
Thy quarry; and I fear me thou hast none.

   Creon. One thing alone I ask thee. Let me speak
As thou hast spoken; then, with knowledge, wreak
Thy judgement. I accept it without fear.

   Oedipus. More skill hast thou to speak than I to hear
Thee. There is peril found in thee and hate.

   Creon. That one thing let me answer ere too late.

   Oedipus. One thing be sure of, that thy plots are known.

   Creon. The man who thinks that bitter pride alone
Can guide him, without thought—his mind is sick.

   Oedipus. Who thinks to slay his brother with a trick
And suffer not himself, his eyes are blind.

   Creon. Thy words are more than just. But say what kind
Of wrong thou fanciest I have done thee. Speak.

Oedipus. Didst urge me, or didst urge me not, to seek
A counsel from that man of prophecies?

Creon. So judged I then, nor now judge otherwise.

Oedipus. (*Suddenly seeing a mode of attack.*)
How many years have passed since Laïus . . .

                       [*The words seem to choke him.*

Creon. Speak on. I cannot understand thee thus.

Oedipus. (*With an effort.*) Passed in that bloody tempest
    from men's sight?

Creon. Long years and old. I scarce can tell them right.

Oedipus. At that time was this seer in Thebes, or how?

Creon. He was; most wise and honoured, even as now.

Oedipus. At that time did he ever speak my name?

Creon. No. To mine ear at least it never came.

Oedipus. Held you no search for those who slew your King?

Creon. For sure we did, but found not anything.

Oedipus. How came the all-knowing seer to leave it so?

Creon. Ask him! I speak not where I cannot know.

Oedipus. One thing thou canst, with knowledge full, I wot.

Creon. Speak it. If true, I will conceal it not.

Oedipus. This: that until he talked with thee, the seer
Ne'er spoke of me as Laïus' murderer.

Creon. I know not if he hath so spoken now.
I heard him not.—But let me ask and thou
Answer me true, as I have answered thee.

Oedipus. Ask, ask! Thou shalt no murder find in me.

Creon. My sister is thy wife this many a day?

Oedipus. That charge it is not in me to gainsay.

Creon. Thou reignest, giving equal reign to her?

Oedipus. Always to her desire I minister.

Creon. Were we not all as one, she, thou and I?

Oedipus. Yes, thou false friend! There lies thy treachery.

Creon. Not so! Nay, do but follow me and scan
Thine own charge close. Think'st thou that any man
Would rather rule and be afraid than rule
And sleep untroubled? Nay, where lives the fool—
I know them not nor am I one of them—
Who careth more to bear a monarch's name
Than do a monarch's deeds? As now I stand
All my desire I compass at thy hand.

Were I the King, full half my deeds were done
To obey the will of others, not mine own.
Were that as sweet, when all the tale were told,
As this calm griefless princedom that I hold
And silent power? Am I so blind of brain
That ease with glory tires me, and I fain
Must change them? All men now give me God-speed,
All smile to greet me. If a man hath need
Of thee, 'tis me he calleth to the gate,
As knowing that on my word hangs the fate
Of half he craves. Is life like mine a thing
To cast aside and plot to be a King?
Doth a sane man turn villain in an hour?

    For me, I never lusted thus for power
Nor bore with any man who turned such lust
To doing.—But enough. I claim but just
Question. Go first to Pytho; find if well
And true I did report God's oracle.
Next, seek in Thebes for any plots entwined
Between this seer and me; which if ye find,
Then seize and strike me dead. Myself that day
Will sit with thee as judge and bid thee Slay!
But damn me not on one man's guess.—'Tis all
Unjust: to call a traitor true, to call
A true man traitor with no cause nor end!
And this I tell thee. He who plucks a friend
Out from his heart hath lost a treasured thing
Dear as his own dear life.

                But Time shall bring
Truth back. 'Tis Time alone can make men know
What hearts are true; the false one day can show.

    Leader. To one that fears to fall his words are wise,
O King; in thought the swift win not the prize.

    Oedipus. When he is swift who steals against my reign
With plots, then swift am I to plot again.
Wait patient, and his work shall have prevailed
Before I move, and mine for ever failed.

    Creon. How then? To banish me is thy intent?

    Oedipus. Death is the doom I choose, not banishment.

    Creon. Wilt never soften, never trust thy friend?

Oedipus. First I would see how traitors meet their end.

Creon. I see thou wilt not think.

Oedipus.   I think to save
My life.

Creon.   Think, too, of mine.

Oedipus.   Thine, thou born knave!

Creon. Yes. . . . What, if thou art blind in everything?

Oedipus. The King must be obeyed.

Creon.   Not if the King
Does evil.

Oedipus.   To your King! Ho, Thebes, mine own!

Creon. Thebes is my country,[3] not the King's alone.

> [OEDIPUS *has drawn his sword; the Chorus
> show signs of breaking into two parties to
> fight for* OEDIPUS *or for* CREON, *when
> the door opens and* JOCASTA *appears on
> the steps.*

Leader. Stay, Princes, stay! See, on the Castle stair
The Queen Jocasta standeth. Show to her
Your strife. She will assuage it as is well.

Jocasta. Vain men, what would ye with this angry swell
Of words heart-blinded? Is there in your eyes
No pity, thus, when all our city lies
Bleeding, to ply your privy hates? . . . Alack,
My lord, come in!—Thou, Creon, get thee back
To thine own house. And stir not to such stress
Of peril griefs that are but nothingness.

Creon. Sister, it is the pleasure of thy lord,
Our King, to do me deadly wrong. His word
Is passed on me: 'tis banishment or death.

Oedipus. I found him . . . I deny not what he saith,
My Queen . . . with craft and malice practising
Against my life.

Creon.   Ye Gods, if such a thing
Hath once been in my thoughts, may I no more
See any health on earth, but, festered o'er
With curses, die!—Have done. There is mine oath.

Jocasta. In God's name, Oedipus, believe him, both
For my sake, and for these whose hearts are all
Thine own, and for my brother's oath withal.

[*Strophe.*

Leader. Yield; consent; think! My Lord, I conjure thee!

Oedipus. What would ye have me do?

Leader. Reject not one who never failed his troth

Of old and now is strong in his great oath.

Oedipus. Dost know what this prayer means?

Leader.   Yea, verily!

Oedipus.   Say then the meaning true.

Leader. I would not have thee cast to infamy

         Of guilt, where none is proved,

One who hath sworn and whom thou once hast loved.

Oedipus. 'Tis that ye seek? For me, then . . . understand

Well . . . ye seek death or exile from the land.

Leader. No, by the God of Gods, the all-seeing Sun!

May he desert me here, and every friend

With him, to death and utterest malison,

    If e'er my heart could dream of such an end!

        But it bleedeth, it bleedeth sore,

           In a land half slain,

        If we join to the griefs of yore

           Griefs of you twain.

Oedipus. Oh, let him go, though it be utterly

My death, or flight from Thebes in beggary.

'Tis thy sad lips, not his, that make me know

Pity. Him I shall hate, where'er he go.

Creon. I see thy mercy moving full of hate

And slow; thy wrath came swift and desperate.

Methinks, of all the pain that such a heart

Spreadeth, itself doth bear the bitterest part.

Oedipus. Oh, leave me and begone!

Creon.   I go, wronged sore

By thee. These friends will trust me as before.

[CREON *goes.* OEDIPUS *stands apart lost in*
trouble of mind.

[*Antistrophe.*

Leader. Queen, wilt thou lead him to his house again?

Jocasta. I will, when I have heard.

Leader. There fell some word, some blind imagining

Between them. Things known foolish yet can sting.

Jocasta. From both the twain it rose?

[22]

Leader.   From both the twain.
Jocasta.   Aye, and what was the word?
Leader. Surely there is enough of evil stirred,
              And Thebes heaves on the swell
Of storm.—Oh, leave this lying where it fell.
Oedipus. So be it, thou wise counsellor! Make slight
My wrong, and blunt my purpose ere it smite.
Leader. O King, not once I have answered. Visibly
              Mad were I, lost to all wise usages,
          To seek to cast thee from us. 'Twas from thee
              We saw of old blue sky and summer seas,
                  When Thebes in the storm and rain
                      Reeled, like to die.
                  Oh, if thou canst, again
                      Blue sky, blue sky . . .!
Jocasta. Husband, in God's name, say what hath ensued
Of ill, that thou shouldst seek so dire a feud.
Oedipus. I will, wife. I have more regard for thee
Than these.—Thy brother plots to murder me.
Jocasta. Speak on. Make all thy charge. Only be clear.
Oedipus. He says that I am Laïus' murderer.
Jocasta. Says it himself? Says he hath witnesses?
Oedipus. Nay, of himself he ventures nothing. 'Tis
This priest, this hellish seer, makes all the tale.
Jocasta. The seer?—Then tear thy terrors like a veil
And take free breath. A seer? No human thing
Born on the earth hath power for conjuring
Truth from the dark of God.
                              Come, I will tell
An old tale. There came once an oracle
To Laïus: I say not from the God
Himself, but from the priests and seers who trod
His sanctuary: if ever son were bred
From him and me, by that son's hand, it said,
Laïus must die. And he, the tale yet stays
Among us, at the crossing of three ways
Was slain by robbers, strangers. And my son—
God's mercy!—scarcely the third day was gone
When Laïus took, and by another's hand
Out on the desert mountain, where the land

[23]

Is rock, cast him to die. Through both his feet
A blade of iron they drove. Thus did we cheat
Apollo of his will. My child could slay
No father, and the King could cast away
The fear that dogged him, by his child to die
Murdered.—Behold the fruits of prophecy!
Which heed not thou! God needs not that a seer
Help him, when he would make his dark things clear.

   Oedipus. Woman, what turmoil hath thy story wrought
Within me! What up-stirring of old thought!

   Jocasta. What thought? It turns thee like a frightened thing.

   Oedipus. 'Twas at the crossing of three ways⁴ this King
Was murdered? So I heard or so I thought.

   Jocasta. That was the tale. It is not yet forgot.

   Oedipus. The crossing of three ways! And in what land?

   Jocasta. Phokis 'tis called. A road on either hand
From Delphi comes and Daulia, in a glen.

   Oedipus. How many years and months have passed since
      then?

   Jocasta. 'Twas but a little time before proclaim
Was made of thee for king, the tidings came.

   Oedipus. My God, what hast thou willed to do with me?

   Jocasta. Oedipus, speak! What is it troubles thee?

   Oedipus. Ask me not yet. But say, what build, what height
Had Laïus? Rode he full of youth and might?

   Jocasta. Tall, with the white new gleaming on his brow
He walked. In shape just such a man as thou.

   Oedipus. God help me! I much fear that I have wrought
A curse on mine own head, and knew it not.

   Jocasta. How sayst thou? O my King, I look on thee
And tremble.

   Oedipus (*to himself*). Horror, if the blind can see!
Answer but one thing and 'twill all be clear.

   Jocasta. Speak. I will answer though I shake with fear.

   Oedipus. Went he with scant array, or a great band
Of armèd followers, like a lord of land?

   Jocasta. Four men were with him, one a herald; one
Chariot there was, where Laïus rode alone.

   Oedipus. Aye me! 'Tis clear now.

                   Woman, who could bring

To Thebes the story of that manslaying?

 Jocasta. A house-thrall, the one man they failed to slay.

 Oedipus. The one man . . .? Is he in the house to-day?

 Jocasta. Indeed no. When he came that day, and found

Thee on the throne where once sat Laïus crowned,

He took my hand and prayed me earnestly

To send him to the mountain heights, to be

A herdsman, far from any sight or call

Of Thebes. And there I sent him. 'Twas a thrall

Good-hearted, worthy a far greater boon.

 Oedipus. Canst find him? I would see this herd, and soon.

 Jocasta. 'Tis easy. But what wouldst thou with the herd?

 Oedipus. I fear mine own voice, lest it spoke a word

Too much; whereof this man must tell me true.

 Jocasta. The man shall come.—My lord, methinks I too

Should know what fear doth work thee this despite.

 Oedipus. Thou shalt. When I am tossed to such an height

Of dark foreboding, woman, when my mind

Faceth such straits as these, where should I find

A mightier love than thine?

       My father—thus

I tell thee the whole tale—was Polybus,

In Corinth King; my mother Meropê

Of Dorian line. And I was held to be

The proudest in Corinthia, till one day

A thing befell: strange was it, but no way

Meet for such wonder and such rage as mine.

A feast it was, and some one flushed with wine

Cried out at me that I was no true son

Of Polybus. Oh, I was wroth! That one

Day I kept silence, but the morrow morn

I sought my parents, told that tale of scorn

And claimed the truth; and they rose in their **pride**

And smote the mocker. . . . Aye, they satisfied

All my desire; yet still the cavil gnawed

My heart, and still the story crept abroad.

 At last I rose—my father knew not, nor

My mother—and went forth to Pytho's floor

To ask. And God in that for which I came

Rejected me, but round me, like a flame,

His voice flashed other answers, things of woe,
Terror, and desolation. I must know
My mother's body and beget thereon
A race no mortal eye durst look upon,
And spill in murder mine own father's blood.

    I heard, and, hearing, straight from where I stood,
No landmark but the stars to light my way,
Fled, fled from the dark south where Corinth lay,
To lands far off, where never I might see
My doom of scorn fulfilled. On bitterly
I strode, and reached the region where, so saith
Thy tale, that King of Thebes was struck to death. . . .
Wife, I will tell thee true. As one in daze
I walked, till, at the crossing of three ways,
A herald, like thy tale, and o'er his head
A man behind strong horses charioted
Met me. And both would turn me from the path,
He and a thrall in front. And I in wrath
Smote him that pushed me—'twas a groom who led
The horses. Not a word the master said,
But watched, and as I passed him on the road
Down on my head his iron-branchèd goad
Stabbed. But, by heaven, he rued it! In a flash
I swung my staff and saw the old man crash
Back from his car in blood. . . . Then all of them
I slew.

        Oh, if that man's unspoken name
Had aught of Laïus in him, in God's eye
What man doth move more miserable than I,
More dogged by the hate of heaven! No man, kin
Nor stranger, any more may take me in;
No man may greet me with a word, but all
Cast me from out their houses. And withal
'Twas mine own self that laid upon my life
These curses.—And I hold the dead man's wife
In these polluting arms that spilt his soul. . . .
Am I a thing born evil? Am I foul
In every vein? Thebes now doth banish me,
And never in this exile must I see
Mine ancient folk of Corinth, never tread

The land that bore me; else my mother's bed
Shall be defiled, and Polybus, my good
Father, who loved me well, be rolled in blood.
If one should dream that such a world began
In some slow devil's heart, that hated man,
Who should deny him? —God, as thou art clean,
Suffer not this, oh, suffer not this sin
To be, that e'er I look on such a day!
Out of all vision of mankind away
To darkness let me fall ere such a fate
Touch me, so unclean and so desolate!

    Leader. I tremble too, O King; but till thou hear
From him who saw, oh, let hope conquer fear.

    Oedipus. One shred of hope I still have, and therefore
Will wait the herdsman's coming. 'Tis no more.

    Jocasta. He shall come. But what further dost thou seek?

    Oedipus. This. If we mark him close and find him speak
As thou hast, then I am lifted from my dread.

    Jocasta. What mean'st thou? Was there something that I
      said . . . ?

    Oedipus. Thou said'st he spoke of robbers, a great band,
That slaughtered Laïus' men. If still he stand
To the same tale, the guilt comes not my way.
One cannot be a band. But if he say
One lonely loin-girt man, then visibly
This is God's finger pointing toward me.

    Jocasta. Be sure of this. He told the story so
When first he came. All they that heard him know,
Not only I. He cannot change again
Now. And if change he should, O Lord of men,
No change of his can make the prophecy
Of Laïus' death fall true. He was to die
Slain by my son. So Loxias spake. . . . My son!
He slew no man, that poor deserted one
That died. . . . And I will no more turn mine eyes
This way nor that for all their prophecies.

    Oedipus. Woman, thou counsellest well. Yet let it not
Escape thee. Send and have the herdsman brought.

    Jocasta. That will I.—Come. Thou knowest I ne'er would do
Nor think of aught, save thou wouldst have it so.

[JOCASTA *and* OEDIPUS *go together into the Palace.*

Chorus.
(They pray to be free from such great sins as they have just heard spoken of.)

[*Strophe.*

Toward God's great mysteries, oh, let me move
    Unstainèd till I die
In speech or doing; for the Laws thereof
Are holy, walkers upon ways above,
    Born in the far blue sky;
Their father is Olympus uncreate;
    No man hath made nor told
Their being; neither shall Oblivion set
Sleep on their eyes, for in them lives a great
    Spirit and grows not old.

(They wonder if these sins be all due to pride and if CREON *has guilty ambitions)* ;

[*Antistrophe.*

'Tis Pride that breeds the tyrant; drunken deep
    With perilous things is she,
Which bring not peace: up, reeling, steep on steep
She climbs, till lo, the rock-edge, and the leap
    To that which needs must be,

The land where the strong foot is no more strong!
    Yet is there surely Pride
That saves a city; God preserve it long!
I judge not. Only through all maze of wrong
    Be God, not man, my guide.

(Or if TIRESIAS *can really be a lying prophet with no fear of God; they feel that all faith in oracles and the things of God is shaken.)*

[*Strophe.*

Is there a priest who moves amid the altars
    Ruthless in deed and word,
Fears not the presence of his god, nor falters
    Lest Right at last be heard?
If such there be, oh, let some doom be given
    Meet for his ill-starred pride,

[28]

Who will not gain his gain where Justice is,
Who will not hold his lips from blasphemies,
Who hurls rash hands amid the things of heaven
　　From man's touch sanctified.

　　In a world where such things be,
　　　　What spirit hath shield or lance
　　To ward him secretly
　　　　From the arrow that slays askance?
　　If honour to such things be,
　　　　Why should I dance my dance?

                                    [*Antistrophe.*

I go no more with prayers and adorations
　　To Earth's deep Heart of Stone,
Nor yet the Abantes' floor, nor where the nations
　　Kneel at Olympia's throne,
Till all this dark be lightened, for the finger
　　Of man to touch and know.
O Thou that rulest—if men rightly call
Thy name on earth—O Zeus, thou Lord of all
And Strength undying, let not these things linger
　　Unknown, tossed to and fro.

　　　　For faint is the oracle,
　　　　　　And they thrust it aside, away;
　　　　And no more visible
　　　　　　Apollo to save or slay;
　　　　And the things of God, they fail
　　　　　　As mist on the wind away.

　　[JOCASTA *comes out from the Palace followed*
　　　　by handmaids bearing incense and flowers.
Jocasta. Lords of the land, the ways my thought hath trod
Lead me in worship to these shrines of God
With flowers and incense flame. So dire a storm
Doth shake the King, sin, dread and every form
Of grief the world knows. 'Tis the wise man's way
To judge the morrow by the yester day;
Which he doth never, but gives eye and ear
To all who speak, will they but speak of fear.
　And seeing no word of mine hath power to heal

His torment, therefore forth to thee I steal,
O Slayer of the Wolf, O Lord of Light,
Apollo: thou art near us, and of right
Dost hold us thine: to thee in prayer I fall.

[She kneels at the altar of Apollo Lukeios.

Oh, show us still some path that is not all
Unclean; for now our captain's eyes are dim
With dread, and the whole ship must follow him.

[While she prays a STRANGER *has entered and
begins to accost the Chorus.*

Stranger. Good masters, is there one of you could bring
My steps to the house of Oedipus, your King?
Or, better, to himself if that may be?

Leader. This is the house and he within; and she
Thou seest, the mother of his royal seed.

*[*JOCASTA *rises, anxious, from her prayer.*

Stranger. Being wife to such a man, happy indeed
And ringed with happy faces may she live!

Jocasta. To one so fair of speech may the Gods give
Like blessing, courteous stranger; 'tis thy due.
But say what leads thee hither. Can we do
Thy wish in aught, or hast thou news to bring?

Stranger. Good news, O Queen, for thee and for the King.

Jocasta. What is it? And from what prince comest thou?

Stranger. I come from Corinth.—And my tale, I trow,
Will give thee joy, yet haply also pain.

Jocasta. What news can have that twofold power? Be plain.

Stranger. 'Tis spoke in Corinth that the gathering
Of folk will make thy lord our chosen King.

Jocasta. How? Is old Polybus in power no more?

Stranger. Death has a greater power. His reign is o'er.

Jocasta. What say'st thou? Dead? . . . Oedipus' father
dead?

Stranger. If I speak false, let me die in his stead.

Jocasta. Ho, maiden! To our master! Hie thee fast
And tell this tale.

[The maiden goes.

Where stand ye at the last
Ye oracles of God? For many a year
Oedipus fled before that man, in fear

[30]

To slay him. And behold we find him thus
Slain by a chance death, not by Oedipus.

[OEDIPUS *comes out from the Palace.*

Oedipus. Jocasta, thou I love to look upon,
Why call'st thou me from where I sat alone?

Jocasta. Give ear, and ponder from what this man tells
How end these proud priests and their oracles.

Oedipus. Whence comes he? And what word hath he
   for us?

Jocasta. From Corinth; bearing news that Polybus
Thy father is no more. He has found his death.

Oedipus. How?—Stranger, speak thyself. This that she
   saith. . .

Stranger. Is sure. If that is the first news ye crave,
I tell thee, Polybus lieth in his grave.

Oedipus. Not murdered? . . . How? Some passing of disease?

Stranger. A slight thing turns an old life to its peace.

Oedipus. Poor father! . . . 'tis by sickness he is dead?

Stranger. The growing years lay heavy on his head.

Oedipus. O wife, why then should man fear any more
The voice of Pytho's dome, or cower before
These birds that shriek above us? They foretold
Me for my father's murderer; and behold,
He lies in Corinth dead, and here am I
And never touched the sword. . . . Or did he die
In grief for me who left him? In that way
I may have wrought his death. . . . But come what may,
He sleepeth in his grave and with him all
This deadly seercraft, of no worth at all.

Jocasta. Dear Lord, long since did I not show thee
   clear . . . ?

Oedipus. Indeed, yes. I was warped by mine own fear.

Jocasta. Now thou wilt cast it from thee, and forget.

Oedipus. Forget my mother? . . . It is not over yet.

Jocasta. What should man do with fear, who hath but Chance
Above him, and no sight nor governance
Of things to be? To live as life may run,
No fear, no fret, were wisest 'neath the sun.
And thou, fear not thy mother. Prophets deem

[31]

A deed wrought that is wrought but in a dream.
And he to whom these things are nothing, best
Will bear his burden.

Oedipus.   All thou counsellest
Were good, save that my mother liveth still.
And, though thy words be wise, for good or ill
Her I still fear.

Jocasta.   Think of thy father's tomb!
Like light across our darkness it hath come.

Oedipus. Great light; but while she lives I fly from her.

Stranger. What woman, Prince, doth fill thee so with fear?

Oedipus. Meropê, friend, who dwelt with Polybus.

Stranger. What in Queen Meropê should fright thee thus?

Oedipus. A voice of God, stranger, of dire import.

Stranger. Meet for mine ears? Or of some secret sort?

Oedipus. Nay, thou must hear, and Corinth. Long ago
Apollo spake a doom, that I should know
My mother's flesh, and with mine own hand spill
My father's blood.—'Tis that, and not my will,
Hath kept me always far from Corinth. So;
Life hath dealt kindly with me, yet men know
On earth no comfort like a mother's face.

Stranger. 'Tis that, hath kept thee exiled in this place?

Oedipus. That, and the fear too of my father's blood.

Stranger. Then, surely, Lord . . . I came but for thy
  good . . .
'Twere well if from that fear I set thee free.

Oedipus. Ah, couldst thou! There were rich reward for thee.

Stranger. To say truth, I had hoped to lead thee home
Now, and myself to get some good therefrom.

Oedipus. Nay; where my parents are I will not go.

Stranger. My son, 'tis clear enough thou dost not know
Thine own road.

Oedipus.   How? Old man, in God's name, say.

Stranger. If this it is, keeps thee so long away
From Corinth.

Oedipus.   'Tis the fear lest that word break
One day upon me true.

Stranger.   Fear lest thou take
Defilement from the two that gave thee birth?

Oedipus. 'Tis that, old man, 'tis that doth fill the earth
With terror.

Stranger.   Then thy terror all hath been
For nothing.

Oedipus.   How? Were not your King and Queen
My parents?

Stranger.   Polybus was naught to thee
In blood.

Oedipus.   How? He, my father!

Stranger.   That was he
As much as I, but no more.

Oedipus   Thou art naught;
'Twas he begot me.

Stranger.   'Twas not I begot
Oedipus, neither was it he.

Oedipus.   What wild
Fancy, then, made him name me for his child?

Stranger. Thou wast his child—by gift. Long years ago
Mine own hand brought thee to him.

Oedipus.   Coming so,
From a strange hand, he gave me that great love?

Stranger. He had no child, and the desire thereof
Held him.

Oedipus.   And thou didst find somewhere—or buy—
A child for him?

Stranger.   I found it in a high
Glen of Kithairon.

> [*Movement of* JOCASTA, *who stands riveted
> with dread, unnoticed by the others.*

Oedipus.   Yonder? To what end
Wast travelling in these parts?

Stranger.   I came to tend
The flocks here on the mountain.

Oedipus.   Thou wast one
That wandered, tending sheep for hire?

Stranger.   My son,
That day I was the saviour of a King.

Oedipus. How saviour? Was I in some suffering
Or peril?

Stranger.   Thine own feet a tale could speak.

Oedipus. Ah me! What ancient pain stirs half awake
Within me!

Stranger.   'Twas a spike through both thy feet.
I set thee free.

Oedipus.   A strange scorn that, to greet
A babe new on the earth!

Stranger.   From that they fain
Must call thee Oedipus, *"Who-walks-in-pain."*

Oedipus. Who called me so—father or mother? Oh,
In God's name, speak!

Stranger.   I know not. He should know
Who brought thee.

Oedipus.   So: I was not found by thee.
Thou hadst me from another?

Stranger.   Aye; to me
One of the shepherds gave the babe, to bear
Far off.

Oedipus.   What shepherd? Know'st thou not? Declare
All that thou knowest.

Stranger.   By my memory, then,
I think they called him one of Laïus' men.

Oedipus. That Laïus who was king in Thebes of old?

Stranger. The same. My man did herding in his fold.

Oedipus. Is he yet living? Can I see his face?

Stranger.   [*Turning to the Chorus.*
Ye will know that, being natives to the place.

Oedipus. How?—Is there one of you within my pale
Standing, that knows the shepherd of his tale?
Ye have seen him on the hills? Or in this town?
Speak! For the hour is come that all be known.

Leader. I think 'twill be the Peasant Man, the same,
Thou hast sought long time to see.—His place and name
Our mistress, if she will, can tell most clear.

                              [JOCASTA *remains as if she heard nothing.*

Oedipus. Thou hear'st him, wife. The herd whose presence
      here
We craved for, is it he this man would say?

Jocasta. He saith . . . What of it? Ask not; only pray
Not to remember. . . . Tales are vainly told.

Oedipus. 'Tis mine own birth. How can I, when I hold

Such clues as these, refrain from knowing all?

Jocasta. For God's love, no! Not if thou car'st at all
For thine own life. . . . My anguish is enough.

Oedipus (*bitterly*). Fear not! . . . Though I be thrice of
    slavish stuff
From my third grand-dam down, it shames not thee.

Jocasta. Ask no more. I beseech thee . . . Promise me!

Oedipus. To leave the Truth half-found? 'Tis not my mood.

Jocasta. I understand; and tell thee what is good.

Oedipus. Thy good doth weary me.

Jocasta.   O child of woe,
I pray God, I pray God, thou never know!

Oedipus (*turning from her*). Go, fetch the herdsman
    straight!—This Queen of mine
May walk alone to boast her royal line.

Jocasta.   [*She twice draws in her breath through her
            teeth, as if in some sharp pain.*

Unhappy one, goodbye! Goodbye before
I go: this once, and never never more!

        [*She comes towards him, then turns and goes
          into the palace.*

Leader. King, what was that? She passed like one who flies
In very anguish. Dread is o'er mine eyes
Lest from this silence break some storm of wrong.

Oedipus. Break what break will! My mind abideth strong
To know the roots, how low soe'er they be,
Which grew to Oedipus. This woman, she
Is proud, methinks, and fears my birth and name
Will mar her nobleness. But I, no shame
Can ever touch me. I am Fortune's child,
Not man's; her mother face hath ever smiled
Above me, and my brethren of the sky,
The changing Moons, have changed me low and high.
There is my lineage true, which none shall wrest
From me; who then am I to fear this quest?

Chorus.
(*They sing of* OEDIPUS *as the foundling of
their own Theban mountain, Kithairon,
and doubtless of divine birth.*)

If I, O Kithairon, some vision can borrow   *[Strophe.*
  From seercraft, if still there is wit in the old,
Long, long, through the deep-orbèd Moon of the morrow—
  So hear me, Olympus!—thy tale shall be told.
O mountain of Thebes, a new Theban shall praise thee,
  One born of thy bosom, one nursed at thy springs;
And the old men shall dance to thy glory, and raise thee
  To worship, O bearer of joy to my kings.
        And thou, we pray,
Look down in peace, O Apollo; I-ê, I-ê!

                        [Antistrophe.

What Oread mother, unaging, unweeping,
  Did bear thee, O Babe, to the Crag-walker Pan;
Or perchance to Apollo? He loveth the leaping
  Of herds on the rock-ways unhaunted of man.
Or was it the lord of Cyllênê, who found thee,
  Or glad Dionysus, whose home is the height,
Who knew thee his own on the mountain, as round the
  The White Brides of Helicon laughed for delight?
        'Tis there, 'tis there,
The joy most liveth of all his dance and prayer.
  Oedipus. If I may judge, ye Elders, who have ne'er
Seen him, methinks I see the shepherd there
Whom we have sought so long. His weight of years
Fits well with our Corinthian messenger's;
And, more, I know the men who guide his way,
Bondsmen of mine own house.
                     Thou, friend, wilt say
Most surely, who hast known the man of old.
  Leader. I know him well. A shepherd of the fold
Of Laïus, one he trusted more than all.

         [The SHEPHERD *comes in, led by two thralls.*
           He is an old man and seems terrified.

  Oedipus. Thou first, our guest from Corinth: say withal
Is this the man?
  Stranger.   This is the man, O King.
  Oedipus.   *[Addressing the* SHEPHERD.
Old man! Look up, and answer everything
I ask thee.—Thou wast Laïus' man of old?
  Shepherd. Born in his house I was, not bought with gold.

[36]

Oedipus. What kind of work, what way of life, was thine?

Shepherd. Most of my days I tended sheep or kine.

Oedipus. What was thy camping ground at midsummer?

Shepherd. Sometimes Kithairon, sometimes mountains near.

Oedipus. Saw'st ever there this man thou seëst now?

Shepherd. There, Lord? What doing?—What man meanest thou?

Oedipus. [*Pointing to the* STRANGER.
Look! Hath he ever crossed thy path before?

Shepherd. I call him not to mind, I must think more.

Stranger. Small wonder that, O King! But I will throw
Light on his memories.—Right well I know
He knows the time when, all Kithairon through,
I with one wandering herd and he with two,
Three times we neighboured one another, clear
From spring to autumn stars, a good half-year.
At winter's fall we parted; he drove down
To his master's fold, and I back to mine own. . . .
Dost call it back, friend? Was it as I say?

Shepherd. It was. It was. . . . 'Tis all so far away,

Stranger. Say then: thou gavest me once, there in the wild,
A babe to rear far off as mine own child?

Shepherd. [*His terror returning.*
What does this mean? To what end askest thou?

Stranger. [*Pointing to* OEDIPUS.
That babe has grown, friend. 'Tis our master now.

Shepherd. [*He slowly understands, then stands for a
moment horror-struck.*
No, in the name of death! . . . Fool, hold thy peace.
[*He lifts his staff at the* STRANGER.

Oedipus. Ha, greybeard! Wouldst thou strike him?—'Tis not his
Offences, 'tis thine own we need to mend.

Shepherd. Most gentle master, how do I offend?

Oedipus. Whence came that babe whereof he questioneth?

Shepherd. He doth not know . . . 'tis folly . , , what he saith.

Oedipus. Thou wilt not speak for love; but pain maybe . . .

Shepherd. I am very old. Ye would not torture me.

Oedipus. Back with his arms, ye bondmen! Hold him so.

[37]

[*The thralls drag back the* SHEPHERD's
arms, ready for torture.

Shepherd. Woe's me! What have I done? . . . What
wouldst thou know?

Oedipus. Didst give this man the child, as he doth say?

Shepherd. I did. . . . Would God that I had died this day!

Oedipus. 'Fore heaven, thou shalt yet, if thou speak not true.

Shepherd. 'Tis more than death and darker, if I do.

Oedipus. This dog, it seems, will keep us waiting.

Shepherd. Nay,
I said at first I gave it.

Oedipus. In what way
Came it to thee? Was it thine own child, or
Another's?

Shepherd. Nay, it never crossed my door:
Another's.

Oedipus. Whose? What man, what house, of these
About thee?

Shepherd. In the name of God who sees,
Ask me no more!

Oedipus. If once I ask again,
Thou diest.

Shepherd. From the folk of Laïus, then,
It came.

Oedipus. A slave, or born of Laïus' blood?

Shepherd. There comes the word I dread to speak, O God!

Oedipus. And I to hear: yet heard it needs must be.

Shepherd. Know then, they said 'twas Laïus' child. But she
Within, thy wife, best knows its fathering.

Oedipus. 'Twas she that gave it?

Shepherd. It was she, O King.

Oedipus. And bade you . . . what?

Shepherd. Destroy it.

Oedipus. Her own child? . . .
Cruel!

Shepherd. Dark words of God had made her wild.

Oedipus. What words?

Shepherd. The babe must slay his father; so
'Twas written.

[38]

Oedipus.   Why didst thou, then, let him go
With this old man?
    Shepherd.   O King, my heart did bleed.
I thought the man would save him, past all need
Of fear, to his own distant home. . . . And he
Did save him, to great evil. Verily
If thou art he whom this man telleth of,
Know, to affliction thou art born.
    Oedipus.   Enough!
All will come true. . . . Thou Light, never again
May I behold thee, I in the eyes of men
Made naked, how from sin my being grew,
In sin I wedded and in sin I slew!

> [*He rushes into the Palace. The* SHEPHERD
> *is led away by the thralls.*

                              [*Strophe.*

Chorus. Nothingness, nothingness,
      Ye Children of Man, and less
          I count you, waking or dreaming!
      And none among mortals, none,
      Seeking to live, hath won
      More than to seem, and to cease
          Again from his seeming.
      While ever before mine eyes
      One fate, one ensample, lies—
      Thine, thine, O Oedipus, sore
          Of God oppressèd—
      What thing that is human more
          Dare I call blessèd?

                             [*Antistrophe.*

      Straight his archery flew
      To the heart of living; he knew
          Joy and the fulness of power,
      O Zeus, when the riddling breath
      Was stayed and the Maid of Death
      Slain, and we saw him through
          The death-cloud, a tower!

      For that he was called my king;
      Yea, every precious thing

Wherewith men are honoured, down
    We cast before him,
And great Thebes brought her crown
    And kneeled to adore him.

                                       [*Strophe.*

But now, what man's story is such bitterness to speak?
  What life hath Delusion so visited, and Pain,
        And swiftness of Disaster?
        O great King, our master,
  How oped the one haven to the slayer and the slain?
And the furrows of thy father, did they turn not nor shriek,
  Did they bear so long silent thy casting of the grain?

                                   [*Antistrophe.*

'Tis Time, Time, desireless, hath shown thee what thou art;
  The long monstrous mating, it is judged and all its race.
        O child of him that sleepeth,
        Thy land weepeth, weepeth,
  Unfathered. . . . Would God, I had never seen thy face!
From thee in great peril fell peace upon my heart,
  In thee mine eye clouded and the dark is come apace.

               [*A* MESSENGER *rushes out from the Palace.*
  Messenger. O ye above this land in honour old
Exalted, what a tale shall ye be told,
What sights shall see, and tears of horror shed,
If still your hearts be true to them that led
Your sires! There runs no river, well I ween,
Not Phasis nor great Ister, shall wash clean
This house of all within that hideth—nay,
Nor all that creepeth forth to front the day,
Of purposed horror. And in misery
That woundeth most which men have willed to be.
  Leader. No lack there was in what we knew before
Of food for heaviness. What bring'st thou more?
  Messenger. One thing I bring thee first. . . . 'Tis quickly
  said.
Jocasta, our anointed queen, is dead.
  Leader. Unhappy woman! How came death to her?
  Messenger. By her own hand. . . . Oh, of what passed in
  there

Ye have been spared the worst. Ye cannot see.
Howbeit, with that which still is left in me
Of mind and memory, ye shall hear her fate.
    Like one entranced with passion, through the gate
She passed, the white hands flashing o'er her head,
Like blades that tear, and fled, unswerving fled,
Toward her old bridal room, and disappeared
And the doors crashed behind her. But we heard
Her voice within, crying to him of old,
Her Laïus, long dead; and things untold
Of the old kiss unforgotten, that should bring
The lover's death and leave the loved a thing
Of horror, yea, a field beneath the plough
For sire and son: then wailing bitter-low
Across that bed of births unreconciled,
Husband from husband born and child from child.
And, after that, I know not how her death
Found her. For sudden, with a roar of wrath,
Burst Oedipus upon us. Then, I ween,
We marked no more what passion held the Queen,
But him, as in the fury of his stride,
"A sword! A sword! And show me here," he cried,
"That wife, no wife, that field of bloodstained earth
Where husband, father, sin on sin, had birth,
Polluted generations!" While he thus
Raged on, some god—for sure 'twas none of us—
Showed where she was; and with a shout away,
As though some hand had pointed to the prey,
He dashed him on the chamber door. The straight
Door-bar of oak, it bent beneath his weight,
Shook from its sockets free, and in he burst
To the dark chamber.

                                    There we saw her first
Hanged, swinging from a noose, like a dead bird.
He fell back when he saw her. Then we heard
A miserable groan, and straight he found
And loosed the strangling knot, and on the ground
Laid her.—Ah, then the sight of horror came!
The pin of gold, broad-beaten like a flame,
He tore from off her breast, and, left and right,

Down on the shuddering orbits of his sight
Dashed it: "Out! Out! Ye never more shall see
Me nor the anguish nor the sins of me.
Ye looked on lives whose like earth never bore,
Ye knew not those my spirit thirsted for:
Therefore be dark for ever!"

                      Like a song
His voice rose, and again, again, the strong
And stabbing hand fell, and the massacred
And bleeding eyeballs streamed upon his beard,
Wild rain, and gouts of hail amid the rain.

  Behold affliction, yea, afflictions twain
From man and woman broken, now made one
In downfall. All the riches yester sun
Saw in this house were rich in verity.
What call ye now our riches? Agony,
Delusion, Death, Shame, all that eye or ear
Hath ever dreamed of misery, is here.

    Leader. And now how fares he? Doth the storm abate?
    Messenger. He shouts for one to open wide the gate
And lead him forth, and to all Thebes display
His father's murderer, his mother's. . . . Nay,
Such words I will not speak. And his intent
Is set, to cast himself in banishment
Out to the wild, not walk 'mid human breed
Bearing the curse he bears. Yet sore his need
Of strength and of some guiding hand. For sure
He hath more burden now than man may endure.

  But see, the gates fall back, and that appears
Which he who loathes shall pity—yea, with tears.

              [OEDIPUS *is led in, blinded and bleeding.*
                The Old Men bow down and hide their
                faces; some of them weep.
    Chorus. Oh, terrible! Oh, sight of all
           This life hath crossed, most terrible!
           Thou man more wronged than tongue can tell,
       What madness took thee? Do there crawl
           Live Things of Evil from the deep
           To leap on man? Oh, what a leap
      Was His that flung thee to thy fall!

Leader. O fallen, fallen in ghastly case,
      I dare not raise mine eyes to thee;
      Fain would I look and ask and see,
   But shudder sickened from thy face.

Oedipus. Oh, pain; pain and woe!
       Whither? Whither?
   They lead me and I go;
    And my voice drifts on the air
      Far away.
    Where, Thing of Evil, where
      Endeth thy leaping hither?

Leader. In fearful ends, which none may hear nor say.

Oedipus. Cloud of the dark mine own   [*Strophe.*
      For ever, horrible,
      Stealing, stealing, silent, unconquerable,
     Cloud that no wind, no summer can dispel!
    Again, again I groan,
  As through my heart together crawl the strong
  Stabs of this pain and memories of old wrong.

Leader. Yea, twofold hosts of torment hast thou there,
   The stain to think on and the pain to bear.

Oedipus. O Friend, thou mine own   [*Antistrophe.*
      Still faithful, minister
      Steadfast abiding alone of them that were,
     Dost bear with me and give the blind man care?
   Ah me! Not all unknown
   Nor hid thou art. Deep in this dark a call
  Comes and I know thy voice in spite of all.

Leader. O fearful sufferer, and could'st thou kill
   Thy living orbs? What God made blind thy will?

Oedipus. 'Tis Apollo; all is Apollo,   [*Strophe.*
  O ye that love me, 'tis he long time hath planned
    These things upon me evilly, evilly,
     Dark things and full of blood.
 I knew not; I did but follow
  His way; but mine the hand
    And mine the anguish. What were mine eyes to me
    When naught to be seen was good?

Leader. 'Tis even so; and Truth doth speak in thee.

[43]

Oedipus. To see, to endure, to hear words kindly spoken,
   Should I have joy in such?
    Out, if ye love your breath,
  Cast me swift unto solitude, unbroken
   By word or touch.
    Am I not charged with death,
     Most charged and filled to the brim
    With curses? And what man saith
    God hath so hated him?
Leader. Thy bitter will, thy hard calamity,
  Would I had never known nor looked on thee!
Oedipus. My curse, my curse upon him, [*Antistrophe.*
  That man whom pity held in the wilderness,
   Who saved the feet alive from the blood-fetter
   And loosed the barb thereof!
 That babe—what grace was done him,
  Had he died shelterless,
   He had not laid on himself this grief to bear,
   And all who gave him love.
Leader. I, too, O Friend, I had been happier.
Oedipus. Found not the way to his father's blood, nor shaken
  The world's scorn on his mother,
    The child and the groom withal;
 But now, of murderers born, of God forsaken,
  Mine own sons' brother;
   All this, and if aught can fall
    Upon man more perilous
   And elder in sin, lo, all
    Is the portion of Oedipus.
Leader. How shall I hold this counsel or thy mind
True? Thou wert better dead than living blind.
 Oedipus. That this deed is not well and wisely wrought
Thou shalt not show me; therefore school me not.
Think, with what eyes hereafter in the place
Of shadows could I see my father's face,
Or my poor mother's? Both of whom this hand
Hath wronged too deep for man to understand.
Or children—born as mine were born, to see
Their shapes should bring me joy? Great God! To me
There is no joy in city nor in tower

Nor temple, from all whom, in this mine hour,
I that was chief in Thebes alone, and ate
The King's bread, I have made me separate
For ever. Mine own lips have bid the land
Cast from it one so evil, one whose hand
To sin was dedicate, whom God hath shown
Birth-branded . . . and my blood the dead King's own!
All this myself have proved. And can I then
Look with straight eyes into the eyes of men?
I trow not. Nay, if any stop there were
To dam this fount that welleth in mine ear
For hearing, I had never blenched nor stayed
Till this vile shell were all one dungeon made,
Dark, without sound. 'Tis thus the mind would fain
Find peace, self-prisoned from a world of pain.

O wild Kithairon, why was it thy will
To save me? Why not take me quick and kill,
Kill, before ever I could make men know
The thing I am, the thing from which I grow?
Thou dead King, Polybus, thou city wall
Of Corinth, thou old castle I did call
My father's, what a life did ye begin,
What splendour rotted by the worm within,
When ye bred me! O Crossing of the Roads,
O secret glen and dusk of crowding woods,
O narrow footpath creeping to the brink
Where meet the Three! I gave you blood to drink.
Do ye remember? 'Twas my life-blood, hot
From my own father's heart. Have ye forgot
What deed I did among you, and what new
And direr deed I fled from you to do?
O flesh, horror of flesh! . . .

But what is shame
To do should not be spoken. In God's name,
Take me somewhere far off and cover me
From sight, or slay, or cast me to the sea
Where never eye may see me any more.

What? Do ye fear to touch a man so sore
Stricken? Nay, tremble not. My misery
Is mine, and shall be borne by none but me.

Leader. Lo, yonder comes for answer to thy prayer
Creon, to do and to decree. The care
Of all our land is his, now thou art weak.

Oedipus. Alas, what word to Creon can I speak,
How make him trust me more? He hath seen of late
So vile a heart in me, so full of hate.

[*Enter* CREON.

Creon. Not to make laughter, Oedipus, nor cast
Against thee any evil of the past
I seek thee, but . . . Ah God! ye ministers,
Have ye no hearts? Or if for man there stirs
No pity in you, fear at least to call
Stain on our Lord the Sun, who feedeth all;
Nor show in nakedness a horror such
As this, which never mother Earth may touch,
Nor God's clean rain nor sunlight. Quick within!
Guide him.—The ills that in a house have been
They of the house alone should know or hear.

Oedipus. In God's name, since thou hast undone the fear
Within me, coming thus, all nobleness,
To one so vile, grant me one only grace.
For thy sake more I crave it than mine own.

Creon. Let me first hear what grace thou wouldst be shown.

Oedipus. Cast me from Thebes . . . now, quick . . . where
        none may see
My visage more, nor mingle words with me.

Creon. That had I done, for sure, save that I still
Tremble, and fain would ask Apollo's will.

Oedipus. His will was clear enough, to stamp the unclean
Thing out, the bloody hand, the heart of sin.

Creon. 'Twas thus he seemed to speak; but in this sore
Strait we must needs learn surer than before.

Oedipus. Thou needs must trouble God for one so low?

Creon. Surely; thyself will trust his answer now.

Oedipus. I charge thee more . . . and, if thou fail, my sin
Shall cleave to thee. . . . For her who lies within,
Make as thou wilt her burial. 'Tis thy task
To tend thine own. But me: let no man ask
This ancient city of my sires to give
Harbour in life to me. Set me to live

On the wild hills and leave my name to those
Deeps of Kithairon which my father chose,
And mother, for my vast and living tomb.
As they, my murderers, willed it, let my doom
Find me. For this my very heart doth know,
No sickness now, nor any mortal blow,
Shall slay this body. Never had my breath
Been thus kept burning in the midst of death,
Save for some frightful end. So, let my way
Go where it listeth.

But my children—Nay,
Creon, my sons will ask thee for no care.
Men are they, and can find them everywhere
What life needs. But my two poor desolate
Maidens. . . . There was no table ever set
Apart for them, but whatso royal fare
I tasted, they were with me and had share
In all. . . . Creon, I pray, forget them not.
And if it may be, go, bid them be brought,

> [CREON *goes and presently returns with the*
> *two princesses.* OEDIPUS *thinks he is there*
> *all the time.*

That I may touch their faces, and so weep. . . .
Go, Prince. Go, noble heart! . . .
If I might touch them, I should seem to keep
And not to have lost them, now mine eyes are gone. . . .
What say I?
In God's name, can it be I hear mine own
Beloved ones sobbing? Creon of his grace
Hath brought my two, my dearest, to this place.
Is it true?

   Creon. 'Tis true. I brought them, for in them I know
Thy joy is, the same now as long ago.

   Oedipus. God bless thee, and in this hard journey give
Some better guide than mine to help thee live.

   Children! Where are ye? Hither; come to these
Arms of your . . . brother, whose wild offices
Have brought much darkness on the once bright eyes
Of him who grew your garden; who, nowise
Seeing nor understanding, digged a ground

The world shall shudder at. Children, my wound
Is yours too, and I cannot meet your gaze
Now, as I think me what remaining days
Of bitter living the world hath for you.
What dance of damsels shall ye gather to,
What feast of Thebes, but quick ye shall turn home,
All tears, or ere the feast or dancers come?
And, children, when ye reach the years of love,
Who shall dare wed you, whose heart rise above
The peril, to take on him all the shame
That cleaves to my name and my children's name?
God knows, it is enough! . . .
My flowers, ye needs must die, waste things, bereft
And fruitless.

           Creon, thou alone art left
Their father now, since both of us are gone
Who cared for them. Oh, leave them not alone
To wander masterless, these thine own kin,
And beggared. Neither think of them such sin
As ye all know in me, but let their fate
Touch thee. So young they are, so desolate—
Of all save thee. True man, give me thine hand,
And promise.

                 [Oedipus *and* Creon *clasp hands.*
            If your age could understand,
Children, full many counsels I could give.
But now I leave this one word: Pray to live
As life may suffer you, and find a road
To travel easier than your father trod.

   Creon. Enough thy heart hath poured its tears; now back
     into thine house repair.

   Oedipus. I dread the house, yet go I must.

   Creon. Fair season maketh all things fair.

   Oedipus. One oath then give me, and I go.

   Creon. Name it, and I will answer thee.

   Oedipus. To cast me from this land.

   Creon. A gift not mine but God's thou askest me.

   Oedipus. I am a thing of God abhorred.

   Creon. The more, then, will he grant thy prayer.

   Oedipus. Thou givest thine oath?

Creon. I see no light; and, seeing not, I may not swear.

Oedipus. Then take me hence. I care not.

Creon. Go in peace, and give these children o'er.

Oedipus. Ah no! Take not away my daughters!

> [*They are taken from him.*

Creon. Seek not to be master more.

Did not thy masteries of old forsake thee when the end was near?

Chorus. Ye citizens of Thebes, behold; 'tis Oedipus that passeth here,

Who read the riddle-word of Death, and mightiest stood of mortal men,

And Fortune loved him, and the folk that saw him turned and looked again.

Lo, he is fallen, and around great storms and the outreaching sea!

Therefore, O Man, beware, and look toward the end of things that be,

The last of sights, the last of days; and no man's life account as gain

Ere the full tale be finished and the darkness find him without pain.

> [OEDIPUS *is led into the house and the doors close on him.*

SOPHOCLES
ANTIGONE

⇛⇚

TRANSLATED
By
ROBERT WHITELAW

CHARACTERS IN THE PLAY

ANTIGONE ⎱ *daughters of Oedipus.*
ISMENE ⎰
CREON, *King of Thebes.*
A WATCHMAN.
HAEMON, *Son of Creon.*
TIRESIAS, *the blind prophet.*
A MESSENGER.
EURYDICE, *the wife of Creon.*
ANOTHER MESSENGER.
CHORUS OF THEBAN ELDERS.

ARGUMENT

Oedipus, blind and degraded, has been exiled from Thebes. He leaves behind him a curse upon his two sons, Polynices and Eteocles, for not having resisted those who expelled him. Creon, brother of Jocasta, governs Thebes as regent, and is persuaded by Eteocles to banish Polynices, the elder brother. The latter takes refuge at Argos, where he marries the daughter of king Adrastus and persuades him to join in invading Thebes. Before the conflict, Polynices goes to Oedipus, now at Colonus, to secure his forgiveness and blessing. The old king only reiterates his curse, and prophesies that victory shall be with neither, but that both shall fall, slain by each other's hands. Antigone implores Polynices to abandon his enterprise but honour forbids. He goes, with a parting prayer that his sisters will see that in death he is not dishonoured, but receives duly his funeral rites. The prophecy is fulfilled and the brothers are transfixed by each other's spears. Since Eteocles had died defending his native city, he was entitled to his funeral rites. But as Polynices had died while invading his native state at the head of an alien army, and was thus guilty of the greatest crime a citizen could commit, it is decreed that his body shall be left a prey to birds and dogs on the spot where he fell—a fate regarded with peculiar horror by the Greeks, since the funeral rites were believed to determine the welfare of the departed in the next world. It is at this point the play opens.

ANTIGONE

SCENE.—*An open space before the royal palace at* THEBES.
    Enter ANTIGONE *and* ISMENE.

    Antigone. Ismene, sister mine, one life with me,
Knowest thou of the burden of our race[1]
Aught that from us yet living Zeus holds back?
Nay, for nought grievous and nought ruinous,
No shame and no dishonour, have I not seen
Poured on our hapless heads, both thine and mine.
And even now what edict hath the prince[2]
Uttered, men say, to all this Theban folk?
Thou knowest it and hast heard? or 'scapes thy sense,
Aimed at thy friends, the mischief of thy foes?
    Ismene. To me of friends, Antigone, no word
Hath come, or sweet or bitter, since that we
Two sisters of two brothers[3] were bereaved,
Both on a day slain by a twofold blow:
And, now that vanished is the Argive host
Ev'n with the night fled hence, I know no more,
If that I fare the better or the worse.
    Antigone. I knew full well, and therefore from the gates
O' the court I led thee hither, alone to hear.
    Ismene. There's trouble in thy looks: thy tidings tell.
    Antigone. Yea, hath not Creon, of our two brothers slain,
Honoured with burial one, disdained the other?
For Eteocles, they say, he in the earth
With all fair rites and ceremony hath laid,
Nor lacks he honour in the world below;
But the poor dust of Polynices dead
Through Thebes, 'tis said, the edict has gone forth
That none may bury, none make moan for him,
But leave unwept, untombed, a dainty prize
For ravening birds that gloat upon their prey.
So hath our good lord Creon to thee and me
Published, men say, his pleasure—ay, to *me*—
And hither comes, to all who know it not

Its purport to make plain, nor deems the thing
Of slight account, but, whoso does this deed,
A public death by stoning is his doom.
Thou hast it now; and quickly shall be proved
If thou art noble, or base from noble strain.

    Ismene. O rash of heart, if this indeed be so,
What help in me, to loosen or to bind?

    Antigone. Consider, toil and pain if thou wilt share.

    Ismene. On what adventure bound? What wouldst thou do?

    Antigone. To lift his body, wilt thou join with me?

    Ismene. Wouldst thou indeed rebel, and bury him?

    Antigone. My brother I will bury, and thine no less,
Whether thou wilt or no: no traitress I.

    Ismene. O all too bold—when Creon hath forbid?

    Antigone. My rights to hinder is no right of his.

    Ismene. Ah, sister, yet think how our father died,
Wrapt in what cloud of hate and ignominy
By his own sins, self-proved, and both his eyes
With suicidal hand himself he stabbed:
Then too his mother-wife, two names in one,
Fordid with twisted noose her woeful life;
Last, our two brothers in one fatal day
Drew sword, O miserable, and each to each
Dealt mutual slaughter with unnatural hands:
And now shall we twain, who alone are left,
Fall like the rest, and worse—in spite of law,
And scorning kings, their edicts and their power?
Oh rather let us think, 'tis not for us,
Who are but women, to contend with men:
And the king's word is mighty, and to this,
And harsher words than this, we needs must bow.
Therefore will I, imploring of the dead
Forgiveness, that I yield but as I must,
Obey the king's commandment: for with things
Beyond our reach 'twere foolishness to meddle.

    Antigone. I'll neither urge thee, nor, if now thou'dst help
My doing, should I thank thee for thine aid.
Do thou after thy kind: thy choice is made:
I'll bury him; doing this, so let me die.
So with my loved one loved shall I abide,

[54]

My crime a deed most holy: for the dead
Longer have I to please than these on earth.
There I shall dwell for ever: be it thine
To have scorned what gods have hallowed, if thou wilt.

Ismene. Nay, nothing do I scorn: but, how to break
My country's law—I am witless of the way.

Antigone. For thee such plea may serve: I go to heap
The earth upon my brother, whom I love.

Ismene. Alas, unhappy, how I fear for thee!

Antigone. Fear not for me: guide thine own fate aright.

Ismene. Yet breathe this purpose to no ear but mine:
Keep thou thy counsel well—and so will I.

Antigone. Oh speak: for much more hatred thou wilt get,
Concealing, than proclaiming it to all.

Ismene. This fever at thy heart by frost is fed.

Antigone. But, whom I most should please, they most are
    pleased.

Ismene. So wouldst thou: but thou canst not as thou wouldst.

Antigone. Why, then, when strength shall fail me, I will
    cease.

Ismene. Not to attempt the impossible is best.

Antigone. Hated by me, and hated by the dead—
To him a hateful presence evermore—
Thou shouldst be, and thou shalt be, speaking thus.
But leave me, and the folly that is mine,
This worst to suffer—not the worst—since still
A worse remains, no noble death to die.

Ismene. Go if thou wilt: but going know thyself
Senseless, yet to thy friends a friend indeed.

                                        [*Exeunt.*
                                        [*Strophe.*

Chorus. Lo, the sun upspringing!
Fairest light we hail thee
Of all dawns that on Thebes the seven-gated
Ever broke! Eye of golden day!
Over Dirce's fount appearing,
Hence the Argive host white-shielded,
That in complete arms came hither,
Headlong homeward thou didst urge
Faster still with shaken rein.

At call of Polynices, stirred
By bitter heat of wrangling claims,
Against our land they gathered, and they swooped
Down on us—like an eagle, screaming hoarse,
White-clad, with wings of snow—
With shields a many and with waving crests.

[Antistrophe.

But above our dwellings,
With his spears that thirsted
For our blood, at each gate's mouth of the seven
Gaping round, paused the foe—and went,
Ere his jaws with blood were sated,
Or our circling towers the torch-flame
Caught and kindled: so behind him
Raged intense the battle-din—
While for life the Serpent[4] fought.
For Zeus the tongue of vaunting pride
Hates with exceeding hate; he marked
That torrent army's onward flood, superb
With clank of gold, and with his brandished fire
Smote down who foremost climbed
To shout his triumph on our ramparts' heights.

[Strophe.

Hurled from that height with swift reverse,
The unpitying earth received him as he fell,
And quenched the brand he fain had flung,
And quelled the mad endeavour,
The frantic storm-gusts of his windy hate.
So fared it then with him;
Nor less elsewhere great Ares dealt
Against the foemen thunderous blows—
Our trace-horse on the right.
For seven chieftains at our seven gates
Met each his equal foe: and Zeus,
Who foiled their onset, claims from all his due,
The brazen arms, which on the field they left:
Save that infuriate pair,
Who, from one father and one mother sprung,
Against each other laid in rest

[56]

Their spears, victorious both,
And each by other share one equal death.

[Antistrophe.

But now of Victory be glad:
She meets our gladness with an answering smile,
And Thebes, the many-charioted,
Hears far resound her praises:
Now then with war have done, and strife forget!
All temples of the gods
Fill we with song and night-long dance;
And, Theban Bacchus, this our mirth
Lead thou, and shake the earth!
But lo the ruler of this Theban land,
Son of Menoeceus, Creon comes,
Crowned by these new and strange events, he comes—
By will of heav'n our new-created king,
What counsel pondering?
Who by his sovereign will hath now convoked,
In solemn conference to meet,
The elders of the state;
Obedient to whose summons, we are here.

[Enter CREON.

Creon. Sirs, it hath pleased the gods to right again
Our Theban fortunes, by sore tempest tossed:
And by my messenger I summoned hither
You out of all the state; first, as I knew you
To the might o' the throne of Laïus loyal ever:
Also, when Oedipus upheld the state,
And when he perished, to their children still
Ye with a constant mind were faithful found:
Now they are gone: both on one fatal field
An equal guilt atoned with equal doom,
Slayers of each other, by each other slain:
And I am left, the nearest to their blood,
To wield alone the sceptre and the realm.
There is no way to know of any man
The spirit and the wisdom and the will,
Till he stands proved, ruler and lawgiver.
For who, with a whole city to direct,
Yet cleaves not to those counsels that are best,

But locks his lips in silence, being afraid,
I held and hold him ever of men most base:
And whoso greater than his country's cause
Esteems a friend, I count him nothing worth.
For, Zeus who seeth all be witness now,
Nor for the safety's sake would I keep silence,
And see the ruin on my country fall,
Nor would I deem an enemy to the state
Friend to myself; remembering still that she,
She only brings us safe: on board of her
Our friends we make—no friends, if she be lost.
So for the good of Thebes her laws I frame:
And such the proclamation I set forth,
Touching the sons of Oedipus, ev'n now—
Eteocles, who fighting for this land
In battle has fall'n, more valiant none than he,
To bury, and no funeral rite omit
To brave men paid—their solace in the grave:
Not so his brother, Polynices: he,
From exile back returning, utterly
With fire his country and his fathers' gods
Would fain have burnt, fain would with kinsmen's blood
Have slaked his thirst, or dragged us captive hence:
Therefore to all this city it is proclaimed
That none may bury, none make moan for him,
But leave him lying all ghastly where he fell,
Till fowls o' the air and dogs have picked his bones.
So am I purposed: not at least by me
Shall traitors be preferred to honest men:
But, whoso loves this city, him indeed
I shall not cease to honour, alive or dead.
    Chorus.   Creon, son of Menoeceus, 'tis thy pleasure
The friend and foe of Thebes so to requite:
And, whatso pleases thee, that same is law,
Both for our Theban dead and us who live.
    Creon.   Look to it, then, my bidding is performed.
    Chorus.   Upon some younger man impose this burden.
    Creon.   To watch the body, sentinels are set.
    Chorus.   What service more then wouldst thou lay on us?
    Creon.   That ye resist whoever disobeys.

Chorus. Who is so senseless that desires to die?

Creon. The penalty is death: yet hopes deceive,
And men wax foolish oft through greed of gain.

[Enter SENTINEL.

Sentinel. That I come hither, king, nimble of foot,
And breathless with my haste, I'll not profess:
For many a doubtful halt upon the way,
And many a wheel to the right-about, I had,
Oft as my prating heart gave counsel, 'Fool,
What ails thee going into the lion's mouth?'
Then, 'Blockhead, wilt thou tarry? if Creon learns
This from another man, shalt thou not smart?'
So doubtfully I fared, reluctant-slow,
And, if the way was short, 'twas long to me.
But to come hither to thee prevailed at last,
And, though the speech be nought, yet I will speak.
For I have come fast clutching at the hope
That nought's to suffer but what fate decrees.

Creon. What is it that hath troubled thus thy mind?

Sentinel. First for myself this let me say: the deed
I neither did, nor saw who was the doer,
And 'twere not just that I should suffer harm.

Creon. Wisely, thyself in covert, at the mark
Thou aimest: some shrewd news, methinks, thou'lt tell.

Sentinel. Danger to face, well may a man be cautious.

Creon. Speak then, and go thy way, and make an end.

Sentinel. Now I will speak. Some one ev'n now hath buried
The body and is gone; with thirsty dust
Sprinkling it o'er, and paying observance due.

Creon. How? By what man was dared a deed so rash?

Sentinel. I cannot tell. No mattock's stroke indeed,
Nor spade's upcast was there: hard was the ground,
Baked dry, unbroken: track of chariot-wheels
Was none, nor any sign who did this thing.
But he who kept the watch at earliest dawn
Showed to us all—a mystery, hard to clear.
Not buried was the dead man, but concealed,
With dust besprinkled, as for fear of sin:
And neither of dog, nor any beast of prey,
That came, that tore the body, found we trace.

[59]

Then bitter words we bandied to and fro,
Denouncing each the other; and soon to blows
Our strife had grown—was none would keep the peace—
For every one was guilty of the deed,
And none confessed, but all denied they knew.
And we were fain to handle red-hot iron,
Or walk through fire barefoot, or swear by heaven,
That neither had we done it, nor had shared
His secret with who planned it or who wrought.
So all in vain we questioned: and at last
One spake, and all who heard him, bowed by fear,
Bent to the earth their faces, knowing not
How to gainsay, nor doing what he said
How we might 'scape mischance. This deed to thee
He urged that we should show, and hide it not.
And his advice prevailed; and by the lot
To luckless me this privilege befell.
Unwilling and unwelcome is my errand,
A bearer of ill news, whom no man loves.

   Chorus. O king, my thought hath counselled me long since,
Haply this deed is ordered by the gods.

   Creon. Cease, ere my wrath is kindled at thy speech,
Lest thou be found an old man and a fool.
Intolerably thou pratest of the gods,
That they to yonder dead man have respect.
Yea, for what service with exceeding honour
Sought they his burial, who came here to burn
Their pillared shrines and temple-offerings,
And of their land and of their laws make havoc?
Or seest thou that the gods allow the wicked?
Not so: but some impatient of my will
Among my people made a murmuring,
Shaking their heads in secret, to the yoke
With stubborn necks unbent, and hearts disloyal.
Full certainly I know that they with bribes
Have on these men prevailed to do this deed.
Of all the evils current in this world
Most mischievous is gold. This hath laid waste
Fair cities, and unpeopled homes of men:
Many an honest heart hath the false lure

Of gold seduced to walk in ways of shame;
And hence mankind are versed in villanies,
And of all godless acts have learnt the lore.
But, who took hire to execute this work,
Wrought to their own undoing at the last.
Since, if the dread of Zeus I still revere,
Be well assured—and what I speak I swear—
Unless the author of this burial
Ye find, and in my sight produce him here,
For you mere death shall not suffice, until
Gibbeted alive this outrage ye disclose,
That ye may know what gains are worth the winning,
And henceforth clutch the wiselier, having learnt
That to seek gain in all things is not well.
For from ill-gotten pelf the lives of men
Ruined than saved more often shall ye see.

    Sentinel. May I speak a word, or thus am I dismissed?
    Creon. Know'st thou not that ev'n now thy voice offends?
    Sentinel. Do I afflict thy hearing or thy heart?
    Creon. Where I am pained, it skills not to define.
    Sentinel. The doer grieves thy mind, but I thine ears.
    Creon. That thou wast born to chatter, 'tis too plain.
    Sentinel. And therefore not the doer of this deed.
    Creon. At thy life's cost thou didst it, bought with gold.
    Sentinel. Alas!
'Tis pity, men should judge, yet judge amiss.
    Creon. Talk you of 'judging' glibly as you may—
Who did this deed, I'll know, or ye shall own
That all your wondrous winnings end in loss.
    Sentinel. With all my heart I wish he may be found:
But found or no—for that's as fortune will—
I shall not show my face to you again.
Great cause I have to thank the gracious gods,
Saved past all hope and reckoning even now.

                        [*Exeunt* CREON *and* SENTINEL.
                                   [*Strophe.*

    Chorus. Many are the wonders of the world,
And none so wonderful as Man.
Over the waters wan

His storm-vext bark he steers,
While the fierce billows break
Round his path, and o'er his head:
And the Earth-mother, first of gods,
The ageless, the indomitable,
With his ploughing to and fro
He wearieth, year by year:
In the deep furrow toil the patient mules.

[*Antistrophe.*

The birds o' the air he snares and takes
All the light-hearted fluttering race:
And tribes of savage beasts,
And creatures of the deep,
Meshed in his woven toils,
Own the master-mind of man.
Free lives of upland and of wild
By human arts are curbed and tamed:
See the horse's shaggy neck
Submissive to the yoke—
And strength untired of mountain-roaming bulls.

[*Strophe.*

Language withal he learnt,
And Thought that as the wind is free,
And aptitudes of civic life:
Ill-lodged no more he lies,
His roof the sky, the earth his bed,
Screened now from piercing frost and pelting rain;
All-fertile in resource, resourceless never
Meets he the morrow; only death
He wants the skill to shun:
But many a fell disease the healer's art hath foiled.

[*Antistrophe.*

So soaring far past hope,
The wise inventiveness of man
Finds diverse issues, good and ill:
If from their course he wrests
The firm foundations of the state,
Laws, and the justice he is sworn to keep—
High in the city, cityless I deem him,
Dealing with baseness: overbold,

May he my hearth avoid,
Nor let my thoughts with his, who does such deeds, agree!

       [*Re-enter* SENTINEL, *bringing in* ANTIGONE.

What strange portentous sight is this,
I doubt my eyes, beholding? This—
How shall I gainsay what I know?—
This maiden *is*—Antigone!
Daughter of Oedipus,
Hapless child of a hapless sire,
What hast thou done?   It cannot be
That thou hast transgressed the king's command—
That, taken in folly, *thee* they bring!

  Sentinel.   This same is she that did the burial:
We caught her in the act.   But where's the king?

  Chorus.   Back from the palace in good time he comes.

                  [*Re-enter* CREON.

  Creon.   What chance is this, to which my steps are timed?

  Sentinel.   Nothing, sir king, should men swear not to do;
For second thoughts to first thoughts give the lie.
Hither, I made full sure, I scarce should come
Back, by your threats beruffled as I was.
Yet here, surprised by most unlooked-for joy,
That trifles all delights that e'er I knew,
I bring you—though my coming breaks my oath—
This maiden, whom, busied about the corpse,
We captured.   This time were no lots to throw:
My own good fortune this, and none but mine.
Now therefore, king, take her yourself and try her,
And question as you will: but I have earned
Full clearance and acquittal of this coil.

  Creon.   Where, on what manner, was your captive taken?

  Sentinel.   Burying the man, we took her: all is told.

  Creon.   Art thou advised of this?   Is it the truth?

  Sentinel.   I say I saw her burying the body,
That you forbade.   Is that distinct and clear?

  Creon.   How!   Was she seen, and taken in the act?

  Sentinel.   So it fell out.   When I had gone from hence
With thy loud threats yet sounding in my ears,
We swept off all the dust that hid the limbs,
And to the light stripped bare the clammy corpse,

[63]

And on the hill's brow sat, and faced the wind,
Choosing a spot clear of the body's stench.
Roundly we chid each other to the work;
'No sleeping at your post there' was our word.
So did we keep the watch, till in mid-heaven
The sun's bright burning orb above us hung,
With fierce noon-heat: and now a sudden blast
Swept, and a storm of dust, that vexed the sky
And choked the plain, and all the leaves o' the trees
O' the plain were marred, and the wide heaven it filled:
We with shut eyes the heaven-sent plague endured.
And, when after long time its force was spent,
We saw this maiden, and a bitter cry
She poured, as of a wailing bird that sees
Her empty nest dismantled of its brood:
So she, when she espied the body bare,
Cried out and wept, and many a grievous curse
Upon their heads invoked by whom 'twas done.
And thirsty dust she sprinkled with her hands,
And lifted up an urn, fair-wrought of brass,
And with thrice-poured[5] libations crowned the dead.
We saw it and we hasted, and at once,
All undismayed, our captive, hemmed her round,
And with the two offences charged her there,
Both first and last. Nothing did she deny,
But made me glad and sorry, owning all.
For to have slipped one's own neck from the noose
Is sweet, yet no one likes to get his friends
In trouble: but my nature is to make
All else of small account, so I am safe.

 Creon. Speak thou, who bendest on the earth thy gaze,
Are these things, which are witnessed, true or false?

  Antigone. I say I did it; I deny it not.

  Creon. So, sirrah, thou art free; go where thou wilt,
Loosed from the burden of this heavy charge.
But tell me thou—and let thy speech be brief—
The edict hadst thou heard, which this forbade?

  Antigone. I could not choose but hear what all men heard.

  Creon. And didst thou dare to disobey the law?

  Antigone. Nowise from Zeus, methought, this edict came,

Nor Justice, that abides among the gods
In Hades, who ordained these laws for men.
Nor did I deem *thine* edicts of such force
That they, a mortal's bidding, should o'erride
Unwritten laws, eternal in the heavens.
Not of to-day or yesterday are these,
But live from everlasting, and from whence
They sprang, none knoweth.   I would not, for the breach
Of these, through fear of any human pride,
To heaven atone.   I knew that I must die:
How else?   Without thine edict, that were so.
And if before my time, why, this were gain.
Compassed about with ills, who lives, as I,
Death, to such life as his, must needs be gain.
So is it to me to undergo this doom
No grief at all: but had I left my brother,
My mother's child, unburied where he lay,
Then I had grieved; but now this grieves me not.
Senseless I seem to thee, so doing?   Belike
A senseless judgement finds me void of sense.

   Chorus.   How in the child the sternness of the sire
Shows stern, before the storm untaught to bend!

   Creon.   Yet know full well that such o'er-stubborn wills
Are broken most of all, as sturdiest steel,
Of an untempered hardness, fresh from forge,
Most surely snapped and shivered should ye see.
Lo how a little curb has strength enough
To tame the restive horse: for to a slave
His masters give no license to be proud.
Insult on insult heaped!   Was't not enough
My promulgated laws to have transgressed,
But, having done it, face to face with me
She boasts of this and glories in the deed?
I surely am the woman, she the man,
If she defies my power, and I submit.
Be she my sister's child, or sprung from one
More near of blood than all my house to me,
Not so shall they escape my direst doom—
She and her sister: for I count her too
Guilty no less of having planned this work.

Go, call her hither: in the house I saw her
Raving ev'n now, nor mistress of her thoughts.
So oft the mind, revolving secret crime,
Makes premature disclosure of its guilt.
But this is hateful, when the guilty one,
Detected, thinks to glorify his fault.

Antigone. To kill me—wouldst thou more with me than this?
Creon. This is enough: I do desire no more.
Antigone. Why dost thou then delay? I have no pleasure
To hear thee speak—have not and would not have:
Nor less distasteful is my speech to thee.
Yet how could I have won myself a praise
More honourable than this, of burying
My brother? This from every voice should win
Approval, might but fear men's lips unseal.
But kings are fortunate—not least in this,
That they may do and speak what things they will.

Creon. All Thebes sees this with other eyes than thine.
Antigone. They see as I, but bate their breath to thee.
Creon. And art thou not ashamed, from them to differ?
Antigone. To reverence a brother is not shameful.
Creon. And was not he who died for Thebes thy brother?
Antigone. One mother bore us, and one sire begat.
Creon. Yet, honouring both, thou dost dishonour him.
Antigone. He in the grave will not subscribe to this.
Creon. How, if no less thou dost revere the guilty?
Antigone. 'Twas not his slave that perished, but his brother.
Creon. The enemy of this land: its champion he.
Antigone. Yet Death of due observance must not fail.
Creon. Just and unjust urge not an equal claim.
Antigone. Perchance in Hades 'tis a holy deed.
Creon. Hatred, not ev'n in death, converts to love.
Antigone. Not in your hates, but in your loves, I'd share.
Creon. Go to the shades, and, if thou'lt love, love there:
No woman, while I live, shall master me.

[*Enter* ISMENE.

Chorus. See, from the palace comes Ismene—
Sisterly drops from her eyes down-shedding:
Clouded her brows droop, heavy with sorrow;
And the blood-red tinge of a burning blush

Covers her beautiful downcast face.

Creon. Thou, who hast crept, a serpent in my home,
Draining my blood, unseen; and I knew not
Rearing two pests, to overset my throne;
Speak—wilt thou too confess that in this work
Thou hadst a hand, or swear thou didst not know?

Ismene. I'll say the deed was mine, if she consents:
My share of the blame I bear, and do not shrink.

Antigone. Justice forbids thy claim: neither didst thou
Agree, nor I admit thee to my counsels.

Ismene. I am not ashamed, in thine extremity,
To make myself companion of thy fate.

Antigone. Whose was the deed, know Hades and the dead:
I love not friends, who talk of friendliness.

Ismene. Sister, disdain me not, but let me pour
My blood with thine, an offering to the dead.

Antigone. Leave me to die alone, nor claim the work
Thou wouldst not help. My death will be enough.

Ismene. What joy have I to live, when thou art gone?

Antigone. Ask Creon that: thou art of kin to him.

Ismene. Why wilt thou grieve me with thy needless taunts?

Antigone. If I mock thee, 'tis with a heavy heart.

Ismene. What may I do to serve thee even now?

Antigone. Look to thyself: I grudge thee not thy safety.

Ismene. And may I not, unhappy, share thy death?

Antigone. Thou didst make choice to live, but I to die.

Ismene. Might I unsay my words, this were not so.

Antigone. Wise seemed we—thou to these, and I to those.

Ismene. But now our fault is equal, thine and mine.

Antigone. Take heart to live: for so thou dost: but I—
Dead is my life long since—to help the dead.

Creon. One of these two, methinks, proves foolish now;
The other's folly with her life began.

Ismene. Nay, for, O king, misfortunes of the wise
To madness turn the wisdom that they have.

Creon. 'Tis so with thee, choosing to share her guilt.

Ismene. How should I live alone, without my sister?

Creon. Call her not thine: thou hast no sister now.

Ismene. But wilt thou tear her from thy son's embrace?

Creon. Are there no women in the world but she?

Ismene. Not as their faith was plighted, each to each.
Creon. An evil wife I like not for my son.
Antigone. Haemon! beloved! hear not thy father's scorn.
Creon. Thou and thy love to me are wearisome.
Chorus. Wilt thou indeed snatch from thy son his bride?
Creon. 'Tis death that will unloose their marriage-bond.
Chorus. It seems thou art resolved that she must die?
Creon. Of that we are agreed. Delay no more:
Ye, servants, lead them in. For from this time
Women they needs must be, and range no more:
Since ev'n the bold may play the runaway,
When death he sees close-creeping on his life.

[ANTIGONE *and* ISMENE *are led into the palace.*

Chorus.   [*Strophe.*
Happy indeed is the life of the man who tastes not of trouble!
For when from the gods a house is shaken,
Fails nevermore the curse,
On most and on least of the race descending:
Like to a rolling wave,
By furious blasts from the Thraceward driven—
Out of the nethermost deeps, out of the fathomless gloom,
Casting up mire and blackness and storm-vext wrack of the
    sea—
And back, with a moan like thunder, from the cliffs the surf
    is hurled.

[*Antistrophe.*
So from of old to the Labdacid race[6] comes sorrow on sorrow:
And, ev'n as the dead, so fare the living:
Respite from ills is none,
Nor one generation redeems another—
All will some god bring low.
Now o'er the last root of the house, fate-stricken,
Woe for the light that had shined, woe for the lingering hope!
Smooth over all is lying the blood-stained dust they have
    spread—
Rash speech, and a frantic purpose, and the gods who reign
    below.

[*Strophe.*
What human trespass, Zeus,
May circumscribe thy power,

Which neither sleep o'ercomes,
That saps the strength of all things else,
Nor months that run their tireless course,
But thou for ever with an ageless sway
The dazzling splendour dost possess
Of thine Olympian home?
'Tis now as it hath ever been,
And still in years to come
The old order will not change:
Never from human life departs
The universal scourge of man,
His own presumptuous pride.

[Antistrophe.

Hope wings her daring flight,
By strong winds borne afar—
And some are blessed; and some
Are cheated of their vain desires,
That learn their folly all too late,
When in the fire they tread with scorchèd feet.
'Twas said of old—and time approves
The wisdom of the saw—
That, when in foolish ways, that end
In ruin, gods would lead
A mortal's mind astray,
Evil that man miscalls his good:
A brief while then he holds his course
By fatuous pride unscathed.
See, thy son Haemon comes hither, of all
Thy children the last. Comes he lamenting
The doom of the maiden, his bride Antigone—
And the frustrated hope of his marriage?

[Enter HAEMON.

Creon. Soon we shall know, better than seers could say.
My son, in anger art thou come to me,
Hearing the sentence, not to be reversed,
Which on thy destined bride I have pronounced?
Or am I still thy friend, do what I may?

Haemon. Father, I am in thy hand: with thy wise counsels
Thou dost direct me; these I shall obey.
Not rightly should I deem of more account

[69]

The winning of a wife than thy good guidance.
   Creon. Be this thy dearest wish and next thy heart,
In all things to uphold thy father's will.
For to this end men crave to see grow up
Obedient children round them in their homes,
Both to requite their enemies with hate,
And render equal honour to their friends.
Whoso begets unprofitable children,
What shall be said of him, but that he gets
Grief for himself, loud laughter for his foes?
Never, my son, let for a woman's sake
Reason give way to sense, but know full well
Cold is the pleasure that he clasps, who woos
An evil woman to his board and bed.
What wounds so deeply as an evil friend?
Count then this maiden as thine enemy,
Loathe her, and give her leave, in that dark world
To which she goes, to marry with another.
For out of all the city since I found
Her only, and her openly, rebellious,
I shall not to the city break my word,
But she shall die. Let her appeal to Zeus,
And sing the sanctity of kindred blood—
What then? If in my own house I shall nurse
Rebellion, how shall strangers not rebel?
He who to his own kith and kin does right,
Will in the state deal righteously with all.
Of such a man I shall not fear to boast,
Well he can rule, and well he would obey,
And in the storm of battle at his post
Firm he would stand, a comrade staunch and true.
But praise from me that man shall never have,
Who either boldly thrusts aside the law
Or takes upon him to instruct his rulers,
Whom, by the state empowered, he should obey,
In little and in much, in right and wrong.
The worst of evils is to disobey.
Cities by this are ruined, homes of men
Made desolate by this; this in the battle
Breaks into headlong rout the wavering line;

The steadfast ranks, the many lives unhurt,
Are to obedience due. We must defend
The government and order of the state,
And not be governed by a wilful girl.
We'll yield our place up, if we must, to men;
To women that we stooped, shall not be said.

    Chorus. Unless an old man's judgement is at fault,
These words of thine, we deem, are words of wisdom.

    Hæmon. Reason, my father, in the mind of man,
Noblest of all their gifts, the gods implant,
And how to find thy reasoning at fault,
I know not, and to learn I should be loth;
Yet for another it might not be amiss.
But I for thee am vigilant to mark
All that men say, or do, or find to blame.
Thy presence awes the simple citizen
From speaking words that shall not please thine ear,
But I hear what they whisper in the dark,
And how the city for this maid laments,
That of all women she the least deserving
Dies for most glorious deeds a death most cruel,
Who her own brother, fall'n among the slain,
Left not unburied there, to be devoured
By ravening dogs or any bird o' the air:—
'Should not her deed be blazoned all in gold?'
Upon the darkness still such whisper grows.
But I of all possessions that I have
Prize most, my father, thy prosperity.
Welldoing and fair fame of sire to son,
Of son to sire, is noblest ornament.
Cleave not, I pray thee, to this constant mind,
That what thou sayest, and nought beside, is truth.
For men who think that only they are wise,
None eloquent, right-minded none, but they,
Often, when searched, prove empty. 'Tis no shame,
Ev'n if a man be wise, that he should yet
Learn many things, and not hold out too stiffly.
Beside the torrent's course, of trees that bend
Each bough, thou seest, and every twig is safe;
Those that resist are by the roots uptorn.

And ships, that brace with stubborn hardihood
Their mainsheet to the gale, pursue their voyage
Keel-uppermost, their sailors' thwarts reversed.
Cease from thy wrath; be not inexorable:
For if despite my youth I too may think
My thought, I'll say that best it is by far
That men should be all-knowing if they may,
But if—as oft the scale inclines not so—
Why then, by good advice 'tis good to learn.

    Chorus. What in thy son's speech, king, is seasonable
'Tis fit thou shouldst receive: and thou in his:
For there is reason in the words of both.

    Creon. Shall I, grown grey with age, be taught indeed—
And by this boy—to think what he thinks right ?

    Haemon. Nothing that is not right: though I am young,
Consider not my years, but how I act.

    Creon. Is this thine act—to honour the unruly?

    Haemon. Wrongdoers, dishonour—outrage, if thou wilt!

    Creon. Hath not this maiden caught this malady?

    Haemon. The general voice of Thebes says no to that.

    Creon. Shall Thebes prescribe to me how I must govern?

    Haemon. How all too young art thou in speaking thus!

    Creon. Whose business is't but mine how Thebes is
        governed?

    Haemon. A city is none, that to one man belongs.

    Creon. Is it not held, the city is the king's?

    Haemon. Finely thou'dst rule, alone, a land dispeopled!

    Creon. It seems this boy will plead the woman's cause.

    Haemon. Woman art thou? my care is all for thee.

    Creon. Shameless—is't right to wrangle with thy father?

    Haemon. I see that wrong for right thou dost mistake.

    Creon. Do I mistake, to reverence my office?

    Haemon. What reverence, heaven's honours to contemn?

    Creon. O hateful spirit, ruled by a woman's will!

    Haemon. To no base service shalt thou prove me bound.

    Creon. Art thou not pleading all the time for her?

    Haemon. For thee and me, and for the gods below.

    Creon. Thou shalt not marry her, this side the grave.

    Haemon. If she must die, she shall: but not alone.

    Creon. Art grown so bold, thou dost fly out in threats?

Haemon. What threats, to argue with a foolish purpose?
Creon. Thou'lt rue—unwise—thy wisdom spent on me.
Haemon. Thou art my father; or wise I scarce had called thee.
Creon. Slave—to thy mistress babble, not to me.
Haemon. Wouldst thou have all the talking for thine own?
Creon. Is't come to this? But, by Olympus yonder,
Know well, thou shalt be sorry for these taunts,
 Wherewith thou dost upbraid me. Slaves, what ho!
Bring that abhorrence hither, that she may die,
 Now, in her bridegroom's sight, whilst here he stands.
  Haemon. Neither in my sight—imagine no such thing—
Shall she be slain; nor shalt thou from this hour
Look with thine eyes upon my face again:
To friends who love thy madness I commit thee.

[*Exit* HAEMON.

Chorus. Suddenly, sire, in anger he is gone:
Young minds grow desperate, by grief distemper'd.
  Creon. More than a man let him conceive and do;
He shall not save these maidens from their doom.
  Chorus. Both sisters art thou purposed to destroy?
  Creon. Not her whose hands sinned not; thou askest well.
  Chorus. What of the other? how shall she be slain?
  Creon. By paths untrodden of men I will conduct her,
And shut her, living, in a vault, rock-hewn,
And there, with food, no more than shall suffice
To avert the guilt of murder from the city,
To Hades, the one god whom she reveres,
She, praying not to die, either shall have
Her asking, or shall learn, albeit too late,
That to revere the dead is fruitless toil.

[*Exit* CREON.
[*Strophe.*

Chorus. O Love, our conqueror, matchless in might,
Thou prevailest, O Love, thou dividest the prey;
In damask cheeks of a maiden
 Thy watch through the night is set.
Thou roamest over the sea;
On the hills, in the shepherds' huts, thou art;

Nor of deathless gods, nor of short-lived men,
From thy madness any escapeth.

[*Antistrophe.*

Unjust, through thee, are the thoughts of the just,
Thou dost bend them, O Love, to thy will, to thy spite.
Unkindly strife thou hast kindled,
This wrangling of son with sire.
For great laws, throned in the heart,
To the sway of a rival power give place,
To the love-light flashed from a fair bride's eyes:
In her triumph laughs Aphrodite.
Me, even now, me also,
Seeing these things, a sudden pity
Beyond all governance transports:
The fountains of my tears
I can refrain no more,
Seeing Antigone here to the bridal chamber
Come, to the all-receiving chamber of Death.

[*Enter* ANTIGONE *surrounded by guards.*

Antigone. Friends and my countrymen, ye see me
Upon the last of all my ways
Set forth, the Sun-god's latest light
Beholding, now and never more:
But Death, who giveth sleep to all,
Yet living leads me hence
To the Acherontian shore,
Of marriage rites amerced,
And me no bridal song hath ever sung,
But Acheron will make of me his bride.

Chorus. Therefore renowned, with praise of men,
To yonder vault o' the dead thou goest,
By no slow-wasting sickness stricken,
Nor doomed to fall with those who win
The wages of the swords they drew,
But mistress of thyself, alive,
Alone of mortals the dark road
To deathward thou shalt tread.

Antigone. I heard of one, most piteous in her ending,
That stranger,[7] child of Phrygian Tantalus,

[74]

On heights of Sipylus enclasped,
And ivy-like enchained,
By clinging tendrils of the branching rock,
Who day and night unceasingly
'Mid drizzle of rain and drift of snow
Slow-wasting in her place
Stands, as the tale is told,
Her lids surcharged with weeping, and her neck
And bosom drenched with falling of her tears:—
A fate most like to hers
Seals up with sleep these eyes of mine.

   Chorus. She was a goddess, sprung from gods:
Mortals, of mortal birth, are we.
But for one dead to win with those
Who rank no lower than the gods—
Living and, after, when she died—
An equal lot, were much to hear.

   Antigone. Ah, I am mocked! Nay, by our fathers' gods,
Withhold thy taunts till I am gone—
Gone and evanished from thy sight.
O Thebes, my city!
O wealthy men of Thebes!
But *ye* will witness—yes, to you I turn—
O fount Dircaean, and this sacred grove
Of Thebè the fair-charioted,
By what stern law, and how of friends unwept,
To that strange grave I go,
The massy dungeon for my burial heaped.
O luckless wight,
Exiled from earth nor housed below,
Both by the living and the dead disowned!

   Chorus. To furthest brink of boldness thou didst stray,
And stumbling there, at foot of Justice' throne,
Full heavily, my daughter, hast thou fallen:
Yet of thy father's fault belike
This suffering pays the price.

   Antigone. Thou hast touched, ev'n there, my bitterest pang
     of all,
A thrice-told tale, my father's grief—
And all our grievous doom that clung

[75]

About the famed Labdacidae.
O that incestuous bed
Of horror, and my father's sin—
The hapless mother who bore him to the light,
By him enclasped—wherefrom I luckless sprang:
With whom, accurst, unwedded,
I must go hence to dwell.
O brother, a bride ill-starred[8]
Who to thy couch didst win,
How, being dead, me living thou hast slain!

    Chorus. Religion prompts the reverent deed:
But power, to whomso power belongs,
Must nowise be transgressed; and thee
A self-willed temper hath o'erthrown

    Antigone. Unwept and unfriended,
Cheered by no song Hymenaeal—
Lo, I am led, heavy-hearted,
This road that awaits me.
The sacred light-giving eye in heaven
Now no more must I see, unhappy:
But for my fate not a tear falls,
Not a friend makes moan.

                    [Re-enter CREON.

    Creon. Know ye not, songs and weepings before death
That none would pretermit, were he allowed?
Hence with her, hence, and tarry not, but deep
In her tomb-prison, even as I have said,
Leave her alone, forsaken: to die, or else
Live, in that vault entombed, if so she will:
Since of this maiden's blood our hands are clean,
Only we ban her sojourn in the light.

    Antigone. O tomb! O nuptial chamber! O house deep-
        delved
In earth, safe-guarded ever! To thee I come,
And to my kin in thee, who many an one
Are with Persephone,[9] dead among the dead:
And last of all, most miserably by far,
I thither am going, ere my life's term be done.
But a good hope I cherish, that, come there,
My father's love will greet me, yea and thine,

[76]

My mother—and thy welcome, brother dear:
Since, when ye died, I with mine own hands laved
And dressed your limbs, and poured upon your graves
Libations; and like service done to thee
Hath brought me, Polynices, now to this.
Yet well I honoured thee, the wise will say:
Since not for children's sake would I, their mother,
Nor for my husband, slain, and mouldering there,
Have travailed thus, doing despite to Thebes.
According to what law, do I speak this?
One husband slain, another might have been,
And children from another, losing this;
But, father and mother buried out of sight,
There can be born no brother any more.
Such was the law whereby I held thee first
In honour; but to Creon all mistaken,
O dear my brother, I seemed, and overbold—
And now, made captive thus, he leads me hence
No wife, no bride for ever—of marriage-joy
And nursery of children quite bereft:
So by my friends forsaken I depart,
Living, unhappy, to dim vaults of death.
Yet I transgressed—what ordinance of heaven?
Why to the gods, ill-fated, any more
Should I look up—whom call to succour—since
Impiety my piety is named?
But, if these things are pleasing to the gods,
I'll freely own I suffered for my fault;
If theirs the fault, who doomed me, may to them
No worse befall than they unjustly do!

   Chorus. Stormily still o'er the soul of the maiden
The selfsame gusts of passion sweep.

   Creon. Therefore, I warn them, ruth for their lingering,
To those who lead her, this shall cause.

   Antigone. Short shrift, swift death—ah! woe is me—
This speech portends.

   Creon. Lay to thy soul no flattering hope,
That unfulfilled this doom may be.

   Antigone. O country of Thebes and my father's city,
And gods my progenitors,

Lo, how they lead me—now, and delay not.
O all ye princes of Thebes, behold me—
Of the race of your kings, me, sole surviving—
What things at the hands of what men I suffer,
For the fear of the gods I feared.

[*Exit* ANTIGONE.

[*Strophe.*

   Chorus. Out of the sunlight so,
In brass-bound prison-courts,
Were pent the limbs of Danaë,[10]
And in a living tomb sealed up from sight;
Albeit, O daughter, she as thou
Came of a noble line,
And that life-quickening treasure of his golden rain
She had in charge from Zeus to keep.
O dread mysterious power of fate,
That neither wealth nor war can quell,
Nor walls shut out, nor ships escape,
Dark-fleeing o'er the foam!

[*Antistrophe.*

And that Edonian king
Was bound, the choleric son
Of Dryas, splenetive and hot,
Fast in the rock by Dionysus chained.
Such fierce and fevered issue streams
From madness at the height.
With splenetive rash speech what madness had assailed
The vengeful god, too late he learned.
To women-worshippers inspired
Their torchlit revels he forbade,
And flutings that the Muses loved
Had silenced with his scorn.

[*Strophe.*

From the dark rock-portals[11] of the divided sea
Here go the cliffs of Bosporus, and there
The savage Thracian coast
Of Salmydessus, where the neighbour-worshipped God
Of Battle saw the blinding blow accurst,
Dealt by that fierce stepdame,[12]
Darkling descend on both the sons

Of Phineus—on their sightless orbs
That plead for vengeance, stricken through and stabbed
By the sharp shuttle in her murderous hands.

[*Antistrophe.*

Wasted with their sorrow, their mother's hapless fate
They hapless wept, and in their mother's shame
Had part, as those base-born:
Yet she[13] from the old Erechtheid blood her birth derived,
And in deep caverns of the hills was nursed,
Amid her father's storms,
Child of the North-wind—up the steep
Hillsides no bounding foal so fleet,
A daughter of the gods: but her, O child,
Fate's everlasting hands availed to reach.

[*Enter* TIRESIAS *a boy leading him.*

Tiresias. Princes of Thebes, we come—one sight for both
Our common road descrying, as behoves
Blind men to find their way by help of others.
Creon. What tidings, old Tiresias, dost thou bring?
Tiresias. Hear then the prophet, and attend his speech.
Creon. Have I aforetime from thy wisdom swerved?
Tiresias. So, clear of shoals, thou pilotest the state.
Creon. The service thou hast rendered I attest.
Tiresias. Once more on razor's edge thy fortunes stand.
Creon. Hearing thy speech, I shudder: tell me more.
Tiresias. My art's prognostications hear and judge.
For in my ancient seat, to watch the birds
In that their general gathering-place, I sat,
And heard an unintelligible noise,
A cry and clangour of birds, confused with rage;
And what fierce fray they waged with murderous claws,
I guessed too surely by the whirr of wings.
Scared by that sound, burnt-offerings I then
Essayed on blazing altars; but no flame
Leapt from the sacrifice; a clammy ooze
Reeked from the thighs, and 'mid the ashes dripped,
Smoking and sputtering; the gall disparted,
And on the air was spent; and the thighbones
Of the enfolding fat fell stripped and bare.

This from this boy I heard, whose eyes beheld
The failing signs of sacrifice obscure:
Others by me are guided, I by him.
And by thy will we are afflicted thus.
For now our hearths and altars every one
Have ravening dogs and birds fouled with the flesh
Of this poor fallen son of Oedipus;
And so no flame of victims burnt may move
Gods any more to hearken to our prayers,
And birds obscene flap thence their bodeful cries,
With fat of human carrion newly gorged.
Slight not, my son, such warning. For all men,
Both great and small, are liable to err:
But he who errs no more unfortunate
Or all unwise shall be, if having tripped
He rights the wrong nor stubbornly persists.
He who persists in folly is the fool.
Give death his due: stab not the fallen foe:
What valour is in this, to slay the slain?
Wisely I speak and well; and sweet it is
To hear good counsel, when it counsels gain.

 Creon. Old man, ye all, as bowmen at a mark,
Shoot at this man, and now with soothsaying
Ye practice on me—ye by whose sort long since
Mere merchandise and salework I am made.
Go to, get gain, and barter, if ye will,
Amber ye buy from Sardis, and fine gold
Of Ind: but him, I say, ye shall not bury:
No, not if eagles, ministers of Zeus
Should bear him piecemeal to their Master's throne,
Will I, for fear of such pollution, grant
Leave for his burial; knowing well that men
Soil not the stainless majesty of heaven.
But, aged seer, the wisest of mankind
Dishonourably may fall, who fairly speak
Dishonourable words, and all for gain.

 Tiresias. Alas!
Who knows, or who considers, in this world—

 Creon. What wilt thou say? What commonplace is this?

 Tiresias. How prudence is the best of all our wealth?

[80]

Creon. As folly, I suppose, our deadliest hurt.
Tiresias. Yet with this malady art thou possest.
Creon. Reproaches I'll not bandy with the prophet.
Tiresias. Saying that I falsely prophesy, thou dost.
Creon. So are all prophets; 'tis a covetous race.
Tiresias. Greed of base gain marks still the tyrant-sort.
Creon. Knowest thou that of thy rulers this is said?
Tiresias. I know; for thou through me didst save the state.
Creon. Wise in thy craft art thou, but false at heart.
Tiresias. Secrets, fast-locked, thou'lt move me to disclose.
Creon. Unlock them, only speaking not for gain.
Tiresias. So, for thy part indeed, methinks I shall.
Creon. Think not that in my purpose thou shalt trade.
Tiresias. But surely know that thou not many more
Revolving courses of the sun shalt pass,
Ere of thine own blood one, to make amends,
Dead for the dead, thou shalt have rendered up,
For that a living soul thou hast sent below,
And with dishonour in the grave hast lodged,
And that one dead thou holdest here cut off
From presence of the gods who reign below,
All rites of death, all obsequies denied—
With whom thou shouldst not meddle, nor the gods
In heaven, but of their due thou robb'st the dead.
Therefore of Hades and the gods for thee
The Avengers wait, with ruin slow yet sure,
To take thee in the pit which thou hast dug.
Do I speak this for gold? Thyself shalt judge:
For, yet a little while, and wailings loud
Of men and women in thy house shall show.
Think, of each city too what gathering rage,
That sees its mangled dead entombed in maws
Of dogs and all fierce beasts, or borne by kites
With stench unhallowed to its hearth-crowned heights.
So like a bowman have I launched at thee
In wrath, for thou provok'st me, shafts indeed
To pierce thy heart, and fail not, from whose smart
Thou'lt not escape. But now, boy, lead me home,
That he may vent his spleen on younger men,
And learn to keep a tongue more temperate,

And in his breast a better mind than now.

[*Exit* TIRESIAS.

Chorus. The man has prophesied dread things, O king,
And gone: and never have I known—not since
These temples changed their raven locks to snow—
That aught of false this city heard from him.

Creon. Yea, this I know, and much am I perplexed:
For hard it is to yield, but standing firm
I fear to pluck swift ruin on my pride.

Chorus. Son of Menoeceus, be advised in time.

Creon. Say then, what must I do? and I'll obey.

Chorus. Go, from her prison in the rock release
The maiden, and the unburied corpse inter.

Creon. Dost thou think this, and wouldst thou have me yield?

Chorus. Yea, king, and quickly; for the gods cut short
With sudden scathe the foolishness of men.

Creon. Hardly indeed, but yet with forced consent
I'll do it, stooping to necessity.

Chorus. Do it, and go; leave not this task to others.

Creon. Even as I am, I'll go; and, servants, haste,
That hear and hear me not[14]: axes in hand,
All to yon spot, far-seen, make good your speed.
But I, since this way now my mind is bent
Whom I myself have bound, myself will loose.
For now my heart misgives me, he lives best,
Whose feet depart not from the ancient ways.

[*Exit.*
[*Strophe.*

Chorus. Worshipped by many names—
Glory of Theban Semele,[15]
Child of loud-thundering Zeus—
Haunting the famed Italian fields,
Whom as a prince the hospitable vale
Of the Eleusinian Dame reveres—
Bacchus, that hast thy home
In Thebes, the home of Bacchanals,
Beside Ismenus' fertile stream,
Where the fell dragon's teeth of old were sown:

[*Antistrophe.*

O'er the two-crested peak,
With nymphs Corycian in thy train,
By springs of Castaly,
The streaming levin lights thy path:
And from steep Nysa's hills, with ivy clad,
And that green slope, with clustering grapes
Empurpled to the sea,
When thou wouldst visit Theban streets,
A jocund company divine
With acclamation loud conducts thee forth,

[*Strophe.*

Thebes of all cities most thou honourest,
Thou with thy mother, whom the lightning slew:
And now, when Thebes is sick,
And all her people the sore plague hath stricken,
Hear us and come with healing feet
O'er the Parnassian hill,
Or the resounding strait:

[*Antistrophe.*

Come, whom fire-breathing stars in dance obey,
The master of the voices of the night,
Of Zeus the puissant son—
Come at our call, girt with thy Thyiad troop,[16]
That follow, with thy frenzy filled,
Dancing the livelong night,
Iacchus, thee their lord.

[*Enter* MESSENGER.

Messenger. Neighbours of Cadmus, and the royal house
Of old Amphion,[17] no man's life would I,
How high or low soever, praise or blame,
Since, who to-day has fortune, good or ill,
To-morrow's fortune lifts or lays him low;
No seer a constant lot foresees for men.
For Creon before was happy, as I deemed,
Who saved this land of Cadmus from its foes,
And the sole sovereignty of Thebes receiving
Prospered therein, with noble children blest.
Now all is lost. For, when the joys of life
Men have relinquished, no more life indeed
I count their living, but a living death.

[83]

For in thy house heap riches, if thou wilt;
Keep kingly state; yet, if no joy withal
Thou hast, for all things else, compared with pleasure,
I would not change the shadow of a smoke.
    Chorus. Of what grief now of princes wilt thou tell?
    Messenger. That one lies dead, whom those who live have
      slain.
    Chorus. Say, who is slain? And what man is the slayer?
    Messenger. Haemon is dead: his death no stranger's act.
    Chorus. Slain by himself, or by his father's hand?
    Messenger. Wroth with his pitiless sire, he slew himself.
    Chorus. O prophet, how thy prophecy comes true!
    Messenger. These things being so, consider of the rest.
    Chorus. Lo, hard at hand the miserable queen,
Eurydice: who from the house comes forth
Either by chance, or hearing of her son.

                      [*Enter* EURYDICE.
    Eurydice. Good townsmen all, your conference I heard,
As to the doors I came, intending now
Of Pallas to entreat her heavenly aid.
Even as I loosed the fastenings of the gate,
That opened wide, there smote my ears a word
Of sorrow all my own: backward I swooned,
Surprised by terror, in my maidens' arms:
But tell me now your tidings once again—
For not unlearned in sorrow, I shall hear.
    Messenger. Dear mistress, I will tell thee what I saw,
And not leave out one word of all the truth.
Why should I flatter thee with glozing words,
Too soon found false? Plain truth is ever best.
Thy husband hence I followed at the heels
To that high plain, where torn by dogs the body
Of Polynices lay, unpitied still.
A prayer we said to Hecate[18] in the way
And Pluto, their displeasure to refrain,
Then, sprinkling with pure water, in new-stript boughs
Wrapped round and burned the fragments that remained.
A lofty funeral-mound of native earth
We heaped for him; then sought the maiden's bed,
Her bridal bed with Hades in the rock,

And from afar a voice of shrill lament
About the unhallowed chamber some one heard,
And came to Creon, and told it to his lord,
And in his ears, approaching, the wild cry
Rang doubtfully, till now there brake from him
A word of sharp despair, 'O wretched man,
What fear is at my heart? and am I going
The woefullest road that ever I have gone?
It is my son's voice greets me. Good servants, go,
Go nearer quickly; and standing by the tomb,
Even to the throat of the vault peer through and look,
Where the wrenched stone-work gapes, if Haemon's voice
I recognise indeed, or by the gods
Am cheated!' Crazed with his fear, he spake; and we
Looked, as he bade; and in the last of the tomb
We saw the maiden—hanged: about her neck
Some shred of linen had served her for a noose
And fallen upon her, clasping her, he lay,
Wailing his wasted passion in the grave,
His fatal father, and his luckless bride.
His father saw, and crying a bitter cry
Went in, and with a lamentable voice
Called him, 'O rash, what is it that thou hast done?
What wouldst thou? On what madness hast thou rushed?
My son, come forth: I pray thee—I implore.'
But with fierce eyes the boy glared at his sire
And looks of loathing, and for answer plucked
Forth a two-hilted sword, and would have struck,
But missed him, as he fled: and in that minute,
Wroth with himself, in his own side amain
Thrust deep the steel, unhappy; and conscious still
Folded the maiden in his fainting arms;
Then, gasping out his life in one sharp breath,
Pelted her pale cheek with the crimson shower.
Dead with the dead he lies, such nuptial rites
In halls of Hades, luckless, having won;
Teaching the world, that of all human ills
With human folly is none that may compare.

                         [*Exit* EURYDICE.

Chorus. How should one deem of this? The queen, without

A word, of good or evil, has gone hence.

Messenger. Indeed, 'tis strange: but yet I feed on hope
That to lament in public for her son
She will not deign; but, as for private sorrow,
Will charge her women in the house to weep.
She is well tried in prudence, not to fail.

Chorus. I know not; but to me the too-much silence,
No less than clamorous grief, seems perilous.

Messenger. I will go hence to the house, and know, if aught
Of secret purpose in her raging heart
She hath kept locked from us. Thou sayest well:
The too-much silence may bode mischief too.

[*Exit* MESSENGER.

Chorus. Lo, the king comes hither himself, in his hands
The record, not doubtful its purport, bearing;
No grief (I dare to say) wrought by another,
But the weight of his own misdoing.

[*Enter* CREON *with the body of Haemon.*
[*Strophe.*

Creon. Alas my purblind wisdom's fatal fault,
Stubborn, and fraught with death!
Ye see us, sire and son,
The slayer and the slain.
O counsels all unblest!
Alas for thee, my son,
So young a life and so untimely quenched—
Gone from me, past recall—
Not by thy folly, but my own!

Chorus. Ah, how too late thou dost discern the truth!

Creon. Yea, to my cost I know: but then, methinks,
Oh then, some god with crushing weight
Leapt on me, drave me into frantic ways,
Trampling, alas for me,
In the base dust my ruined joy.
O toil and trouble of mortals—trouble and toil!

[*Enter* SECOND MESSENGER.

Second Messenger. Trouble, O king, thine own and none
but thine,
Thou comest, methinks, part bearing in thy hands;
Part—in the house thou hast, and soon shalt see.

[86]

Creon. What more, what worse than evil, yet remains?

Second Messenger. Thy wife is dead, with desperate hand
  ev'n now
Self-slain, for this dead son for whom she lived.

[*Antistrophe.*

Creon. O harbour of Hades, never to be appeased,
Why art thou merciless?
What heavy news is this?
Harsh news to me of grief,
That slays me, slain before!
Ah me, the woeful news!
What sayest thou, what latest word is this?
Slaughter on slaughter heaped—
Slain both together, son and wife!

Chorus. Behold and see: for now the doors stand wide.

Creon. This second grief, ah me, my eyes behold.
What fate, ah what, remains behind?
My son I hold already in my arms:
And now, ah woe is me,
This other in my sight lies dead:
Mother and child—most piteous both to see!

Second Messenger. Heartstricken at the altar as she fell,
She veiled her swooning eyelids, wailing loud
For Megareus,[19] her son, who nobly died
Before, and for this other, and with her last
Breath cursed, the slayer of her children, thee.

Creon. Ah me, will no one aim
Against my heart, made wild with fear,
With two-edged sword a deadly thrust?
O wretched that I am,
Fulfilled with sorrow, and made one with grief!

Second Messenger. She did reproach thee, truly, ere she died,
And laid on thee the blame of both their deaths.

Creon. What was the manner of her violent end?

Second Messenger. Pierced to the heart, by her own hand,
  she died,
Hearing her son's most lamentable fate.

Creon. All, all on me this guilt must ever rest,
And on no head but mine.
O my poor son, I slew thee, even I:

Let no one doubt but that the deed was mine.
O servants, lead me quickly, lead me hence;
And let me be as one who is no more.

    Chorus. 'Tis counselled well, if well with ill can be:
For bad is best, when soonest out of sight.

    Creon. I care not, let it come:
Let come the best of all my fate,
The best, the last, that ends my days:
What care I? come what will—
That I no more may see another day.

    Chorus. Let be the future: mind the present need,
And leave the rest to whom the rest concerns.

    Creon. No other wish have I; that prayer is all.

    Chorus. Pray not at all: all is as fate appoints:
'Tis not in mortals to avert their doom.

    Creon. Oh lead me hence, unprofitable; who thee
Unwittingly have slain,
Child, and my wife, unhappy; and know not now
Which way to look to either: for all things
Are crooked that I handle, and a fate
Intolerable upon my life hath leapt.

                             [CREON *is led away.*

    Chorus. First of all happiness far is wisdom,
And to the gods that one fail not of piety.
But great words of the overweening
Lay great stripes to the backs of the boasters:
Taught by adversity,
Old age learns, too late, to be wise.

                                   [*Exeunt.*

AESCHYLUS
AGAMEMNON

❧❧❧

TRANSLATED
By
GILBERT MURRAY

CHARACTERS IN THE PLAY

AGAMEMNON, *son of Atreus and King of Argos and Mycenae; Commander-in-Chief of the Greek armies in the War against Troy.*

CLYTEMNESTRA, *daughter of Tyndareus, sister of Helen; wife to Agamemnon.*

AEGISTHUS, *son of Thyestes, cousin and blood-enemy to Agamemnon, lover to Clytemnestra.*

CASSANDRA, *daughter of Priam, King of Troy, a prophetess; now slave to Agamemnon.*

A WATCHMAN.

A HERALD.

CHORUS of Argive Elders, faithful to AGAMEMNON.

The play was produced in the archonship of Philocles (458 B.C.).

The first prize was won by Aeschylus with the "Agamemnon," "Choëphoroe," "Eumenides," and the Satyr Play "Proteus."

ARGUMENT

At the opening of the *Agamemnon* we find Clytemnestra alienated from her husband and secretly befriended by his ancestral enemy, Aegisthus. The air is heavy and throbbing with hate; hate which is evil but has its due cause. Agamemnon, obeying the prophet Calchas, when the fleet lay storm-bound at Aulis, had given his own daughter, Iphigenia, as a human sacrifice.

AGAMEMNON

The Scene represents a space in front of the Palace of Agamemnon in Argos, with an Altar of Zeus in the centre and many other altars at the sides. On a high terrace of the roof stands a WATCHMAN. *It is night.*

Watchman. This waste of year-long vigil I have prayed
God for some respite, watching elbow-stayed,
As sleuthhounds watch, above the Atreidae's hall,
Till well I know yon midnight festival
Of swarming stars, and them that lonely go,
Bearers to man of summer and of snow,
Great lords and shining, throned in heavenly fire.

   And still I await the sign, the beacon pyre
That bears Troy's capture on a voice of flame
Shouting o'erseas. So surely to her aim
Cleaveth a woman's heart, man-passionèd!
And when I turn me to my bed—my bed
Dew-drenched and dark and stumbling, to which near
Cometh no dream nor sleep, but alway Fear
Breathes round it, warning, lest an eye once fain
To close may close too well to wake again;
Think I perchance to sing or troll a tune
For medicine against sleep, the music soon
Changes to sighing for the tale untold
Of this house, not well mastered as of old.

   Howbeit, may God yet send us rest, and light
The flame of good news flashed across the night.

        [*He is silent, watching. Suddenly at a distance in
           the night there is a glimmer of fire, increasing
           presently to a blaze.*

Ha!
O kindler of the dark, O daylight birth
Of dawn and dancing upon Argive earth
For this great end! All hail!—What ho, within!
What ho! Bear word to Agamemnon's queen
To rise, like dawn, and lift in answer strong
To this glad lamp her women's triumph-song,

If verily, verily, Ilion's citadel
Is fallen, as yon beacons flaming tell.
  And I myself will tread the dance before
All others; for my master's dice I score
Good, and mine own to-night three sixes plain.

> *[Lights begin to show in the Palace.*

Oh, good or ill, my hand shall clasp again
My dear lord's hand, returning! Beyond that
I speak not. A great ox hath laid his weight
Across my tongue. But these stone walls know well,
If stones had speech, what tale were theirs to tell.
For me, to him that knoweth I can yet
Speak; if another questions I forget.

> *[Exit into the Palace. The woman's "Ololûgê,"
> or triumph-cry, is heard within and then re-
> peated again and again farther off in the City.
> Handmaids and Attendants come from the
> Palace, bearing torches, with which they
> kindle incense on the altars. Among them
> comes* CLYTEMNESTRA, *who throws herself on
> her knees at the central Altar in an agony of
> prayer.*
>
> *Presently from the further side of the open
> space appear the* CHORUS *of* ELDERS *and move
> gradually into position in front of the Palace.
> The day begins to dawn.*

Chorus. Ten years since Ilion's righteous foes,
      The Atreidae strong
  Menelaus and eke Agamemnon arose,
  Two thrones, two sceptres, yokèd of God;
  And a thousand galleys of Argos trod
    The seas for the righting of wrong;
  And wrath of battle about them cried,
      As vultures cry,
  Whose nest is plundered, and up they fly
  In anguish lonely, eddying wide,
  Great wings like oars in the waste of sky,
  Their task gone from them, no more to keep
  Watch o'er the vulture babes asleep.
  But One there is who heareth on high

[92]

Some Pan or Zeus, some lost Apollo—
That keen bird-throated suffering cry
Of the stranger wronged in God's own sky;
And sendeth down, for the law transgressed,
    The Wrath of the Feet that follow.

So Zeus the Watcher of Friend and Friend,
Zeus who Prevaileth, in after quest
For One Belovèd by Many Men
On Paris sent the Atreidae twain;
Yea, sent him dances before the end
      For his bridal cheer,
Wrestlings heavy and limbs forespent
For Greek and Trojan, the knee earth-bent,
The bloody dust and the broken spear.
He knoweth, that which is here is here,
And that which Shall Be followeth near;
He seeketh God with a great desire,
He heaps his gifts, he essays his pyre
With torch below and with oil above,
With tears, but never the wrath shall move
Of the Altar cold that rejects his fire.

We saw the Avengers go that day,
And they left us here; for our flesh is old
And serveth not; and these staves uphold
A strength like the strength of a child at play.
For the sap that springs in the young man's hand
And the valour of age, they have left the land.
And the passing old, while the dead leaf blows
And the old staff gropeth his three-foot way,
Weak as a babe and alone he goes,
A dream left wandering in the day.

    [*Coming near the Central Altar they see* CLY-
        TEMNESTRA, *who is still rapt in prayer.*
But thou, O daughter of Tyndareus,
Queen Clytemnestra, what need? What news?
What tale or tiding hath stirred thy mood
To send forth word upon all our ways
For incensed worship? Of every god

[93]

That guards the city, the deep, the high,
Gods of the mart, gods of the sky,
    The altars blaze.
    One here, one there,
To the skyey night the firebrands flare,
Drunk with the soft and guileless spell
Of balm of kings from the inmost cell.
Tell, O Queen, and reject us not,
All that can or that may be told,
And healer be to this aching thought,
Which one time hovereth, evil-cold,
And then from the fires thou kindlest
Will Hope be kindled, and hungry Care
Fall back for a little while, nor tear
The heart that beateth below my breast.

[CLYTEMNESTRA *rises silently, as though unconscious
    of their presence, and goes into the House. The*
    CHORUS *take position and begin their first Stasi-
    mon, or Standing-song.*

Chorus.
(*The sign seen on the way; Eagles tearing a hare with young.*)
It is ours to tell of the Sign of the War-way given,
    To men more strong,
(For a life that is kin unto ours yet breathes from heaven
    A spell, a Strength of Song:)
How the twin-throned Might of Achaia, one Crown divided
    Above all Greeks that are,
With avenging hand and spear upon Troy was guided
    By the Bird of War.
'Twas a King among birds to each of the Kings of the Sea,
One Eagle black, one black but of fire-white tail,
By the House, on the Spear-hand, in station that all might see;
And they tore a hare, and the life in her womb that grew,
Yea, the life unlived and the races unrun they slew.
    Sorrow, sing sorrow: but good prevail, prevail!

(*How Calchas read the sign; his Vision of the Future.*)
And the War-seer wise, as he looked on the Atreïd Yoke
    Twain-tempered, knew

[94]

Those fierce hare-renders the lords of his host; and spoke,
    Reading the omen true.
"At the last, the last, this Hunt hunteth Ilion down,
    Yea, and before the wall
Violent division the fulness of land and town
    Shall waste withal;
If only God's eye gloom not against our gates,
    And the great War-curb of Troy, fore-smitten, fail.
For Pity lives, and those wingèd Hounds she hates,
    Which tore in the Trembler's body the unborn beast.
And Artemis abhorreth the eagles' feast."
    Sorrow, sing sorrow: but good prevail, prevail!

(*He prays to Artemis to grant the fulfilment of the Sign, but,
    as his vision increases, he is afraid and calls on Paian, the
    Healer, to hold her back.*)
    "Thou beautiful One, thou tender lover
      Of the dewy breath of the Lion's child;
    Thou the delight, through den and cover,
      Of the young life at the breast of the wild,
Yet, oh, fulfill, fulfill the Sign of the Eagles' Kill!
Be the vision accepted, albeit horrible. . . .
But I-ê, I-ê! Stay her, O Paian, stay!
For lo, upon other evil her heart she setteth,
  Long wastes of wind, held ship and unventured sea,
On, on, till another Shedding of Blood be wrought:
They kill but feast not; they pray not; the law is broken;
Strife in the flesh, and the bride she obeyeth not,
And beyond, beyond, there abideth in wrath re-awoken—
It plotteth, it haunteth the house, yea, it never forgetteth—
    Wrath for a child to be."
So Calchas, reading the wayside eagles' sign,
  Spake to the Kings, blessings and words of bale;
    And like his song be thine,
Sorrow, sing sorrow: but good prevail, prevail!

(*Such religion belongs to old and barbarous gods, and brings
    no peace. I turn to Zeus, who has shown man how to Learn
    by Suffering.*)
      Zeus! Zeus, whate'er He be,
      If this name He love to hear

This He shall be called of me.
Searching earth and sea and air
Refuge nowhere can I find
Save Him only, if my mind
Will cast off before it die
The burden of this vanity.

One there was who reigned of old,
Big with wrath to brave and blast,
Lo, his name is no more told!
And who followed met at last
His Third-thrower, and is gone.
Only they whose hearts have known
Zeus, the Conqueror and the Friend,
They shall win their vision's end;

Zeus the Guide, who made man turn
Thought-ward, Zeus, who did ordain
Man by Suffering shall Learn.
So the heart of him, again
Aching with remembered pain,
Bleeds and sleepeth not, until
Wisdom comes against his will.
'Tis the gift of One by strife
Lifted to the throne of life.

(AGAMEMNON *accepted the sign. Then came long
delays and storm while the fleet lay at Aulis.*)

So that day the Elder Lord,
Marshal of the Achaian ships,
Strove not with the prophet's word,
Bowed him to his fate's eclipse,
When with empty jars and lips
Parched and seas impassable
Fate on that Greek army fell,
Fronting Chalcis as it lay,
By Aulis in the swirling bay.

(*Till at last Calchas answered that Artemis was wroth
and demanded the death of* AGAMEMNON'S *daughter. The King's doubt and grief.*)

And winds, winds   blew from Strymon[1] River,
Unharboured, starving,   winds of waste endeavour,
Man-blinding, pitiless   to cord and bulwark,
　　And the waste of days   was made long, more long,
Till the flower of Argos   was aghast and withered;
　　Then through the storm   rose the War-seer's song,
And told of medicine   that should tame the tempest,
　　But bow the Princes   to a direr wrong.
Then "Artemis" he whispered, he named the name[2];
And the brother Kings they shook in the hearts of them,
And smote on the earth their staves, and the tears came.

But the King, the elder,   hath found voice and spoken:
"A heavy doom, sure,   If God's will were broken;
But to slay mine own child,   who my house delighteth,
　　Is that not heavy?   That her blood should flow
　　On her father's hand,   hard beside an altar?
　　My path is sorrow   wheresoe'er I go.
Shall Agamemnon   fail his ships and people,
　　And the hosts of Hellas   melt as melts the snow?
They cry, they thirst, for a death that shall break the spell,
For a Virgin's blood: 'tis a rite of old, men tell.
And they burn with longing.—O God may the end be well!"

　　(*But ambition drove him, till he consented to the sin of
　　　　slaying his daughter, Iphigenia, as a sacrifice.*)
To the yoke of Must-Be   he bowed him slowly,
　　And a strange wind   within his bosom tossed,
A wind of dark thought,   unclean, unholy;
　　And he rose up, daring   to the uttermost.
For men are boldened   by a Blindness, straying
　　Toward base desire,   which brings grief hereafter,
　　　　Yea, and itself is grief;
So this man hardened   to his own child's slaying,
　　As help to avenge him   for a woman's laughter
　　　　And bring his ships relief!

Her "Father, Father,"   her sad cry that lingered,
　　Her virgin heart's breath   they held all as naught,
Those bronze-clad witnesses   and battle-hungered;
　　And there they prayed, and   when the prayer was wrought

[97]

He charged the young men   to uplift and bind her,
  As ye lift a wild kid,   high above the altar,
      Fierce-huddling forward,   fallen, clinging sore
To the robe that wrapt her; yea, he bids them hinder
  The sweet mouth's utterance,   the cries that falter,
      —His curse for evermore!—

With violence and a curb's voiceless wrath.
  Her stole of saffron then to the ground she threw,
And her eye with an arrow of pity found its path
      To each man's heart that slew:
A face in a picture, striving amazedly;
  The little maid who danced at her father's board,
The innocent voice man's love came never nigh,
Who joined to his her little paean-cry
      When the third cup was poured. . . .

What came thereafter I saw not neither tell.
  But the craft of Calchas failed not.—'Tis written, He
Who Suffereth Shall Learn; the law holdeth well.
      And that which is to be,
Ye will know at last; why weep before the hour?
  For come it shall, as out of darkness dawn.
Only may good from all this evil flower;
So prays this Heart of Argos, this frail tower[3]
      Guarding the land alone.

> [*As they cease,* CLYTEMNESTRA *comes from the
> Palace with Attendants. She has finished her
> prayer and sacrifice, and is now wrought up
> to face the meeting with her husband. The
> Leader approaches her.*

Leader. Before thy state, O Queen, I bow mine eyes.
'Tis written, when the man's throne empty lies,
The woman shall be honoured.—Hast thou heard
Some tiding sure? Or is it Hope, hath stirred
To fire these altars? Dearly though we seek
To learn, 'tis thine to speak or not to speak.
  Clytemnestra. Glad-voiced, the old saw telleth, comes this
    morn,

The Star-child of a dancing midnight born,
And beareth to thine ear a word of joy
Beyond all hope: the Greek hath taken Troy.
    Leader. How?
Thy word flies past me, being incredible.
    Clytemnestra. Ilion is ours. No riddling tale I tell.
    Leader. Such joy comes knocking at the gate of tears.
    Clytemnestra. Aye, 'tis a faithful heart that eye declares.
    Leader. What warrant hast thou? Is there proof of this?
    Clytemnestra. There is; unless a God hath lied there is.
    Leader. Some dream-shape came to thee in speaking guise?
    Clytemnestra. Who deemeth me a dupe of drowsing eyes?
    Leader. Some word within that hovereth without wings?
    Clytemnestra. Am I a child to hearken to such things?
    Leader. Troy fallen?—But how long? When fell she, say?
    Clytemnestra. The very night that mothered this new day.
    Leader. And who of heralds with such fury came?
    Clytemnestra. A Fire-god, from Mount Ida scattering flame.
Whence starting, beacon after beacon burst
In flaming message hitherward. Ida first
Told Hermes' Lemnian Rock, whose answering sign
Was caught by towering Athos, the divine,
With pines immense—yea, fishes of the night
Swam skyward, drunken with that leaping light,
Which swelled like some strange sun, till dim and **far**
Makistos' watchman marked a glimmering star;
They, nowise loath nor idly slumber-won,
Spring up to hurl the fiery message on,
And a far light beyond the Eurîpus tells
That word hath reached Messapion's sentinels.
They beaconed back, then onward with a high
Heap of dead heather flaming to the sky.
And onward still, not failing nor aswoon,
Across the Asopus like a beaming moon
The great word leapt, and on Kithairon's height
Uproused a new relay of racing light.
His watchers knew the wandering flame, nor hid
Their welcome, burning higher than was bid.
Out over Lake Gorgopis then it floats,
To Aigiplanctos, waking the wild goats,

Crying for "Fire, more Fire!" And fire was reared,
Stintless and high, a stormy streaming beard,
That waved in flame beyond the promontory
Rock-ridged, that watches the Saronian sea,
Kindling the night: then one short swoop to catch
The Spider's Crag, our city's tower of watch;
Whence hither to the Atreidae's roof it came,
A light true-fathered of Idaean flame.
Torch-bearer after torch-bearer, behold
The tale thereof in stations manifold,
Each one by each made perfect ere it passed,
And Victory in the first as in the last.
These be my proofs and tokens that my lord
From Troy hath spoke to me a burning word.

   Leader. Woman, speak on. Hereafter shall my prayer
Be raised to God; now let me only hear,
Again and full, the marvel and the joy.

   Clytemnestra. Now, even now, the Achaian holdeth Troy!
Methinks there is a crying in her streets
That makes no concord. When sweet unguent meets
With vinegar in one phial, I warrant none
Shall lay those wranglers lovingly at one.
So conquerors and conquered shalt thou hear,
Two sundered tones, two lives of joy or fear.

   Here women in the dust about their slain,
Husbands or brethren, and by dead old men
Pale children who shall never more be free,
For all they loved on earth cry desolately.
And hard beside them war-stained Greeks, whom stark
Battle and then long searching through the dark
Hath gathered, ravenous, in the dawn, to feast
At last on all the plenty Troy possessed,
No portion in that feast nor ordinance,
But each man clutching at the prize of chance.
Aye, there at last under good roofs they lie
Of men spear-quelled, no frosts beneath the sky,
No watches more, no bitter moony dew. . . .
How blessèd they will sleep the whole night through!
Oh, if these days they keep them free from sin
Toward Ilion's conquered shrines and Them within

Who watch unconquered, maybe not again
The smiter shall be smit, the taker ta'en.
May God but grant there fall not on that host
The greed of gold that maddeneth and the lust
To spoil inviolate things! But half the race
Is run which windeth back to home and peace.
Yea, though of God they pass unchallengèd,
Methinks the wound of all those desolate dead
Might waken, groping for its will. . . .

                        Ye hear
A woman's word, belike a woman's fear.
May good but conquer in the last incline
Of the balance! Of all prayers that prayer is mine.

   Leader. O Woman, like a man faithful and wise
Thou speakest. I accept thy testimonies
And turn to God with praising, for a gain
Is won this day that pays for all our pain.

              [CLYTEMNESTRA *returns to the Palace. The*
                CHORUS *take up their position for the*
                Second Stasimon.

  An Elder. O Zeus, All-ruler, and Night the Aid,
          Gainer of glories, and hast thou thrown
          Over the towers of Ilion
            Thy net close-laid,
          That none so nimble and none so tall
          Shall escape withal
          The snare of the slaver that claspeth all?

  Another. And Zeus the Watcher of Friend and Friend
          I also praise, who hath wrought this end.
          Long since on Paris his shaft he drew,
            And hath aimèd true,
          Not too soon falling nor yet too far,
          The fire of the avenging star.

Chorus. (*This is God's judgement upon Troy. May it not be too*
     fierce! Gold cannot save one who spurneth Justice.)
    The stroke of Zeus hath found them! Clear this day
        The tale, and plain to trace.
    He judged, and Troy hath fallen.—And have men said
    That God not deigns to mark man's hardihead,

Trampling to earth the grace
Of holy and delicate things?—Sin lies that way.
For visibly Pride doth breed its own return
  On prideful men, who, when their houses swell
    With happy wealth, breathe ever wrath and blood.
Yet not too fierce let the due vengeance burn;
  Only as deemeth well
    One wise of mood.

Never shall state nor gold
  Shelter his heart from aching
Whoso the Altar of Justice old
  Spurneth to Night unwaking.

(*The Sinner suffers in his longing till at last Temptation overcomes him; as longing for Helen overcame Paris.*)
The tempting of misery forceth him, the dread
    Child of fore-scheming Woe!
And help is vain; the fell desire within
Is veilèd not, but shineth bright like Sin:
    And as false gold will show
Black where the touchstone trieth, so doth fade
His honour in God's ordeal. Like a child,
  Forgetting all, he hath chased his wingèd bird,
    And planted amid his people a sharp thorn.
And no God hears his prayer, or, have they heard,
  The man so base-beguiled
    They cast to scorn.

Paris to Argos came;
  Love of a woman led him;
So God's altar he brought to shame,
  Robbing the hand that fed him.

(*Helen's flight; the visions seen by the King's seers;
the phantom of Helen and the King's grief.*)
She hath left among her people   a noise of shield and sword,
  A tramp of men armèd   where the long ships are moored;
She hath ta'en in her goings   Desolation as a dower;

She hath stept, stept quickly,   through the great gated Tower,
    And the thing that could not be,   it hath been!
And the Seers they saw visions,   and they spoke of strange ill:
    "A Palace, a Palace;   and a great King thereof:
    A bed, a bed empty,   that was once pressed in love:
And thou, thou, what art thou?   Let us be, thou so still,
    Beyond wrath, beyond beseeching,   to the lips reft of thee!"
    For she whom he desireth   is beyond the deep sea,
    And a ghost in his castle   shall be queen.

        Images in sweet guise
            Carven shall move him never,
        Where is Love amid empty eyes?
            Gone, gone for ever!

    (*His dreams and his suffering; but the War that he
        made caused greater and wider suffering.*)
But a shape that is a dream,   'mid the breathings of the night,
Cometh near, full of tears, bringing vain vain delight:
For in vain when, desiring, he can feel the joy's breath
—Nevermore! Nevermore!—from his arms it vanisheth,
    As a bird along the wind-ways of sleep.
In the mid castle hall,   on the hearthstone of the Kings,
These griefs there be,   and griefs passing these,
But in each man's dwelling   of the host that sailed the seas,
A sad woman waits;   she has thoughts of many things,
    And patience in her heart lieth deep.

        Knoweth she them she sent,
            Knoweth she? Lo, returning,
        Comes in stead of the man that went
            Armour and dust of burning.

    (*The return of the funeral urns; the murmurs of the
        People.*)
And the gold-changer, Ares,   who changeth quick for dead,
Who poiseth his scale   in the striving of the spears,
Back from Troy sendeth dust,   heavy dust, wet with tears,
Sendeth ashes with men's names   in his urns neatly spread.
And they weep over the men,   and they praise them one by one,
How this was a wise fighter,   and this nobly slain—

"Fighting to win back another's wife!"
Till a murmur is begun,
 And there steals an angry pain
  Against Kings too forward in the strife.

   There by Ilion's gate
    Many a soldier sleepeth,
   Young men beautiful; fast in hate
    Troy her conqueror keepeth.

  (For the Shedder of Blood is in great peril, and
   not unmarked by God. May I never be a
   Sacker of Cities!)

But the rumour of the People, it is heavy, it is chill;
And tho' no curse be spoken, like a curse doth it brood;
And my heart waits some tiding which the dark holdeth still,
For of God not unmarked is the shedder of much blood.
And who conquers beyond right . . . Lo, the life of man
  decays;
 There be Watchers dim his light in the wasting of the years;
  He falls, he is forgotten, and hope dies.
There is peril in the praise
  Over-praisèd that he hears;
   For the thunder it is hurled from God's eyes.

   Glory that breedeth strife,
    Pride of the Sacker of Cities;
   Yea, and the conquered captive's life,
    Spare me, O God of Pities!

Divers Elders. The fire of good tiding it hath sped the city
  through,
But who knows if a god mocketh? Or who knows if all be
  true?
   'Twere the fashion of a child,
   Or a brain dream-beguiled,
   To be kindled by the first
   Torch's message as it burst,
And thereafter, as it dies, to die too.

'Tis like a woman's sceptre, to ordain
Welcome to joy before the end is plain!

Too lightly opened are a woman's ears; ⎫
Her fence downtrod by many trespassers, ⎬
   And quickly crossed; but quickly lost ⎪
The burden of a woman's hopes or fears. ⎭

> *Here a break occurs in the action,*[4] *like the descent
> of the curtain in a modern theatre. A space of
> some days is assumed to have passed and we
> find the Elders again assembled.*

Leader. Soon surely shall we read the message right;
Where fire and beacon-call and lamps of light
True speakers, or but happy things that seem
And are not, like sweet voices in a dream.
I see a Herald yonder by the shore,
Shadowed with olive sprays. And from his sore
Rent raiment cries a witness from afar,
Dry Dust, born brother to the Mire of war,
That mute he comes not, neither through the smoke
Of mountain forests shall his tale be spoke;
But either shouting for a joyful day,
Or else. . . . But other thoughts I cast away.
As good hath dawned, may good shine on, we pray!
  And whoso for this City prayeth aught
  Else, let him reap the harvest of his thought!

> [*Enter the* HERALD, *running. His garments are
> torn and war-stained. He falls upon his knees
> and kisses the Earth, and salutes each Altar in
> turn.*

Herald. Land of my fathers! Argos! Am I here . . .
Home, home at this tenth shining of the year,
And all Hope's anchors broken save this one!
For scarcely dared I dream, here in mine own
Argos at last to fold me to my rest. . . .
But now—All Hail, O Earth! O Sunlight blest!
And Zeus Most High!

> [*Checking himself as he sees the altar of Apollo.*

And thou, O Pythian Lord[5];
No more on us be thy swift arrows poured!
Beside Scamander well we learned how true
Thy hate is. Oh, as thou art Healer too,
Heal us! As thou art Saviour of the Lost,
Save also us, Apollo, being so tossed
With tempest! . . . All ye Daemons of the Pale!
And Hermes! Hermes, mine own guardian, hail!
Herald beloved, to whom all heralds bow. . . .
Ye Blessèd Dead that sent us, receive now
In love your children whom the spear hath spared.

O House of Kings, O roof-tree thrice-endeared,
O solemn thrones! O gods that face the sun!
Now, now, if ever in the days foregone,
After these many years, with eyes that burn,
Give hail and glory to your King's return!
For Agamemnon cometh! A great light
Cometh to men and gods out of the night.

Grand greeting give him—aye, it need be grand—
Who, God's avenging mattock in his hand,
Hath wrecked Troy's towers and digged her soil beneath,
Till her gods' houses, they are things of death;
Her altars waste, and blasted every seed
Whence life might rise! So perfect is his deed,
So dire the yoke on Ilion he hath cast,
The first Atreides, King of Kings at last,
And happy among men! To whom we give
Honour most high above all things that live.

For Paris nor his guilty land can score
The deed they wrought above the pain they bore.
"Spoiler and thief," he heard God's judgement pass;
Whereby he lost his plunder, and like grass
Mowed down his father's house and all his land;
And Troy pays twofold for the sin she planned.

   Leader. Be glad, thou Herald of the Greek from Troy!
   Herald. So glad, I am ready, if God will, to die!
   Leader. Did love of this land work thee such distress?
   Herald. The tears stand in mine eyes for happiness.
   Leader. Sweet sorrow was it, then, that on you fell.
   Herald. How sweet? I cannot read thy parable.

Leader. To pine again for them that loved you true.
Herald. Did ye then pine for us, as we for you?
Leader. The whole land's heart was dark, and groaned for thee.
Herald. Dark? For what cause? Why should such darkness be?
Leader. Silence in wrong is our best medicine here.
Herald. Your kings were gone. What others need you fear?
Leader. 'Tis past! Like thee now, I could gladly die.
Herald. Even so! 'Tis past, and all is victory.
And, for our life in those long years, there were
Doubtless some grievous days, and some were fair.
Who but a god goes woundless all his way? . . .
Oh, could I tell the sick toil of the day,
The evil nights, scant decks ill-blanketed;
The rage and cursing when our daily bread
Came not! And then on land 'twas worse than all.
Our quarters close beneath the enemy's wall;
And rain—and from the ground the river dew—
Wet, always wet! Into our clothes it grew,
Plague-like, and bred foul beasts in every hair.
Would I could tell how ghastly midwinter
Stole down from Ida till the birds dropped dead!
Or the still heat, when on his noonday bed
The breathless blue sea sank without a wave! . . .
Why think of it? They are past and in the grave,
All those long troubles. For I think the slain
Care little if they sleep or rise again;
And we, the living, wherefore should we ache
With counting all our lost ones, till we wake
The old malignant fortunes? If Good-bye
Comes from their side, Why, let them go, say I.
Surely for us, who live, good doth prevail
Unchallenged, with no wavering of the scale;
Wherefore we vaunt unto these shining skies,
As wide o'er sea and land our glory flies:
"By men of Argolis who conquered Troy,
These spoils, a memory and an ancient joy,
Are nailed in the gods' houses throughout Greece."
Which whoso readeth shall with praise increase

Our land, our kings, and God's grace manifold
Which made these marvels be.—My tale is told.

   Leader. Indeed thou conquerest me. Men say, the light
In old men's eyes yet serves to learn aright.
But Clytemnestra and the House should hear
These tidings first, though I their health may share.

           [*During the last words* CLYTEMNESTRA *has en-*
           tered from the Palace.

   Clytemnestra. Long since I lifted up my voice in joy,
When the first messenger from flaming Troy
Spake through the dark of sack and overthrow.
And mockers chid me: "Because beacons show
On the hills, must Troy be fallen? Quickly born
Are women's hopes!" Aye, many did me scorn;
Yet gave I sacrifice; and by my word
Through all the city our woman's cry was heard,
Lifted in blessing round the seats of God,
And slumbrous incense o'er the altars glowed.
In fragrance.
         And for thee, what need to tell
Thy further tale? My lord himself shall well
Instruct me. Yet, to give my lord and king
All reverent greeting at his homecoming—
What dearer dawn on woman's eyes can flame
Than this, which casteth wide her gate to acclaim
The husband whom God leadeth safe from war?—
Go, bear my lord his prayer: That fast and far
He haste him to this town which loves his name;
And in his castle may he find the same
Wife that he left, a watchdog of the hall,
True to one voice and fierce to others all;
A body and soul unchanged, no seal of his
Broke in the waiting years.—No thought of ease
Nor joy from other men hath touched my soul,
Nor shall touch, until bronze be dyed like wool.

   A boast so faithful and so plain, I wot,
Spoke by a royal Queen doth shame her not.

                   [*Exit* CLYTEMNESTRA.

   Leader. Let thine ear mark her message. 'Tis of fair
Seeming, and craves a clear interpreter. . . .

But, Herald, I would ask thee; tell me true
Of Menelaus. Shall he come with you,
Our land's belovèd crown, untouched of ill?
    Herald. I know not how to speak false words of weal
For friends to reap thereof a harvest true.
    Leader. Canst speak of truth with comfort joined? Those two
Once parted, 'tis a gulf not lightly crossed.
    Herald. Your king is vanished from the Achaian host,
He and his ship! Such comfort have I brought.
    Leader. Sailed he alone from Troy? Or was he caught
By storms in the midst of you, and swept away?
    Herald. Thou hast hit the truth; good marksman, as men say!
And long to suffer is but brief to tell.
    Leader. How ran the sailors' talk? Did there prevail
One rumour, showing him alive or dead?
    Herald. None knoweth, none hath tiding, save the head
Of Helios, ward and watcher of the world.
    Leader. Then tell us of the storm. How, when God hurled
His anger, did it rise? How did it die?
    Herald. It likes me not, a day of presage high
With dolorous tongue to stain. Those twain, I vow,
Stand best apart. When one with shuddering brow,
From armies lost, back beareth to his home
Word that the terror of her prayers is come;
One wound in her great heart, and many a fate
For many a home of men cast out to sate
The two-fold scourge that worketh Ares' lust,
Spear crossed with spear, dust wed with bloody dust;
Who walketh laden with such weight of wrong,
Why, let him, if he will, uplift the song
That is Hell's triumph. But to come as I
Am now come, laden with deliverance high,
Home to a land of peace and laughing eyes,
And mar all with that fury of the skies
Which made our Greeks curse God—how should this be?

    Two enemies most ancient, Fire and Sea,
A sudden friendship swore, and proved their plight
By war on us poor sailors through that night
Of misery, when the horror of the wave
Towered over us, and winds from Strymon drave

Hull against hull, till good ships, by the horn
Of the mad whirlwind gored and overborne,
One here, one there, 'mid rain and blinding spray,
Like sheep by a devil herded, passed away.
And when the blessèd Sun upraised his head,
We saw the Aegean waste a-foam with dead,
Dead men, dead ships, and spars disasterful.
Howbeit for us, our one unwounded hull
Out of that wrath was stolen or begged free
By some good spirit—sure no man was he!—
Who guided clear our helm; and on till now
Hath Saviour Fortune throned her on the prow,
No surge to mar our mooring, and no floor
Of rock to tear us when we made for shore.
Till, fled from that sea-hell, with the clear sun
Above us and all trust in fortune gone,
We drove like sheep the thoughts about our brain
Of that lost army, broken and scourged amain
With evil.   And, methinks, if there is breath
In them, they talk of us as gone to death—
How else?—and so say we of them! For thee,
Since Menelaus thy first care must be,
If by some word of Zeus, who wills not yet
To leave the old house for ever desolate,
Some ray of sunlight on a far-off sea
Lights him, yet green and living . . . we may see
His ship some day in the harbour!—'Twas the word
Of truth ye asked me for, and truth ye have heard!

> [*Exit* HERALD.   *The* CHORUS *take position for
> the Third Stasimon.*

Chorus.   (*Surely there was mystic meaning in the name*
HELENA, *meaning which was fulfilled when she fled
to Troy.*)
> Who was He who found for thee
> That name, truthful utterly—
> Was it One beyond our vision
> Moving sure in pre-decision
> > Of man's doom his mystic lips?—
> > Calling thee, the Battle-wed,
> > Thee, the Strife-encompassèd,

Helen? Yea, in fate's derision,
  Hell in cities, Hell in ships,
Hell in hearts of men they knew her,
  When the dim and delicate fold
  Of her curtains backward rolled,
And to sea, to sea, she threw her
  In the West Wind's giant hold;
And with spear and sword behind her
  Came the hunters in a flood,
Down the oarblade's viewless trail
  Tracking, till in Simoïs' vale
Through the leaves they crept to find her,
  A Wrath, a seed of blood.

*(The Trojans welcomed her with triumph and praised
Alexander, till at last their song changed and they
saw another meaning in Alexander's name also.)*
        So the Name to Ilion came
        On God's thought-fulfilling flame,
She a vengeance and a token
Of the unfaith to bread broken,
    Of the hearth of God betrayed,
        Against them whose voices swelled
        Glorying in the prize they held
And the Spoiler's vaunt outspoken
    And the song his brethren made
'Mid the bridal torches burning;
    Till, behold, the ancient City
Of King Priam turned, and turning
Took a new song for her learning,
A song changed and full of pity,
With the cry of a lost nation;
    And she changed the bridegroom's name:
Called him Paris Ghastly-wed;
For her sons were with the dead,
And her life one lamentation,
    'Mid blood and burning flame.

*(Like a lion's whelp reared as a pet and turning after-
wards to a great beast of prey.)*

[111]

Lo, once there was a herdsman reared
   In his own house, so stories tell,
A lion's whelp, a milk-fed thing
And soft in life's first opening
Among the sucklings of the herd;
   The happy children loved him well,
And old men smiled, and oft, they say,
In men's arms, like a babe, he lay,
Bright-eyed, and toward the hand that teased him
   Eagerly fawning for food or play.

Then on a day outflashed the sudden
   Rage of the lion brood of yore;
He paid his debt to them that fed
With wrack of herds and carnage red,
Yea, wrought him a great feast unbidden,
   Till all the house-ways ran with gore;
A sight the thralls fled weeping from,
   A great red slayer, beard a-foam,
High-priest of some blood-cursèd altar
   God had uplifted against that home.

   (*So was it with Helen in Troy.*)
And how shall I call the thing that came
   At the first hour to Ilion city?
Call it a dream of peace untold,
A secret joy in a mist of gold,
A woman's eye that was soft, like flame,
   A flower which ate a man's heart with pity.

But she swerved aside and wrought to her kiss a bitter ending,
And a wrath was on her harbouring, a wrath upon her friending,
   When to Priam and his sons she fled quickly o'er the deep,
With the god to whom she sinned for her watcher on the wind,
   A death-bride, whom brides long shall weep.

   (*Men say that Good Fortune wakes the envy of God;
   not so; Good Fortune may be innocent, and then
   there is no vengeance.*)
A grey word liveth, from the morn
   Of old time among mortals spoken,

That man's Wealth waxen full shall fall
Not childless, but get sons withal;
And ever of great bliss is born
    A tear unstanched and a heart broken.

But I hold my thought alone and by others unbeguiled;
'Tis the deed that is unholy shall have issue, child on child,
Sin on sin, like his begetters; and they shall be as they were.
But the man who walketh straight, and the house thereof, tho'
    Fate
    Exalt him, the children shall be fair.

    (*It is Sin, it is Pride and Ruthlessness, that beget chil-
        dren like themselves till Justice is fulfilled upon
        them.*)
But Old Sin loves, when comes the hour again,
    To bring forth New,
Which laugheth lusty amid the tears of men;
Yea, and Unruth, his comrade, wherewith none
May plead nor strive, which dareth on and on,
    Knowing not fear nor any holy thing;
Two fires of darkness in a house, born true,
    Like to their ancient spring.

But Justice shineth in a house low-wrought
    With smoke-stained wall,
And honoureth him who filleth his own lot;
But the unclean hand upon the golden stair
With eyes averse she flieth, seeking where
    Things innocent are; and, recking not the power
Of wealth by man misgloried, guideth all
    To her own destined hour.

          [*Here amid a great procession enter* AGAMEM-
            NON *on a Chariot. Behind him on another
            Chariot is* CASSANDRA. *The* CHORUS *ap-
            proach and make obeisance. Some of* AGA-
            MEMNON'S *men have on their shields a
            White Horse, some a Lion. Their arms are
            rich and partly barbaric.*

    Leader. All hail, O King! Hail, Atreus' Son!
Sacker of Cities! Ilion's bane!

               [113]

With what high word shall I greet thee again,
How give thee worship, and neither outrun
The point of pleasure, nor stint too soon?
For many will cling to fair seeming
The faster because they have sinned erewhile;
And a man may sigh with never a sting
Of grief in his heart, and a man may smile
With eyes unlit and a lip that strains.
But the wise Shepherd knoweth his sheep,
  And his eyes pierce deep
The faith like water that fawns and feigns.

But I hide nothing, O King. That day
When in quest of Helen our battle array
Hurled forth, thy name upon my heart's scroll
Was deep in letters of discord writ;
  And the ship of thy soul,
Ill-helmed and blindly steered was it,
Pursuing ever, through men that die,
One wild heart that was fain to fly.
  But on this new day,
From the deep of my thought and in love, I say
 "Sweet is a grief well ended;"
And in time's flow Thou wilt learn and know
  The true from the false,
Of them that were left to guard the walls
 Of thine empty Hall unfriended.

      [*During the above* CLYTEMNESTRA *has appeared
        on the Palace steps, with a train of Attend-
        ants, to receive her Husband.*

 Agamemnon. To Argos and the gods of Argolis
All hail, who share with me the glory of this
Home-coming and the vengeance I did wreak
On Priam's City! Yea, though none should speak,
The great gods heard our cause, and in one mood
Uprising, in the urn of bitter blood,
That men should shriek and die and towers should burn,
Cast their great vote; while over Mercy's urn
Hope waved her empty hands and nothing fell.
 Even now in smoke that City tells her tale;

The wrack-wind liveth, and where Ilion died
The reek of the old fatness of her pride
From hot and writhing ashes rolls afar.

    For which let thanks, wide as our glories are,
Be uplifted; seeing the Beast of Argos hath
Round Ilion's towers piled high his fence of wrath
And, for one woman ravished, wrecked by force
A City. Lo, the leap of the wild Horse
In darkness when the Pleiades were dead;
A mailèd multitude, a Lion unfed,
Which leapt the tower and lapt the blood of Kings!

    Lo, to the Gods I make these thanksgivings.
But for thy words: I marked them, and I mind
Their meaning, and my voice shall be behind
Thine. For not many men, the proverb saith,
Can love a friend whom fortune prospereth
Unenvying; and about the envious brain
Cold poison clings, and doubles all the pain
Life brings him. His own woundings he must nurse,
And feels another's gladness like a curse.
    Well can I speak. I know the mirrored glass
Called friendship, and the shadow shapes that pass
And feign them a King's friends. I have known but one—
Odysseus, him we trapped against his own
Will!—who once harnessed bore his yoke right well . . .
Be he alive or dead of whom I tell
The tale. And for the rest, touching our state
And gods, we will assemble in debate
A concourse of all Argos, taking sure
Counsel, that what is well now may endure
Well, and if aught needs healing medicine, still
By cutting and by fire, with all good will,
I will essay to avert the after-wrack
Such sickness breeds.

              Aye, Heaven hath led me back;
And on this hearth where still my fire doth burn
I will go pay to heaven my due return,
Which guides me here, which saved me far away.
    O Victory, now mine own, be mine alway!

[115]

[CLYTEMNESTRA, *at the head of her retinue, steps forward. She controls her suspense with difficulty but gradually gains courage as she proceeds.*

Clytemnestra. Ye Elders, Council of the Argive name
Here present, I will no more hold it shame
To lay my passion bare before men's eyes.
There comes a time to a woman when fear dies
For ever. None hath taught me. None could tell,
Save me, the weight of years intolerable
I lived while this man lay at Ilion.
That any woman thus should sit alone
In a half-empty house, with no man near,
Makes her half-blind with dread! And in her ear
Alway some voice of wrath; now messengers
Of evil; now not so; then others worse,
Crying calamity against mine and me.

  Oh, had he half the wounds that variously
Came rumoured home, his flesh must be a net,
All holes from heel to crown! And if he met
As many deaths as I met tales thereon,
Is he some monstrous thing, some Geryon
Three-souled, that will not die, till o'er his head,
Three robes of earth be piled, to hold him dead?

  Aye, many a time my heart broke, and the noose
Of death had got me; but they cut me loose.
It was those voices alway in mine ear.

For that, too, young Orestes is not here
Beside me, as were meet, seeing he above
All else doth hold the surety of our love;
Let not thy heart be troubled. It fell thus:
Our loving spear-friend took him, Strophios
The Phocian, who forewarned me of annoy
Two-fronted, thine own peril under Troy,
And ours here, if the rebel multitude
Should cast the Council down. It is men's mood
Alway, to spurn the fallen. So spake he,
And sure no guile was in him.

[116]

For them thou lovest in the grave,
For them on Earth, be blind, be brave:
Uphold the cloak before thine eyes
And see not while thy Gorgon dies;
But him who sowed the seed of wrong,
Go, look him in the face and slay!

All. Oh, in courage and in power,
When the deed comes and the hour,
As she crieth to thee "Son,"
Let thy "Father" quell her breath!
But a stroke and it is done,
The unblamèd deed of death[7].

[*Enter from the country* AEGISTHUS.

Aegisthus. A message called me; else I scarce had thought
To have come so quick. 'Tis a strange rumour, brought,
They tell me, by some Phocian wayfarers
In passing: strange, nor grateful to our ears.
Orestes dead! A galling load it were
And dripping blood for this poor House to bear,
Still scored and festerous with its ancient wound.
How shall I deem it? Living truth and sound?
Or tales of women, born to terrify,
That wildly leap, and up in mid-air die?
What know ye further? I would have this clear.

Leader. We heard the tale; but go within and hear
With thine own ears. A rumoured word hath weak
Force, when the man himself is there to speak.

Aegisthus. Hear him I will, and question him beside.
Was this man with Orestes when he died,
Or speaks he too from rumour? If he lies . . .
He cannot cheat a mind that is all eyes.

[*He enters the House.*

Chorus. Zeus, Zeus, how shall I speak, and how
Begin to pray thee and beseech?
How shall I ever mate with speech
This longing, and obtain my vow?
The edges of the blades that slay
Creep forth to battle: shall it be
Death, death for all eternity,
On Agamemnon's House this day;

[171]

Or sudden a new light of morn,
 A beacon fire for freedom won,
 The old sweet rule from sire to son,
And golden Argolis reborn?
Against two conquerors all alone,
 His last death-grapple, deep in blood,
 Orestes joineth. . . . O great God,
Give victory!

      [*Death-cry of* AEGISTHUS *within.*
    Ha! The deed is done!
 Leader. How? What is wrought? Stand further from the door
Till all is over. Move apart before
Men mark, and deem us sharers in the strife.
For after this 'tis war, for death or life.

    [*The Women stand back almost unseen. A House-*
     hold SLAVE *rushes out from the main Door,*
     and beats at the door of the Women's House.

 Slave. Ho!
Treason! Our master! Treason! Haste amain!
Treason within. Aegisthus lieth slain.
Unbar, unbar, with all the speed ye may
The women's gates! Oh, tear the bolts away! . . .
God, but it needs a man, a lusty one,
To help us, when all time for help is gone!
What ho!
I babble to deaf men, and labouring cry,
To ears sleep-charmèd, words that fail and die.
Where art thou, Clytemnestra? What dost thou? . . .
'Fore God, 'tis like to be her own neck now,
In time's revenge, that shivers to its fate.

        [*Enter* CLYTEMNESTRA.
 Clytemnestra. What wouldst thou? Why this clamour at
  our gate?
 Slave. The dead are risen, and he that liveth slain.
 Clytemnestra. Woe's me! The riddle of thy speech is plain.
By treason we shall die, even as we slew. . . .
Ho, there, mine axe of battle! Let us try
Who conquereth and who falleth, he or I . . .
To that meseemeth we are come, we two.

    [*Enter from the House* ORESTES *with drawn sword.*

      [172]

Orestes. 'Tis thou I seek. With him my work is done.

Clytemnestra (suddenly failing). Woe's me!
Aegisthus, my beloved, my gallant one!

Orestes. Thou lovest him! Go then and lay thine head
Beside him. Thou shalt not betray the dead.

[*Makes as if to stab her.*

Clytemnestra. Hold, O my son! My child, dost thou not fear
To strike this breast? Hast thou not slumbered here,
Thy gums draining the milk that I did give?

Orestes (lowering his sword). Pylades!
What can I? Dare I let my mother live?

Pylades. Where is God's voice from out the golden cloud
At Pytho? Where the plighted troth we vowed?
Count all the world thy foe, save God on high.

Orestes. I will obey. Thou counsellest righteously.
Follow! Upon his breast thou shalt expire
Whom, living, thou didst hold above my sire.
Go, lie in his dead arms! . . . This was the thing
Thou lovedst, loathing thine anointed King.

Clytemnestra. I nursed thee. I would fain grow old with
thee.

Orestes. Shall one who slew my father house with me?

Clytemnestra. Child, if I sinned, Fate had her part therein.

Orestes. Then Fate is here, with the reward of sin.

Clytemnestra. Thou reck'st not of a Mother's Curse, my
child?

Orestes. Not hers who cast me out into the wild.

Clytemnestra. Cast out? I sent thee to a war-friend's Hall.

Orestes. A free man's heir, ye sold me like a thrall.

Clytemnestra. If thou wast sold, where is the price I got?

Orestes. The price! . . . For very shame I speak it not.

Clytemnestra. Speak. But tell, too, thy father's harlotries.

Orestes. Judge not the toiler, thou who sitt'st at ease!

Clytemnestra. A woman starves with no man near, my son.

Orestes. Her man's toil wins her bread when he is gone.

Clytemnestra. To kill thy mother, Child: is that thy will?

Orestes. I kill thee not: thyself it is doth kill.

Clytemnestra. A mother hath her Watchers: think and quail!

Orestes. How shall I 'scape my Father's if I fail?

Clytemnestra (*to herself*). Living, I cry for mercy to a tomb!
Orestes.   Yea, from the grave my father speaks thy doom.
Clytemnestra.   Ah God! The serpent that I bare and fed!
Orestes.   Surely of truth prophetic is the dread
That walketh among dreams.   Most sinfully
Thou slewest: now hath Sin her will of thee.

> [*He drives* CLYTEMNESTRA *before him into the palace.   The* CHORUS *come forward again.*

Leader.   For these twain also in their fall I weep.
Yet, seeing Orestes now through mire so deep
Hath climbed the crest, I can but pray this eye
Of the Great House be not made blind and die.

[*Strophe.*

Chorus.   Judgement came in the end
> To Troy and the Trojans' lord,
> (O Vengeance, heavy to fall!)
> There came upon Atreus' Hall
> Lion and lion friend,
> A sword came and a sword.
> A walker in Pytho's way
> On the neck of her kings hath trod,
> A beggar and outcast, yea,
> But led by God.

[*Antistrophe*

> Came He of the laughing lure,
> The guile and the secret blow,
> (O Vengeance, subtle to slay!)
> But there held his hand that day
> The Daughter of Zeus, the pure,
> Justice yclept below.
> Justice they called her name,
> For where is a goodlier?
> And her breath is a sword of flame
> On the foes of her.

All.   Cry, Ho for the perils fled,
> For the end of the long dismay!
> Cry, Ho for peace and bread;
> For the Castle's lifted head,

[174]

For the two defilers dead,
  And the winding of Fortune's way!

[*Strophe.*

Even as Apollo gave
  His charge on the Mountain, He
Who holdeth the Earth-heart Cave,
  Hast thou wrought innocently
Great evil, hindered long,
  Tracking thy mother's sin . . .
  Is the power of God hemmed in
So strangely to work with wrong?
  Howbeit, let praise be given
  To that which is throned in Heaven:
    The Gods are strong.

[*Antistrophe.*

And soon shall the Perfect Hour
  O'er the castle's threshold stone
Pass with his foot of power,
  When out to the dark is thrown
The sin thereof and the stain
  By waters that purify.
  Now, now with a laughing eye
God's fortune lieth plain;
  And a cry on the wind is loud:
"The stranger that held us bowed
    Is fallen again!"

All.   O light of the dawn to be!
  The curb is broken in twain,
And the mouth of the House set free.
Up, O thou House, and see!
Too long on the face of thee
  The dust hath lain!

[*The doors are thrown open, and* ORESTES *discovered standing over the dead bodies of* AEGISTHUS *and* CLYTEMNESTRA. *The Household is grouped about him and Attendants hold the great red robe in which Agamemnon was murdered.*

[175]

Orestes. (*He speaks with ever-increasing excitement*).
Behold your linkèd conquerors! Behold
My Father's foes, the spoilers of the fold!
Oh, lordly were these twain, when thronèd high,
And lovely now, as he who sees them lie
Can read, two lovers faithful to their troth!
They vowed to slay my father, or that both
As one should die, and both the vows were true!
And mark, all ye who hear this tale of rue,
This robe, this trap that did my father greet,
Irons of the hand and shackling of the feet!
Outstretch it north and south: cast wide for me
This man-entangler, that our Sire may see—
Not mine, but He who watcheth all deeds done,
Yea, all my mother's wickedness, the Sun—
And bear me witness, when they seek some day
To judge me, that in justice I did slay
This woman: for of him I take no heed.
He hath the adulterer's doom, by law decreed.
But she who planned this treason 'gainst her own
Husband, whose child had lived beneath her zone—
Oh, child of love, now changed to hate and blood!—
What is she? Asp or lamprey of the mud,
That, fangless, rotteth with her touch, so dire
That heart's corruption and that lust like fire?
Woman? Not woman, though I speak right fair.
                    [*His eyes are caught by the great red robe.*
A dead man's winding-sheet? A hunter's snare?
A trap, a toil, a tangling of the feet. . . .
I think a thief would get him this, a cheat
That robs the stranger. He would snare them so,
And kill them, kill them, and his heart would glow. . . .
Not in my flesh, not in my house, O God,
May this thing live! Ere that, Oh, lift thy rod
And smiting blast me, dead without a child!
                          [*He stops exhausted.*

   Chorus.   O deeds of anger and of pain!
             O woman miserably slain!
             Alas, Alas!
             And he who lives shall grieve again.

Orestes. Did she the deed or no? This robe defiled
Doth bear me witness, where its web is gored,
How deep the dye was of Aegisthus' sword;
And blood hath joined with the old years, to spoil
The many tinctures of the broidered coil.
Oh, now I weep, now praise him where he died,
And calling on this web that pierced his side. . . .
Pain, pain is all my doing, all my fate,
My race, and my begetting: and I hate
This victory that sears me like a brand. . . .

   Chorus. No mortal thro' this life shall go
       For ever portionless of woe.
       Alas! Alas!
       It comes to all, or swift or slow.

   Orestes. Yet wait: for I would have you understand.
The end I know not. But methinks I steer
Unseeing, like some broken charioteer,
By curbless visions borne. And at my heart
A thing of terror knocketh, that will start
Sudden a-song, and she must dance to hear.
But while I am still not mad, I here declare
To all who love me, and confess, that I
Have slain my mother, not unrighteously;
Who with my father's blood hath stained the sod
Of Argos and drawn down the wrath of God.
And the chief spell that wrought me to the deed
Is Loxias, Lord of Pytho, who decreed
His high commandment: if this thing I dare,
He lays on me no sin: if I forbear . . .
I cannot speak his judgement: none can know
The deeps thereof, no arrow from the bow
Out-top it. Therefore here ye see me, how
I go prepared, with wreaths and olive bough,
To kneel in supplication on the floor
Of Loxias, touch the fire that evermore
Men call the undying, and the midmost stone
Of earth, flying this blood which is mine own.
And how these evil things were wrought, I pray
All men of Argos on an after day
Remember, and bear witness faithfully

When Menelaus comes. . . . And take from me,
Living or dead, a wanderer and outcast
For ever, this one word, my last, my last. . . .
   Leader. Nay, all is well. Leave no ill omen here,
Nor bind upon thy lips the yoke of fear.
All Argos thou hast freed, and with one sweep
Two serpents' heads hurled reeking to the deep.
   Orestes (*overcome with sudden terror*). Ah! Ah!
Ye bondmaids! They are here: like Gorgons, gowned
In darkness; all bewreathed and interwound
With serpents! . . . I shall never rest again.
   Leader. What fantasies, most father-loved of men,
Haunt thee?   Be strong, thou conqueror!   Have no fear!
   Orestes. These are no fantasies.   They are here; they are
      here,
The Hounds of my dead Mother, hot to kill.
   Leader. The blood upon thine hand is reeking still:
For that the turmoil in thy heart is loud.
   Orestes. O Lord Apollo! More and more they crowd
Close, and their eyes drip blood, most horrible!
   Leader. One cleansing hast thou.   Loxias can quell
Thy tempest with his touch, and set thee free.
   Orestes. You cannot see them. I alone can see.
I am hunted. . . . I shall never rest again.

[*Exit* ORESTES

   Chorus. Farewell. May blessing guide thee among men.
         May God with love watch over thee, and heed
         Thy goings and be near thee at thy need.
   All.   Behold a third great storm made wild
            By winds of wrath within the race,
            Hath shook this castle from its place.
         The ravin of the murdered child
         First broke Thyestes in his pride:
            Second, a warrior and a King,
            Chief of Achaia's warfaring,
         Was smitten in the bath and died.
         And Third, this Saviour or this last
            Doom from the deep.   What end shall fall,
            Or peace, or death outsweeping all,
         When night comes and the Wrath is past?   [*Exeunt.*

[178]

AESCHYLUS
THE EUMENIDES

⋙⋘

TRANSLATED
By
GILBERT MURRAY

CHARACTERS IN THE PLAY

The PYTHIAN PROPHETESS.
ORESTES.
The God APOLLO.
The Goddess PALLAS ATHENA.
The Ghost of CLYTEMNESTRA.
CHORUS *of* FURIES (*Eumenides*).
CHORUS OF ATHENIAN CITIZENS.

The play was first produced in 458 B.C. at the same time as the other two plays in the trilogy, Agamemnon and Choëphoroe.

ARGUMENT

At the end of the *Choëphoroe*, Orestes goes mad, overcome by the horror of the deed he has been obliged, by divine command, to commit. He is already haunted by the Furies, "his mother's wrathful hounds," who are destined to pursue him over the earth until the sin is expiated through suffering. When the play opens, Orestes has taken refuge at the temple of Apollo where he seeks the protection of the god whose will he has performed.

THE EUMENIDES

The scene[1] represents the front of the Temple of APOLLO
*at Delphi; great doors at the back lead to the inner shrine
and the central Altar. The Pythian* PROPHETESS *is standing
before the Doors.*

   Prophetess. First of all Gods I worship in this prayer
Earth, the primeval prophet; after her
Themis, the Wise, who on her mother's throne—
So runs the tale—sat second; by whose own
Accepted will, with never strife nor stress,
Third reigned another earth-born Titaness,
Phoebe; from whom (for that he bears her name)
To Phoebus as a birthtide gift it came.
   He left his isle, he left his Delian seas,
He passed Athena's wave-worn promontories,
In haste this great Parnassus to possess
And Delphi, thronèd in the wilderness.
And with him came, to escort him and revere,
A folk born of Hephaistos, pioneer
Of God's way, making sweet a bitter land.
And much this people and the King whose hand
Then steered them, Delphos, glorified his name,
Till Zeus into his heart put mystic flame
And prophet here enthroned him, fourth in use:
So Loxias' lips reveal the thought of Zeus[2].
   These gods be foremost in all prayers of mine,
Who have held the Throne. Next, She before the shrine,
Pallas, is praisèd, and the Nymphs who keep
Yon old Corycian bird-belovèd steep,
Deep-caverned, where things blessèd come and go.
And Bromios walks the mountain, well I know,
Since first he led his Maenad host on high
And doomed King Pentheus like a hare to die.
And Pleistos' fountains and Poseidon's power
I call, and Him who brings the Perfect Hour,
Zeus, the Most Highest. With which prayers I go

To seat me, priestess, on the Throne.   And, oh,
May God send blessing on mine entrance, more
And deeper than He e'er hath sent of yore!
   If there be present men of Greece but not
Of Delphi, let them enter as the lot
Ordains; I speak but as God leadeth me.

> *[She enters the Inner Shrine, and the stage*
> *is for a moment empty.   Then she re-*
> *turns, grasping at the wall for support.*

Ah! Horrors, horrors, dire to speak or see,
From Loxias' chamber drive me reeling back.
My knees are weak beneath me, and I lack
The strength to fly. . . . O hands, drag me from here,
If feet fail! . . . An old woman, and in fear,
A thing of naught, a babe in helplessness!
I made my way into the Holy Place,
And there, at the inmost Altar of the world,
A man abhorred of God, his body hurled
Earthward in desperate prayer; blood on his hand
Yet reeking, and a naked new-drawn brand
Wreathed in beseeching wool, a suppliant's weed
Of snow-white fleece . . . so much mine eyes could read.
But out in front of him a rout unknown
Of women sleepeth, flung from throne to throne.
Women?   Nay, never women!   Gorgons more:
And yet not like the Gorgon shapes of yore. . . .
I saw a picture once of woman things
That ravished Phineus' banquet.   But no wings
Have these; all shadows, black, abominable.
The voices of their slumber rise and swell,
Back-beating, and their eyes drop gouts of gore.
Their garb, it is no garb to show before
God's altar nor the hearths of human kind.
I cannot read what lineage lies behind
These shapes, nor what land, having born such breed,
Hath trembled not before and shall not bleed
Hereafter.   Let Apollo great in power
Take to his care the peril of this hour:
Being Helper, Prophet, Seer of things unseen,
The stainèd hearth he knoweth to make clean.

[*The* PROPHETESS *departs. The doors open and
reveal the inner shrine,* ORESTES *at the Altar,
the* FURIES *asleep about him, and* APOLLO
standing over them.

Apollo. I fail thee not. For ever more I stay,
Or watching at thy side or far away,
Thy guard, and iron against thine enemies.
Even now my snares have closèd upon these.
The ragers sleep: the Virgins without love,
So grey, so old, whom never god above
Hath kissed, nor man, nor from the wilderness
One wild beast. They were born for wickedness
And sorrow; for in evil night they dwell,
And feed on the great darkness that is Hell,
Most hated by the Gods and human thought.
But none the less, fly thou and falter not.
For these shall hunt thee, ever on through earth
Unwandered, through the vast lands of the North,
The sea-ways and the cities ringed with sea.
But faint not. Clasp thy travail unto thee;
On till thou come to Pallas' Rock[3], and fold
Thine arms in prayer about her image old.
In Athens there be hearts to judge, there be
Words that bring peace; and I shall set thee free
At last from all this woe.—If thou didst kill
Thy mother, was it not my word and will?

Orestes. Not to betray thou knowest. Oh, ponder yet
One other lesson, Lord—not to forget!
Thy strength in doing can be trusted well.

[ORESTES *departs.*

Apollo. Remember! Let no fear thy spirit quell!
Do thou, O Hermes[4], brother of my blood,
Watch over him. Thou guide of man, make good
The name thou bearest, shepherding again
My suppliant. Him who pitieth suffering men
Zeus pitieth, and his ways are sweet on earth.

[*Exit* APOLLO. *Presently enter the* GHOST
of CLYTEMNESTRA. *She watches the
sleeping* FURIES.

[183]

Ghost[5]. Ye sleep, O God, and what are sleepers worth?
'Tis you, have left me among all the dead
Dishonoured. Always, for that blood I shed,
Rebuke and hissing cease not, and I go
Wandering in shame. Oh, hear! . . . For that old blow
I struck still I am hated, but for his
Who smote me, being of my blood, there is
No wrath in all the darkness: there is none
Cares for a mother murdered by her son.
   Open thine heart to see this gash!—
               (*She shows the wound in her throat.*) In sleep
The heart hath many eyes and can see deep:
'Tis daylight makes man's fate invisible.
   Oft of my bounty ye have lapt your fill;
Oft the sad peace of wineless cups to earth
I have poured, and midmurk feastings on your hearth
Burned, when no other god draws near to eat.
   And all these things ye have cast beneath your feet,
And he is fled, fled lightly like a fawn
Out of your nets! With mocking he is gone
And twisting of the lips. . . . I charge you, hark!
This is my life, my death. Oh, shake the dark
From off you, Children of the Deep. 'Tis I,
Your dream, I, Clytemnestra, stand and cry.
                  [*Moaning among the* FURIES.

Moan on, but he is vanished and forgot.
So strong the prayers of them that love me not!
                            [*Moaning.*

Too sound ye sleep.—And have ye for the dead
No pity? . . . And my son, my murderer, fled!
                            [*Groaning.*

Ye groan; ye slumber. Wake! . . . What task have ye
To do on earth save to work misery?
                            [*Groaning.*

Can sleep and weariness so well conspire
To drain the fell she-dragon of her fire?
           [*Sharp repeated muttering: then words "At
                him! At him! Catch, catch, catch! Ah,
                beware!"*

Ah, hunting in your dreams, and clamorous yet,
Tired bloodhounds that can sleep but not forget!
  How now? Awake! Be strong! And faithful keep
Thy lust of pain through all the drugs of sleep.
  Thou feelst my scorn? Aye, feel and agonize
Within; such words are scourges to the wise.
Thy blood-mist fold about him, like a doom.
Waste him with vapour from thy burning womb.
A second chase is death! . . . Pursue! Pursue!

> [*The* GHOST *vanishes as the* FURIES *gradually wake.*

Leader of the Furies. Awake! Quick, waken her as I wake
  you!
Thou sleepest? Rise; cast slumber from thy brain
And search. Is our first hunt so all in vain?

Furies (*speaking severally*). O rage, rage and wrath!
    Friends, they have done me wrong!
      Many and many a wrong I have suffered,
        mockeries all!
Evil and violent deeds, a shame that lingereth long
      And bitter, bitter as gall!
The beast is out of the toils, out of the toils and away!
      I slept, and I lost my prey.

What art thou, O Child of Zeus? A thief and a cozener!
      Hast broken beneath thy wheels them that were holy
        and old?
A godless man and an evil son, he but kneels in prayer,
      And straight he is ta'en to thy fold.
Thou hast chosen the man who spilt his mother's blood!
      Are these things just, thou God:

As a raging charioteer mid-grippeth his goad to bite
      Beneath the belly, beneath the flank, where the smart
        is hot,
There riseth out of my dreams Derision with hands to smite;
As a wretch at the block is scourged when the scourger hateth
    aright,
      And the shuddering pain dies not.

These be the deeds ye do, ye Gods of the younger race:
    Ye break the Law at your will; your high throne drips
        with gore,
The foot is wet and the head. There is blood in the Holy
        Place!
The Heart of Earth uplifteth its foulness in all men's face,
    Clean nevermore, nevermore!

Blood, thou holy Seer, there is blood on thy burning hearth.
    Thine inmost place is defiled, and thine was the will
        and the word.
Thou has broken the Law of Heaven, exalted the things of
        Earth;
    The hallowed Portions of old thine hand hath blurred.

Thou knowest to hurt my soul; yea, but shalt save not him.
    The earth may open and hide, but never shall he be
        freed.
Defiling all he goes, there where in exile dim
    Many defilers more wait and bleed.

                                        [*Enter* APOLLO.

Apollo. Avaunt, I charge you! Get ye from my door![6]
Darken this visionary dome no more!
Quick, lest ye meet that snake of bitter wing
That leaps a-sudden from my golden string,
And in your agony spue forth again
The black froth ye have sucked from tortured men!
    This floor shall be no harbour to your feet.
Are there not realms where Law upon her seat
Smites living head from trunk? Where prisoners bleed
From gougèd eyes? Children with manhood's seed
Blasted are there; maimed foot and severed hand,
And stoning, and a moan through all the land
Of men impaled to die. There is the board
Whereat ye feast, and, feasting, are abhorred
Of heaven.—But all the shapes of you declare
Your souls within. Some reeking lion's lair
Were your fit dwelling, not this cloistered Hall
Of Mercy, which your foulness chokes withal.
    Out, ye wild goats unherded! Out, ye drove
Accursed, that god nor devil dares to love!

[During this speech the FURIES *fly confusedly from the Temple down into the Orchestra. The* LEADER *turns.*

Leader. Phoebus Apollo, in thy turn give heed!
I hold thee not a partner in this deed;
Thou hast wrought it all. The guilt is thine alone.
  Apollo. What sayst thou there?—One word, and then begone.
  Leader. Thou spakest and this man his mother slew.
  Apollo. I spoke, and he avenged his father. True.
  Leader. Thou stoodest by, to accept the new-shed gore.
  Apollo. I bade him turn for cleansing to my door.
  Leader. Ha! And revilest us who guide his feet?
  Apollo. Ye be not clean to approach this Mercy Seat.
  Leader. We be by Law eternal what we be.
  Apollo. And what is that? Reveal thy dignity.
  Leader. We hunt from home his mother's murderer.
  Apollo. A husband-murdering woman, what of her?
  Leader. 'Twas not one blood in slayer and in slain.
  Apollo. How? Would ye count as a light thing and vain
The perfect bond of Hera and high Zeus?
Yea, and thy word dishonoureth too the use
Of Cypris, whence love groweth to his best.
The fate-ordainèd meeting, breast to breast,
Of man and woman is a tie more sure
Than oath or pact, if Justice guards it pure.
If them so joined ye heed not when they slay,
Nor rise in wrath, nor smite them on their way,
Unrighteous is thine hunting of this man,
Orestes. Why on him is all thy ban
Unloosed? The other never broke thy rest . . .
But Pallas, child of Zeus, shall judge this quest.
  Leader. I cleave to him. I leave him never more.
  Apollo. Oh, hunt thy fill! Make sorrow doubly sore.
  Leader. Abridge not thou the Portions of my lot.
  Apollo. Keep thou thy portions. I will touch them not.
  Leader. Thou hast thy greatness by the throne of God;
I . . . But the scent draws of that mother's blood.
I come! I come! I hunt him to the grave. . . .

[The FURIES *go out on the track of* ORESTES.

[187]

Apollo. 'Tis mine then to bring succour, and to save
My suppliant. Earth and Heaven are both afraid
For God's wrath, if one helpless is betrayed.

> [APOLLO *returns behind the shrine, and the*
> *doors close. When they open again, they*
> *reveal, in place of* APOLLO's *Central Altar,*
> *the Statue of* ATHENA PARTHENOS: *the*
> *scene now represents the Temple of*
> *Athena in Athens. Enter* ORESTES, *worn*
> *with travel and suffering.*

Orestes. Pallas Athena, from Apollo's wing
I come; receive in peace this hunted thing
My sin no more polluteth, nor with hand
Unpurified before thy throne I stand.
A blunted edge, grief-worn and sanctified
By pain, where'er men traffic or abide,
On, on, o'er land and sea I have made my way,
True-purposed Loxias' bidding to obey.
At last I have found thy House; thine image I
Clasp, and here wait thy judgement till I die.

> [*He throws himself down at the feet of the*
> *Statue, but no answer comes. Presently*
> *enter the* FURIES, *following him.*

Leader. Ha! Here he has passed. Spot reeketh upon spot.
Blood is a spy that points and babbles not.
Like hounds that follow some sore-wounded fawn,
We smell the way that blood and tears are gone,
And follow.—Oh, my belly gaspeth sore
With toils man-wasting; I can chase no more.
Through all the ways of the world I have shepherded
My lost sheep, and above the salt sea sped,
Wingless pursuing, swift as any sail.
And now 'tis here, meseemeth, he doth quail
And cower.—Aye, surely it is here; the smell
Of man's blood laughs to meet me. All is well.

Furies (*searching*). Ha, search, search again!
　　　　Seek for him far and wide.
　　　　Shall this man fly or hide
　　　And the unatonèd stain
　　　Of his mother's blood be vain?

Haha! Lo where he lies!
And comfort is in his eyes!
He hath made his arms a wreath
    For the knees of the Deathless One,
And her judgement challengeth
    On the deed his hands have done.
In vain! All in vain!
    When blood on the earth is shed,
    Blood of a mother dead,
Ye shall gather it not again.
    'Tis wet, 'tis vanishèd,
Down in the dust like rain.

    Thyself shalt yield instead,
Living, from every vein,
    Thine own blood, rich and red,
For our parchèd mouths to drain,
    Till my righteous heart be fed
With thy blood and thy bitter pain;
    Till I waste thee like the dead,
And cast thee among the slain,
    Till her wrong be comforted
And her wound no longer stain.

The Law thou then shalt see;
    That whoso of men hath trod
In sin against these three,
    Parent or Guest or God,
That sin is unforgot,
And the payment faileth not.
There liveth, for every man,
    Below, in the realm of Night,
A judge who straighteneth
The crooked; his name is Death.
All life his eye doth scan
    And recordeth right.

Orestes. I have known much evil, and have learnt therein
What divers roads man goes to purge his sin,
And when to speak and when be dumb; and eke
In this thing a wise master bids me speak.
The blood upon this hand is fallen asleep

[189]

And fades. And though a sin be ne'er so deep
'Twill age with the aging years. When this of mine
Was fresh, on Phoebus' hearth with blood of swine
'Twas washed and blurred. 'Twere a long tale since then,
To tell how I have spoke with many men
In scatheless parle. And now, with lips of grace,
Once more I pray the Lady of this place,
Athena, to mine aid. Let her but come;
Myself, mine Argive people and my home
Shall without war be hers, hers true of heart
And changeless. Therefore, whereso'er thou art,
In some far wilderness of Libyan earth,
By those Tritonid waters of thy birth;
Upgirt for deeds or veilèd on thy throne;
Or is it Phlegra's field thou brood'st upon,
Guiding the storm, like some bold Lord of War,
Oh, hear! A goddess heareth though afar:
Bring me deliverance in this mine hour!

[*He waits expectant, but there is no answer.*

Leader. Not Lord Apollo's, not Athena's power
Shall reach thee any more. Forgot, forgot,
Thou reelest back to darkness, knowing not
Where in man's heart joy dwelleth; without blood,
A shadow, flung to devils for their food!

Wilt answer not my word? Wilt spurn thereat,
Thou that art mine, born, doomed, and consecrate
My living feast, at no high altar slain?
Hark thou this song to bind thee like a chain!

Furies (*as they move into position for the Dance*).
   Up, let us tread the dance, and wind—
      The hour is come!—our shuddering spell.
      Show how this Band apportions well
   Their fated burdens to mankind.

   Behold, we are righteous utterly.
      The man whose hand is clean, no wrath
      From us shall follow: down his path
   He goeth from all evil free.

But whoso slays and hides withal
   His red hand, swift before his eyes
   True witness for the dead we rise:
We are with him to the end of all.

[*Being now in position they begin the Binding Song.*

Some Furies. Mother, who didst bear a being
   Dread to the eyeless and the seeing,
      Night, my Mother!
   Leto's Child would wrong me, tear
   From my clutch this trembling hare,
   My doomèd prey: he bore to slay,
   And shall he not the cleansing bear,
      He, none other?

Chorus. But our sacrifice to bind,
   Lo, the music that we wind,
   How it dazeth and amazeth
      And the will it maketh blind,
   As it moves without a lyre
   To the throb of my desire;
   'Tis a chain about the brain,
      'Tis a wasting of mankind.

Other Furies. Thus hath Fate, through weal and woe,
   For our Portion as we go
     Spun the thread:
   Whenso mortal man in sin
   'Brueth hand against his kin,
   Mine till death He wandereth,
   And freedom never more shall win,
     Not when dead.

Chorus. But our sacrifice to bind,
   Lo, the music that we wind,
   How it dazeth and amazeth
      And the will it maketh blind,
   As it moves without a lyre
   To the throb of my desire;
   'Tis a chain about the brain,
      'Tis a wasting of mankind.

Some Furies. Since the hour we were begot
        Of this rite am I the priest;
  Other gods may share it not;
        Nor is any man nor beast
  That dare eat the food we eat
  Nor among us take his seat;
  For no part have I nor lot
        In the white robe of the feast.

Chorus. For the tale I make mine own
  Is of houses overthrown,
  When the Foe within the Dwelling
        Slays a brother and is flown:
  Up and after him, Io!
  While the blood is still a-flow,
  Though his strength be full and swelling,
        We shall waste him, flesh from bone!

Other Furies. Would they take thee from the care
        We have guarded thee withal?
  Would the Gods disown our prayer
        Till no Law be left at all?
  Yea, because of blood that drips
  As aforetime from our lips,
  And the world's hate that we bear,
        God hath cast us from His hall!

Chorus. I am on them as they fly,
  With a voice out of the sky,
  And my armèd heel is o'er them
        To fall crashing from on high.
  There be fliers far and fast,
  But I trip them at the last,
  And my arms are there before them,
        And shall crush them ere they die!

Divers Furies. The glories of Man that were proud where
  the sunlight came,
    Below in the dark are wasted and cast to shame;
      For he trembles at the hearing
      Of the Black Garments nearing,

And the beating of the feet, like flame
He falls and knows not; the blow hath made blind
      his eyes;
And above hangs Sin, as a darkening of the skies,
      And a great voice swelling
      Like a mist about his dwelling,
And sobbing in the mist and cries.

For so it abideth: subtle are we to plan,
      Sure to fulfil, and forget not any Sin;
      And Venerable they call us, but none can win
            Our pardon for child of man.
Unhonoured and undesired though our kingdom be,
      Where the sun is dead and no god in all the skies,
Great crags and trackless, alike for them that see,
      And them of the wasted eyes;

What mortal man but quaketh before my power,
      And boweth in worship to hear my rule of doom,
      God-given of old, fate-woven on the ageless loom
            And ripe to the perfect hour?
To the end of all abideth mine ancient Right,
      Whose word shall be never broke nor its deed undone,
Though my seat is below the Grave, in the place where sight
      Fails and there is no Sun.

                                    [*Enter* ATHENA.
Athena. Far off I heard the calling of my name,
Beside Scamander[7], where I took in claim
The new land which the Achaean lords and kings,
In royal spoil for many warfarings,
Gave, root and fruit for ever, as mine own
Exempted prize, to Theseus' sons alone.
Thence came I speeding, while behind me rolled
My wingless aegis, floating fold on fold.
   But these strange visitants . . . I tremble not
Beholding, yet I marvel. Who and what
Are ye? I speak to all. And who is he
Who round mine image clings so desperately?
   But ye are like no earth-seed ever sown,
No goddess-shape that Heaven hath looked upon,

Nor any semblance born of human kind . . .
  Howbeit, ye have not wronged me. I were blind
To right and custom did I speak you ill.
  Leader. Virgin of God most high, have all thy will.
Still-weeping Night knows us the brood she bears;
The wronged ones in the darkness call us Prayers.
  Athena. I know your lineage and the names ye hold.
  Leader. Our office and our lot can soon be told.
  Athena. Make clear thy word, that all be understood.
  Leader. We hunt from home the shedder of man's blood.
  Athena. What end appoint ye to that flight of his?
  Leader. A land where none remembereth what joy is.
  Athena. And such a chase on this man thou wilt cry?
  Leader. Who dared to be his mother's murderer, aye.
  Athena. What goaded him? Some fear, some unseen wrath?
  Leader. What goad could drive a man on such a path?
  Athena (*looking at Orestes*). Why speaketh one alone, when
    two are there?
  Leader. He will not swear, nor challenge me to swear.
  Athena. Which wouldst thou, to seem righteous, or to be?
  Leader. What meanst thou there? Speak out thy subtlety.
  Athena. Let no bare oath the deeper right subdue.
  Leader. Try thou the cause, then, and give judgement true.
  Athena. Ye trust me this whole issue to decide?
  Leader. Who would not trust thee? True thou art and tried.
  Athena (*turning to Orestes*). Strange man, and what in turn
    hast thou to advance?
Thy land and lineage, and thy long mischance
Show first, then make thine answer to their laws.
If truly in the justice of thy cause
Trusting, thou clingest here in need so dire
To mine own shape, hard by my deathless fire,
In fearful prayer, as lost Ixîon prayed,
Make to all these thine answer unafraid.
  Orestes. Most high Athena, let me from the last
Of these thy questionings one fear outcast.
Pollution is not in me, nor with hand
Blood-reeking cleave I to thine altar-strand;
In sign whereof, behold, I have cast away
That silence which the man of blood alway

[194]

Observeth, till some hand, that hath the power
To cleanse the sins of man, new blood shall shower
Of swine upon him, drowning the old stain.
I have been cleansed again and yet again
In others' dwellings, both by blood that fell
And running rivers that have washed me well.
Be that care then forgot.   My name and birth
Are quickly told.   I am sprung of Argive earth;
My father's name was known upon thy lips,
Agamemnon, marshall of a thousand ships,
With whom thou madest Troy, that city of pride,
No more a city.   He returning died,
Not kingly.   'Twas my mother black of heart
Met him and murdered, snaring him with art
Of spangled webs. . . . Alas, that robe of wrath,
That cried to heaven the blood-stain of the bath!
Then came long exile; then, returning, I
Struck dead my mother.   Nought will I deny;
So, for my sire belovèd, death met death.

    And Loxias in these doings meriteth
His portion, who foretold strange agonies
To spur me if I left unsmitten these
That slew him. . . . Take me thou, and judge if ill
I wrought or righteously.   I will be still
And praise thy judgement, whatsoe'er betide.
    Athena.   This is a mystery graver to decide
Than mortal dreameth.   Nor for me 'twere good
To sift the passionate punishments of blood.
Since thou hast cast thee on my altar stair
Perfect by suffering, from thy stains that were
Made clean and harmless, suppliant at my knee,
I, in my City's name, must pity thee
And chide not.   Yet these too, I may not slight;
They have their portion in the Orb of Right
Eternal.   If they are baffled of their will,
The wrath of undone Justice shall distil
Through all the air a poison; yea, a pall
Intolerable about the land shall fall
And groaning sickness.   Doubtful thus it lies:
To cast them out or keep them in mine eyes

Were equal peril, and I must ponder sore.
Yet, seeing fate lays this matter at my door,
Myself not judging, I will judges find
In mine own City, who will make no blind
Oath-challenge to pursuer and pursued,
But follow this new rule, by me indued
As law for ever. Proofs and witnesses
Call ye on either side, and set to these
Your oaths. Such oath helps Justice in her need.
　　I will go choose the noblest of the breed
Of Athens, and here bring them to decide
This bloody judgement even as truth is tried,
And then, their oath accomplished, to depart,
Right done, and no transgression in their heart.

> [*Exit* ATHENA. *The Shrine is closed.*
> ORESTES *remaining inside at the foot*
> *of the Image.*

Furies. This day there is a new Order born.
　　　　If this long coil of judging and of strife
　　　　Shall uplift the mother-murderer to life,
Shall the World not mark it, and in scorn
　　　　Go forth to do evil with a smile?
　　　　Yea, for parents hereafter there is guile
　　　　　　That waiteth, and great anguish; by a knife
In a child's hand their bosom shall be torn.

No wrath shall be stirred by any deed,
　　　　No doom from the Dark Watchers any more.
　　　　Lo, to all death I cast wide the door!
And men, while they whisper of the need
　　Of their neighbour, shall pray tremblingly within
　　For some rest and diminishing of sin.
　　　　They will praise the old medicine that of yore
Brought comfort, and marvel as they bleed.

　　　　　　Vainly will they make their moan?
　　　　　　Vainly cry in sore despite,
　　　　"Help, ye Watchers on your throne,
　　　　　　Help, O Right!"
　　　　Many a father so shall cry,

Many a mother, new in pain;
Their vain sobbing floateth by:
"The great House is fallen again!
        Law shall die!"

Times there be when Fear is good,
    And the Watcher in the breast
Needs must reign in masterhood.
            Aye, tis best
Through much straitening to be wise.
    Who that hath no fear at all
In the sunlight of his eyes,
    Man or City, but shall fall
            From Right somewise?

The life that walketh without rule,
The life that is a tyrant's fool,
            Thou shalt not praise.
O'er all man's striving variously
God looketh, but, where'er it be.
Gives to the Mean his victory.
And therefore know I and confess,
The doomèd child of Godlessness
Is Pride of Man, and Pride's excess;
Only from health of heart shall spring
What men desire, what poets sing,
            Stormless days.

Whate'er befall, the Throne of Right
Fear thou, and let no lucre bright
            Seen suddenly,
To spurn that Altar make thee blind;
For chastisement is hid behind,
And the End waiteth, and shall bind.
Wherefore I charge thee, through all stress
Thy mother and thy father bless:
Herein, O Man, lies holiness.
And next, of all within thy fold,
The stranger and the friendless hold
            In sanctity.

He that is righteous uncompelled and free
     His life's way taketh
Not without happiness; and utterly
Cast to destruction shall he never be.
But he who laugheth and is bold in sin,
From every port great gain he gathers in,
Rejoicing; but methinks shall cast away
All, with much haste and trembling, on the day
    When sails are stript by the edge of wind and sea
       And yard-arm breaketh.

He yearns, he strives, amid the whirling sea,
    But none shall hear;
And loud his Daemon laughs, saying "This is he
    Who vaunted him these things should never be!"
Who now is weeping, weak in the endless foam,
And sees the foreland where beyond is home,
But shall not pass it: on the rocks of Right
Wrecked is his life's long glory; and the night
     Falls, and there lives from all his agony
      No word nor tear.

*The scene[8] is now set with seats for the Council of
    the Areopagus. Enter* ATHENA, *the* JUDGES, *a*
    HERALD, *a crowd of* CITIZENS, *the* FURIES,
    ORESTES.

Athena. Herald, thine office! See that yonder crowds
Hold back, and let this piercer of the clouds,
Filled with man's breath, the Tuscan trumpet, blow
His fiery summons to the host below.
Then all be silence, while the people fill
This Council Hall. Thus shall my sovran will
And ordinance to this people, great and small,
Be known for ever, and upheld by all
Within our gates; and thus my wardens do
Justice this day, discerning false from true.

                         [*Enter* APOLLO.

    Leader. Apollo, thou! Go, reign where thou art king!
What portion hast thou in this doom-saying?
    Apollo. I come to bear my witness. This is one

Who in great anguish came to me alone
For refuge, and knelt suppliant at my shrine.
Therefore the cleansing of his stain is mine.
Likewise I share his plea, and on me take
What guilt he bears for that dead mother's sake.
  Ope thou the court, O Pallas, and, as well
Thou canst, establish justice durable.
    Athena. Ho! Opened is the Court; and yours the speech.
      (*To the* FURIES)
He who pursueth, speaking first, can teach
Best his whole grief, and how the evil grew.
    Leader. Many are we, yet shall our words be few.
Make answer thou, point against point. And say
First this one thing: thy mother didst thou slay?
    Orestes. I slew her. . . . Aye. Denied it cannot be.
    Leader. Aha! The first of the three bouts to me!
    Orestes. Too soon ye vaunt. I am not yet outsped.
    Leader. How didst thou slay? That also must be said.
    Orestes (*with an effort*). I will say it. I drew sword and
      clave her throat.
    Leader. Who and what tempted thee? Who laid the plot?
    Orestes. He who is with me now, and witnesseth.
    Leader. God's prophet bade thee plot thy mother's death?
    Orestes. Yes: and hath never failed me to this day.
    Leader. And when the vote is cast, what wilt thou say?
    Orestes. I fear not. Helpers from my father's grave.
    Leader. Go, mother-murderer! Call the dead to save!
    Orestes. Two stains of death lay mingled on her hand.
    Leader. How two? Let these who judge thee understand.
    Orestes. A husband and a father, both, she slew.
    Leader. And death hath purged her. Shalt not thou die too?
    Orestes. Ye never hunted her, for all her stain.
    Leader. 'Twas not one blood in slayer and in slain.
    Orestes. And are my mother's blood and my blood one?
    Leader. How did she feed thee else beneath her zone?
Caitiff! Thy mother's blood wilt thou deny?
    Orestes (*overcome*). I can no more. . . . Give witness, and
      reply.
Lord Phoebus, in my stead, if righteously
I slew. . . . I slew: denied it cannot be:

But rightly, or most foully—as thine own
Heart speaks, give judgement, and let all be known.

   Apollo. Ye judges of Athena's Court most high,
I come to speak before you faithfully,
Being God's prophet: therefore truth is mine.
Nor ever spake I from my throne divine
Of man nor woman, land nor city wall,
Save by command of Him who ruleth all,
Zeus, the Olympian Father. Is there Right
Holier than this, I charge ye think, or Might
More mighty? Follow ye the All-Father's will:
If oaths be strong, is Zeus not stronger still?

   Leader. 'Twas Zeus, thou tellest, laid this duty large
Upon thy lips? 'Twas Zeus who bade thee charge
This man to avenge his father and cast down,
As nothing worth, his mother's sacred crown?

   Apollo. Are these the same? That a great man, raised high
By royal sceptre, given of God, should die,
And die by a woman's hand—and not in war
By Amazonian arrow, sped from far, . . .
But—Hear my tale, O Pallas, and ye too
Who sit enthronèd to sift false from true;
He came from battle after sufferings sore
But greater glories, and she stood before
The gate to greet and praise him, strewed his path
With crimson robes and led him to his bath—
A marble bed!—and o'er the end thereof
Laid the great web and curtained it above,
To ensnare him as he rose; then, in the wide
Unending folds, she smote him and he died!
So died a man, ye hear it from my lips,
All-honoured, War-Lord of a thousand ships;
And such a wife was she! Be stern, and smite
The guilty, ye who sit to establish right!

   Leader. Doth Zeus count fatherhood so high a thing?
Who cast in bonds his father and his king,
Old Cronos? Are these things not contrary?
I charge ye, judges, hearken his reply.

   Apollo. Ye worms of hate, O ye that Gods abhor,
Bonds can be loosened; there is cure therefor,

[200]

And many and many a plan in God's great mind
To free the prisoners whom he erst did bind.
But once the dust hath drunk the blood of men
Murdered, there is no gathering it again.
For that no magic doth my Father know,
Though all things else he changeth high and low
Or fixeth, and no toil is in his breath.

 Leader. Is that thy pleading against this man's death?
The kindred blood, his mother's blood, the well
Of his own life, he hath spilt. How shall he dwell
In Argos? In his home? What altar-stair,
When Argos worships, will receive his prayer?
What love-bowl of the brethren cleanse his hand?

 Apollo. That too I answer; mark and understand.
The mother to the child that men call hers
Is no true life-begetter, but a nurse
Of live seed. 'Tis the sower of the seed
Alone begetteth. Woman comes at need,
A stranger, to hold safe in trust and love
That bud of new life—save when God above
Wills that it die. And would ye proof of this,
There have been fathers where no mother is.
Whereof a perfect witness standeth nigh,
Athena Pallas, child of the Most High,
A thought-begotten unconceivèd bloom,
No nursling of the darkness of the womb,
But such a flower of life as goddess ne'er
Hath born in heaven nor ever more shall bear.

 Pallas, in all things it is mine to swell
In power thy people and thy citadel;
And therefore to thine Altar did I send
This suppliant, that hereafter to the end
Of mortal time he may be true to thee,
And plant his spear by thine unfalteringly,
And on through generations yet unborn
Argos observe the pact her King hath sworn.

 Athena. Now shall I charge upon their faith these men
To cast true stones, or would ye speak again?

 Leader. Shot is our every arrow: I but stay
To learn how ends the issue of the day.

Athena. How shall I cast a judgement in this cause
Unblamed of you, and of the eternal laws?

Apollo. Ye have heard what ye have heard. Strangers, revere
Your oaths, and cast your judgement without fear.

Athena. Hear now mine ordinance, ye who have striven
This day to give, what none before hath given,
True judgement o'er spilt blood. O Attic Folk,
Henceforth for ever, under Aegeus' yoke,
This Council and this Judgement Seat by me
Are stablisht. On this mountain shall it be,
Here in the Amazon's most virgin hold,
Who came in wrath for Theseus' wrongs of old
Embattled, and this fortress against ours,
Hill against hill, towers against soaring towers,
Built, and to Ares on the rock with flame
Gave sacrifice: whence comes its awful name,
The Rock, the Mount, of Ares. All things here
Being holy, Reverence and her sister, Fear,
In darkness as in daylight shall restrain
From all unrighteousness the sons of men,
While Athens' self corrupt not her own law.
With mire and evil influx ye can flaw
Fair water till no lips may drink thereof.
I charge you, citizens, enfold and love
That spirit that nor anarch is nor thrall;
And casting away Fear, yet cast not all;
For who that hath no fear is safe from sin?
That Fear which is both Ruth and Law within
Be yours, and round your city and your land
Shall be upraised a rampart, yea, a hand
Of strong deliverance, which no sons of men,
From the Isle of Pelops to the Scythian fen,
Possess nor know, this Council of the Right,
Untouched of lucre, terrible to smite,
And swift and merciful, a guard to keep
Vigil above my people while they sleep.
Which here I establish. Let these words advise
My city evermore.—I charge you, rise
And lift your stones of doom and judge, alway
Your oath remembering. I have said my say.

[*The* Judges *rise and go one by one past the
two urns, casting their stones as they pass.*

Leader. Behold, an awful presence moveth yet
Within your land, which mock not nor forget!

Apollo. The will of Zeus, by my lips ministered,
I charge you make not fruitless nor unfeared!

Leader. And what wouldst thou with blood, having therein
No place? Henceforth thine altars are unclean!

Apollo. Did Zeus, then, sin, who bowed his head to spare
Blood-red Ixîon for his burning prayer?

Leader. Thou speakest: but my Law, if it be broke,
Shall come again in wrath to haunt this folk.

Apollo. Thou hast no honour more 'mid things divine,
Or old or new: the victory shall be mine.

Leader. So in Admetus' House thou didst betray
The Fates, to make man deathless past his day.

Apollo. Shall not a god regard his worshipper
Then chiefliest, when in peril and in prayer?

Leader. The ancient boundaries thou didst desecrate,
Thou mad'st a drunkard of Eternal Fate!

Apollo. True Justice thou canst know not. Thou shalt spue
Thy venom forth, and none give heed thereto.

Leader. Women are we, and old; and thou dost ride
Above us, trampling, in thy youth and pride.
Howbeit, I wait to know the end, being still
In doubt to work this City good or ill.

Athena. One judgement still remains. I, at the last,
To set Orestes free this stone will cast:
For, lo, no mother bare me: I approve
In all—save only that I know not love—
The man's way. Flesh and spirit I am His
Who gave me life. And in this coil it is
No dire deed that a woman, who had slain
Her mate and house-lord, should be quelled again.
Wherefore I judge that here, if equal be
The votes ye cast, Orestes shall go free.
Ye judges, haste: on you this office turns:
And cast the gathered sea-stones from the urns.

Orestes. Apollo, Lord, what shall the issue be?

Leader. O Night, O dark-eyed Mother, dost thou see?

[203]

Orestes. Is it the noose of death, or life and light?

Leader. My law down-trodden or enthroned in right?

Apollo. Divide the fallen sea-stones as is due,
Strangers, and in the count see all be true.
An absent voice hath made life ruinous,
And one cast pebble built a fallen house.

> [*The scrutineers bring their results to* ATHENA.

Athena. This prisoner, since the stones for ill and good
Are equal, hath escaped the doom of blood.

Orestes. O Pallas, O deliverer of my race[9],
Thou hast led back the wanderer to his place,
The homeless to his home; and men shall say
"Once more he is an Argive, and this day
Dwells in his father's riches, by the word
Of Pallas, Loxias, and Zeus the Third,
Who saveth all and all accomplisheth."
'Twas He of old who saw my father's death,
And pitied; He who saw pursuing me
My mother's ministers, and set me free.

Pallas, to this thy people and thy clime
Through all the long years of ensuing Time
I swear, ere I depart to mine own land,
This oath. No captain of an Argive band
Shall ever against Athens raise his spear.
Yea, and if any break this law, I swear
Myself out of the grave bewilderment
Shall set before their host, and discontent,
Disheartened roads and rivers evil-starred,
Till back they turn, bowed down by toils too hard
For bearing. But if still with vow unbroke,
Through storm or shine, for Pallas and her folk
Their lance is lifted, then to Argos too
My love shall be the greater, and hold true.
And fare thee well, O Pallas; fare you well,
All that within her ancient rampart dwell;
Iron may your grasp against all evil be,
And strong to save, and big with victory!

> [*Exit* ORESTES.

Furies. Woe on you, woe, ye younger gods!
Ye have trampled the great Laws of old

Beneath your chariots! Ye have broke the rods
    Of justice, yea and torn them from my hold!
Mine office gone, unhappy and angered sore,
I rage alone. What have I any more
  To do? Or be? Shall not mine injury turn
    And crush this people? Shall not poison rain
    Upon them, even the poison of this pain
      Wherewith my heart doth burn?
  And up therefrom there shall a lichen creep,
    A leafless, childless, blight,
A stain in the earth man-slaying. . . O just Throne of Right!
    Have ye not suffered deep,
Deep, ye unhappy children of old Night,
    Born to be scorned and weep!
Athena. I pray you, nay! Make not this bitter moan;
Ye are not conquered. Equal, stone for stone,
The judgement fell, in honesty of thought,
Not scorn of thee. From Zeus on high was brought
A shining witness; and the god, who gave
The word to slay, himself was here to save,
Lest this man for obedience to his will
Should perish. . . . And for this ye fain would spill
Your poison? Ah, take thought! Nor on our heads
Rain the strange dew a spirit's anger sheds,
Seed-ravening blight and mildews merciless,
Till all the land lie waste in fruitlessness.
Spare us, and, lo, I promise: here shall be
A home your own, a caverned mystery,
Where alway ye shall sit, enthroned in pride
And shining, by my people glorified.
Furies. Woe on you, woe, ye younger gods!
      Ye have trampled the great Laws of old
Beneath your chariots! Ye have broke the rods
    Of justice, yea and torn them from my hold!
Mine office gone, unhappy and angered sore,
I rage alone. What have I any more
  To do? Or be? Shall not mine injury turn
    And crush this people? Shall not poison rain
    Upon them, even the poison of this pain
      Wherewith my heart doth burn?

And up therefrom there shall a lichen creep,
    A leafless, childless, blight,
A stain in the earth man-slaying. . . O just Throne of Right!
    Have ye not suffered deep,
Deep, ye unhappy children of old Night,
    Born to be scorned and weep!

Athena. Ah, rage not. No dishonour comes you nigh;
Nor, being immortal, blast for these who die
Their little life and land. I, even as you,
Obey the supreme Father, yea, I too.
What boots it to say more? To me alone
The keys of that great treasure-house are known
Where sleep the lightnings.—But He needs them not!
Accept my word, and cast not here the hot
Fruits of a passion that turns all to ill:
Bid the dark tempest's bitter surge be still,
Thou great in glory, partner of my home!
From many miles of land to thee shall come
First-fruits for maidens wed, for children born;
Then shall ye bless this peace that we have sworn.

Furies.   That this should fall on me,
      Me of the ancient way,
      The faithful of heart! To be
      Unclean, abominable,
      In the darkness where I dwell,
      And mine honour shorn away!
My breath is as a fire flung far and wide,
And a strange anguish stabbeth at my side.
Hear thou my wrath, O Mother, Night, mine own,
Hear what these young false-handed gods have wrought!
Mine immemorial honour is overthrown,
    And I am naught!

Athena. Thine heaviness myself will help thee bear.
Older thou art than I, and surely ware
Of wisdom that I wot not: yet also
To me Zeus giveth both to think and know.
And if ye leave us for the stranger's shore,
This know I, that your heart shall still be sore
For Athens. Time's great river in its flow
From darkness shall but make her glory grow.

And here in honour at Erechtheus' side
Enthronèd, thou shalt garner gifts of pride
From men and women worshippers, in fair
Procession moving, richer and more rare
Than eye of man hath seen in other lands.
Such offering now awaits thee at my hands:
Blessing and blest, 'mid glories gladly given,
To share this land, the best beloved of Heaven.

    Furies.   That this should fall on me,
             Me of the ancient way,
             The faithful of heart! To be
             Unclean, abominable,
             In the darkness where I dwell,
             And mine honour shorn away!
My breath is as a fire flung far and wide,
And a strange anguish stabbeth at my side.
Hear thou my wrath, O Mother, Night, mine own,
Hear what these young false-handed gods have wrought!
Mine immemorial honour is overthrown,
             And I am naught!

    Athena. I will not cease thine anger to assuage
With good words. None shall say that, in thine age
By younger gods and city-building men
Thou and thy law were mocked, cast out again
To walk the wilderness, exiles from hence.
If thou canst hold that spirit in reverence
Which hears Persuasion and which thinks again,
Whose understanding and whose peace doth reign
By God's appointment in my word and thought,
Here thou wilt stay. Or, if that please thee not,
Thou shalt not justly lay upon this land
Or wrath, or vengeance, or afflicting hand.
Stay, if ye will. Let this soil be your own
With Right made perfect and an ageless throne.

    Leader. Great Pallas, what abode shall be my lot?
    Athena. A throne unwashed by tears; reject it not.
    Leader. Say I consent; what shall mine office be?
    Athena. No house shall prosper save by aid of thee.
    Leader. Such greatness mine! Wilt thou thereof have care?
    Athena. Yea; and through life uphold thy worshipper.

Leader. For dateless time thou giv'st me warranty?

Athena. How should I speak the thing that shall not be?

Leader. Thou wilt soften me. . . . Methinks mine anger
   bends.

Athena. Stay, and that softened mood will find thee friends.

Leader. What spell upon the land wouldst have me lay?

Athena. All that brings Victory and not Dismay.

From earth and dewy sea—be this thy prayer—
From moving winds and the still dome of air
Let breaths of gladness and sweet sunlight come;
The fruit of flocks and fields round every home
Abundant flow and, year by year, be true.
The seeds of human life make fruitful, too,
Save in the ungodly: them thy Rule of Right
Shall uproot, as of old. For I delight,
Like one that tends his garden, to uprear
These plants of righteousness, untouched by fear
Of evil. Cast not on this soil of mine
Thy whet-stones of the blood, like poisonous wine
In young men's hearts, till rage and death be stirred.
Oh, take not from the fierce mate-murdering bird
The heart to give my people, the blind war
Within, that burneth most where brethren are.
War with the stranger, yes; no stint thereof;
Terror is there, and glory, and great love;
But not the mad bird-rage that slays at home.
Such let thine office be. And if there come
True-hearted war, I will not fail to uphold
This land victorious where great deeds are told.

> [*At a sign from the* LEADER, *the* FURIES *take
>   formation for a Song of Blessing.*

.*Furies.* A home with Pallas shall be mine.
   I will not give this City nay,
The Fort of Heaven, which Zeus divine
   And faithful Ares hold in sway,
A shining loveliness to enfold
The altars of the gods of old.

For whom—so do I weave my prayer
And move with words of presage good—

All fortunes whereby life is fair,
Like springing fountains, up shall flood,
From Earth's deep-bosomed caverns won
By wooing of the enthronèd Sun.

Athena. I love my City; and with plan
    Aforethought here have welcomed these,
    The Awarders great and hard to appease,
Whose realm is all the estate of man.

Justice is theirs: though many an one
    May meet their wrath in innocence,
    Not knowing why the wound nor whence,
That striketh. Some great evil done

Aforetime, with no payment just,
    Cast him to These. Strange wrath and hate
    Are round him, and he cries: but Fate,
Unanswering, grindeth him to dust.

Furies. No storm-wind—so I speak my prize—
    Shall breathe the blight that poisoneth trees;
No burning things that blind the eyes
    Of plants, shall pass her boundaries:
The groaning pest shall come not nigh,
Nor fruit upon the branches die.

The flocks shall browse in happy cheer,
    And Pan, the Shepherd, guard them true,
With twofold increase, as the year
    Repays her seeds in season due;
And deep-hid treasures of the ground
Shall be in God's due order found.

Athena. Ye Guardians, hear the word she hath said,
    And shall fulfil! Most potent hands
    Hath great Erînys, in the lands
Where dwell the deathless and the dead.

And all this world of men declares
    Her visible act on right and wrong;
    How one man's life she makes a song,
Another's a long mist of tears.

[209]

Furies. Let manhood's glory by no doom
    Of death untimely be defiled;
  Let life to maidens in their bloom
    Bring each a lover and a child.
O whatsoever Gods have power,
And Fates eternal, grant this dower!

  Ye Fates, our Mother's Sisterhood,
    Assigners true to all that be,
To every house its ill and good,
    To every hour its potency.
Righteous participants through all,
Of Gods the most majestical.

Athena. With joy I hear their prescient song
    Touching my land; and much in pride
    I praise Persuasion gentle-eyed,
Who guarded well my lips and tongue,

  When these were wrathful and denied;
    But Zeus, whose Word is in the Mart,
    Prevailed; and of our strife no part,
Save strife in blessing, shall abide.

Furies. Let her who hungereth still for wrong,
    Faction, in Athens ne'er again
  Lift on the air her ravening song;
    Let not the dust of Pallas' Plain
Drink the dark blood of any son
By fury of revenge fordone.

  Rage not to smite the smiter, lest
    By rage the City's heart be torn:
  Bless him that blesseth: in each breast
    So shall a single love be born,
And 'gainst Her foes a single hate.
This also maketh firm a state.

Athena. Wise are they and have found the way
    Of peace. And in each awful face
    I see for you, my People, grace:
If ye are gentle, even as they,

[210]

And do them worship, this shall be
　　Your work: to guide through ill, through good,
　　Both land and town in that pure mood
Of truth that shuns iniquity.

[*The* JUDGES *and the concourse of* ATHENIANS
*have now formed into procession, to escort
the* FURIES *to their Cavern.*

Chorus of Athenians. Rejoice, rejoice! And as ye go your
　　ways
　　　　In rich apportionment of blissful days,
　　　　　　Farewell, farewell!

Furies. Ye folk within the wall, approved
　　　　To neighbour Jove's eternal eyes,
　　Ye lovers of the Well-beloved,
　　　　The Virgin Spirit, timely wise,
　　The wings of Pallas fold above you,
　　Therefore shall Zeus the Father love you.

Athena. Fare ye well also. I must go
　　　　Before you, guiding, to make bright
　　　　Your secret chambers[10] with the light,
　　The holy light, they dared not know.

Come, and when deep beneath the veil
　　　　Of earth ye pass, 'mid offering high,
　　　　Hold down the evil that shall die,
　　Send up the good that shall prevail.

Ye sons of Cranaos, guide them, till
　　　　These Wanderers rest within your doors:
　　　　With them one City now is yours;
　　Be one in working and in will!

Chorus of Athenians. Rejoice, rejoice! I raise my voice
　　again,
　　　　To speak that bliss that overtowereth pain.
　　　　　　Farewell, farewell!

Furies. All things within the Wall that dwell,
　　　All gods and men, that are or were;
　　All life from Pallas' citadel
　　　Which draws its being, I am here:
　　These Dwellers in your gates adore,
　　And fear the tides of Life no more!

Athena. The prayers they have uttered o'er my land I praise;
And speed them on, 'mid many a torch's blaze,
To that most deep and subterranean end
Of wandering. Let these ministers, who tend
Mine image, follow; righteous warders they.
Let all the fulness of the land this day,
Children, and wives and women bent with years,
Come forth: do worship to these Wanderers
Accepted in their robes of crimson dye.
Let leap the flash of fire. This great Ally
Shall be revealed and proven in the fate
Of Athens, if her men be true and great.
　　Chorus of Athenians. Gather ye home; are ye great, do ye
　　　crave adoration,
　　O childless Children of Night in the pride of your going?
　　　　(Give good words, O Folk of the Fold!)
Aeonian caverns of glory are yours, and oblation
　　Of worship, and sacrifice high, and praise overflowing.
　　　　(Give good words, O young men and old!)
Come with the Law that can pardon, the Judgement that knoweth,
　　O Semnai, Semnai, watchers o'er people and land;
And joy be a-stream in your ways, as the fire that bloweth
　　　A-stream from beacon and brand.
　　　　　　　　　[*A cry of joy rises above the singing.*
Outpour ye the Chalice of Peace where the torches are blending:
　　In Pallas the place it is found and the task it is done.
The Law that is Fate and the Father the All-Comprehending
　　　Are here met together as one.
　　　　　　　　[*Again a cry of joy as the Procession passes
　　　　　　　　out of sight.*

EURIPIDES
ELECTRA

❊❊❊

TRANSLATED
By
GILBERT MURRAY

CHARACTERS IN THE PLAY

CLYTEMNESTRA, *Queen of Argos and Mycenae; widow of Agamemnon.*
ELECTRA, *daughter of Agamemnon and Clytemnestra.*
ORESTES, *son of Agamemnon and Clytemnestra, now in banishment.*
A PEASANT, *husband of Electra.*
AN OLD MAN, *formerly servant to Agamemnon.*
PYLADES, *son of Strophios, King of Phokis; friend to Orestes.*
AEGISTHUS, *usurping King of Argos and Mycenae, now husband of Clytemnestra.*
The Heroes CASTOR and POLYDEUCES.
CHORUS of Argive Women, with their LEADER.
FOLLOWERS of ORESTES; HANDMAIDS of CLYTEMNESTRA.

The scene is laid in the mountains of Argos. The play was first produced between the years 414 and 412 B.C.

ARGUMENT

The vengeance of Orestes has been treated by each of the three tragedians: by Sophocles in his *Electra*, by Aeschylus in the *Agamemnon*, and by Euripides in the present play. In Aeschylus' play it is the dead king, Agamemnon, who dominates the action, called forth from his sleep by the chants of the Libation-Bearers and the prayers of his children. But to Euripides, as to Sophocles, Electra is the central figure, "a woman shattered in childhood by the shock of an experience too terrible for a girl to bear; a poisoned and a haunted woman, eating her heart in ceaseless broodings of hate and love, alike unsatisfied"—*A-lektra*, "the Unmated."

ELECTRA

The scene represents a hut on a desolate mountain side; the river Inachus is visible in the distance. The time is the dusk of early dawn, before sunrise. The PEASANT *is discovered in front of the hut.*

Peasant. Old gleam on the face of the world, I give thee
    hail,
River of Argos land, where sail on sail
The long ships met, a thousand, near and far.
When Agamemnon walked the seas in war;
Who smote King Priam in the dust, and burned
The storied streets of Ilion, and returned
Above all conquerors, heaping tower and fane
Of Argos high with spoils of Eastern slain.

So in far lands he prospered; and at home
His own wife trapped and slew him. 'Twas the doom
Aegisthus wrought, son of his father's foe[1].

Gone is that King, and the old spear laid low
That Tantalus wielded when the world was young.
Aegisthus hath his queen, and reigns among
His people. And the children here alone,
Orestes and Electra, buds unblown
Of man and womanhood, when forth to Troy
He shook his sail and left them—lo, the boy
Orestes, ere Aegisthus' hand could fall,
Was stolen from Argos—borne by one old thrall,
Who served his father's boyhood, over seas
Far off, and laid upon King Strophios' knees
In Phokis, for the old king's sake. But here
The maid Electra waited, year by year,
Alone, till the warm days of womanhood
Drew nigh and suitors came of gentle blood
In Hellas. Then Aegisthus was in fear
Lest she be wed in some great house, and bear
A son to avenge her father. Close he wrought
Her prison in his house, and gave her not
To any wooer. Then, since even this

[215]

Was full of peril, and the secret kiss
Of some bold prince might find her yet, and rend
Her prison walls, Aegisthus at the end
Would slay her. Then her mother, she so wild
Aforetime, pled with him and saved her child.
Her heart had still an answer for her lord
Murdered, but if the child's blood spoke, what word
Could meet the hate thereof? After that day
Aegisthus thus decreed: whoso should slay
The old king's wandering son, should win rich meed
Of gold; and for Electra, she must wed
With me, not base of blood—in that I stand
True Mycenaean—but in gold and land
Most poor, which maketh highest birth as naught.
So from a powerless husband shall be wrought
A powerless peril. Had some man of might
Possessed her, he had called perchance to light
Her father's blood, and unknown vengeances
Risen on Aegisthus yet.

                Aye, mine she is:
But never yet these arms—the Cyprian knows
My truth!—have clasped her body, and she goes
A virgin still. Myself would hold it shame
To abase this daughter of a royal name.
I am too lowly to love violence. Yea,
Orestes too doth move me, far away,
Mine unknown brother! Will he ever now
Come back and see his sister bowed so low?

   Doth any deem me fool, to hold a fair
Maid in my room and seek no joy, but spare
Her maidenhood? If any such there be,
Let him but look within. The fool is he
In gentle things, weighing the more and less
Of love by his own heart's untenderness.

        [*As he ceases* ELECTRA *comes out of the hut. She is in
           mourning garb, and carries a large pitcher on her
           head. She speaks without observing the* PEASANT'S
           presence.*

    Electra. Dark shepherdess of many a golden star,
Dost see me, Mother Night? And how this jar

Hath worn my earth-bowed head, as forth and fro
For water to the hillward springs I go?
Not for mere stress of need, but purpose set,
That never day nor night God may forget
Aegisthus' sin: aye, and perchance a cry
Cast forth to the waste shining of the sky
May find my father's ear. . . . The woman bred
Of Tyndareus, my mother—on her head
Be curses!—from my house hath outcast me;
She hath borne children to our enemy;
She hath made me naught, she hath made Orestes naught. . . .

> [*As the bitterness of her tone increases, the*
> PEASANT *comes forward.*

Peasant. What wouldst thou now, my sad one, ever fraught
With toil to lighten my toil? And so soft
Thy nurture was! Have I not chid thee oft,
And thou wilt cease not, serving without end?
 Electra (*turning to him with impulsive affection*).
O friend, my friend, as God might be my friend,
Thou only hast not trampled on my tears.
Life scarce can be so hard, 'mid many fears
And many shames, when mortal heart can find
Somewhere one healing touch, as my sick mind
Finds thee. . . . And should I wait thy word, to endure
A little for thine easing, yea, or pour
My strength out in thy toiling fellowship?
Thou hast enough with fields and kine to keep;
'Tis mine to make all bright within the door.
'Tis joy to him that toils, when toil is o'er,
To find home waiting, full of happy things.
 Peasant. If so it please thee, go thy way. The springs
Are not far off. And I before the morn
Must drive my team afield, and sow the corn
In the hollows.—Not a thousand prayers can gain
A man's bare bread, save an he work amain.

> [ELECTRA *and the* PEASANT *depart on their several
> ways. After a few moments there enter stealthily
> two armed men,* ORESTES *and* PYLADES.

[217]

Orestes. Thou art the first that I have known in deed
True and my friend, and shelterer of my need.
Thou only, Pylades, of all that knew,
Hast held Orestes of some worth, all through
These years of helplessness, wherein I lie
Downtrodden by the murderer—yea, and by
The murderess, my mother! . . . I am come,
Fresh from the cleansing of Apollo, home
To Argos—and my coming no man yet
Knoweth—to pay the bloody twain their debt
Of blood. This very night I crept alone
To my dead father's grave, and poured thereon
My heart's first tears and tresses of my head
New-shorn, and o'er the barrow of the dead
Slew a black lamb, unknown of them that reign
In this unhappy land. . . . I am not fain
To pass the city gates, but hold me here
Hard on the borders. So my road is clear
To fly if men look close and watch my way;
If not, to seek my sister. For men say
She dwelleth in these hills, no more a maid
But wedded. I must find her house, for aid
To guide our work, and learn what hath betid
Of late in Argos.—Ha, the radiant lid
Of Dawn's eye lifteth! Come, friend; leave we now
This trodden path. Some worker of the plough,
Or serving damsel at her early task
Will presently come by, whom we may ask
If here my sister dwells. But soft! Even now
I see some bondmaid there, her death-shorn brow
Bending beneath its freight of well-water.
Lie close until she pass; then question her.
A slave might help us well, or speak some sign
Of import to this work of mine and thine.

> [*The two men retire into ambush.* ELECTRA *enters,*
> *returning from the well.*

Electra.　　　　Onward, O labouring tread,
　　　　　　As on move the years;
　　　　　　Onward amid thy tears,
　　　　　　　O happier dead!

[218]

Let me remember. I am she,   *[Strophe.*
Agamemnon's child, and the mother of me
Clytemnestra, the evil Queen,
Helen's sister. And folk, I ween,
That pass in the streets call yet my name
Electra. . . . God protect my shame!
   For toil, toil is a weary thing,
      And life is heavy about my head;
   And thou far off, O Father and King,
      In the lost lands of the dead.
A bloody twain made these things be;
One was thy bitterest enemy,
And one the wife that lay by thee.

                [Antistrophe.

Brother, brother, on some far shore
Hast thou a city, is there a door
That knows thy football, Wandering One?
Who left me, left me, when all our pain
Was bitter about us, a father slain,
And a girl that wept in her room alone.
   Thou couldst break me this bondage sore,
      Only thou, who art far away,
   Loose our father, and wake once more. . . .
      Zeus, Zeus, dost hear me pray? . . .
The sleeping blood and the shame and the doom!
O feet that rest not, over the foam
Of distant seas, come home, come home!

                [Strophe.

What boots this cruse that I carry?
   O, set free my brow!
For the gathered tears that tarry
      Through the day and the dark till now,
Now in the dawn are free,
      Father, and flow beneath
The floor of the world, to be
      As a song in the house of Death:
From the rising up of the day
They guide my heart alway,
   The silent tears unshed,
And my body mourns for the dead;

My cheeks bleed silently,
  And these bruisèd temples keep
Their pain, remembering thee
  And thy bloody sleep.

Be rent, O hair of mine head!

 As a swan crying alone
  Where the river windeth cold.
For a loved, for a silent one,
  Whom the toils of the fowler hold,
I cry, Father, to thee,
O slain in misery!

[Antistrophe.

The water, the wan water,
  Lapped him, and his head
Drooped in the bed of slaughter
  Low, as one wearièd;
Woe for the edgèd axe,
  And woe for the heart of hate,
Houndlike about thy tracks,
  O conqueror desolate,
From Troy over land and sea,
Till a wife stood waiting thee;
Not with crowns did she stand,
Nor flowers of peace in her hand;
With Aegisthus' dagger drawn
  For her hire she strove,
Through shame and through blood alone;
  And won her a traitor's love.

  [*As she ceases there enter from right and left
      the* Chorus, *consisting of women of Argos,
      young and old, in festal dress.*

[Strophe.

Chorus. (*Some Women.*)
    Child of the mighty dead,
      Electra, lo, my way
    To thee in the dawn hath sped,
      And the cot on the mountain grey,
      For the Watcher hath cried this day:
    He of the ancient folk,

The walker of waste and hill,
Who drinketh the milk of the flock;
　And he told of Hera's will;
For the morrow's morrow now
　They cry her festival,
And before her throne shall bow
　Our damsels all.

Electra.　Not unto joy, nor sweet
　Music, nor shining of gold,
The wings of my spirit beat.
　Let the brides of Argos hold
　Their dance in the night, as of old;
I lead no dance; I mark
　No beat as the dancers sway;
With tears I dwell in the dark,
　And my thought is of tears alway,
　To the going down of the day.
Look on my wasted hair
And raiment. . . . This that I bear,
Is it meet for the King my sire,
　And her whom the King begot?
For Troy, that was burned with fire
　And forgetteth not?

Chorus.　(*Other Women.*)　　　　　　　[*Antistrophe.*

Hera is great!—Ah, come,
　Be kind; and my hand shall bring
Fair raiment, work of the loom,
　And many a golden thing,
　For joyous robe-wearing.
Deemest thou this thy woe
　Shall rise unto God as prayer,
Or bend thine haters low?
　Doth God for thy pain have care?
Not tears for the dead nor sighs,
　But worship and joy divine
Shall win thee peace in thy skies,
　O daughter mine!

Electra.　No care cometh to God
　For the voice of the helpless; none
For the crying of ancient blood.

[221]

> Alas for him that is gone,
> And for thee, O wandering one:
> That now, methinks, in a land
> Of the stranger must toil for hire,
> And stand where the poor men stand,
> A-cold by another's fire,
> O son of the mighty sire:
> While I in a beggar's cot
> On the wrecked hills, changing not,
> Starve in my soul for food;
> But our mother lieth wed
> In another's arms, and blood
> Is about her bed.

Leader. On all of Greece she wrought great jeopardy,
Thy mother's sister, Helen,—and on thee.

> [ORESTES *and* PYLADES *move out from their conceal-*
> *ment;* ORESTES *comes forward:* PYLADES *beckons*
> *to two* ARMED SERVANTS *and stays with them in the*
> *background.*

Electra. Woe's me! No more of wailing! Women, flee!
Strange armèd men beside the dwelling there
Lie ambushed! They are rising from their lair.
Back by the road, all you. I will essay
The house; and may our good feet save us!

Orestes (*between* ELECTRA *and the hut*). Stay,
Unhappy woman! Never fear my steel.

Electra (*in utter panic*). O bright Apollo! Mercy! See, I
    kneel;
Slay me not.

Orestes.   Others I have yet to slay
Less dear than thou.

Electra.   Go from me! Wouldst thou lay
Hand on a body that is not for thee?

Orestes. None is there I would touch more righteously.

Electra. Why lurk'st thou by my house? And why a sword?

Orestes. Stay. Listen! Thou wilt not gainsay my word.

Electra. There—I am still. Do what thou wilt with me.
Thou art too strong.

Orestes.   A word I bear to thee . . .
Word of thy brother.

But for me,
The old stormy rivers of my grief are dead
Now at the spring; not one tear left unshed.
Mine eyes are sick with vigil, endlessly
Weeping the beacon-piles that watched for thee
For ever answerless.   And did I dream,
A gnat's thin whirr would start me, like a scream
Of battle, and show me thee by terrors swept,
Crowding, too many for the time I slept.

From all which stress delivered and free-souled,
I greet my lord: O watchdog of the fold,
O forestay sure that fails not in the squall,
O strong-based pillar of a towering hall;
O single son to a father age-ridden;
O land unhoped for seen by shipwrecked men;
Sunshine more beautiful when storms are fled;
Spring of quick water in a desert dead. . . .
How sweet to be set free from any chain!

These be my words to greet him home again.
No god shall grudge them.   Surely I and thou
Have suffered in time past enough! And now
Dismount, O head with love and glory crowned,
From this high car; yet plant not on bare ground
Thy foot, great King, the foot that trampled Troy.
   Ho, bondmaids, up! Forget not your employ,
A floor of crimson broideries to spread
For the King's path.   Let all the ground be red
Where those feet pass; and Justice, dark of yore,
Home light him to the hearth he looks not for!
   What followeth next, our sleepless care shall see
Ordered as God's good pleasure may decree.

> [*The attendants spread tapestries of crimson and*
> *gold from the Chariot to the Door of the*
> *Palace.* AGAMEMNON *does not move.*

Agamemnon. Daughter of Leda, watcher of my fold,
In sooth thy welcome, grave and amply told,
Fitteth mine absent years.   Though it had been
Seemlier, methinks, some other, not my Queen,

Had spoke these honours. For the rest, I say,
Seek not to make me soft in woman's way;
Cry not thy praise to me wide-mouthed, nor fling
Thy body down, as to some barbarous king.
Nor yet with broidered hangings strew my path,
To awake the unseen ire. 'Tis God that hath
Such worship; and for mortal man to press
Rude feet upon this broidered loveliness . . .
I vow there is danger in it. Let my road
Be honoured, surely; but as man, not god.
Rugs for the feet and yonder broidered pall . . .
The names ring diverse! . . . Aye, and not to fall
Suddenly blind is of all gifts the best
God giveth, for I reckon no man blest
Ere to the utmost goal his race be run.

So be it; and if, as this day I have done,
I shall do always, then I fear no ill.

 Clytemnestra. Tell me but this, nowise against thy will . . .
 Agamemnon. My will, be sure, shall falter not nor fade.
 Clytemnestra. Was this a vow in some great peril made?
 Agamemnon. Enough! I have spoke my purpose, fixed and plain.
 Clytemnestra. Were Priam the conqueror . . . Think, would he refrain?
 Agamemnon. Oh, stores of broideries would be trampled then!
 Clytemnestra. Lord, care not for the cavillings of men!
 Agamemnon. The murmur of a people hath strange weight.
 Clytemnestra. Who feareth envy, feareth to be great.
 Agamemnon. 'Tis graceless when a woman strives to lead.
 Clytemnestra. When a great conqueror yields, 'tis grace indeed.
 Agamemnon. So in this war thou must my conqueror be?
 Clytemnestra. Yield! With good will to yield is victory!
 Agamemnon. Well, if I needs must . . . Be it as thou hast said!

Quick! Loose me these bound slaves on which I tread,
And while I walk yon wonders of the sea
God grant no eye of wrath be cast on me
From far!

[*The Attendants untie his shoes.*

            For even now it likes me not
To waste mine house, thus marring underfoot
The pride thereof, and wondrous broideries
Bought in far seas with silver. But of these
Enough.—And mark, I charge thee, this princess
Of Ilion; tend her with all gentleness.
God's eye doth see, and loveth from afar,
The merciful conqueror. For no slave of war
Is slave by his own will. She is the prize
And chosen flower of Ilion's treasuries,
Set by the soldiers' gift to follow me.

    Now therefore, seeing I am constrained by thee
And do thy will, I walk in conqueror's guise
Beneath my Gate, trampling sea-crimson dyes.

        [*As he dismounts and sets foot on the Tapestries*
          Clytemnestra's *women utter again their*
          Cry of Triumph. The people bow or kneel
          as he passes.

Clytemnestra. There is the sea—its caverns who shall drain?
Breeding of many a purple-fish the stain
Surpassing silver, ever fresh renewed,
For robes of kings. And we, by right indued,
Possess our fill thereof. Thy house, O King,
Knoweth no stint, nor lack of anything.

    What trampling of rich raiment, had the cry
So sounded in the domes of prophesy,
Would I have vowed these years, as price to pay
For this dear life in peril far away!
Where the root is, the leafage cometh soon
To clothe an house, and spread its leafy boon
Against the burning star; and, thou being come,
Thou, on the midmost hearthstone of thy home,
Oh, warmth in winter leapeth to thy sign.
And when God's summer melteth into wine
The green grape, on that house shall coolness fall
Where the true man, the master, walks his hall.

Zeus, Zeus! True Master, let my prayers be true!
And, oh, forget not that thou art willed to do!

[She follows AGAMEMNON *into the Palace. The retinues of both King and Queen go in after them.* CASSANDRA *remains.*

[*Strophe.*

Chorus. What is this that evermore,
    A cold terror at the door
Of this bosom presage-haunted,
Pale as death hovereth?
While a song unhired, unwanted,
By some inward prophet chanted,
    Speaks the secret at its core;
    And to cast it from my blood
    Like a dream not understood
    No sweet-spoken Courage now
    Sitteth at my heart's dear prow.

    Yet I know that manifold
    Days, like sand, have waxen old
Since the day those shoreward-thrown
    Cables flapped and line on line
Standing forth for Ilion
    The long galleys took the brine.

[*Antistrophe.*

    And in harbour—mine own eye
    Hath beheld—again they lie;
Yet that lyreless music hidden
    Whispers still words of ill,
'Tis the Soul of me unbidden,
Like some Fury sorrow-ridden,
    Weeping over things that die.
    Neither waketh in my sense
    Ever Hope's dear confidence;
    For this flesh that groans within,
    And these bones that know of Sin,
    This tossed heart upon the spate
    Of a whirlpool that is Fate,
    Surely these lie not. Yet deep
        Beneath hope my prayer doth run,
    All will die like dreams, and creep
        To the unthought of and undone.   [*Strophe.*

[120]

Surely of great Weal at the end of all
Comes not Content; so near doth Fever crawl,
Close neighbour, pressing hard the narrow wall.
Woe to him who fears not fate!
'Tis the ship that forward straight
Sweepeth, strikes the reef below;
He who fears and lightens weight,
Casting forth, in measured throw
From the wealth his hand hath got
His whole ship shall founder not,
With abundance overfraught.
Nor deep seas above him flow.
Lo, when famine stalketh near,
One good gift of Zeus again
From the furrows of one year
Endeth quick the starving pain.

[*Antistrophe.*

But once the blood of death is fallen, black
And oozing at a slain man's feet, alack!
By spell or singing who shall charm it back?

One there was of old[6] who showed
    Man the path from death to day;
But Zeus, lifting up his rod,
    Spared not, when he charged him stay.

Save that every doom of God
    Hath by other dooms its way
Crossed, that none may rule alone,
In one speech-outstripping flood
Forth had all this passion flown,
    Which now murmuring hides away,
Full of pain, and hoping not
Ever one clear thread to unknot
From the tangle of my soul,
From a heart of burning coal.

[*Suddenly* CLYTEMNESTRA *appears
standing in the Doorway.*

Clytemnestra.   Thou likewise, come within! I speak thy
name,

Cassandra; [CASSANDRA *trembles, but continues to stare in*
front of her, as though not hearing CLYTEM-
NESTRA.

        seeing the Gods—why chafe at them?—
Have placed thee here, to share within these walls
Our lustral waters, 'mid a crowd of thralls
Who stand obedient round the altar-stone
Of our Possession.   Therefore come thou down,
And be not over-proud.   The tale is told
How once Alcmena's son[7] himself, being sold,
Was patient, though he liked not the slaves' mess.

    And more, if Fate must bring thee to this stress,
Praise God thou art come to a House of high report
And wealth from long ago.   The baser sort,
Who have reaped some sudden harvest unforeseen,
Are ever cruel to their slaves, and mean
In the measure.   We shall give whate'er is due.

                          [CASSANDRA *is silent.*

   Leader.   To thee she speaks, and waits . . . clear words and
     true!
Oh, doom is all around thee like a net;
Yield, if thou canst. . . . Belike thou canst not yet.

   Clytemnestra.   Methinks, unless this wandering maid is one
Voiced like a swallow-bird, with tongue unknown
And barbarous, she can read my plain intent.
I use but words, and ask for her consent.

   Leader.   Ah, come! 'Tis best, as the world lies to-day.
Leave this high-thronèd chariot, and obey!

   Clytemnestra.   How long must I stand dallying at the Gate?
Even now the beasts to Hestia consecrate
Wait by the midmost fire, since there is wrought
This high fulfilment for which no man thought.
Wherefore, if 'tis thy pleasure to obey
Aught of my will, prithee, no more delay!
If, deaf to sense, thou wilt not understand . . .
Thou show her, not with speech but with brute hand!

                 [*To the Leader of the* CHORUS.

   Leader.   The strange maid needs a rare interpreter.
She is trembling like a wild beast in a snare.

Clytemnestra. 'Fore God, she is mad, and heareth but her own
Folly! A slave, her city all o'erthrown,
She needs must chafe her bridle, till this fret
Be foamed away in blood and bitter sweat.
I waste no more speech, thus to be defied.

[*She goes back inside the Palace.*

Leader. I pity thee so sore, no wrath nor pride
Is in me.—Come, dismount! Bend to the stroke
Fate lays on thee, and learn to feel thy yoke.
[*He lays his hand softly on* CASSANDRA'S *shoulder.*
Cassandra (*moaning to herself*). Otototoi . . . Dreams.
Dreams.
Apollo. O Apollo!
Second Elder. Why sob'st thou for Apollo? It is writ,
He loves not grief nor lendeth ear to it.
Cassandra. Otototoi . . . Dreams. Dreams.
Apollo. O Apollo!
Leader. Still to that god she makes her sobbing cry
Who hath no place where men are sad, or die.
Cassandra. Apollo, Apollo! Light of the Ways of Men!
Mine enemy!
Hast lighted me to darkness yet again?
Second Elder. How? Will she prophesy about her own
Sorrows? That power abides when all is gone!
Cassandra. Apollo, Apollo! Light of all that is!
Mine enemy!
Where hast thou led me? . . . Ha! What house is this?
Leader. The Atreidae's castle. If thou knowest not, I
Am here to help thee, and help faithfully.
Cassandra (*whispering*). Nay, nay. This is the house that
God hateth.
There be many things that know its secret; sore
And evil things; murders and strangling death.
'Tis here they slaughter men . . . A splashing floor.
Second Elder. Keen-sensed the strange maid seemeth, like a
hound
For blood.—And what she seeks can sure be found!
Cassandra. The witnesses . . . I follow where they lead.
That weeping: here quite close: children are there,

    Weeping: and wounds that bleed.

    The smell of the baked meats their father tare.

Second Elder (*recognizing her vision, and repelled*). Word
    of thy mystic power had reached our ear

    Long since. Howbeit we need no prophets here.

Cassandra. Ah, ah! What would they? A new dreadful
    thing.

    A great great sin plots in the house this day;

    Too strong for the faithful, beyond medicining . . .

    And help stands far away.

Leader. This warning I can read not, though I knew
    That other tale. It rings the city through.

Cassandra. O Woman, thou! The lord who lay with thee!
    Wilt lave with water, and then . . . How speak the end?

    It comes so quick, A hand . . . Another hand . . .

    That reach, reach gropingly . . .

Leader. I see not yet. These riddles, pierced with blind
    Gleams of foreboding but bemuse my mind.

Cassandra. Ah, ah! What is it? There; it is coming clear.
    A net . . . some net of Hell.

    Nay, she that lies with him . . . is she the snare?

    And half of his blood upon it. It holds well . : .

    O Crowd of ravening Voices, be glad, yea, shout

    And cry for the stoning, cry for the casting out!

Second Elder. What Fury Voices call'st thou to be hot
    Against this castle? Such words like me not.

    And deep within my breast I feel that sick

      And saffron drop, which creepeth to the heart.

    To die as the last rays of life depart.

      Misfortune comes so quick.

Cassandra. Ah, look! Look! Keep his mate from the Wild
    Bull!

      A tangle of raiment, see;

    A black horn, and a blow, and he falleth, full

    In the marble amid the water. I counsel ye.

    I speak plain. . . . Blood in the bath and treachery!

Leader. No great interpreter of oracles
    Am I; but this, I think, some mischief spells.

      What spring of good hath seercraft ever made

        Up from the dark to flow?

      'Tis but a weaving of words, a craft of woe,
        To make mankind afraid.

Cassandra. Poor woman! Poor dead woman! . . Yea, it is I,
Poured out like water among them. Weep for me. . . .
Ah! What is this place? Why must I come with thee . . .
        To die, only to die?

Leader. Thou art borne on the breath of God, thou spirit
   wild,
      For thine own weird to wail,
    Like to that winged voice,[8] that heart so sore
    Which, crying alway, hungereth to cry more,
    "Itylus, Itylus," till it sing her child
      Back to the nightingale.

Cassandra. Oh, happy Singing Bird, so sweet, so clear!
      Soft wings for her God made,
    And an easy passing, without pain or tear . . .
    For me 'twill be torn flesh and rending blade.

Second Elder. Whence is it sprung, whence wafted on God's
   breath,
      This anguish reasonless?
    This throbbing of terror shaped to melody,
    Moaning of evil blent with music high?
    Who hath marked out for thee that mystic path
      Through thy woe's wilderness?

Cassandra. Alas for the kiss, the kiss of Paris, his people's
   bane!
   Alas for Scamander Water, the water my fathers drank!
    Long, long ago, I played about thy bank,
      And was cherished and grew strong;
   Now by a River of Wailing, by shores of Pain,
      Soon shall I make my song.

Leader. How sayst thou? All too clear,
    This ill word thou hast laid upon thy mouth!
      A babe could read thee plain.
    It stabs within me like a serpent's tooth,
    The bitter thrilling music of her pain:
      I marvel as I hear.

Cassandra. Alas for the toil, the toil of a City, worn unto
   death!

Alas for my father's worship before the citadel,
The flocks that bled and the tumult of their breath!
    But no help from them came
To save Troy Towers from falling as they fell! . . .
And I on the earth shall writhe, my heart aflame.
Second Elder. Dark upon dark, new ominous words of ill!
    Sure there hath swept on thee some Evil Thing.
      Crushing, which makes thee bleed
      And in the torment of thy vision sing
    These plaining death-fraught oracles . . . Yet still, still,
    Their end I cannot read!
Cassandra. (*By an effort she regains mastery of herself, and
    speaks directly to the Leader.*)
'Fore God, mine oracles shall no more hide
With veils his visage, like a new-wed bride!
A shining wind out of this dark shall blow,
Piercing the dawn, growing as great waves grow,
To burst in the heart of sunrise . . . stronger far
Than this poor pain of mine. I will not mar
With mists my wisdom.
               Be near me as I go,
Tracking the evil things of long ago,
And bear me witness. For this roof, there clings
Music about it, like a choir which sings
One-voiced, but not well-sounding, for not good
The words are. Drunken, drunken, and with blood,
To make them dare the more, a revelling rout
Is in the rooms, which no man shall cast out,
Of sister Furies. And they weave to song,
Haunting the House, its first blind deed of wrong,
Spurning in turn that King's bed desecrate,
Defiled, which paid a brother's sin with hate. . . .
    Hath it missed or struck, mine arrow? Am I a poor
Dreamer, that begs and babbles at the door?
Give first thine oath in witness, that I know
Of this great dome the sins wrought long ago.
    Elder. And how should oath of mine, though bravely sworn,
Appease thee? Yet I marvel that one born
Far over seas, of alien speech, should fall
So apt, as though she had lived here and seen all.

Cassandra. The Seer Apollo made me too to see.
Elder (*in a low voice*). Was the God's heart pierced with de-
sire for thee?
Cassandra. Time was, I held it shame hereof to speak.
Elder. Ah, shame is for the mighty, not the weak.
Cassandra. We wrestled, and his breath to me was sweet.
Elder. Ye came to the getting of children, as is meet?
Cassandra. I swore to Loxias, and I swore a lie.
Elder. Already thine the gift of prophecy?
Cassandra. Already I showed my people all their path.
Elder. And Loxias did not smite thee in his wrath?
Cassandra. After that sin . . . no man believed me more.
Elder. Nay, then, to us thy wisdom seemeth sure.
Cassandra. Oh, oh! Agony, agony!
Again the awful pains of prophecy
Are on me, maddening as they fall. . . .
Ye see them there . . . beating against the wall?
So young . . . like shapes that gather in a dream . . .
Slain by a hand they loved. Children they seem,
Murdered . . . and in their hands they bear baked meat:
I think it is themselves. Yea, flesh; I see it;
And inward parts. . . . Oh, what a horrible load
To carry! And their father drank their blood.
    From these, I warn ye, vengeance broodeth still,
A lion's rage, which goes not forth to kill
But lurketh in his lair, watching the high
Hall of my war-gone master . . . Master? Aye;
Mine, mine! The yoke is nailed about my neck. . . .
Oh, lord of ships and trampler on the wreck
Of Ilion, knows he not this she-wolf's tongue,
Which licks and fawns, and laughs with ear up-sprung.
To bite in the end like a secret death?—And can
The woman? Slay a strong and armèd man? . . .
    What fangèd reptile like to her doth creep?
Some serpent amphisbene, some Skylla, deep
Housed in the rock, where sailors shriek and die,
Mother of Hell blood-raging, which doth cry
On her own flesh war, war without alloy . . .
God! And she shouted in his face her joy,
Like men in battle when the foe doth break.

And feigns thanksgiving for his safety's sake!
  What if no man believe me? 'Tis all one.
The thing which must be shall be; aye, and soon
Thou too shalt sorrow for these things, and here
Standing confess me all too true a seer.
  Leader. The Thyestean feast of children slain
I understood, and tremble. Aye, my brain
Reels at these visions, beyond guesswork true.
But after, though I heard, I had lost the clue.
  Cassandra. Man, thou shalt look on Agamemnon dead.
  Leader. Peace, Mouth of Evil! Be those words unsaid!
  Cassandra. No god of peace hath watch upon that hour.
  Leader. If it must come. Forefend it, Heavenly Power!
  Cassandra. They do not think of prayer; they think of death.
  Leader. They? Say, what man this foul deed compasseth?
  Cassandra. Alas, thou art indeed fallen far astray!
  Leader. How could such deed be done? I see no way.
  Cassandra. Yet know I not the Greek tongue all too well?
  Leader. Greek are the Delphic dooms, but hard to spell.
  Cassandra. Ah! Ah! There!
What a strange fire! It moves . . . It comes at me.
O Wolf Apollo, mercy! O agony! . . .
Why lies she with a wolf, this lioness lone,
Two-handed, when the royal lion is gone?
God, she will kill me! Like to them that brew
Poison, I see her mingle for me too
A separate vial in her wrath, and swear,
Whetting her blade for him, that I must share
His death . . . because, because he hath dragged me here!
  Oh, why these mockers at my throat? This gear
Of wreathèd bands, this staff of prophecy?
I mean to kill you first, before I die.
Begone!

> [*She tears off her prophetic habiliments; and pres-
> ently throws them on the ground, and stamps
> on them.*

  Down to perdition! . . . Lie ye so?
So I requite you! Now make rich in woe
Some other Bird of Evil, me no more!

> [*Coming to herself.*

[128]

Ah, see! It is Apollo's self, hath tore
His crown from me! Who watched me long ago
In this same prophet's robe, by friend, by foe,
All with one voice, all blinded, rocked to scorn:
"A thing of dreams" "a beggar-maid outworn,"
Poor, starving and reviled, I endured all;
And now the Seer, who called me till my call
Was perfect, leads me to this last dismay. . . .
'Tis not the altar-stone where men did slay
My father; 'tis a block, a block with gore
Yet hot, that waits me, of one slain before.

    Yet not of God unheeded shall we lie.
There cometh after, one who lifteth high
The downfallen; a branch where blossometh
A sire's avenging and a mother's death.
Exiled and wandering, from this land outcast,
One day He shall return, and set the last
Crown on these sins that have his house downtrod.
For, lo, there is a great oath sworn of God,
His father's upturned face shall guide him home.

    Why should I grieve? Why pity these men's doom?
I who have seen the City of Ilion
Pass as she passed; and they who cast her down
Have thus their end, as God gives judgement sure. . . .
    I go to drink my cup. I will endure
To die. O Gates, Death-Gates, all hail to you!
Only, pray God the blow be stricken true!
Pray God, unagonized, with blood that flows
Quick unto friendly death, these eyes may close!
    Leader. O full of sorrows, full of wisdom great,
Woman, thy speech is a long anguish; yet,
Knowing thy doom, why walkst thou with clear eyes,
Like some god-blinded beast, to sacrifice?
    Cassandra. There is no escape, friends; only vain delay.
    Leader. Is not the later still the sweeter day?
    Cassandra. The day is come. Small profit now to fly.
    Leader. Through all thy griefs, Woman, thy heart is high.
    Cassandra. Alas! None that is happy hears that praise.
    Leader. Are not the brave dead blest in after days?
    Cassandra. O Father! O my brethren brave, I come!

[129]

[*She moves towards the House, but recoils shuddering.*

Leader. What frights thee? What is that thou startest from?

Cassandra. Ah, faugh! Faugh!

Leader.   What turns thee in that blind
Horror? Unless some loathing of the mind . . .

Cassandra. Death drifting from the doors, and blood like
   rain!

Leader. 'Tis but the dumb beasts at the altar slain.

Cassandra. And vapours from a charnel-house . . . See
   there!

Leader. 'Tis Tyrian incense clouding in the air.

Cassandra. (*recovering herself again*). So be it!—I will go,
   in yonder room
To weep mine own and Agamemnon's doom.
May death be all! Strangers, I am no bird
That pipeth trembling at a thicket stirred
By the empty wind. Bear witness on that day
When woman for this woman's life shall pay,
And man for man ill-mated low shall lie:
I ask this boon, as being about to die.

   Leader. Alas, I pity thee thy mystic fate!

   Cassandra. One word, one dirge-song would I utter yet
O'er mine own corpse. To this last shining Sun
I pray that, when the Avenger's work is done,
His enemies may remember this thing too,
This little thing, the woman slave they slew!
O world of men, farewell! A painted show
Is all thy glory; and when life is low
The touch of a wet sponge out-blotteth all.
Oh, sadder this than any proud man's fall!

                               [*She goes into the House.*

Chorus.   Great Fortune is an hungry thing,
              And filleth no heart anywhere,
         Though men with fingers menacing
              Point at the great house, none will dare,
       When Fortune knocks, to bar the door
       Proclaiming: "Come thou here no more!"
       Lo, to this man the Gods have given
              Great Ilion in the dust to tread
       And home return, emblazed of heaven;

If it is writ, he too shall go
Through blood for blood spilt long ago;
If he too, dying for the dead,
 Should crown the deaths of alien years,
 What mortal afar off, who hears,
Shall boast him Fortune's Child, and led
 Above the eternal tide of tears?

        [*A sudden Cry from within.*

Voice. Ho! Treason in the house! I am wounded: slain.
Leader. Hush! In the castle! 'Twas a cry
 Of some man wounded mortally.
Voice. Ah God, another! I am stricken again.
Leader. I think the deed is done. It was the King
Who groaned. . . Stand close, and think of any thing . . .

   [*The Old Men gather together under the shock,
    and debate confusedly.*

Elder B. I give you straight my judgement. Summon all
The citizens to rescue. Sound a call!
Elder C. No, no! Burst in at once without a word!
In, and convict them by their dripping sword!
Elder D. Yes; that or something like it. Quick, I say,
Be doing! 'Tis a time for no delay.
Elder E. We have time to think. This opening . . . They
 have planned
Some scheme to make enslavement of the land.
Elder F. Yes, while we linger here! They take no thought
Of lingering, and their sword-arm sleepeth not!
Elder G. I have no counsel. I can speak not. Oh,
Let him give counsel who can strike a blow!
Elder H. I say as this man says. I have no trust
In words to raise a dead man from the dust.
Elder I. How mean you? Drag out our poor lives, and stand
Cowering to these defilers of the land?
Elder J. Nay, 'tis too much! Better to strive and die!
Death is an easier doom than slavery.
Elder K. We heard a sound of groaning, nothing plain,
How know we—are we seers?—that one is slain?
Elder L. Oh, let us find the truth out, ere we grow
Thus passionate! To surmise is not to know.

Leader. Break in, then! 'Tis the council ye all bring,
And learn for sure, how is it with the King.

> [*They cluster up towards the Palace Door, as
> though to force an entrance, when the great
> Door swings open, revealing* CLYTEMNESTRA,
> *who stands, axe in hand, over the dead bodies
> of* AGAMEMNON *and* CASSANDRA. *The body
> of* AGAMEMNON *is wrapped in a rich crim-
> son web. There is blood on* CLYTEMNES-
> TRA'S *brow, and she speaks in wild triumph.*

Clytemnestra. Oh, lies enough and more have I this day
Spoken, which now I shame not to unsay.
How should a woman work, to the utter end,
Hate on a damnèd hater, feigned a friend;
How pile perdition round him, hunter-wise,
Too high for overleaping, save by lies?
To me this hour was dreamed of long ago;
A thing of ancient hate. 'Twas very slow
In coming, but it came. And here I stand
Even where I struck, with all the deed I planned
Done! 'Twas so wrought—what boots it to deny?—
The man could neither guard himself nor fly.
An endless web, as by some fisher strung,
A deadly plenteousness of robe, I flung
All round him, and struck twice; and with two cries
His limbs turned water and broke; and as he lies
I cast my third stroke in, a prayer well-sped
To Zeus of Hell, who guardeth safe his dead!
So there he gasped his life out as he lay;
And, gasping, the blood spouted . . . Like dark spray
That splashed, it came, a salt and deathly dew;
Sweet, sweet as God's dear rain-drops ever blew
O'er a parched field, the day the buds are born! . . .

Which things being so, ye Councillors high-born,
Depart in joy, if joy ye will. For me,
I glory. Oh, if such a thing might be
As o'er the dead thank-offering to outpour,
On this dead it were just, aye, just and more,
Who filled the cup of the House with treacheries
Curse-fraught, and here hath drunk it to the lees!

[132]

Leader. We are astonied at thy speech. To fling,
Wild mouth! such vaunt over thy murdered King!
   Clytemnestra. Wouldst fright me, like a witless woman? Lo,
This bosom shakes not. And, though well ye know,
I tell you . . . Curse me as ye will, or bless,
'Tis all one . . . This is Agamemnon; this,
My husband, dead by my right hand, a blow
Struck by a righteous craftsman. Aye, 'tis so.
   Chorus. Woman, what evil tree,
         What poison grown of the ground
      Or draught of the drifting sea
         Way to thy lips hath found,
      Making thee clothe thy heart
         In rage, yea, in curses burning
      When thine own people pray?
      Thou hast hewn, thou hast cast away;
      And a thing cast away thou art,
         A thing of hate and a spurning!
   Clytemnestra. Aye, now, for me, thou hast thy words of fate;
Exile from Argos and the people's hate
For ever! Against him no word was cried,
When, recking not, as 'twere a beast that died,
With flocks abounding o'er his wide domain,
He slew his child, my love, my flower of pain.
Great God, as magic for the winds of Thrace!
Why was not he man-hunted from his place,
To purge the blood that stained him? . . . When the deed
Is mine, oh, then thou art a judge indeed!
But threat thy fill. I am ready, and I stand
Content; if thy hand beateth down my hand,
Thou rulest. If aught else be God's decree,
Thy lesson shall be learned, though late it be.
   Chorus. Thy thought, it is very proud;
         Thy breath is the scorner's breath;
      Is not the madness loud
         In thy heart, being drunk with death?
      Yea, and above thy brow
         A star of the wet blood burneth!
      Oh, doom shall have yet her day,
      The last friend cast away,

[133]

When lie doth answer lie
And a stab for a stab returneth!
Clytemnestra. And hark what Oath-gods gather to my
side!
By my dead child's Revenge, now satisfied,
By Mortal Blindness, by all Powers of Hell
Which Hate, to whom in sacrifice he fell,
My Hope shall walk not in the house of Fear,
While on my hearth one fire yet burneth clear,
One lover, one Aegisthus[9], as of old!
What should I fear, when fallen here I hold
This foe, this scorner of his wife, this toy
And fool of each Chryseïs under Troy;
And there withal his soothsayer and slave,
His chanting bed-fellow, his leman brave,
Who rubbed the galleys' benches at his side?
But, oh, they had their guerdon as they died!
For he lies thus, and she, the wild swan's way,
Hath trod her last long weeping roundelay,
And lies, his lover, ravisht o'er the main
For his bed's comfort and my deep disdain.
Chorus. (*Some Elders.*)
Would God that suddenly
With no great agony,
No long sick-watch to keep,
My hour would come to me,
My hour, and presently
Bring the eternal, the
Unwaking sleep,
Now that my Shepherd, he
Whose love watched over me,
Lies in the deep!
Another. For woman's sake he endured and battled well,
And by a woman's hand he fell.
Others. What hast thou done, O Helen blind of brain,
O face that slew the souls on Ilion's plain,
One face, one face, and many a thousand slain?
The hate of old that on this castle lay,
Builded in lust, a husband's evil day,
Hath bloomed for thee a perfect flower again

And unforgotten, an old and burning stain
　　　Never to pass away.
Clytemnestra.　Nay, pray not for the hour of death, being
　tried
　　　Too sore beneath these blows,
　Neither on Helen turn my wrath aside,
　The Slayer of Men, the face which hath destroyed
　Its thousand Danaan souls, and wrought a wide
　　　Wound that no leech can close.
Chorus.　Daemon[10], whose heel is set
　　　　On the House and the twofold kin
　　　　　Of the high Tantalidae,
　　　　A power, heavy as fate,
　　　　　Thou wieldest through woman's sin,
　　　　　　Piercing the heart of me!
　　　Like a raven swoln with hate
　　　　He hath set on the dead his claw,
　　　He croaketh a song to sate
　　　His fury, and calls it Law!
Clytemnestra.　Ah, call upon Him! Yea, call—
　　　　And thy thought hath found its path—
　　　The Daemon who haunts this hall,
　　　　The thrice-engorgèd Wrath;
　　　From him is the ache of the flesh
　　　　For blood born and increased;
　　　Ere the old sore hath ceased
　　　　It oozeth afresh.
Chorus.　　　Indeed He is very great,
　　　　　And heavy his anger, He,
　　　　　The Daemon who guides the fate
　　　　　　Of the old Tantalidae:
　　　Alas, alas, an evil tale ye tell
　　　Of desolate angers and insatiable!
　　　Ah me,
　　　And yet 'tis all as Zeus hath willed,
　　　　Doer of all and Cause of all;
　　　By His Word every chance doth fall,
　　　　No end without Him is fulfilled;
　　　　　What of these things
　　　But cometh by high Heaven's counsellings?

[*A band of Mourners has gathered*
within the House.

Mourners. Ah, sorrow, sorrow! My King, my King!
How shall I weep, what word shall I say?
Caught in the web of this spider thing,
In foul death gasping thy life away!
Woe's me, woe's me, for this slavish lying,
The doom of craft and the lonely dying,
The iron two-edged and the hands that slay!

Clytemnestra. And criest thou still this deed hath been
My work? Nay, gaze, and have no thought
That this is Agamemnon's Queen.
'Tis He, 'tis He, hath round him wrought
This phantom of the dead man's wife;
He, the old Wrath, the Driver of Men astray,
Pursuer of Atreus for the feast defiled;
To assoil an ancient debt he hath paid this life;
A warrior and a crownèd King this day
Atones for a slain child.

Chorus. That thou art innocent herein
What tongue dare boast? It cannot be,
Yet from the deeps of ancient sin
The Avenger may have wrought with thee.
On the red Slayer crasheth, groping wild
For blood, more blood, to build his peace again,
And wash like water the old frozen stain
Of the torn child.

Mourners. Ah, sorrow, sorrow! My King, my King!
How shall I weep, what word shall I say?
Caught in the web of this spider thing,
In foul death gasping thy life away.
Woe's me, woe's me, for this slavish lying,
The doom of craft and the lonely dying,
The iron two-edged and the hands that slay!

Clytemnestra. And what of the doom of craft that first
He planted, making the House accurst?
What of the blossom from this root riven,
Iphigenia, the unforgiven?
Even as the wrong was, so is the pain:
He shall not laugh in the House of the slain,

When the count is scored;
He hath but spoilèd and paid again
The due of the sword.

Chorus. I am lost; my mind dull-eyed
Knows not nor feels
Whither to fly nor hide
While the House reels.
The noise of rain that falls
On the roof affrighteth me,
Washing away the walls;
Rain that falls bloodily.
Doth ever the sound abate?
Lo, the next Hour of Fate
Whetting her vengeance due
On new whet-stones, for new
Workings of hate.

Mourners. Would thou hadst covered me, Earth, O Earth,
Or e'er I had looked on my lord thus low,
In the pallèd marble of silvern girth!
What hands may shroud him, what tears may flow?
Not thine, O Woman who dared to slay him,
Thou durst not weep to him now, nor pray him,
Nor pay to his soul the deep unworth
Of gift or prayer to forget thy blow.
Oh, who with heart sincere
Shall bring praise or grief
To lay on the sepulchre
Of the great chief?

Clytemnestra. His burial is not thine to array.
By me he fell, by me he died,
I watch him to the grave, not cried
By mourners of his housefolk; nay,
His own child for a day like this
Waits, as is seemly, and shall run
By the white waves of Acheron
To fold him in her arms and kiss!

Chorus. Lo, she who was erst reviled
Revileth: and what is true?
Spoil taken from them that spoiled,
Life-blood from them that slew!

Surely while God ensueth
  His laws, while Time doth run
'Tis written: On him that doeth
  It shall be done.
This is God's law and grace,
Who then shall hunt the race
Of curses from out this hall?
The House is sealed withal
  To dreadfulness.

Clytemnestra. Aye, thou hast found the Law,.and stept
  In Truth's way.—Yet even now I call
  The Living Wrath which haunts this hall
To truce and compact. I accept
All the affliction he doth heap
  Upon me, and I charge him go
  Far off with his self-murdering woe
To strange men's houses. I will keep
Some little dower, and leave behind
  All else, contented utterly.
  I have swept the madness from the sky
Wherein these brethren slew their kind.

[*As she ceases, exhausted and with the fire gone out
of her,* AEGISTHUS, *with Attendants, bursts tri-
umphantly in.*

Aegisthus. O shining day, O dawn of righteousness
Fulfilled! Now, now indeed will I confess
That divine watchers o'er man's death and birth
Look down on all the anguish of the earth,
Now that I see him lying, as I love
To see him, in this net the Furies wove,
To atone the old craft of his father's hand.

For Atreus, this man's father, in this land
Reigning, and by Thyestes in his throne
Challenged—he was his brother and mine own
Father—from home and city cast him out;
And he, after long exile, turned about
And threw him suppliant on the hearth, and won
Promise of so much mercy, that his own
Life-blood should reek not in his father's hall.
Then did that godless brother, Atreus, call,

[138]

To greet my sire—More eagerness, O God,
Was there than love!—a feast of brotherhood.
And, feigning joyous banquet, laid as meat
Before him his dead children. The white feet
And finger-fringèd hands apart he set,
Veiled from all seeing, and made separate
The tables. And he straightway, knowing naught,
Took of those bodies, eating that which wrought
No health for all his race. And when he knew
The unnatural deed, back from the board he threw,
Spewing that murderous gorge, and spurning brake
The table, to make strong the curse he spake:
"Thus perish all of Pleisthenês[11] begot!"

For that lies this man here; and all the plot
Is mine, most righteously. For me, the third,
When butchering my two brethren, Atreus spared
And cast me with my broken sire that day,
A little thing in swaddling clothes, away
To exile; where I grew, and at the last
Justice hath brought me home! Yea, though outcast
In a far land, mine arm hath reached this king;
My brain, my hate, wrought all the counselling;
And all is well. I have seen mine enemy
Dead in the snare, and care not if I die!

Leader. Aegisthus, to insult over the dead
I like not. All the counsel, thou has said,
Was thine alone; and thine the will that spilled
This piteous blood. As justice is fulfilled,
Thou shalt not 'scape—so my heart presageth—
The day of cursing and the hurlèd death.

Aegisthus. How, thou poor oarsman of the nether row,
When the main deck is master? Sayst thou so? . . .
To such old heads the lesson may prove hard,
I fear me, when Obedience is the word.
But hunger, and bonds, and cold, help men to find
Their wits.—They are wondrous healers of the mind!
Hast eyes and seest not this?—Against a spike
Kick not, for fear it pain thee if thou strike.

Leader (*turning from him to Clytemnestra*). Woman! A
    soldier fresh from war! To keep

[139]

Watch o'er his house and shame him in his sleep . . .
To plot this craft against a lord of spears . . .

[CLYTEMNESTRA, *as though in a dream, pays no
heed.* AEGISTHUS *interrupts.*

Aegisthus. These be the words, old man, that lead to tears!
Thou hast an opposite to Orpheus' tongue,
Who chained all things with his enchanting song,
For thy mad noise will put the chains on thee.
Enough! Once mastered thou shalt tamer be.

Leader. Thou master? Is old Argos so accurst?
Thou plotter afar off, who never durst
Raise thine own hand to affront and strike him down . . .

Aegisthus. To entice him was the wife's work. I was known
By all men here, his old confessed blood-foe.
Howbeit, with his possessions I will know
How to be King. And who obeys not me
Shall be yoked hard, no easy trace-horse he,
Corn-flushed. Hunger, and hunger's prison mate,
The clammy murk, shall see his rage abate.

Leader. Thou craven soul! Why not in open strife
Slay him? Why lay the blood-sin on his wife,
Staining the Gods of Argos, making ill
The soil thereof? . . . But young Orestes still
Liveth. Oh, Fate will guide him home again,
Avenging, conquering, home to kill these twain!

Aegisthus. 'Fore God, if 'tis your pleasure thus to speak and
do, ye soon shall hear!
Ho there, my trusty pikes, advance! There cometh business for
the spear.

[*A body of Spearmen, from concealment outside,
rush in and dominate the stage.*

Leader. Ho there, ye Men of Argos! Up! Stand and be ready,
sword from sheath!

Aegisthus. By Heaven, I also, sword in hand, am ready, and
refuse not death!

Leader. Come, find it! We accept thy word. Thou offerest
what we hunger for.

[*Some of the Elders draw swords with the Leader;
others have collapsed with weakness. Men
from* AGAMEMNON'S *retinue have gathered*

and prepare for battle, when, before they can
come to blows, CLYTEMNESTRA *breaks from*
her exhausted silence.

Clytemnestra. Nay, peace, O best-belovèd! Peace! And let
us work no evil more.

Surely the reaping of the past is a full harvest, and not good,

And wounds enough are everywhere.—Let us not stain ourselves with blood.

Ye reverend Elders, go your ways, to his own dwelling every
one,

Ere things be wrought for which men suffer.—What we did
must needs be done.

And if of all these strifes we now may have no more, oh, I
will kneel

And praise God, bruisèd though we be beneath the Daemon's
heavy heel.

This is the word a woman speaks, to hear if any man will
deign.

Aegisthus. And who are these to burst in flower of folly thus
of tongue and brain,

And utter words of empty sound and perilous, tempting Fortune's frown,

And leave wise counsel all forgot, and gird at him who wears
the crown?

Leader. To cringe before a caitiff's crown, it squareth not with
Argive ways.

Aegisthus (*sheathing his sword and turning from them*).
Bah, I will be a hand of wrath to fall on thee in after days.

Leader. Not so, if God in after days shall guide Orestes home
again!

Aegisthus. I know how men in exile feed on dreams . . . and
know such food is vain.

Leader. Go forward and wax fat! Defile the right for this
thy little hour!

Aegisthus. I spare thee now. Know well for all this folly
thou shalt feel my power.

Leader. Aye, vaunt thy greatness, as a bird beside his mate
doth vaunt and swell.

Clytemnestra. Vain hounds are baying round thee; oh, forget
them! Thou and I shall dwell

[141]

As Kings in this great House. We two at last will order all
    things well.

                [The Elders and the remains of AGAMEMNON'S
                      retinue retire sullenly, leaving the Spear-
                      men in possession. CLYTEMNESTRA *and*
                      AEGISTHUS *turn and enter the Palace.*

AESCHYLUS
CHOËPHOROE

➤➤➤‹‹‹

TRANSLATED
By
GILBERT MURRAY

CHARACTERS IN THE PLAY.

ORESTES, *son of Agamemnon and Clytemnestra.*

ELECTRA, *daughter of Agamemnon and Clytemnestra.*

CLYTEMNESTRA, *formerly wife to Agamemnon, now wedded to Aegisthus.*

AEGISTHUS, *son of Thyestês, blood-foe to Agamemnon, and now Tyrant of Argos.*

PYLADES, *son of Strophios, King of Phokis, friend to Orestes.*

THE OLD NURSE *of Orestes.*

A SLAVE *of Aegisthus.*

CHORUS *of Bondmaids in the House of Clytemnestra and Aegisthus.*

The play was first in the archonship of Philocles (458 B.C.). The First Prize was won by Aeschylus with Agamemnon, Choëphoroe, Eumenides *and the Satyr-play* Proteus.

ARGUMENT

In the preceding play, *Agamemnon*, we witnessed the murder of Agamemnon by his wife Clytemnestra and her lover Aegisthus. Orestes was absent from Mycenae when the murder took place, having been rescued as a child from the hands of Clytemnestra who desired to kill him. With the help of Electra he was conveyed to Mount Parnassus where King Strophios took charge of him. Seven years later, at the age of twenty, he is commanded by the Delphic oracle to return and avenge his father's death.

CHOËPHOROE

The scene represents the Grave of Agamemnon, a mound of earth in a desolate expanse. The time is afternoon. ORESTES *and* PYLADES *in the garb of travellers, with swords at their sides, are discovered.* ORESTES' *hair is cut short, that of* PYLADES *streams down his back. Both look grim and travel-stained.* ORESTES *holds a long tress of hair in his hand.*

Orestes. O Warder Hermes of the world beneath,
Son of the Father who is Lord of Death;
Saviour, be thou my saviour; Help in War,
Help me! I am returned from lands afar
To claim mine own. And on this headland steep
Of death, I call my Father o'er the deep
To hearken, to give ear.—Behold, I bring
Out of my poverty one little thing,
To adorn thy grave, though who can touch the dead
Or wake from sleep that unuplifted head?
Yet long ago in Phokis, where I lay
With Strophios in the hills, being cast away
In childhood, plundered by mine enemies,
And friendless, save for this man, Pylades,
I sware an oath which should for ever set
In memory those they taught me to forget:
If once I came to manhood, so I sware,
In tresses twain I would divide mine hair,
One tress for Inachos[1] river, by whose grace
I live, and one for mourning at this place.
Which oath I here fulfil.

> *[He lays the tress of hair upon the upper part of the grave mound.*

                                    O Herald, lay
Before his sight the gift I bring this day,
Who stood not by to mourn him as he fell,
Nor reached mine arms to bid the dead farewell.
> *[As he turns, he sees the Libation-Bearers approaching.*

Ha!
What sight is this? What stricken multitude
Of women here in raiment sable-hued
Far-gleameth? How shall I interpret it?
Hath some new death upon my lineage lit?
Or is it to my father's grave they go
With offerings, to appease the wrath below?
It must be. Surely 'tis Electra there,
My sister, moves alone, none like to her
In sorrow. Zeus, Oh, grant to me this day
My vengeance, and be near me in the fray!
Come, Pylades, stand further, till we know
More sure, what means this embassy of woe.

> [ORESTES *and* PYLADES *withdraw, as* ELECTRA
> *with the* CHORUS *of women bearing offerings*
> *for the Grave enters from the other side.*

[*Strophe.*

Chorus.   Driven, yea, driven
  I come: I bear Peace-offering to the dead,
Mine hands as blades that tear, my tresses riven,
      And cheek ploughed red.
But all my years, before this day as after,
    Have been fed full with weeping as with bread.
    And this dumb cry of linen, as in pain,
    Deep rent about my bosom, speaketh plain
Of a life long since wounded, where no laughter
      Sounds nor shall sound again.

[*Antistrophe.*

    Dread, very dread,
And hair upstarting and the wrath that streams
From the heart of sleep, have first interpreted
     What manner of dreams
This house hath dreamed; a voice of terror, blasting
  The midnight, up from the inmost place it grew,
  Shaking the women's chambers; and the Seer,
  Being sworn of God, made answer, there is here
Anger of dead men wronged, and hate outlasting
     Death, against them that slew.

[*Strophe.*

Craving to fly that curse
With graceless gift hither she urgeth me
　　—O Earth, Mother and Nurse!—
She whom God hateth. But my spirit fears
　　　To speak the word it bears.
When blood is spilt, how shall a gift set free?
　　O hearthstone wet with tears!
O pillars of a house broken in twain!
　　　Without sun, without love,
Murk in the heart thereof and mist above,
　　　For a lord slain!

[*Antistrophe.*

　　The reverence of old years
Is gone, which not by battle nor by strife,
　　Stealing through charmèd ears,
Lifted the people's hearts to love their King;
　　　Gone, yet the land still fears.
For Fortune is a god and rules men's life.
　　Who knows the great Wheel's swing,
How one is smitten swift in the eyes of light;
　　　For one affliction cries
Slow from the border of sunset; and one lies
　　　In deedless night?

[*Strophe.*

　　Has Earth once drunk withal
The blood of her child, Man, the avenging stain
　　Hardens, nor flows again.
A blind pain draweth the slayer, draweth him,
On, on, till he is filled even to the brim
With sickness of the soul to atone for all.

[*Antistrophe.*

　　The shrine of maidenhood
Once broken ne'er may be unbroke again.
　　And where man's life hath flowed
All the world's rivers in their multitude
　　Rolling shall strive in vain
To clean from a brother's hand that ancient blood.
　　For me, God in far days
Laid hand upon my city, and herded me

From my old home to the House of Slavery,
Where all is violence, and I needs must praise,
   Just or unjust,
The pleasure of them that rule, and speechless hold
The ache of a heart that rageth in the dust.
   Only behind the fold
Of this still veil for a little I hide my face
And weep for the blind doings of this race,
And secret tears are in my heart, ice-cold.

Electra. Ye thrallèd women, tirers of the bower,
Since ye are with me in this suppliant hour,
Your escort giving, give your counsel too.
What speech have I for utterance, when I sue
With offerings to the dead? What word of love
What prayer to reach my father from above?
"To dear Lord," shall I say, "due gifts I bear
From loving mistress" . . . when they come from her?
I dare not. And I cannot find the word
To speak, when offerings like these are poured. . . .
Or shall I pray him, as men's custom is,
To send to them who pay these offices
Requital due . . . for murder and for pride?
Or, as in silence and in shame he died,
In shame and silence shall I pour this urn
Of offering to the dust, and pouring turn,
As men cast out some foulness they abhor,
And fling the cup, and fly, and look no more?
 Share with me, Friends, this burden of strange thought.
One hate doth make us one. Oh, hide not aught
For fear of what may fall us! Destiny
Waiteth alike for them that men call free,
And them by others mastered. At thine ease.
Speak, if thou knowest of wiser words than these.

 Leader. As at God's altar, since so fain thou art,
Before this Tomb I will unveil my heart.

 Electra. Speak, by his grave and in the fear thereof.

 Leader. Pray as thou pourest: To all hearts of love . . .

 Electra. And who is such of all around us, who?

 Leader. Thyself, and whoso hates Aegisthus true.

 Electra. For thee and me alone am I to pray?

Leader. Ask thine own understanding. It will say.
Electra. Who else? What heart that with our sorrow grieves?
Leader. Forget not that—far off—Orestes lives.
Electra. Oh, bravely spoke! Thou counsellest not in vain.
Leader. Next; on the sinners pray, their sin made plain. . . .
Electra. Pray what? I know not. Oh, make clear my road!
Leader. Pray that there come to them or man or god. . . .
Electra. A judge? Or an avenger? Speak thy prayer.
Leader. Plain be thy word: one who shall slay the slayer.
Electra. But dare I? Is it no sin thus to pray?
Leader. How else? With hate thine hater to repay.

> [ELECTRA *mounts upon the Grave Mound and*
> *makes sacrifice.*

Electra. Herald most high of living and of dead,
Thou midnight Hermes, hear; and call the dread
Spirits who dwell below the Earth, my vows
To hearken and to watch my father's house;
And Earth our Mother, who doth all things breed
And nurse, and takes again to her their seed.
And I too with thee, as I pour these streams
To wash dead hands, will call him in his dreams:
O Father, pity me; pity thine own
Orestes, and restore us to thy throne;
We are lost, we are sold like slaves: and in our stead
Lo, she hath brought thy murderer to her bed,
Aegisthus. I am like one chained alway;
Orestes wandering without house or stay;
But they are full of pride, and make turmoil
And banquet of the treasures of thy toil.
Guide thou Orestes homeward, let there be
Some chance to aid him:—Father, hark to me!
And, oh, give me a heart to understand
More than my mother, and a cleaner hand!
These prayers for us; but for our enemies
This also I speak: O Father, let there rise
Against them thine Avenger, and again
The slayer in just recompense be slain.—
Behold, I pray great evil, and I lay
These tokens down; yea, midmost as I pray
Against thine enemies I lay them—so.

Do thou to us send blessing from below
With Zeus, and Earth, and Right which conquereth all.
　　These be the prayers on which mine offerings fall.
Do ye set lamentation like a wreath
Round them, and cry the triumph-song of death.

> [*She proceeds with the pouring of offerings and
> presently finds on the tomb the Lock of Hair.
> The* CHORUS *makes lamentation before the
> grave.*

Chorus.　Let fall the tear that plashes as it dies,
　　　　Where the dead lies,
　　　Fall on this barrèd door,
　　Where Good nor Evil entereth any more,
　　　This holy, abhorrèd thing,
　We turn from, praying—Lo, the milk and wine
　　Are poured.　Awake and hear, thou awful King;
Hear in thy darkened soul, O Master mine!

Oh, for some man of might
To aid this land, some high and visible lord
Of battle, shining bright
Against Death; the great lance
Bearing deliverance,
The back-bent Scythian bow, the hilted sword
Close-held to smite and smite!

Electra (*excitedly returning from the Grave.*)
Behold,
The offerings of the dust are ministered:
But counsel me.　I bear another word.

Leader.　Speak on.　My spirit leaps for eagerness.
Electra.　Cast on the tomb I found this shaven tress.
Leader.　Who cast it there?　What man or zonèd maid?
Electra.　Methinks that is a riddle quickly read!
Leader.　Thy thought is swift; and may thine elder know?
Electra.　What head save mine would blazon thus its woe?
Leader.　She that should mourn him is his enemy.
Electra (*musing, to herself*).　Strange bird, but of one feather
　　to mine eye. . . .
Leader.　With what?　Oh, speak.　Make thy comparison.
Electra.　Look; think ye not 'tis wondrous like mine own?

[150]

Leader. Thy brother's! . . . Sent in secret! Can it be?

Electra. 'Tis like his long locks in my memory.

Leader. Orestes! Would he dare to walk this land?

Electra. Belike he sent it by another's hand!

Leader. That calls for tears no less, if never more
His footstep may be set on Argos shore.

    Electra. At my heart also bitterer than gall
A great wave beats. The iron hath passed thro' all
My being; and the stormy drops that rise
Fall unforbidden from these starvèd eyes,
Gazing upon this hair. 'Tis past belief
That any Argive tree hath shed this leaf.
And sure she shore it not who wrought his death,
My mother, godless, with no mother's faith
Or kindness for her child.—And yet to swear
Outright that this glad laughter is the hair
Of my beloved Orestes. . . . Oh, I am weak
With dreaming! Had it but a voice to speak
Like some kind messenger, I had not been
This phantom tossing in the wind between
Two fancies. Either quick it would proclaim
Its hate, if from some hater's head it came;
Or, if it were our own, with me 'twould shed
Tears for this tomb and our great father dead. . . .
Surely they know, these gods to whom we pray,
Through what wild seas our vessel beats her way,
And, if to save us is their will, may breed
A mighty oak-trunk from a little seed. . . .

                [*She goes back to the Tomb, searching.*

    Ah see, the print of feet, a second sign!
The same feet: surely they are shaped like mine.
Surely! Two separate trails of feet are there:
He and perchance some fellow traveller.
The heels; the mark of the long muscle thrown
Athwart them on the sand—just like mine own
In shape and measure. What? . . . Oh, all is vain;
Torment of heart and blinding of the brain!

          [*She buries her face in her hands.* ORESTES *rises
            from his hiding-place and stands before her.*

Orestes. Thy prayer hath borne its fruit. Hereafter tell
The gods thy thanks, and may the end be well!
   Electra. What meanest thou? What hath God done for me?
   Orestes. Shown thee a face which thou hast longed to see.
   Electra. What face? What know'st thou of my secret heart?
   Orestes. Orestes'. For that name all fire thou art.
   Electra. If that be so, how am I near mine end?
   Orestes. Here am I, Sister. Seek no closer friend.
   Electra. Stranger! It is a plot thou lay'st for me!
   Orestes. Against mine own dear life that plot would be.
   Electra. Thou mock'st me! Thou would'st laugh to hear me
moan!
   Orestes. Who mocks thy tribulation mocks mine own.
   Electra. My heart half dares foretell that thou art he . . .
   Orestes. Nay, when I face thee plain thou wilt not see!
Oh, seeing but that shorn tress of funeral hair
Thy soul took wings and seemed to hold me there;
Then peering in my steps . . . thou knew'st them mine,
Thy brother's, moulded feet and head like thine.
Set the lock here, where it was cut. Behold
This cloak I wear, thy woven work of old,
The battened ridges and the broidered braid
Of lions . . .

        [ELECTRA *throws herself into his arms.*
          Hold! Ah, be not all dismayed
With joy! Our nearest is our deadliest foe.
   Electra. O best beloved, O dreamed of long ago,
Seed of deliverance washed with tears as rain,
By thine own valour thou shalt build again
Our father's House! O lightener of mine eyes,
Four places in my heart, four sanctities,
Are thine. My father in thy face and mien
Yet living: thine the love that might have been
My mother's—whom I hate, most righteously—
And my poor sister's, fiercely doomed to die,
And thou my faithful brother, who alone
Hast cared for me. . . . O Victory, be our own
This day, with Justice who doth hold us fast,
And Zeus most high, who saveth at the last!
   Orestes. O Zeus, O Zeus, look down on our estate!

Hast seen thine eagle's brood left desolate,
The father in the fell toils overborne
Of some foul serpent, and the young forlorn
And starved with famine, still too weak of wing
To bear to the nest their father's harvesting?
Even so am I, O Zeus, and even so
This woman, both disfathered long ago,
Both to one exile cast, both desolate.
He was thy worshipper, thy giver great
Of sacrifice.   If thou tear down his nest,
What hand like his shall glorify thy feast?
Blot out the eagle's brood, and where again
Hast thou thy messenger to speak to men?
Blast this most royal oak, what shade shall cool
Thine altars on the death-day of the Bull?
But cherish us, and from a little seed
Thou shalt make great a House now fallen indeed.

   Leader.   O Children, Saviours of your father's House,
Be silent!   Children, all is perilous;
And whoso hears may idly speak of ye
To our masters; whom may I yet live to see
Dead where the pine logs ooze in fragrant fire!

   Orestes.   (*He speaks with increasing horror as he proceeds.*)
Oh, Loxias shall not mock my great desire,
Who spoke his divine promise, charging me
To thread this peril to the extremity:
Yea, raised his awful voice and surging told
To my hot heart of horrors stormy-cold
Till I seek out those murderers, by the road
Themselves have shown—so spake he—blood for blood,
In gold-rejecting rage, the wild bull's way!
If not, for their offending I must pay
With mine own life, in torment manifold.
Of many things that rise from earth he told,
To appease the angry dead: yea, and strange forms,
On thee and me, of savage-fangèd worms,
Climbing the flesh; lichens, which eat away
Even unto nothingness our natural clay.
And when they leave him, a man's hair is white.
For him that disobeys, he said, the night

Hath Furies, shapen of his father's blood;
Clear-seen, with eyeball straining through the hood
Of darkness. The blind arrows of dead men
Who cried their kin for mercy and were slain,
And madness, and wild fear out of the night,
Shall spur him, rack him, till from all men's sight
Alone he goes, out to the desert dim,
And that bronze horror clanging after him!

    For such as he there is no mixing bowl,
No dear libation that binds soul to soul:
From every altar fire the unseen rage
Outbars him: none shall give him harbourage,
Nor rest beneath one roof with such an one;
Till, without worship, without love, alone
He crawls to his death, a carcase to the core
Through-rotted, and embalmed to suffer more.
                                        [*Collecting himself.*

    So spake he . . . God, and is one to believe
Such oracles as these? Nay, though I give
No credence, the deed now must needs be done.
So many things of power work here as one:
The God's command; grief for my father slain;
And mine own beggary urgeth me amain,
That never shall these Argives, famed afar,
High conquerors of Troy in joyous war
Cower to . . . two women. For he bears, I know,
A woman's heart. . . . If not, this day will show.
            [*He kneels at the Grave:* ELECTRA *kneels opposite
              him and the* CHORUS *gather behind.*

Chorus.   Ye great Apportionments of God,
            The road of Righteousness make straight:
            "For tongue of hate be tongue of hate
        Made perfect": thus, as falls her rod,
        God's justice crieth: "For the blow
            Of death the blow of death atone"
        "On him that doeth shall be done":
        Speaks a grey word of long ago.
                                        [*Strophe* 1.

Orestes. O Father, Father of Doom,
            What word, what deed from me,

[154]

Can waft afar to the silent room
   Where thy sleep holdeth thee
A light that shall rend thy gloom?
   Yet surely, the tale is told,
That tears are comfort beneath the tomb
   To the great Kings of old.

                             [*Strophe* 2.

Leader. No fire ravening red,
   O Son, subdueth quite
The deep life of the dead;
   His wrath breaks from the night.
When they weep for one who dies
His Avenger doth arise,
   Yea, for father and life-giver
There is Justice, when the cries
   And the tears run as a river.

                             [*Antistrophe* 1.

Electra. O Father, hearken and save,
   For my sore sorrow's sake!
Children twain are above thy grave
   Seeking for thee: Oh, wake!
Thy grave is their only home,
   The beggared and out-cast.
What here is well? What is saved from doom?
   O Atê strong to the last!

Chorus. Yet still it may be—God is strong—
   A changèd music shall be born
   To sound above this dirge forlorn,
And the King's House with Triumph-song
   Lead home a Friend in love new-sworn.

                             [*Strophe* 3.

Orestes. Would that in ancient days,
   Father, some Lycian lance
      Had slain thee by Ilion's wall;
Then hadst thou left great praise
   In thy House, and thy children's glance
      In the streets were marked of all:
Men had upreared for thee
   A high-piled burial hill

In a land beyond the sea;
    And the House could have borne its ill.

                                [Antistrophe 2.

Leader. And all they who nobly died
    Would have loved him in that place,
    And observed him in his pride
    As he passed with royal pace
    To a throne at the right hand
    Of the Kings of the Dark Land:
    For a king he was when living,
    Above all who crownèd stand
    With the sceptre of lawgiving.

                                [Antistrophe 3.

Electra. Nay, would thou hadst died not ever!
      Not by the Ilion Gate,
        Not when the others fell
    Spear-broken beside the river!
      If they who wrought thee hate
        Had died, it had all been well:
    A strange death, full of fear,
      That the folk beyond far seas
    Should enquire thereof, and hear;
      Not of our miseries!

Chorus. My daughter, rare as gold is rare,
    And blither than the skies behind
    The raging of the northern wind
    Are these thy prayers: for what is prayer?
    Yet, be thou sure, this twofold scourge
    Is heard: it pierceth to the verge
    Of darkness, and your helpers now
    Are wakening. These encharioted
    Above us, lo, their hand is red!
    Abhorrèd are they by the dead;
    But none so hates as he and thou!

                                [Strophe 4.

Orestes. Ah me, that word, that word
      Stabbeth my heart, as a sword!
    God, God, who sendest from below
      Blind vengeance in the wake

Of sin, what deed have I to do,
With hand most weak and full of woe?
   'Tis for my father's sake!

Leader. May it be mine, may it be mine,   *[Strophe 5.*
   To dance about the blazing pine
     Crying, crying,
   "A man is slain, a woman dying!"
   It hideth in my bosom's core,
    It beats its wings for death, for death,
   A bitter wind that blows before
    The prow, a hate that festereth,
   A thing of horror, yet divine!

Electra. Zeus of the orphan, when   *[Antistrophe 4.*
    Wilt lift thy hand among men?
   Let the land have a sign. Be strong,
    And smite the neck from the head.
   I ask for right after much wrong.
   Hear me, O God! Hark to my song,
    Ye Princedoms of the Dead!

Chorus. 'Tis written: the shed drop doth crave
    For new blood. Yea, the murdered cry
   Of dead men shrieketh from the grave
    To Her who out of sins gone by
    Makes new sin, that the old may die.

                        [Strophe 6.
Orestes. How? Are ye dumb, Ye Princedoms of the Dead?
   O Curses of Them that perish, come hither, hither!
  Look on this wreck of kings, the beaten head,
  Bowed in despair, roofless, disherited!
   Whither to turn, O Lord Zeus? Whither, whither?

                      [Antistrophe 5.
Leader. My heart, my heart is tossed again
   To see thee yielded up to pain,
    Failing, failing;
   Then mist is on my eyes and wailing
   About mine ears, and tears as rain.
   But when once more I look on thee
   With power exalted, sudden-swift

A hope doth all my burden lift,
　　And light, and signs of things to be.
　　　　　　　　　　　　　　　　[*Antistrophe* 6.

Electra.　What best shall pierce thine ear; the wrongs she
　　wrought,
　　Wrought upon us, upon us, she and none other?
Oh, fawn and smile: but the wrongs shall soften not,
Wrongs with a wolfish heart, by a wolf begot:
　　They see no smile, they reck not the name of Mother!
　　　　　　　　　　　　　　　　[*Strophe* 7.

Chorus.　With the dirge of Agbatana I beat my breast:
　　Like the Keeners of Kissia, I make songs of pain.
Lo, yearning of arms abundant, east and west:
　　Tearing they smite, again and yet again,
From above, from high; yea, God hath smitten red
This bitter bleeding bosom, this bended head.
　　　　　　　　　　　　　　　　[*Strophe* 8.

Electra.　Ho, Mother! Ho, thou, Mother,
　　　　Mine enemy, daring all!
　　　　　　What burial made ye here?
　　　　His people followed not,
　　　　Mourned him not, knew him not:
　　　　　　Enemies bare his pall:
　　　　His wife shed no tear!
　　　　　　　　　　　　　　　　[*Strophe* 9.

Orestes.　All, all dishonour, so thy story telleth it!
　　And for that dishonour shall the woman pay,
As the gods have willed it, as my right hand willeth it!
　　Then Death may take me, let me only slay!
　　　　　　　　　　　　　　　　[*Antistrophe* 9.

Leader.　His hands and feet, they were hacked away from
　　him!
　　Yea, she that buried him, she wrought it so.
To make thy life blasted, without help or stay from him.
　　Thou hast it all, the defiling and shame and woe!
　　　　　　　　　[ORESTES *breaks down in speechless tears.*
　　　　　　　　　　　　　　　　[*Antistrophe* 7.

Electra.　Thou tellest the doom he died, but I saw him not;
　　I was far off, dishonoured and nothing worth.
Like a dog they drove me back, and the door was shut,

And alone I poured my tears to him through the earth.
I laughed not, yet rejoiced that none saw me weep.
Write this in thine heart, O Father; grave it deep.

[*Antistrophe* 8.

Leader. Write! Yea, and draw the word
    Deep unto that still land
      Where thy soul dwells in peace.
  What is, thou hast this day heard;
    What shall be, reach forth thine hand
    And take it! Be hard, be hard
      To smite and not cease!
    (ORESTES, ELECTRA, *and the* LEADER.)

[*Strophe* 10.

Orestes. Thee, thee I call. Father, be near thine own.
Electra. I also cry thee, choked with the tears that flow.
Leader. Yea, all this band, it crieth to thee as one.
All. O great King, hear us. Awake thee to the sun.
      Be with us against thy foe!

[*Antistrophe* 10.

Orestes. The slayer shall meet the slayer, wrong smite with
  wrong.
Electra. O Zeus, bless thou the murder to be this day.
Leader. (Dost hear? Oh, fear is upon me and trembling
  strong.)
All. The day of Fate is old, it hath lingered long,
      It cometh to them that pray.

[*Strophe* 11.

Divers Women.
Alas, alas, for the travail born in the race,
  Alas for the harp of Atê, whose strings run blood,
    The beaten bosom, the grief too wild to bear.
    The pain that gnaweth, and will not sink to sleep.

[*Antistrophe* 11.

The House hath healing[2] for its own bitterness;
  It is here within. None other can stay the flood;
    Through bitter striving, through hate and old despair.
    Behold the Song of the Daemons of the deep!
Orestes. O Father mine, O most unkingly slain,
Grant me the lordship of thy House again.

Electra. A boon for me likewise, O Father, give;
To lay Aegisthus in his blood and live.

Orestes. So men shall honour thee with wassail high;
Else without meat or incense shalt thou lie,
Unhonoured when the dead their banquets call.

Electra. And I will pour thee offerings wondrous fair
From my stored riches for a marriage-prayer,
And this thy grave will honour more than all.

Orestes. Send back, O Earth, my sire to comfort me.

Electra. In power, in beauty, Great Persephone!

Orestes. Remember, Father, how they laved thee there!

Electra. Remember the strange weaving thou didst wear!

Orestes. A snarèd beast in chains no anvil wrought!

Electra. In coilèd webs of shame and evil thought!

Orestes. Scorn upon scorn!   Oh, art thou wakenèd?

Electra. Dost rear to sunlight that belovèd head?

Orestes. Or send thine helping Vengeance to the light
To aid the faithful: or let even fight
Be joined in the same grapple as of yore,
If, conquered, thou wouldst quell thy conqueror.

Electra. Yet one last cry: O Father, hear and save!
Pity thy children cast upon thy grave:
The woman pity, and the weeping man.

Orestes. And blot not out the old race that began
With Pelops: and though slain thou art not dead!

Electra. Children are living voices for a head
Long silent, floats which hold the net and keep
The twisted line unfoundered in the deep.

Orestes. Listen: 'tis thou we weep for, none but thou:
Thyself are saved if thou save us now.

Leader. Behold, ye have made a long and yearning praise,
This sepulchre for unlamented days
Requiting to the full.   And for the rest,
Seeing now thine heart is lifted on the crest
Of courage, get thee to the deed, and see
What power the Daemon[3] hath which guardeth thee.

Orestes. So be it.   Yet methinks to know one thing
Were well.   Why sent she this drink-offering?
Hoped she by late atonement to undo
That wrong eternal?   A vain comfort, too,

[160]

Sent to one dead, and feeling not!   My mind
Stumbles to understand what lies behind
These gifts, so puny for the deed she hath done.
Yea, though man offer all he hath to atone
For one life's blood, 'tis written, he hath lost
That labour.—But enough.   Say all thou know'st.

   Leader.   Son, I was near her, and could mark aright.
A dream, a terror wandering in the night,
Shook her dark spirit till she spoke that word.

   Orestes.   What was the dream she dreamed?   Speak, if ye
     heard.

   Leader.   She bore to life, she said, a Serpent Thing.

   Orestes.   And after?   To its head thy story bring.

   Leader.   In swathing clothes she lapt it like a child.

   Orestes.   It craved for meat, that dragon of the wild?

   Leader.   Yes; in the dream she gave it her own breast.

   Orestes.   And took no scathing from the evil beast?

   Leader.   The milk ran into blood.   So deep it bit.

   Orestes.   The dream is come.   The man shall follow it.

   Leader.   And   she,   appalled,   came   shrieking   out   of
     sleep;
And many a torch, long blinded in the deep
Of darkness, in our chambers burst afire
To cheer the Queen.   Then spake she her desire,
To send, as a swift medicine for the dread
That held her, these peace offerings to the dead.

   Orestes.   Behold, I pray this everlasting Earth,
I pray my father's grave, they bring to birth
In fullness all this dream.   And here am I
To read its heart and message flawlessly.
Seeing that this serpent, born whence I was born,
Wore the same swathing-bands these limbs had worn,
Fanged the same breast that suckled me of yore,
And through the sweet milk drew that gout of gore,
And seeing she understood, and sore afeared
Shrieked: therefore it must be that, having reared
A birth most ghastly, she in wrath shall die:
And I, the beast, the serpent, even I
Shall slay her! Be it so. The dream speaks clear.

   Leader.   I take thyself for mine interpreter,

And pray that this may be. But speak thy will;
Who shall be doing, say, and who be still?

    Orestes. 'Tis simply told. This woman makes her way
Within, and ye my charges shall obey,
That they who slew by guile a man most rare,
By guile, and snarèd in the self-same snare,
May die, as Lord Apollo hath foretold,
Loxias the Seer, who never failed of old.

    First, I array me in a stranger's guise,
With all the gear of travel, and likewise
This man—their guest and battle-guest of yore!
Then hither shall we come, and stand before
The courtyard gate, and call. Aye, we will teach
Our tongues an accent of Parnassian speech,
Like men in Phokis born. And say, perchance
None of the warders with glad countenance
Will ope to us, the House being so beset
With evil: aye, what then? Then obdurate
We shall wait on, till all who pass that way
Shall make surmise against the House, and say
"What ails Aegisthus? Wherefore doth he close
His door against the traveller, if he knows
And is within?" So comes it, soon or late,
I cross the threshold of the courtyard gate;
And entering find him on my father's throne. . . .
Or, say he is abroad and comes anon,
And hears, and calls for me—and there am I
Before him, face to face and eye to eye;
"Whence comes the traveller?" ere he speaks it, dead
I lay him, huddled round this leaping blade!
Then shall the Curse have drunken of our gore
Her third, last, burning cup, and thirst no more.

    Therefore go thou within, and watch withal
That all this chance may well and aptly fall.
For you, I charge ye of your lips take heed:
Good words or silence, as the hour may need.
While One Below[4] his counsel shall afford
And ope to me the strait way of the sword.

             [ORESTES *and* PYLADES *depart,* ELECTRA *goes int*
               the House.

Chorus. Host on host, breedeth Earth[5]   [*Strophe* 1.
　　Things of fear and ghastly birth;
　　Arm on arm spreads the Sea
　　That full of coilèd horrors be;
　　And fires the sky doth multiply;
　　And things that crawl, and things that fly,
　　And they that are born in the wind can tell of the perils
　　　Of tempest and the Wrath on high.

                                        [*Antistrophe* 1.

　　But, ah, the surge over-bold
　　Of man's passion who hath told?
　　Who the Love, wild as hate,
　　In woman's bosom desperate,
　　Which feedeth in the fields of Woe?
　　Where lives of mortals linkèd go
　　The heart of a woman is perilous past all perils
　　　Of stars above or deeps below.

                                        [*Strophe* 2.

　　Wist ye not, O light of mind,
　　　Her who slew her son with hate,
　　　Thestios' daughter desolate,
　　How she wrought All her thought
　　　To one counsel, fiery-blind,
　　　　When she burned the brand of fate,
　　　That was twin to him and brother
　　　　From the hour of that first cry
　　　When the babe came from the mother
　　　　Till the strong man turned to die?

                                        [*Antistrophe* 2.

　　Wist ye not one loathed of old,
　　　Who to win a foe did sell,
　　　Cruel, him who loved her well;
　　Skylla, dyed with blood and pride,
　　　Who craved the rings of Cretan gold
　　　　That Minos gave, too rich to tell;
　　　Like a wolf at night she came
　　　　Where he lay with tranquil breath,
　　　And she cut the Crest of Flame:
　　　　And, a-sudden, all was death.

But o'er all terrors on man's tongue   *[Strophe* 3.
   The woman's deed of Lemnos lies;
It echoes, like an evil song,
   Far off, and whensoe'er there rise
   New and strange sins, in dire surmise,
Men mind them of the Lemnian wrong.
Yet surely by the Sin God's eye
Abhorreth, mortal man shall die,
   And all the glory that was his.
For who shall lift that thing on high
   Which God abaseth?   Not amiss
I garner to my crown of woe
These sins of Woman long ago.

                           [Antistrophe 3.

O lust so old, so hard of heart!
   I lose me in the stories told,
Untimely.   Have these walls no part
   In ravening of desire, as bold
   And evil as those deeds of old?
The House with dread thereof doth start
   From dreaming.   On, through woe or weal
A woman brooding planned her path,
   Against a warrior robed in steel,
And armies trembled at his wrath.
   And he is gone; and we must kneel
On a cold hearth and bow in fear
Before a woman's trembling spear.

                           [Strophe 4.

Lo, the sword hovereth at the throat
For Justice' sake.   It scorneth not
   What the proud man to earth has trod.
Its edge is bitter to the bone;
It stabbeth on, thro' iron, thro' stone,
Till it reach him who hath forgot
   That Ruth which is the law of God.

                           [Antistrophe 4.

For Justice is an oak that yet
Standeth; and Doom the Smith doth whet
   His blade in the dark.   But what is this?
A child led to the House from lands

Far off, and blood upon his hands!
The great Erinys wreaks her debt,
    Whose thought is as the vast abyss.

*The scene now represents the front of the Palace of
    the Atridae, with one door leading to the main
    palace, another to the Women's House. Dusk is
    approaching. Enter* ORESTES *and* PYLADES, *dis-
    guised as merchants from Phokis, with Attendants.*

Orestes. Ho, Warder! Hear! One knocketh at your gate! ...
Ho, Warder, yet again! I knock and wait. . . .
A third time, ye within! I call ye forth;
Or counts your lord the stranger nothing worth?
    A Porter (*within, opening the main door*).
Enough! I hear. What stranger and wherefrom?
    Orestes. Go, rouse your masters. 'Tis to them I come,
Bearing great news. And haste, for even now
Night's darkling chariot presseth to the brow
Of heaven, and wayfarers like us must find
Quick anchorage in some resthouse for our kind.
Let one come forth who bears authority;
A woman, if God will; but if it be
A man, 'twere seemlier. With a woman, speech
Trembles and words are blinded. Man can teach
Man all his purpose and make clear his thought.
                    [*Enter* CLYTEMNESTRA *from the House.*
    Clytemnestra. Strangers, your pleasure? If ye have need
        of aught
All that beseems this House is yours to-day,
Warm bathing and the couch that soothes away
Toil, and the tendering of righteous eyes.
Else, if ye come on some grave enterprise,
That is man's work; and I will find the man.
    Orestes. I come from Phokis, of the Daulian clan,
And, travelling hither, bearing mine own load
Of merchandise, toward Argos, as the road
Branched, there was one who met me, both of us
Strangers to one another: Strophios,
A Phocian prince, men called him. On we strode
Together, till he asked me of my road

[165]

And prayed me thus: "Stranger, since other care
Takes thee to Argos, prithee find me there
The kin of one Orestes. . . . Plainly said
Is best remembered: tell them he is dead.
Forget not. And howe'er their choice may run,
To bear his ashes home, or leave their son
In a strange grave, in death an exile still,
Discover, and bring back to me their will.
Tell them his ashes lie with me, inurned
In a great jar of bronze, and richly mourned."
So much I tell you straight, being all I heard.
Howbeit, I know not if I speak my word
To the right hearers, princess of this old
Castle. Methinks his father should be told.

 Clytemnestra. Ah me,
So cometh the last wreck in spite of all!
Curse of this House, thou foe that fear'st no fall,
How dost thou spy my hidden things and mar
Their peace with keen-eyed arrows from afar,
Till all who might have loved me, all, are gone!
And now Orestes; whom I had thought upon
So wisely, walking in free ways, his gait
Unsnarèd in this poison-marsh of hate!
The one last hope, the healing and the prayer
Of this old House, 'twas writ on empty air!

 Orestes. For me, in a great House and favoured thus
By fortune, 'tis by tidings prosperous
I fain were known and welcomed. Pleasantest
Of all ties is the tie of host and guest.
But my heart told me 'twere a faithless thing
To fail a comrade in accomplishing
His charge, when I had pledged both word and hand.

 Clytemnestra. Not for our sorrow shall thy portion stand
The lowlier, nor thyself be less our friend.
Another would have told us; and the end
Is all one. But 'tis time that strangers who
Have spent long hours in travel should have due
Refreshment. Ho, there! Lead him to our broad
Guest-chambers, and these comrades of his road
Who follow. See they find all comfort there

To assuage their way-worn bodies. And have care
That in their tendance naught be found amiss.
  Ourselves shall with our Lord consult of this
Distress, and, having yet good friends, who know
My heart, take counsel how to affront the blow.

> [CLYTEMNESTRA *goes back into the Women's*
> *House; Attendants lead* ORESTES *and his*
> *followers through the main door.*

Leader. Ye handmaidens, arise, be bold:
      See if our moving lips have power
      To aid Orestes in his hour;
    For sure ye loved this House of old.

Chorus. Thou holy Earth, thou holy shore
      Beyond the grave, where rests his head
      The Lord of Ships, the King, the Dead,
    Now list, now aid, or never more!
    The hour is full. The Guileful Word
      Descends to wrestle for the right,
      And Hermes guards the hour of night
    For him that smiteth with the sword.

> [*The* NURSE *enters from the Women's House,*
> *weeping.*

Leader. The stranger works some mischief, it would seem!
Yonder I see Orestes' Nurse, a-stream
With tears.—How now, Kilissa, whither bound,
And Grief the unbidden partner of thy round?
Nurse. The mistress bids me call Aegisthus here
Quickly, to see these two, and learn more clear,
As man from man, the truth of what they tell.
Oh, to us slaves she makes it pitiable
And grievous, and keeps hid behind her eyes
The leaping laughter. Aye, 'tis a rich prize
For her, and for the House stark misery,
This news the travellers tell so trippingly.
And, Oh, Aegisthus, he, you may be sure,
Will laugh to hear it! . . . Ah, I am a poor
Old woman! Such a tangle as they were,
The troubles in this House, and hard to bear,

Long years back, and all aching in my breast!
But none that hurt like this! Through all the rest . . .
Well, I was sore, but lived them down and smiled.
But little Orestes, my heart's care, the child
I took straight from his mother; and save me
He had no other nurse! And, Oh, but he
Could scream and order me to tramp the dark!
Aye, times enough, and trouble enough, and stark
Wasted at that! A small thing at the breast,
That has no sense, you tend it like a beast,
By guesswork. For he never speaks, not he,
A babe in swaddling clothes, if thirst maybe
Or hunger comes, or any natural need.
The little belly takes its way. Indeed,
'Twas oft a prophet he wanted, not a nurse;
And often enough my prophecies, of course,
Came late, and then 'twas clothes to wash and dry,
And fuller's work as much as nurse's. Aye,
I followed both trades, from the day when first
His father gave me Orestes to be nursed. . . .
And now he is dead; and strangers come and tell
The news to me. And this poor miserable
Old woman must go tell the plunderer
Who shames this house! Oh, glad he will be to hear!
   Leader. How doth she bid him come? In what array?
   Nurse. I take thee not. . . . What is it ye would say?
   Leader. Comes he with spears to guard him or alone?
   Nurse. She bids him bring the spearmen of the throne.
   Leader. Speak not that bidding to our loathèd Lord!
"Alone, quick, fearing nothing" is the word.
So speak, and in thy heart let joy prevail!
The teller straighteneth many a crookèd tale.
   Nurse. What ails thee? Are these tidings to thy mind?
   Leader. The wind is cold, but Zeus may change the wind.
   Nurse. How, when Orestes, our one hope, is dead?
   Leader. Not yet! So much the dullest seer can read.
   Nurse. What mean'st thou? There is something ye have
      heard!
   Leader. Go, tell thy tale. Obey thy mistress' word!
God, where He guardeth, guardeth faithfully.

Nurse. I go.—May all be well, God helping me!

[*The* NURSE *goes out.*

Chorus.   Lo, I pray God, this day[6]:   [*Strophe.*
   Father of Olympus, hear!
  Grant thy fortunes healingly
  Fall for them who crave to see
   In this House of lust and fear,
    Purity, purity.
  I have sinned not, I have spoken
  In the name of Law unbroken;
  Zeus, as thou art just, we pray thee
   Be his guard!

All.   There is One within the Gate
   Of his foemen, where they wait;
  Oh, prefer him, Zeus, before them
   And exalt and make him great:
  Two- and threefold shall he pay thee
   Love's reward.

          [*Antistrophe.*

  Seest thou one lost, alone,
   Child of him who loved thee well?
  As a young steed he doth go,
  Maddened, in the yoke of woe:
  Oh, set measure on the swell,
   Forth and fro, forth and fro,
 Of the beating hoofs that bear him
 Through this bitter course. Oh, spare him!
  By his innocence we pray thee
   Be his guard!

All.   There is One within the Gate
   Of his foemen, where they wait;
  Oh, prefer him, Zeus, before them
   And exalt and make him great:
  Two- and threefold shall he pay thee
   Love's reward.

  Gods of the treasure-house within,   [*Strophe.*
   One-hearted, where the bronzen door
  On darkness gloateth and on gold:

With present cleansing wash the old
Blight of this house: and aged Sin
    Amid the gloom shall breed no more!

All. And, O light of the Great Cavern, let it be
That this Man's house look up again, and see,
    Till the dead veil of scorn
    And long darkness shall be torn,
And the kind faces shine and old Argolis be free!

[*Antistrophe*

    And, Oh, let Hermes, Maia-born,
    Be near, who moveth in his kind,
    As the wind blows, to help at need:
    The word he speaketh none may read:
    Before his eyes the Day is torn
        With darkness and the Night is blind.

    All. And, O Light of the Great Cavern, let it be
That this Man's house look up again, and see,
    Till the dead veil of scorn
    And long darkness shall be torn,
And the kind faces shine and old Argolis be free!

[*Strophe*

    Then, then the prison shall unclose:
        A wind of Freedom stream above:
    A flood which faileth not, a voice
    Telling of women that rejoice,
    One harp in many souls, one spell
    Enchanted. Ho, the ship goes well!
    For me, for me, this glory grows.
        And Evil flies from those I love.

    All. Oh, in courage and in power,
    When the deed comes and the hour,
    As she crieth to thee "Son"
        Let thy "Father" quell her breath!
    But a stroke and it is done,
        The unblamèd deed of death.

[*Antistrophe*

    The heart of Perseus, darkly strong,
        Be lifted in thy breast to-day:

[170]

Electra.   Oh, friend! More than friend!
Living or dead?
Orestes.   He lives; so let me send
My comfort foremost, ere the rest be heard.
Electra. God love thee for the sweetness of thy word!
Orestes. God love the twain of us, both thee and me.
Electra. He lives! Poor brother! In what land weareth he
His exile?
Orestes.   Not one region nor one lot
His wasted life hath trod.
Electra.   He lacketh not
For bread?
Orestes.   Bread hath he; but a man is weak
In exile.
Electra. What charge laid he on thee? Speak.
Orestes. To learn if thou still live, and how the storm,
Living, hath struck thee.
Electra.   That thou seest; this form
Wasted . . .
Orestes.   Yea, riven with the fire of woe.
I sigh to look on thee.
Electra.   My face; and, lo,
My temples of their ancient glory shorn.
Orestes. Methinks thy brother haunts thee, being forlorn;
Aye, and perchance thy father, whom they slew. . .
Electra. What should be nearer to me than those two?
Orestes. And what to him, thy brother, half so dear
As thou?
Electra.   His is a distant love, not near
At need.
Orestes.   But why this dwelling place, this life
Of loneliness?
Electra (*with sudden bitterness*). Stranger, I am a wife. . . .
O better dead!
Orestes.   That seals thy brother's doom!
What Prince of Argos . . . ?
Electra.   Not the man to whom
My father thought to give me.
Orestes.   Speak; that I
May tell thy brother all.

[223]

Electra.   'Tis there, hard by,
His dwelling, where I live, far from men's eyes.

  Orestes. Some ditcher's cot, or cowherd's, by its guise!

  Electra (*struck with shame for her ingratitude*).
A poor man; but true-hearted, and to me
God-fearing.

  Orestes.   How? What fear of God hath he?

  Electra. He hath never held my body to his own.

  Orestes. Hath he some vow to keep? Or is it done
To scorn thee?

  Electra.   Nay; he only scorns to sin
Against my father's greatness.

  Orestes.   But to win
A princess! Doth his heart not leap for pride?

  Electra. He honoureth not the hand that gave the bride.

  Orestes. I see. He trembles for Orestes' wrath?

  Electra. Aye, that would move him. But beside, he hath
A gentle heart.

  Orestes.   Strange! A good man. . . , I swear
He well shall be requited.

  Electra.   Whensoe'er
Our wanderer comes again!

  Orestes.   Thy mother stays
Unmoved 'mid all thy wrong?

  Electra.   A lover weighs
More than a child in any woman's heart.

  Orestes. But what end seeks Aegisthus, by such art
Of shame?

  Electra.   To make mine unborn children low
And weak, even as my husband.

  Orestes.   Lest there grow
From thee the avenger?

  Electra.   Such his purpose is:
For which may I requite him!

  Orestes.   And of this
Thy virgin life—Aegisthus knows it?

  Electra.   Nay,
We speak it not. It cometh not his way.

  Orestes. These women hear us. Are they friends to thee?

  Electra. Aye, friends and true. They will keep faithfully

All words of mine and thine.

    Orestes (*trying her*).   Thou art well stayed
With friends. And could Orestes give thee aid
In aught, if e'er . . .

    Electra.   Shame on thee! Seest thou not?
Is it not time?

    Orestes (*catching her excitement*).   How time? And if
      he sought
To slay, how should he come at his desire?

    Electra. By daring, as they dared who slew his sire!

    Orestes. Wouldst thou dare with him, if he came, thou too,
To slay her?

    Electra.   Yes; with the same axe that slew
My father!

    Orestes.   'Tis thy message? And thy mood
Unchanging?

    Electra.   Let me shed my mother's blood,
And I die happy.

    Orestes.   God! . . . I would that now
Orestes heard thee here.

    Electra.   Yet, wottest thou,
Though here I saw him, I should know him not.

    Orestes. Surely. Ye both were children, when they wrought
Your parting.

    Electra.   One alone in all this land
Would know his face.

    Orestes.   The thrall, methinks, whose hand
Stole him from death—or so the story ran?

    Electra. He taught my father, too, an old old man
Of other days than these.

    Orestes.   Thy father's grave . . .
He had due rites and tendance?

    Electra.   What chance gave,
My father had, cast out to rot in the sun.

    Orestes. God, 'tis too much! . . . To hear of such things done
Even to a stranger, stings a man. . . . But speak,
Tell of thy life, that I may know, and seek
Thy brother with a tale that must be heard
Howe'er it sicken. If mine eyes be blurred,
Remember, 'tis the fool that feels not. Aye,

[225]

EURIPIDES

Wisdom is full of pity; and thereby
Men pay for too much wisdom with much pain.

    Leader. My heart is moved as this man's. I would fain
Learn all thy tale. Here dwelling on the hills
Little I know of Argos and its ills.

    Electra. If I must speak—and at love's call, God knows,
I fear not—I will tell thee all; my woes,
My father's woes, and—O, since thou hast stirred
This storm of speech, thou bear him this my word—
His woes and shame! Tell of this narrow cloak
In the wind; this grime and reek of toil, that choke
My breathing; this low roof that bows my head
After a king's. This raiment . . . thread by thread,
'Tis I must weave it, or go bare—must bring,
Myself, each jar of water from the spring.
No holy day for me, no festival,
No dance upon the green! From all, from all
I am cut off. No portion hath my life
'Mid wives of Argos, being no true wife.
No portion where the maidens throng to praise
Castor—my Castor, whom in ancient days,
Ere he passed from us and men worshipped him,
They named my bridegroom!—

                  And she, she! . . . The grim
Troy spoils gleam round her throne, and by each hand
Queens of the East, my father's prisoners, stand,
A cloud of Orient webs and tangling gold.
And there upon the floor, the blood, the old
Black blood, yet crawls and cankers, like a rot
In the stone! And on our father's chariot
The murderer's foot stands glorying, and the red
False hand uplifts that ancient staff, that led
The armies of the world! . . . Aye, tell him how
The grave of Agamemnon, even now,
Lacketh the common honour of the dead;
A desert barrow, where no tears are shed,
No tresses hung, no gift, no myrtle spray.
And when the wine is in him, so men say,
Our mother's mighty master leaps thereon,
Spurning the slab, or pelteth stone on stone,

[226]

Flouting the lone dead and the twain that live:
"Where is thy son Orestes? Doth he give
Thy tomb good tendance? Or is all forgot?"
So is he scorned because he cometh not. . . .
   O stranger, on my knees, I charge thee, tell
This tale, not mine, but of dumb wrongs that swell
Crowding—and I the trumpet of their pain,
This tongue, these arms, this bitter burning brain;
These dead shorn locks, and he for whom they died!
His father slew Troy's thousands in their pride:
He hath but one to kill. . . . O God, but one!
Is he a man, and Agamemnon's son?

   Leader. But hold: is this thy husband from the plain,
His labour ended, hasting home again?

                             [*Enter the* PEASANT.

   Peasant. Ha, who be these? Strange men in arms before
My house! What would they at this lonely door?
Seek they for me?—Strange gallants should not stay
A woman's going.

   Electra.   Friend and helper!—Nay,
Think not of any evil. These men be
Friends of Orestes, charged with words for me! . . .
Strangers, forgive his speech.

   Peasant.   What word have they
Of him? At least he lives and sees the day?

   Electra. So fares their tale—and sure I doubt it not!

   Peasant. And ye two still are living in his thought,
Thou and his father?

   Electra.   In his dreams we live.
An exile hath small power.

   Peasant.   And did he give
Some privy message?

   Electra.   None: they come as spies
For news of me.

   Peasant.   Thine outward news their eyes
Can see; the rest, methinks, thyself will tell.

   Electra. They have seen all, heard all. I trust them well.

   Peasant. Why were our doors not open long ago?
Be welcome, strangers both, and pass below
My lintel. In return for your glad words

Be sure all greeting that mine house affords
Is yours.—Ye followers, bear in their gear!—
Gainsay me not; for his sake are ye dear
That sent you to our house; and though my part
In life be low, I am no churl at heart.

> [*The* PEASANT *goes to the* ARMED SERVANTS *at
> the back, to help them with the baggage.*

Orestes (*aside to Electra*). Is this the man that shields thy
    maidenhood
Unknown, and will not wrong thy father's blood?

    Electra. He is called my husband. 'Tis for him I toil.

    Orestes. How dark lies honour hid! And what turmoil
In all things human: sons of mighty men
Fallen to naught, and from ill seed again
Good fruit: yea, famine in the rich man's scroll
Writ deep, and in poor flesh a lordly soul.
As, lo, this man, not great in Argos, not
With pride of house uplifted, in a lot
Of unmarked life hath shown a prince's grace.

> [*To the* PEASANT, *who has returned.*

All that is here of Agamemnon's race,
And all that lacketh yet, for whom we come,
Do thank thee, and the welcome of thy home
Accept with gladness.—Ho, men; hasten ye
Within!—This open-hearted poverty
Is blither to my sense than feasts of gold.

    Lady, thine husband's welcome makes me bold;
Yet would thou hadst thy brother, before all
Confessed, to greet us in a prince's hall!
Which may be, even yet. Apollo spake
The word; and surely, though small store I make
Of man's divining, God will fail us not.

> [ORESTES *and* PYLADES *go in, following the*
> SERVANTS.

    Leader. O never was the heart of hope so hot
Within me. How? So moveless in time past,
Hath Fortune girded up her loins at last?

    Electra. Now know'st thou not thine own ill furniture,
To bid these strangers in, to whom for sure
Our best were hardship, men of gentle breed?

[228]

Peasant. Nay, if the men be gentle, as indeed
I deem them, they will take good cheer or ill
With even kindness.

Electra.   'Twas ill done; but still—
Go, since so poor thou art, to that old friend
Who reared my father. At the realm's last end
He dwells, where Tanaos river foams between
Argos and Sparta. Long time hath he been
An exile 'mid his flocks. Tell him what thing
Hath chanced on me, and bid him haste and bring
Meat for the strangers' tending.—Glad, I trow,
That old man's heart will be, and many a vow
Will lift to God, to learn the child he stole
From death, yet breathes.—I will not ask a dole
From home; how should my mother help me? Nay,
I pity him that seeks that door, to say
Orestes liveth!

Peasant.   Wilt thou have it so?
I will take word to the old man. But go
Quickly within, and whatso there thou find
Set out for them. A woman, if her mind
So turn, can light on many a pleasant thing
To fill her board. And surely plenishing
We have for this one day.—'Tis in such shifts
As these, I care for riches, to make gifts
To friends, or lead a sick man back to health
With ease and plenty. Else small aid is wealth
For daily gladness; once a man be done
With hunger, rich and poor are all as one.

> [*The* PEASANT *goes off to the left;* ELECTRA *goes
> into the house.*

> [*Strophe.*

Chorus. O for the ships of Troy, the beat
            Of oars that shimmered
      Innumerable, and dancing feet
            Of Nereids glimmered;
      And dolphins, drunken with the lyre,
      Across the dark blue prows, like fire,
            Did bound and quiver,
      To cleave the way for Thetis' son,

Fleet-in-the-wind Achilles, on
To war, to war, till Troy be won
    Beside the reedy river.

[Antistrophe.

Up from Eubœa's caverns came
    The Nereids, bearing
Gold armour from the Lords of Flame,
    Wrought for his wearing:
Long sought those daughters of the deep,
Up Pelion's glen, up Ossa's steep
    Forest enchanted,
Where Peleus reared alone, afar,
His lost sea-maiden's child, the star
Of Hellas, and swift help of war
    When weary armies panted.

[Strophe.

There came a man from Troy, and told
    Here in the haven,
How, orb on orb, to strike with cold
The Trojan, o'er that targe of gold,
    Dread shapes were graven.
All round the level rim thereof
Perseus, on wingèd feet, above
    The long seas hied him;
The Gorgon's wild and bleeding hair
He lifted; and a herald fair,
He of the wilds, whom Maia bare,
    God's Hermes, flew beside him.

[Antistrophe.

But midmost, where the boss rose higher,
    A sun stood blazing,
And wingèd steeds, and stars in choir,
Hyad and Pleiad, fire on fire,
    For Hector's dazing:
Across the golden helm, each way,
Two taloned Sphinxes held their prey,
    Song-drawn to slaughter:
And round the breastplate ramping came
A mingled breed of lion and flame,

Hot-eyed to tear that steed of fame
    That found Pirene's water.

The red red sword with steeds four-yoked   *[Epode.*
    Black-maned, was graven,
That laboured, and the hot dust smoked
    Cloudwise to heaven.
Thou Tyndarid woman! Fair and tall
Those warriors were, and o'er them all
    One king great-hearted,
Whom thou and thy false love did slay:
Therefore the tribes of Heaven one day
For these thy dead shall send on thee
An iron death: yea, men shall see
The white throat drawn, and blood's red spray,
    And lips in terror parted.

    *[As they cease, there enters from the left a very old
    man, bearing a lamb, a wineskin, and a wallet.*
Old Man. Where is my little Princess? Ah, not now;
But still my queen, who tended long ago
The lad that was her father. . . . How steep-set
These last steps to her porch! But faint not yet:
Onward, ye failing knees and back with pain
Bowed, till we look on that dear face again.
                        [Enter ELECTRA.
Ah, daughter, is it thou?—Lo, here I am,
With gifts from all my store; this suckling lamb
Fresh from the ewe, green crowns for joyfulness,
And creamy things new-curdled from the press.
And this long-storèd juice of vintages
Forgotten, cased in fragrance: scant it is,
But passing sweet to mingle nectar-wise
With feebler wine.—Go, bear them in; mine eyes . . .
Where is my cloak?—They are all blurred with tears.
    Electra. What ails thine eyes, old friend? After these years
Doth my low plight still stir thy memories?
Or think'st thou of Orestes, where he lies
In exile, and my father? Aye, long love
Thou gavest him, and seest the fruit thereof
Wasted, for thee and all who love thee!

Old Man.   All

Wasted! And yet 'tis that lost hope withal
I cannot brook. But now I turned aside
To see my master's grave. All, far and wide,
Was silence; so I bent these knees of mine
And wept and poured drink-offerings from the wine
I bear the strangers, and about the stone
Laid myrtle sprays. And, child, I saw thereon
Just at the censer slain, a fleecèd ewe,
Deep black, in sacrifice: the blood was new
About it: and a tress of bright brown hair
Shorn as in mourning, close. Long stood I there
And wondered, of all men what man had gone
In mourning to that grave.—My child, 'tis none
In Argos. Did there come . . . Nay, mark me now . . .
Thy brother in the dark, last night, to bow
His head before that unadorèd tomb?

   O come, and mark the colour of it. Come
And lay thine own hair by that mourner's tress!
A hundred little things make likenesses
In brethren born, and show the father's blood.

   Electra (*trying to mask her excitement and resist the contagion of his*). Old heart, old heart, is this a wise man's
      mood? . . .

O, not in darkness, not in fear of men,
Shall Argos find him, when he comes again,
Mine own undaunted . . . Nay, and if it were,
What likeness could there be? My brother's hair
Is as a prince's and a rover's, strong
With sunlight and with strife: not like the long
Locks that a woman combs. . . . And many a head
Hath this same semblance, wing for wing, tho' bred
Of blood not ours. . . . 'Tis hopeless. Peace, old man.

   Old Man. The footprints! Set thy foot by his, and scan
The track of frame and muscles, how they fit!

   Electra. That ground will take no footprint! All of it
Is bitter stone. . . . It hath? . . . And who hath said
There should be likeness in a brother's tread
And sister's? His is stronger every way.

   Old Man. But hast thou nothing . . . ? If he came this day

And sought to show thee, is there no one sign
Whereby to know him? . . . Stay; the robe was thine,
'Work of thy loom, wherein I wrapt him o'er
That night, and stole him through the murderers' door.

Electra. Thou knowest, when Orestes was cast out
I was a child. . . . If I did weave some clout
Of raiment, would he keep the vesture now
He wore in childhood? Should my weaving grow
As his limbs grew? . . . 'Tis lost long since. No more!
O, either 'twas some stranger passed, and shore
His locks for very ruth before that tomb:
Or, if he found perchance, to seek his home,
Some spy . . .

Old Man. The strangers! Where are they? I fain
Would see them, aye, and bid them answer plain . . .

Electra. Here at the door! How swift upon the thought!

[*Enter* ORESTES *and* PYLADES.

Old Man. High-born: albeit for that I trust them not.
The highest oft are false. . . . Howe'er it be,

[*Approaching them.*

I bid thee strangers hail!

Orestes.   All hail to thee,
Greybeard!—Prithee, what man of all the King
Trusted of old, is now this broken thing?

Electra. 'Tis he that trained my father's boyhood.

Orestes.   How?
And stole from death thy brother? Sayest thou?

Electra. This man was his deliverer, if it be
Deliverance.

Orestes.   How his old eye pierceth me,
As one that testeth silver and alloy!
Sees he some likeness here?

Electra.   Perchance 'tis joy,
To see Orestes' comrade, that he feels.

Orestes. None dearer.—But what ails the man? He reels
Dizzily back.

Electra.   I marvel. I can say
No more.

Old Man (*in a broken voice*). Electra, mistress, daughter,
      pray!

[233]

Pray unto God!

Electra.   Of all the things I crave,
The thousand things, or all that others have,
What should I pray for?

Old Man.   Pray thine arms may hold
At last this treasure-dream of more than gold
God shows us!

Electra. God, I pray thee! . . . Wouldst thou more?

Old Man. Gaze now upon this man, and bow before
Thy dearest upon earth!

Electra.   I gaze on thee!
O, hath time made thee mad?

Old Man.   Mad, that I see
Thy brother?

Electra.   My . . . I know not what thou say'st:
I looked not for it . . .

Old Man.   I tell thee, here confessed
Standeth Orestes, Agamemnon's son!

Electra. A sign before I trust thee! O, but one!
How dost thou know . . . ?

Old Man.   There, by his brow, I see
The scar he made, that day he ran with thee
Chasing thy fawn, and fell.

Electra (*in a dull voice*).   A scar? 'Tis so.
I see a scar.

Old Man.   And fearest still to throw
Thine arms round him thou lovest?

Electra.   O, no more!
Thy sign hath conquered me. . . . (*throwing herself into*
Orestes' *arms*).   At last, at last!
Thy face like light! And do I hold thee fast,
Unhoped for?

Orestes.   Yea, at last! And I hold thee.

Electra. I never knew . . .

Orestes.   I dreamed not.

Electra.   Is it he,
Orestes?

Orestes.   Thy defender, yea, alone
To fight the world! Lo, this day have I thrown
A net, which once unbroken from the sea

Drawn home, shall . . . O, and it must surely be!
Else men shall know there is no God, no light
In Heaven, if wrong to the end shall conquer right.

   Chorus.   Comest thou, comest thou now,
              Chained by the years and slow,
                 O Day long sought?
              A light on the mountains cold
              Is lit, yea, a fire burneth.
              'Tis the light of one that turneth
              From roamings manifold,
              Back out of exile old
                 To the house that knew him not.

              Some spirit hath turned our way,
                Victory visible,
              Walking at thy right hand,
              Belovèd; O lift this day
              Thine arms, thy voice, as a spell;
              And pray for thy brother, pray,
              Threading the perilous land,
                 That all be well!

  Orestes. Enough; this dear delight is mine at last
Of thine embracing; and the hour comes fast
When we shall stand again as now we stand,
And stint not.—Stay, Old Man: thou, being at hand
At the edge of time, advise me, by what way
Best to requite my father's murderers. Say,
Have I in Argos any still to trust;
Or is the love, once borne me, trod in dust,
Even as my fortunes are? Whom shall I seek?
By day or night? And whither turn, to wreak
My will on them that hate us? Say.

  Old Man.   My son,
In thine adversity, there is not one
Will call thee friend. Nay, that were treasure-trove,
A friend to share, not faltering from love,
Fair days and foul the same. Thy name is gone
Forth to all Argos, as a thing o'erthrown
And dead. Thou hast not left one spark to glow
With hope in one friend's heart! Hear all, and know:

Thou hast God's fortune and thine own right hand,
Naught else, to conquer back thy fatherland.

 Orestes. The deed, the deed! What must we do?

 Old Man.   Strike down
Aegisthus . . . and thy mother.

 Orestes.   'Tis the crown
My race is run for. But how find him?

 Old Man.   Not
Within the city walls, however hot
Thy spirit.

 Orestes.   Ha! With watchers doth he go
Begirt, and mailèd pikemen?

 Old Man.   Even so:
He lives in fear of thee, and night nor day
Hath slumber.

 Orestes.   That way blocked!—'Tis thine to say
What next remains.

 Old Man.   I will; and thou give ear.
A thought has found me!

 Orestes.   All good thoughts be near,
For thee to speak and me to understand!

 Old Man. But now I saw Aegisthus, close at hand
As here I journeyed.

 Orestes.   That good word shall trace
My path for me! Thou saw'st him? In what place?

 Old Man. Out on the pastures where his horses stray.

 Orestes. What did he there so far?—A gleam of day
Crosseth our darkness.

 Old Man.   'Twas a feast, methought,
Of worship to the wild-wood nymphs he wrought.

 Orestes. The watchers of men's birth? Is there a son
New born to him, or doth he pray for one
That cometh?   [*Movement of* ELECTRA.

 Old Man.   More I know not; he had there
A wreathèd ox, as for some weighty prayer.

 Orestes. What force was with him? Not his serfs alone?

 Old Man. No Argive lord was there; none but his own
Household.

 Orestes.   Not any that might know my race,
Or guess?

Old Man. Thralls, thralls; who ne'er have seen thy
face.

Orestes. Once I prevail, the thralls will welcome me!

Old Man. The slaves' way, that; and no ill thing for thee!

Orestes. How can I once come near him?

Old Man. Walk thy ways
Hard by, where he may see thee, ere he slays
His sacrifice.

Orestes. How? Is the road so nigh?

Old Man. He cannot choose but see thee, passing by,
And bid thee stay to share the beast they kill.

Orestes. A bitter fellow-feaster, if God will!

Old Man. And then . . . then swift be heart and brain, to
see
God's chances!

Orestes. Aye. Well hast thou counselled me.
But . . . where is she?

Old Man. In Argos now, I guess;
But goes to join her husband, ere the press
Of the feast.

Orestes. Why goeth not my mother straight
Forth at her husband's side?

Old Man. She fain will wait
Until the gathered country-folk be gone.

Orestes. Enough! She knows what eyes are turned upon
Her passings in the land!

Old Man. Aye, all men hate
The unholy woman.

Orestes. How then can I set
My snare for wife and husband in one breath?

Electra (*coming forward*). Hold! It is I must work our
mother's death.

Orestes. If that be done, I think the other deed
Fortune will guide.

Electra. This man must help our need,
One friend alone for both.

Old Man. He will, he will!
Speak on. What cunning hast thou found to fill
Thy purpose?

Electra. Get thee forth, Old Man, and quick

Tell Clytemnestra . . . tell her I lie sick,
New-mothered of a man-child.

Old Man.   Thou hast borne
A son! But when?

    Electra. Let this be the tenth morn.
Till then a mother stays in sanctity,
Unseen.

    Old Man.   And if I tell her, where shall be
The death in this?

    Electra.   That word let her but hear,
Straight she will seek me out!

    Old Man.   The queen! What care
Hath she for thee, or pain of thine?

    Electra.   She will;
And weep my babe's low station!

    Old Man.   Thou hast skill
To know her, child; say on.

    Electra.   But bring her here,
Here to my hand; the rest will come.

    Old Man.   I swear,
Here at the gate she shall stand palpable!

    Electra. The gate: the gate that leads to me and Hell.

    Old Man. Let me but see it, and I die content.

    Electra. First, then, my brother: see his steps be bent . . .

    Old Man. Straight yonder where Aegisthus makes his
       prayer!

    Electra. Then seek my mother's presence, and declare
My news.

    Old Man. Thy very words, child, as tho' spoke
From thine own lips!

    Electra.   Brother, thine hour is struck.
Thou standest in the van of war this day.

    Orestes (*rousing himself*). Aye, I am ready. . . . I will go
      my way,
If but some man will guide me.

    Old Man.   Here am I,
To speed thee to the end, right thankfully.

    Orestes (*turning as he goes and raising his hands to heaven*).
Zeus of my sires, Zeus of the lost battle,

    Electra. Have pity; have pity; we have earned it well!

Old Man. Pity these twain, of thine own body sprung!
Electra. O Queen o'er Argive altars, Hera high,
Orestes. Grant us thy strength, if for the right we cry.
Old Man. Strength to these twain, to right their father's
    wrong!
Electra. O Earth, deep Earth, to whom I yearn in vain,
Orestes. And deeper thou, O father darkly slain,
Old Man. Thy children call, who love thee: hearken thou!
Orestes. Girt with thine own dead armies, wake, O wake!
Electra. With all that died at Ilion for thy sake . . .
Old Man. And hate earth's dark defilers; help us now!
Electra. Dost hear us yet, O thou in deadly wrong,
Wronged by my mother?
Old Man.   Child, we stay too long.
He hears; be sure he hears!
    Electra.   And while he hears,
I speak this word for omen in his ears:
"Aegisthus dies, Aegisthus dies." . . . Ah me,
My brother, should it strike not him, but thee,
This wrestling with dark death, behold, I too
Am dead that hour. Think of me as one true,
Not one that lives. I have a sword made keen
For this, and shall strike deep.
                        I will go in
And make all ready. If there come from thee
Good tidings, all my house for ecstasy
Shall cry; and if we hear that thou art dead,
Then comes the other end!—Lo, I have said.
    Orestes. I know all, all.
    Electra.   Then be a man to-day!
                [ORESTES *and the* OLD MAN *depart.*
O Women, let your voices from this fray
Flash me a fiery signal, where I sit,
The sword across my knees, expecting it.
For never, though they kill me, shall they touch
My living limbs!—I know my way thus much.
                        [*She goes into the house.*
    Chorus. When white-haired folk are met [*Strophe.*
                In Argos about the fold,
            A story lingereth yet,

[239]

A voice of the mountains old,
    That tells of the Lamb of Gold:
A lamb from a mother mild,
    But the gold of it curled and beat;
And Pan, who holdeth the keys of the wild,
    Bore it to Atreus' feet:
His wild reed pipes he blew,
    And the reeds were filled with peace,
And a joy of singing before him flew,
    Over the fiery fleece:
And up on the basèd rock,
    As a herald cries, cried he:
"Gather ye, gather, O Argive folk,
    The King's Sign to see,
The sign of the blest of God,
    For he that hath this, hath all!"
Therefore the dance of praise they trod
    In the Atreïd brethren's hall.

                        [Antistrophe.

They opened before men's eyes
    That which was hid before,
The chambers of sacrifice,
    The dark of the golden door,
    And fires on the altar floor.
And bright was every street,
    And the voice of the Muses' tree,
The carven lotus, was lifted sweet;
    When afar and suddenly,
Strange songs, and a voice that grew:
    "Come to your king, ye folk!
Mine, mine, is the Golden Ewe!"
    'Twas dark Thyestes spoke.
For, lo, when the world was still,
    With his brother's bride he lay,
And won her to work his will,
    And they stole the Lamb away!
Then forth to the folk strode he,
    And called them about his fold,
And showed that Sign of the King to be,
    The fleece and the horns of gold.

[240]

Then, then, the world was changed;
  And the Father, where they ranged,
Shook the golden stars and glowing,
  And the great Sun stood deranged
In the glory of his going.

  Lo, from that day forth, the East
  Bears the sunrise on his breast,
And the flaming Day in heaven
  Down the dim ways of the West
Driveth, to be lost at even.

  The wet clouds to Northward beat;
  And Lord Ammon's desert seat
Crieth from the South, unslaken,
  For the dews that once were sweet,
For the rain that God hath taken.   [*Antistrophe.*

  'Tis a children's tale, that old
  Shepherds on far hills have told;
And we reck not of their telling,
  Deem not that the Sun of gold
Ever turned his fiery dwelling,

  Or beat backward in the sky,
  For the wrongs of man, the cry
Of his ailing tribes assembled,
  To do justly, ere they die!
Once, men told the tale, and trembled;

  Fearing God, O Queen: whom thou
  Hast forgotten, till thy brow
With old blood is dark and daunted.
  And thy brethren, even now,[2]
Walk among the stars, enchanted.

Leader. Ha, friends, was that a voice? Or some dream
    sound
Of voices shaketh me, as underground
God's thunder shuddering? Hark, again, and clear!
It swells upon the wind.—Come forth and hear!
Mistress, Electra!

          [ELECTRA, *a bare sword in her hand, comes
              from the house.*

Electra.   Friends!   Some news is brought?
How hath the battle ended?
    Leader.   I know naught.
There seemed a cry as of men massacred!
    Electra. I heard it too. Far off, but still I heard.
    Leader. A distant floating voice . . . Ah, plainer now!
    Electra. Of Argive anguish!—Brother, is it thou?
    Leader. I know not. Many confused voices cry . . .
    Electra. Death, then for me! That answer bids me die.
    Leader. Nay, wait! We know not yet thy fortune. Wait!
    Electra. No messenger from him!—Too late, too late!
    Leader. The message yet will come. 'Tis not a thing
So light of compass, to strike down a king.

                          [*Enter a* MESSENGER, *running.*
    Messenger. Victory, Maids of Argos, Victory!
Orestes . . . all that love him, list to me! . . .
Hath conquered! Agamemnon's murderer lies
Dead! O give thanks to God with happy cries!
    Electra. Who art thou? I mistrust thee. . . . 'Tis a plot!
    Messenger. Thy brother's man. Look well. Dost know me
      not?
    Electra. Friend, friend; my terror made me not to see
Thy visage. Now I know and welcome thee.
How sayst thou? He is dead, verily dead,
My father's murderer . . . ?
    Messenger.   Shall it be said
Once more? I know again and yet again
Thy heart would hear. Aegisthus lieth slain!
    Electra. Ye Gods! And thou, O Right, that seest all,
Art come at last? . . . But speak; how did he fall?
How swooped the wing of death? . . . I crave to hear.
    Messenger. Forth of this hut we set our faces clear
To the world, and struck the open chariot road;
Then on toward the pasture lands, where stood
The great Lord of Mycenae. In a set
Garden beside a channelled rivulet,
Culling a myrtle garland for his brow,
He walked: but hailed us as we passed: "How now,
Strangers! Who are ye? Of what city sprung,
And whither bound?" "Thessalians," answered young

[242]

Orestes: "to Alpheüs journeying,
With gifts to Olympian Zeus." Whereat the King:
"This while, beseech you, tarry, and make full
The feast upon my hearth. We slay a bull
Here to the Nymphs. Set forth at break of day
To-morrow, and 'twill cost you no delay.
But come"—and so he gave his hand, and led
The two men in——"I must not be gainsaid;
Come to the house. Ho, there; set close at hand
Vats of pure water, that the guests may stand
At the altar's verge, where falls the holy spray."
Then quickly spake Orestes: "By the way
We cleansed us in a torrent stream. We need
No purifying here. But if indeed
Strangers may share thy worship, here are we
Ready, O King, and swift to follow thee."
 So spoke they in the midst. And every thrall
Laid down the spears they served the King withal,
And hied him to the work. Some bore amain
The death-vat, some the corbs of hallowed grain;
Or kindled fire, and round the fire and in
Set cauldrons foaming; and a festal din
Filled all the place. Then took thy mother's lord
The ritual grains, and o'er the altar poured
Its due, and prayed: "O Nymphs of Rock and Mere,
With many a sacrifice for many a year,
May I and she who waits at home for me,
My Tyndarid Queen, adore you. May it be
Peace with us always, even as now; and all
Ill to mine enemies"—meaning withal
Thee and Orestes. Then my master prayed
Against that prayer, but silently, and said
No word, to win once more his fatherland.
Then in the corb Aegisthus set his hand,
Took the straight blade, cut from the proud bull's head
A lock, and laid it where the fire was red;
Then, while the young men held the bull on high,
Slew it with one clean gash; and suddenly
Turned on thy brother: "Stranger, every true
Thessalian, so the story goes, can hew

A bull's limbs clean, and tame a mountain steed.
Take up the steel, and show us if indeed
Rumour speak true." Right swift Orestes took
The Dorian blade, back from his shoulders shook
His brochèd mantle, called on Pylades
To aid him, and waved back the thralls. With ease
Heelwise he held the bull, and with one glide
Bared the white limb; then stripped the mighty hide
From off him, swifter than a runner runs
His furlongs, and laid clean the flank. At once
Aegisthus stooped, and lifted up with care
The ominous parts, and gazed. No lobe was there;
But lo, strange caves of gall, and, darkly raised,
The portal vein boded to him that gazed
Fell visitations. Dark as night his brow
Clouded. Then spake Orestes: "Why art thou
Cast down so sudden?" "Guest," he cried, "there be
Treasons from whence I know not, seeking me.
Of all my foes, 'tis Agamemnon's son;
His hate is on my house, like war." "Have done!"
Orestes cried: "thou fear'st an exile's plot,
Lord of a city? Make thy cold heart hot
With meat.—Ho, fling me a Thessalian steel!
This Dorian is too light. I will unseal
The breast of him." He took the heavier blade,
And clave the bone. And there Aegisthus stayed,
The omens in his hand, dividing slow
This sign from that; till, while his head bent low,
Up with a leap thy brother flashed the sword,
Then down upon his neck, and cleft the cord
Of brain and spine. Shuddering the body stood
One instant in an agony of blood,
And gasped and fell. The henchmen saw, and straight
Flew to their spears, a host of them to set
Against those twain. But there the twain did stand
Unfaltering, each his iron in his hand,
Edge fronting edge. Till "Hold," Orestes calls:
"I come not as in wrath against these walls
And mine own people. One man righteously
I have slain, who slew my father. It is I,

The wronged Orestes! Hold, and smite me not,
Old housefolk of my father!" When they caught
That name, their lances fell. And one old man,
An ancient in the house, drew nigh to scan
His face, and knew him. Then with one accord
They crowned thy brother's temples, and outpoured
Joy and loud songs.   And hither now he fares
To show the head, no Gorgon, that he bears,
But that Aegisthus whom thou hatest! Yea,
Blood against blood, his debt is paid this day.

        *[He goes off to meet the others—*ELECTRA *stands
           as though stupefied.*

Chorus. Now, now thou shalt dance in our dances,
    Beloved, as a fawn in the night!
The wind is astir for the glances
    Of thy feet; thou art robed with delight.
He hath conquered, he cometh to free us
      With garlands new-won,
More high than the crowns of Alpheüs,
      Thine own father's son:
    Cry, cry, for the day that is won!
Electra. O Light of the Sun, O chariot wheels of flame,
O Earth and Night, dead Night without a name
That held me! Now mine eyes are raised to see,
And all the doorways of my soul flung free.
Aegisthus dead! My father's murderer dead!
  What have I still of wreathing for the head
Stored in my chambers? Let it come forth now
To bind my brother's and my conqueror's brow.

        [Some garlands are brought out from the house to
          ELECTRA.

Chorus. Go, gather thy garlands, and lay them
    As a crown on his brow, many-tressed,
But our feet shall refrain not nor stay them:
    'Tis the joy that the Muses have blest.
For our king is returned as from prison,
      The old king, to be master again,
Our belovèd in justice re-risen:
      With guile he hath slain . . .
    But cry, cry in joyance again!

[*There enter from the left* ORESTES *and* PYLADES,
followed by some thralls.

Electra. O conqueror, come! The king that trampled Troy
Knoweth his son Orestes. Come in joy,
Brother, and take to bind thy rippling hair
My crowns! . . . O what are crowns, that runners wear
For some vain race? But thou in battle true
Hast felled our foe Aegisthus, him that slew
By craft thy sire and mine.   [*She crowns* ORESTES.
                                And thou no less,
O friend at need, O reared in righteousness,
Take, Pylades, this chaplet from my hand.
'Twas half thy battle. And may ye two stand
Thus alway, victory-crowned, before my face!
                                [*She crowns* PYLADES.

Orestes. Electra, first as workers of this grace
Praise thou the Gods, and after, if thou will,
Praise also me, as chosen to fulfil
God's work and Fate's.—Aye, 'tis no more a dream;
In very deed I come from slaying him.
Thou hast the knowledge clear, but lo, I bring
More also. See himself, dead!

          [*Attendants bring in the body of* AEGISTHUS *on a bier.*
                                Wouldst thou fling
This lord on the rotting earth for beasts to tear?
Or up, where all the vultures of the air
May glut them, pierce and nail him for a sign
Far off? Work all thy will. Now he is thine.

Electra. It shames me; yet, God knows, I hunger sore—

Orestes. What wouldst thou? Speak; the old fear nevermore
Need touch thee.

Electra.   To let loose upon the dead
My hate! Perchance to rouse on mine own head
The sleeping hate of the world?

Orestes.   No man that lives
Shall scathe thee by one word.

Electra.   Our city gives
Quick blame; and little love have men for me.

Orestes. If aught thou hast unsaid, sister, be free
And speak. Between this man and us no bar

Cometh nor stint, but the utter rage of war.

> [*She goes and stands over the body. A moment's silence.*

   Electra. Ah me, what have I? What first flood of hate
To loose upon thee? What last curse to sate
My pain, or river of wild words to flow
Bank-high between? . . . Nothing? . . . And yet I know
There hath not passed one sun, but through the long
Cold dawns, over and over, like a song,
I have said them—words held back, O, some day yet
To flash into thy face, would but the fret
Of ancient fear fall loose and let me free.
And free I am, now; and can pay to thee
At last the weary debt.

                  Oh, thou didst kill
My soul within. Who wrought thee any ill,
That thou shouldst make me fatherless? Aye, me
And this my brother, loveless, solitary?
'Twas thou, didst bend my mother to her shame:
Thy weak hand murdered him who led to fame
The hosts of Hellas—thou, that never crossed
O'erseas to Troy! . . . God help thee, wast thou lost
In blindness, long ago, dreaming, some-wise,
She would be true with thee, whose sin and lies
Thyself had tasted in my father's place?
And then, that thou wert happy, when thy days
Were all one pain? Thou knewest ceaselessly
Her kiss a thing unclean, and she knew thee
A lord so little true, so dearly won!
So lost ye both, being in falseness one,
What fortune else had granted; she thy curse,
Who marred thee as she loved thee, and thou hers . . .
And on thy ways thou heardst men whispering,
"Lo, the Queen's husband yonder"—not "the King."

   And then the lie of lies that dimmed thy brow,
Vaunting that by thy gold, thy chattels, Thou
Wert Something; which themselves are nothingness,
Shadows, to clasp a moment ere they cease.
The thing thou art, and not the things thou hast,
Abideth, yea, and bindeth to the last

Thy burden on thee: while all else, ill-won
And sin-companioned, like a flower o'erblown,
Flies on the wind away.

       Or didst thou find
In women . . . Women? . . . Nay, peace, peace! The blind
Could read thee. Cruel wast thou in thine hour,
Lord of a great king's house, and like a tower
Firm in thy beauty.   [*Starting back with a look of loathing.*
     Ah, that girl-like face!
God grant, not that, not that, but some plain grace
Of manhood to the man who brings me love:
A father of straight children, that shall move
Swift on the wings of War.

        So, get thee gone!
Naught knowing how the great years, rolling on,
Have laid thee bare, and thy long debt full paid.
 O vaunt not, if one step be proudly made
In evil, that all Justice is o'ercast:
Vaunt not, ye men of sin, ere at the last
The thin-drawn marge before you glimmereth
Close, and the goal that wheels 'twixt life and death.

 Leader. Justice is mighty. Passing dark hath been
His sin: and dark the payment of his sin.

 Electra (*with a weary sigh, turning from the body*). Ah me!
 Go some of you, bear him from sight,
That when my mother come, her eyes may light
On nothing, nothing, till she know the sword . . .

   [*The body is borne into the hut.* PYLADES *goes with it.*

 Orestes (*looking along the road*). Stay, 'tis a new thing!
 We have still a word
To speak . . .

 Electra.   What? Not a rescue from the town
Thou seëst?

 Orestes.   'Tis my mother comes: my own
Mother, that bare me.   [*He takes off his crown.*

 Electra (*springing, as it were, to life again, and moving
  where she can see the road*). Straight into the snare!
Aye, there she cometh.—Welcome in thy rare
Chariot! All welcome in thy brave array!

Orestes. What would we with our mother? Didst thou say
Kill her?

Electra (*turning on him*). What? Is it pity? Dost thou fear
To see thy mother's shape?

Orestes.   'Twas she that bare
My body into life. She gave me suck.
How can I strike her?

Electra.   Strike her as she struck
Our father!

Orestes (*to himself, brooding*). Phoebus, God, was all thy
    mind
Turned unto darkness?

Electra.   If thy God be blind,
Shalt thou have light?

Orestes (*as before*). Thou, thou, didst bid me kill
My mother: which is sin.

Electra.   How brings it ill
To thee, to raise our father from the dust?

Orestes. I was a clean man once. Shall I be thrust
From men's sight, blotted with her blood?

Electra.   Thy blot
Is black as death if him thou succour not!

Orestes. Who shall do judgement on me, when she dies?

Electra. Who shall do judgement, if thy father lies
Forgotten?

Orestes (*turning suddenly to* ELECTRA). Stay! How if some
    fiend of Hell,
Hid in God's likeness, spake that oracle?

Electra. In God's own house? I trow not.

Orestes.   And I trow
It was an evil charge!   [*He moves away from her.*

Electra (*almost despairing*). To fail me now!
To fail me now! A coward!—O brother, no!

Orestes. What shall it be, then? The same stealthy blow …

Electra. That slew our father! Courage! thou hast slain
Aegisthus.

Orestes.   Aye. So be it.—I have ta'en
A path of many terrors: and shall do
Deeds horrible. 'Tis God will have it so. . . .
Is this the joy of battle, or wild woe?

[*He goes into the House.*

Leader. O Queen o'er Argos thronèd high,
O Woman, sister of the twain,
God's Horsemen, stars without a stain,[3]
Whose home is in the deathless sky,
Whose glory in the sea's wild pain,
Toiling to succour men that die:
Long years above us hast thou been,
God-like for gold and marvelled power:
Ah, well may mortal eyes this hour
Observe thy state: All hail, O Queen!

[*Enter from the right* CLYTEMNESTRA *on a chariot, accompanied by richly dressed Handmaidens.*

Clytemnestra. Down from the wain, ye dames of Troy, and hold
Mine arm as I dismount. . . .

[*Answering* ELECTRA'S *thought.*
                              The spoils and gold
Of Ilion I have sent out of my hall
To many shrines. These bondwomen are all
I keep in mine own house . . . Deemst thou the cost
Too rich to pay me for the child I lost—
Fair though they be?

Electra.   Nay, Mother, here am I
Bond likewise, yea, and homeless, to hold high
Thy royal arm!

Clytemnestra. Child, the war-slaves are here;
Thou needst not toil.

                    Electra. What was it but the spear
Of war, drove me forth too? Mine enemies
Have sacked my father's house, and, even as these,
Captives and fatherless, made me their prey.

Clytemnestra. It was thy father cast his child away,[4]
A child he might have loved! . . . Shall I speak out?
(*Controlling herself*) Nay; when a woman once is caught about
With evil fame, there riseth in her tongue
A bitter spirit—wrong, I know! Yet, wrong
Or right, I charge ye look on the deeds done;
And if ye needs must hate, when all is known,

[250]

Hate on! What profits loathing ere ye know?
  My father gave me to be his. 'Tis so.
But was it his to kill me, or to kill
The babes I bore? Yet, lo, he tricked my will
With fables of Achilles' love: he bore
To Aulis and the dark ship-clutching shore,
He held above the altar-flame, and smote,
Cool as one reaping, through the strainèd throat,
My white Iphigenia. . . . Had it been
To save some falling city, leaguered in
With foemen; to prop up our castle towers,
And rescue other children that were ours,
Giving one life for many, by God's laws
I had forgiven all! Not so. Because
Helen was wanton, and her master knew
No curb for her: for that, for that, he slew
My daughter!—Even then, with all my wrong,
No wild beast yet was in me. Nay, for long,
I never would have killed him. But he came,
At last, bringing that damsel, with the flame
Of God about her, mad and knowing all:
And set her in my room; and in one wall
Would hold two queens!—O wild are woman's eyes
And hot her heart. I say not otherwise.
But, being thus wild, if then her master stray
To love far off, and cast his own away,
Shall not her will break prison too, and wend
Somewhere to win some other for a friend?
And then on us the world's curse waxes strong
In righteousness! The lords of all the wrong
Must hear no curse!—I slew him. I trod then
The only road: which led me to the men
He hated. Of the friends of Argos whom
Durst I have sought, to aid me to the doom
I craved?—Speak if thou wouldst, and fear not me,
If yet thou deemst him slain unrighteously.

  Leader. Thy words be just, yet shame their justice brings;
A woman true of heart should bear all things
From him she loves. And she who feels it not,
I cannot reason of her, nor speak aught.

Electra. Remember, Mother, thy last word of grace,
Bidding me speak, and fear not, to thy face.
    Clytemnestra. So said I truly, child, and so say still.
    Electra. Wilt softly hear, and after work me ill?
    Clytemnestra. Not so, not so. I will but pleasure thee.
    Electra. I answer then. And, Mother, this shall be
My prayer of opening, where hangs the whole:
Would God that He had made thee clean of soul!
Helen and thou—O, face and form were fair,
Meet for men's praise; but sisters twain ye were,
Both things of naught, a stain on Castor's star.
And Helen slew her honour, borne afar
In wilful ravishment: but thou didst slay
The highest man of the world. And now wilt say
'Twas wrought in justice for thy child laid low
At Aulis? . . . Ah, who knows thee as I know?
Thou, thou, who long ere aught of ill was done
Thy child, when Agamemnon scarce was gone,
Sate at the looking-glass, and tress by tress
Didst comb the twinèd gold in loneliness.
When any wife, her lord being far away,
Toils to be fair, O blot her out that day
As false within! What would she with a cheek
So bright in strange men's eyes, unless she seek
Some treason? None but I, thy child, could so
Watch thee in Hellas: none but I could know
Thy face of gladness when our enemies
Were strong, and the swift cloud upon thine eyes
If Troy seemed falling, all thy soul keen-set
Praying that he might come no more! . . . And yet
It was so easy to be true. A king
Was thine, not feebler, not in anything
Below Aegisthus; one whom Hellas chose
For chief beyond all kings. Aye, and God knows,
How sweet a name in Greece, after the sin
Thy sister wrought, lay in thy ways to win.
Ill deeds make fair ones shine, and turn thereto
Men's eyes.—Enough: but say he wronged thee; slew
By craft thy child:—what wrong had I done, what
The babe Orestes? Why didst render not

Back unto us, the children of the dead,
Our father's portion? Must thou heap thy bed
With gold of murdered men, to buy to thee
Thy strange man's arms? Justice! Why is not he
Who cast Orestes out, cast out again?
Not slain for me whom doubly he hath slain,
In living death, more bitter than of old
My sister's? Nay, when all the tale is told
Of blood for blood, what murder shall we make,
I and Orestes, for our father's sake?

Clytemnestra. Aye, child; I know thy heart, from long ago.
Thou hast alway loved him best. 'Tis oft-time so:
One is her father's daughter, and one hot
To bear her mother's part. I blame thee not . . .
Yet think not I am happy, child; nor flown
With pride now, in the deeds my hand hath done . . .

> [*Seeing* ELECTRA *unsympathetic, she checks herself.*

But thou art all untended, comfortless
Of body and wild of raiment; and thy stress
Of travail scarce yet ended! . . . Woe is me!
'Tis all as I have willed it. Bitterly
I wrought against him, to the last blind deep
Of bitterness. . . . Woe's me!

Electra.   Fair days to weep,
When help is not! Or stay: though he lie cold
Long since, there lives another of thy fold
Far off; there might be pity for thy son?

Clytemnestra. I dare not! . . Yes, I fear him. 'Tis mine own
Life, and not his, comes first. And rumour saith
His heart yet burneth for his father's death.

Electra. Why dost thou keep thine husband ever hot
Against me?

Clytemnestra. 'Tis his mood. And thou art not
So gentle, child!

Electra.   My spirit is too sore!
Howbeit, from this day I will no more
Hate him.

Clytemnestra (*with a flash of hope*). O daughter!—Then,
     indeed, shall he,
I promise, never more be harsh to thee!

Electra. He lieth in my house, as 'twere his own.
'Tis that hath made him proud.

Clytemnestra.   Nay, art thou flown
To strife again so quick, child?

Electra.   Well; I say
No more; long have I feared him, and alway
Shall fear him, even as now!

Clytemnestra.   Nay, daughter, peace!
It bringeth little profit, speech like this . . .
Why didst thou call me hither?

Electra.   It reached thee,
My word that a man-child is born to me?
Do thou make offerings for me—for the rite
I know not—as is meet on the tenth night.
I cannot; I have borne no child till now.

Clytemnestra. Who tended thee? 'Tis she should make the
    vow.

Electra. None tended me. Alone I bare my child.

Clytemnestra. What, is thy cot so friendless? And this wild
So far from aid?

Electra.   Who seeks for friendship sake
A beggar's house?

Clytemnestra.   I will go in, and make
Due worship for thy child, the Peace-bringer.
To all thy need I would be minister.
Then to my lord, where by the meadow side
He prays the woodland nymphs.

                    Ye handmaids, guide
My chariot to the stall, and when ye guess
The rite draws near its end, in readiness
Be here again. Then to my lord! . . . I owe
My lord this gladness, too.

          [*The Attendants depart;* Clytemnestra, *left alone,
               proceeds to enter the house.*

Electra.   Welcome below
My narrow roof! But have a care withal,
A grime of smoke lies deep upon the wall.
Soil not thy robe! . . .

                    Not far now shall it be,
The sacrifice God asks of me and thee.

[254]

The bread of Death is broken, and the knife
Lifted again that drank the Wild Bull's life:
And on his breast . . . Ha, Mother, hast slept well
Aforetime? Thou shalt lie with him in Hell.
That grace I give to cheer thee on thy road;
Give thou to me—peace from my father's blood!

[*She follows her mother into the house.*

Chorus. Lo, the returns of wrong.
            The wind as a changèd thing
        Whispereth overhead
        Of one that of old lay dead
        In the water lapping long:
            My King, O my King!

        A cry in the rafters then
            Rang, and the marble dome:
        "Mercy of God, not thou,
        "Woman! To slay me now,
        "After the harvests ten
            "Now, at the last, come home!"

        O fate shall turn as the tide,
            Turn, with a doom of tears
        For the flying heart too fond;
        A doom for the broken bond.
        She hailed him there in his pride,
            Home from the perilous years,

        In the heart of his wallèd lands,
            In the Giants' cloud-capt ring;[5]
        Herself, none other, laid
        The hone to the axe's blade;
        She lifted it in her hands,
            The woman, and slew her king.
        Woe upon spouse and spouse,

            Whatso of evil sway
        Held her in that distress!
        Even as a lioness
        Breaketh the woodland boughs
            Starving, she wrought her way.

[255]

Voice of Clytemnestra. O Children, Children; in the name of
      God,
Slay not your mother!
      A Woman.   Did ye hear a cry
Under the rafters?
      Another.   I weep too, yea, I;
Down on the mother's heart the child hath trod!
                                    [*A death-cry from within.*
      Another. God bringeth Justice in his own slow tide.
            Aye, cruel is thy doom; but thy deeds done
            Evil, thou piteous woman, and on one
                  Whose sleep was by thy side!
                  [*The doors burst open, and* ORESTES *and* ELECTRA
                        come forth in disorder. Attendants bring out the
                        bodies of CLYTEMNESTRA *and* AEGISTHUS.
      Leader. Lo, yonder, in their mother's new-spilt gore
            Red-garmented and ghastly, from the door
            They reel. . . . O horrible! Was it agony
            Like this, she boded in her last wild cry?
            There lives no seed of man calamitous,
            Nor hath lived, like this seed of Tantalus.
Orestes. O Dark of the Earth, O God,
                  Thou to whom all is plain;
            Look on my sin, my blood,
                  This horror of dead things twain:
            Gathered as one they lie
            Slain; and the slayer was I,
                  I, to pay for my pain!
Electra. Let tear rain upon tear,
                  Brother: but mine is the blame.
            A fire stood over her,
                  And out of the fire I came,
            I, in my misery. . . .
            And I was the child at her knee.
                  'Mother' I named her name.
Chorus.   Alas for Fate, for the Fate of thee,
            O Mother, Mother of Misery:
            And Misery, lo, hath turned again,
            To slay thee, Misery and more,
            Even in the fruit thy body bore.

Yet hast thou Justice, Justice plain,
    For a sire's blood spilt of yore!

Orestes. Apollo, alas for the hymn
      Thou sangest, as hope in mine ear!
The Song was of Justice dim,
    But the Deed is anguish clear;
And the Gift, long nights of fear,
    Of blood and of wandering,
      Where cometh no Greek thing,
Nor sight, nor sound on the air.
Yea, and beyond, beyond,
      Roaming—what rest is there?
Who shall break bread with me?
Who, that is clean, shall see
And hate not the blood-red hand,
    His mother's murderer?

Electra. And I? What clime shall hold
      My evil, or roof it above?
I cried for dancing of old,
    I cried in my heart for love:
What dancing waiteth me now?
What love that shall kiss my brow
    Nor blench at the brand thereof?

Chorus. Back, back, in the wind and rain
    Thy driven spirit wheeleth again.
Now is thine heart made clean within
That was dark of old and murder-fraught.
But, lo, thy brother; what hast thou wrought . . .
Yea, though I love thee . . . what woe, what sin,
    On him, who willed it not!

Orestes. Saw'st thou her raiment there,
      Sister, there in the blood?
      She drew it back as she stood,
    She opened her bosom bare,
      She bent her knees to the earth,
      The knees that bent in my birth . . .
    And I . . . Oh, her hair, her hair . . .
          [*He breaks into inarticulate weeping.*

Chorus. Oh, thou didst walk in agony,
      Hearing thy mother's cry, the cry

[257]

          Of wordless wailing, well know I.

Electra. She stretched her hand to my cheek,
        And there brake from her lips a moan;
      'Mercy, my child, my own!'
    Her hand clung to my cheek;
    Clung, and my arm was weak;
      And the sword fell and was gone.

Chorus. Unhappy woman, could thine eye
    Look on the blood, and see her lie,
    Thy mother, where she turned to die?

Orestes. I lifted over mine eyes
      My mantle: blinded I smote,
    As one smiteth a sacrifice;
      And the sword found her throat.

Electra. I gave thee the sign and the word;
    I touched with mine hand thy sword.

Leader.   Dire is the grief ye have wrought.

Orestes. Sister, touch her again:
      Oh, veil the body of her;
      Shed on her raiment fair,
    And close that death-red stain.
      Mother! And didst thou bear,
    Bear in thy bitter pain,
      To life, thy murderer?

    [*The two kneel over the body of* CLYTEMNESTRA,
      and cover her with raiment.

Electra. On her that I loved of yore,
      Robe upon robe I cast:
    On her that I hated sore.

Chorus. O House that hath hated sore,
      Behold thy peace at the last!

Leader. Ha, see: above the roof-tree high
      There shineth . . . Is some spirit there
      Of earth or heaven? That thin air
    Was never trod by things that die!
      What bodes it now that forth they fare,
    To men revealèd visibly?

      [*There appears in the air a vision of* CASTOR *and*
        POLYDEUCES. *The mortals kneel or veil*
        their faces.

Castor. Thou Agamemnon's Son, give ear! 'Tis we,
Castor and Polydeuces, call to thee,
God's Horsemen and thy mother's brethren twain.
An Argive ship, spent with the toiling main,
We bore but now to peace, and, here withal
Being come, have seen thy mother's bloody fall,
Our sister's. Righteous is her doom this day,
But not thy deed. And Phoebus, Phoebus . . . Nay;
He is my lord; therefore I hold my peace.
Yet though in light he dwell, no light was this
He showed to thee, but darkness! Which do thou
Endure, as man must, chafing not. And now
Fare forth where Zeus and Fate have laid thy life.

The maid Electra thou shalt give for wife
To Pylades; then turn thy head and flee
From Argos' land. 'Tis never more for thee
To tread this earth where thy dead mother lies.
And, lo, in the air her Spirits, bloodhound eyes,
Most horrible yet Godlike, hard at heel
Following shall scourge thee as a burning wheel,[6]
Speed-maddened. Seek thou straight Athena's land,
And round her awful image clasp thine hand,
Praying: and she will fence them back, though hot
With flickering serpents, that they touch thee not,
Holding above thy brow her gorgon shield.

There is a hill in Athens, Ares' field,
Where first for that first death by Ares done
On Halirrhothius, Poseidon's son,
Who wronged his daughter, the great Gods of yore
Held judgement: and true judgements evermore
Flow from that Hill, trusted of man and God.
There shalt thou stand arraignèd of this blood;
And of those judges half shall lay on thee
Death, and half pardon; so shalt thou go free.
For Phoebus in that hour, who bade thee shed
Thy mother's blood, shall take on his own head
The stain thereof. And ever from that strife
The law shall hold, that when, for death or life
Of one pursued, men's voices equal stand,
Then Mercy conquereth.—But for thee, the band

Of Spirits dread, down, down, in very wrath,
Shall sink beside that Hill, making their path
Through a dim chasm, the which shall aye be trod
By reverent feet, where men may speak with God.
But thou forgotten and far off shalt dwell,
By great Alpheüs waters, in a dell
Of Arcady, where that gray Wolf-God's wall
Stands holy. And thy dwelling men shall call
Orestes' Town. So much to thee be spoke.
But this dead man, Aegisthus, all the folk
Shall bear to burial in a high green grave
Of Argos. For thy mother, she shall have
Her tomb from Menelaus, who hath come
This day, at last, to Argos, bearing home
Helen. From Egypt comes she, and the hall
Of Proteus, and in Troy hath ne'er at all
Set foot. 'Twas but a wraith of Helen, sent
By Zeus, to make much wrath and ravishment.

So forth for home, bearing the virgin bride,
Let Pylades make speed, and lead beside
Thy once-named brother, and with golden store
Stablish his house far off on Phokis' shore.

Up, gird thee now to the steep Isthmian way,
Seeking Athena's blessèd rock; one day,
Thy doom of blood fulfilled and this long stress
Of penance past, thou shalt have happiness.

Leader (*looking up*). Is it for us, O Seed of Zeus,
       To speak and hear your words again?
Castor.   Speak: of this blood ye bear no stain.
Electra. I also, sons of Tyndareus,

       My kinsmen; may my word be said?
Castor.   Speak: on Apollo's head we lay
       The bloody doings of this day.
Leader. Ye Gods, ye brethren of the dead,

       Why held ye not the deathly herd
         Of Kêrês' back from off this home?
Castor.   There came but that which needs must come
       By ancient Fate and that dark word

       That rang from Phoebus in his mood.

Electra.   And what should Phoebus seek with me,
            Or all God's oracles that be,
          That I must bear my mother's blood?

Castor.   Thy hand was as thy brother's hand,
            Thy doom shall be as his. One stain,
            From dim forefathers on the twain
          Lighting, hath sapped your hearts as sand.

Orestes (*who has never raised his head, nor spoken to the
  Gods*). After so long, sister, to see
            And hold thee, and then part, then part,
            By all that chained thee to my heart
          Forsaken, and forsaking thee!

Castor.   Husband and house are hers. She bears
              No bitter judgement, save to go
              Exiled from Argos.
Electra.   And what woe,
          What tears are like an exile's tears?

Orestes. Exiled and more am I; impure,
              A murderer in a stranger's hand!
Castor.   Fear not. There dwells in Pallas' land
          All holiness. Till then endure!
                        [ORESTES *and* ELECTRA *embrace.*
Orestes. Aye, closer; clasp my body well,
              And let thy sorrow loose, and shed,
              As o'er the grave of one new dead,
          Dead evermore, thy last farewell!
                                    [*A sound of weeping.*
Castor.   Alas, what would ye? For that cry
              Ourselves and all the sons of heaven
              Have pity. Yea, our peace is riven
          By the strange pain of these that die.

Orestes. No more to see thee! *Electra.* Nor thy breath
              Be near my face! *Orestes.* Ah, so it ends.
Electra.   Farewell, dear Argos. All ye friends,
          Farewell! *Orestes.* O faithful unto death,

[261]

Thou goest? *Electra.* Aye, I pass from you,
   Soft-eyed at last. *Orestes.* Go, Pylades,
   And God go with you! Wed in peace
My tall Electra, and be true.

          [ELECTRA *and* PYLADES *depart to the left.*

Castor. Their troth shall fill their hearts.—But on:
   Dread feet are near thee, hounds of prey,
   Snake-handed, midnight-visaged, yea,
And bitter pains their fruit! Begone!

          [ORESTES *departs to the right.*

But hark, the far Sicilian sea
   Calls, and a noise of men and ships
   That labour sunken to the lips
In bitter billows; forth go we,

Through the long leagues of fiery blue,
   With saving; not to souls unshriven;
   But whoso in his life hath striven
To love things holy and be true,

Through toil and storm we guard him; we
   Save, and he shall not die!—Therefore,
   O praise the lying man no more,
Nor with oath-breakers sail the sea:
   Farewell, ye walkers on the shore
Of death! A God hath counselled ye.

          [CASTOR *and* POLYDEUCES *disappear.*

Chorus. Farwell, farwell!—But he who can so fare,
   And stumbleth not on mischief anywhere,
     Blessèd on earth is he!

EURIPIDES
IPHIGENIA IN TAURIS

⇒⇒》《《⇐

TRANSLATED
By
GILBERT MURRAY

CHARACTERS IN THE PLAY

IPHIGENIA, *eldest daughter of Agamemnon, King of Argos; supposed to have been sacrificed by him to Artemis at Aulis.*

ORESTES, *her brother; pursued by Furies for killing his mother, Clytemnestra, who had murdered Agamemnon.*

PYLADES, *Prince of Phokis, friend to Orestes.*

THOAS, *King of Tauris, a savage country beyond the Symplêgades.*

A HERDSMAN.

A MESSENGER.

CHORUS of Captive Greek Women, handmaids to Iphigenia.

The Goddess PALLAS ATHENA.

The play was first performed between the years 414 and 412 B.C.

ARGUMENT

It will be remembered that Agamemnon, when ready to sail with all the powers of Greece against Troy, was bound by weather at Aulis. The medicine-man, Calchas, explained that Artemis demanded the sacrifice of his daughter, Iphigenia, who was then at home with her mother, Clytemnestra. Odysseus and Agamemnon sent for the maiden on the pretext that she was to be married to the famous young hero, Achilles; she was brought to Aulis and treacherously slaughtered—or, at least, so the people thought. In reality Artemis at the last moment saved Iphigenia, rapt her away from mortal eyes, and set her down in the land of the Tauri to be her priestess. These Tauri possessed an image of Artemis which had fallen from heaven, and kept up a savage rite of sacrificing to it all strangers who were cast on their shores. Iphigenia, obedient to her goddess, and held by "the spell of the altar," had to consecrate the victims as they went in to be slain. So far only barbarian strangers had come; she waited half in horror, half in a rage of revenge, for the day when she should have to sacrifice a Greek. The first Greek that came was her own brother, Orestes, who had been sent by Apollo to take the image of Artemis and bear it to Attica, where it should no more be stained with human sacrifice.

IPHIGENIA IN TAURIS

*The Scene shows a great and barbaric Temple on a desolate
sea-coast. An altar is visible stained with blood. There are
spoils of slain men hanging from the roof.* IPHIGENIA, *in the
dress of a Priestess, comes out from the Temple.*

Iphigenia. Child of the man of torment and of pride[1]
Tantalid Pelops bore a royal bride
On flying steeds from Pisa. Thence did spring
Atreus: from Atreus, linkèd king with king,
Menelaus, Agamemnon. His am I
And Clytemnestra's child: whom cruelly
At Aulis, where the strait of shifting blue
Frets with quick winds, for Helen's sake he slew,
Or thinks to have slain; such sacrifice he swore
To Artemis on that deep-bosomed shore.

    For there Lord Agamemnon, hot with joy
To win for Greece the crown of conquered Troy,
For Menelaus' sake through all distress
Pursuing Helen's vanished loveliness,
Gathered his thousand ships from every coast
Of Hellas: when there fell on that great host
Storms and despair of sailing. Then the King
Sought signs of fire, and Calchas answering
Spake thus: "O Lord of Hellas, from this shore
No ship of thine may move for evermore,
Till Artemis receive in gift of blood
Thy child, Iphigenia. Long hath stood
Thy vow, to pay to Her that bringeth light
Whatever birth most fair by day or night
The year should bring. That year thy queen did bear
A child—whom here I name of all most fair.
See that she die."
                So from my mother's side
By lies Odysseus won me, to be bride
In Aulis to Achilles. When I came,
They took me and above the altar flame

[265]

Held, and the sword was swinging to the gash,
When, lo, out of their vision in a flash
Artemis rapt me, leaving in my place
A deer to bleed; and on through a great space
Of shining sky upbore and in this town
Of Tauris the Unfriended set me down;
Where o'er a savage people savagely
King Thoas rules. This is her sanctuary
And I her priestess. Therefore, by the rite
Of worship here, wherein she hath delight—
Though fair in naught but name. . . . But Artemis
Is near; I speak no further. Mine it is
To consecrate and touch the victim's hair;
Doings of blood unspoken are the care
Of others, where her inmost chambers lie.
Ah me!
But what dark dreams, thou clear and morning sky,
I have to tell thee, could that bring them ease!
Meseemed in sleep, far over distant seas,
I lay in Argos, and about me slept
My maids: and, lo, the level earth was swept
With quaking like the sea. Out, out I fled,
And, turning, saw the cornice overhead
Reel, and the beams and mighty door-trees down
In blocks of ruin round me overthrown.
One single oaken pillar, so I dreamed,
Stood of my father's house; and hair, meseemed,
Waved from its head all brown: and suddenly
A human voice it had, and spoke. And I,
Fulfilling this mine office, built on blood
Of unknown men, before that pillar stood,
And washed him clean for death, mine eyes astream
With weeping.
        And this way I read my dream.
Orestes is no more: on him did fall
My cleansing drops.—The pillar of the hall
Must be the man first-born; and they on whom
My cleansing falls, their way is to the tomb.
  Therefore to my dead brother will I pour
Such sacrifice, I on this bitter shore

[266]

And he beyond great seas, as still I may,
With all those maids whom Thoas bore away
In war from Greece and gave me for mine own.
But wherefore come they not? I must be gone
And wait them in the temple, where I dwell.

                      [*She goes into the Temple.*

Voice. Did some one cross the pathway? Guard thee well.

Another Voice. I am watching. Every side I turn mine eye.

           [*Enter* ORESTES *and* PYLADES. *Their dress*
                shows they are travellers: ORESTES *is*
                shaken and distraught.

Orestes. How, brother? And is this the sanctuary
At last, for which we sailed from Argolis?

Pylades. For sure, Orestes. Seest thou not it is?

Orestes. The altar, too, where Hellene blood is shed.

Pylades. How like long hair those blood-stains, tawny red!

Orestes. And spoils of slaughtered men—there by the thatch.

Pylades. Aye, first-fruits of the harvest, when they catch
Their strangers!—'Tis a place to search with care.

              [*He searches, while* ORESTES *sits.*

Orestes. O God, where hast thou brought me? What new snare
Is this?—I slew my mother; I avenged
My father at thy bidding; I have ranged
A homeless world, hunted by shapes of pain,
And circling trod in mine own steps again.
At last I stood once more before thy throne
And cried thee question, what thing should be done
To end these miseries, wherein I reel
Through Hellas, mad, lashed like a burning wheel;
And thou didst bid me seek . . . what land but this
Of Tauri, where thy sister Artemis
Her altar hath, and seize on that divine
Image which fell, men say, into this shrine
From heaven. This I must seize by chance or plot
Or peril—clearer word was uttered not—
And bear to Attic earth. If this be done,
I should have peace from all my malison.

  Lo, I have done thy will. I have pierced the seas
Where no Greek man may live.—Ho, Pylades,

Sole sharer of my quest: hast seen it all?
What can we next? Thou seest this circuit wall
Enormous?   Must we climb the public stair,
With all men watching?   Shall we seek somewhere
Some lock to pick, some secret bolt or bar—
Of all which we know nothing? Where we are,
If one man mark us, if they see us prize
The gate, or think of entrance anywise,
'Tis death.—We still have time to fly for home:
Back to the galley quick, ere worse things come!
    Pylades. To fly we dare not, brother. 'Twere a thing
Not of our custom; and ill work, to bring
God's word to such reviling.—Let us leave
The temple now, and gather in some cave
Where glooms the cool sea ripple. But not where
The ship lies; men might chance to see her there
And tell some chief; then certain were our doom.
But when the fringèd eye of Night be come
Then we must dare, by all ways foul or fine,
To thieve that wondrous Image from its shrine.
Ah, see; far up, between each pair of beams
A hollow one might creep through! Danger gleams
Like sunshine to a brave man's eyes, and fear
Of what may be is no help anywhere.
    Orestes. Aye; we have never braved these leagues of way
To falter at the end. See, I obey
Thy words. They are ever wise. Let us go mark
Some cavern, to lie hid till fall of dark.
God will not suffer that bad things be stirred
To mar us now, and bring to naught the word
Himself hath spoke. Aye, and no peril brings
Pardon for turning back to sons of kings.

            [*They go out towards the shore. After they
               are gone, enter gradually the* WOMEN OF
               THE CHORUS.

    Chorus. Peace! Peace upon all who dwell
        By the Sister Rocks that clash in the swell
           Of the Friendless Seas.[2]
        O Child of Leto, thou,
        Dictynna mountain-born,

To the cornice gold-inlaid,
To the pillared sanctities,
We come in the cold of morn,
We come with virgin brow,
Pure as our oath was sworn,
Handmaids of thine handmaid
Who holdeth the stainless keys.

From Hellas, that once was ours,
We come before thy gate,
From the land of the western seas,
The horses and the towers,
The wells and the garden trees,
And the seats where our fathers sate.

Leader. What tidings, ho? With what intent
Hast called me to thy shrine and thee,
O child of him who crossed the sea
To Troy with that great armament,
The thousand prows, the myriad swords?
I come, O child of Atreid Lords.

[IPHIGENIA, *followed by* ATTENDANTS,
comes from the Temple.

Iphigenia. Alas, O maidens mine,
I am filled full of tears:
My heart filled with the beat
Of tears, as of dancing feet,
A lyreless joyless line,
And music meet for the dead.

For a whisper is in mine ears,
By visions borne on the breath
Of the Night that now is fled,
Of a brother gone to death.
Oh sorrow and weeping sore,
For the house that no more is,
For the dead that were kings of yore
And the labour of Argolis!

[*She begins the Funeral Rite.*

O Spirit, thou unknown,
Who bearest on dark wings

[269]

My brother, my one, mine own,
  I bear drink-offerings,
And the cup that bringeth ease
  Flowing through Earth's deep breast;
Milk of the mountain kine,
The hallowed gleam of wine,
The toil of murmuring bees:
  By these shall the dead have rest.

                         [*To an* ATTENDANT.
The golden goblet let me pour,
And that which Hades thirsteth for.

O branch of Agamemnon's tree
  Beneath the earth, as to one dead,
This cup of love I pour to thee.
    Oh, pardon, that I may not shed
One lock of hair to wreathe thy tomb,
  One tear; so far, so far am I
From what to me and thee was home,
    And where in all men's fantasy,
    Butchered, O God! I also lie.

Chorus. Woe; woe: I too with refluent melody,
  An echo wild of the dirges of the Asian,
I, thy bond maiden, cry to answer thee:
  The music that lieth hid in lamentation,
The song that is heard in the deep hearts of the dead,
  That the Lord of dead men 'mid his dancing singeth,
  And never joy-cry, never joy it bringeth;
  Woe for the house of Kings in desolation,
Woe for the light of the sceptre vanishèd.

From kings in Argos of old, from joyous kings,
      The beginning came:
Then peril swift upon peril, flame on flame:
The dark and wheeling coursers,[3] as wild with wings,
The cry of one betrayed on a drowning shore,
The sun that blanched in heaven, the world that changed—
Evil on evil and none alone!—deranged
By the Golden Lamb and the wrong grown ever more;
Blood following blood, sorrow on sorrow sore!

So come the dead of old, the dead in wrath,
Back on the seed of the high Tantalidae;
Surely the Spirit of Life an evil path
      Hath hewed for thee.

Iphigenia. From the beginning the Spirit of my life
Was an evil spirit. Alas for my mother's zone,
And the night that bare me! From the beginning Strife,
As a book to read, Fate gave me for mine own.
They wooed a bride for the strikers down of Troy—
Thy first-born, Mother: was it for this, thy prayer?—
A hind of slaughter to die in a father's snare,
Gift of a sacrifice where none hath joy.

    They set me on a royal wain;
      Down the long sand they led me on,
    A bride new-decked, a bride of bane,
      In Aulis to the Nereid's son.
    And now estranged for evermore
      Beyond the far estranging foam
    I watch a flat and herbless shore,
      Unloved, unchilded, without home
    Or city: never more to meet
      For Hera's dance with Argive maids,
    Nor round the loom 'mid singing sweet
      Make broideries and storied braids,
    Of writhing giants overthrown
    And clear-eyed Pallas. . . . All is gone!
    Red hands and ever-ringing ears:
    The blood of men that friendless die,
    The horror of the strangers' cry
    Unheard, the horror of their tears.

    But now, let even that have rest:
    I weep for him in Argos slain,
    The brother whom I knew, Ah me,
    A babe, a flower; and yet to be—
    There on his mother's arms and breast—
    The crowned Orestes, lord of men!

[271]

Leader of the Chorus. Stay, yonder from some headland **of**
the sea
There comes—methinks a herdsman, seeking thee.
                    [*Enter a* HERDSMAN. IPHIGENIA *is still on her knees.*
Herdsman. Daughter of Clytemnestra and her king,
Give ear! I bear news of a wondrous thing.
    Iphigenia. What news, that should so mar my obsequies?
    Herdsman. A ship hath passed the blue Symplêgades,
And here upon our coast two men are thrown,
Young, bold, good slaughter for the altar-stone
Of Artemis!   [*She rises.*
            Make all the speed ye may;
'Tis not too much. The blood-bowl and the spray!
    Iphigenia. Men of what nation? Doth their habit show?
    Herdsman. Hellenes for sure, but that is all we know.
    Iphigenia. No name? No other clue thine ear could seize?
    Herdsman. We heard one call his comrade "Pylades."
    Iphigenia. Yes. And the man who spoke—his name was
        what?
    Herdsman. None of us heard. I think they spoke it not.
    Iphigenia. How did ye see them first, how make them fast?
    Herdsman. Down by the sea, just where the surge is cast. . . .
    Iphigenia. The sea? What is the sea to thee and thine?
    Herdsman. We came to wash our cattle in the brine.
    Iphigenia. Go back, and tell how they were taken; show
The fashion of it, for I fain would know
All.—'Tis so long a time, and never yet,
Never, hath Greek blood made this altar wet.
    Herdsman. We had brought our forest cattle where the **seas**
Break in long tides from the Symplêgades.
A bay is there, deep eaten by the surge
And hollowed clear, with cover near the verge
Where purple-fishers camp. These twain were there
When one of mine own men, a forager,
Spied them, and tiptoed whispering back: "God **save**
Us now! Two things unearthly by the wave
Sitting!" We looked, and one of pious mood
Raised up his hands to heaven and praying stood:
"Son of the white Sea Spirit, high in rule,
Storm-lord Palaemon, Oh, be merciful:

[272]

Or sit ye there the warrior twins of Zeus,
Or something loved of Him, from whose great thews
Was born the Nereids' fifty-fluted choir."
   Another, flushed with folly and the fire
Of lawless daring, laughed aloud and swore
'Twas shipwrecked sailors skulking on the shore,
Our rule and custom here being known, to slay
All strangers. And most thought this was the way
To follow, and seek out for Artemis
The blood-gift of our people.
                                        Just at this
One of the strangers started from his seat,
And stood, and upward, downward, with a beat
His head went, and he groaned, and all his arm
Trembled. Then, as a hunter gives alarm,
He shrieked, stark mad and raving: "Pylades,
Dost see her there?—And there—Oh, no one sees!—
A she-dragon of Hell, and all her head
Agape with fangèd asps, to bite me dead.
She hath no face, but somewhere from her cloak
Bloweth a wind of fire and bloody smoke:
The wings' beat fans it: in her arms, Ah see!
My mother, dead grey stone, to cast on me
And crush. . . . Help, help! The crowd on me behind. . . ."
   No shapes at all were there. 'Twas his sick mind
Which turned the herds that lowed and barking hounds
That followed, to some visionary sounds
Of Furies. For ourselves, we did but sit
And watch in silence, wondering if the fit
Would leave him dead. When suddenly out shone
His sword, and like a lion he leaped upon
Our herds, to fight his Furies! Flank and side
He stabbed and smote them, till the foam was dyed
Red at the waves' edge. Marry, when we saw
The cattle hurt and falling, no more law
We gave, but sprang to arms and blew the horn
For help—so strong they looked and nobly born
For thralls like us to meet, that pair unknown.
   Well, a throng gathered ere much time was gone;
When suddenly the whirl of madness slips

From off him and he falls, quite weak, his lips
Dropping with foam. When once we saw him fall
So timely, we were at him one and all
To pelt and smite. The other watched us come,
But knelt and wiped those lips all dank with foam
And tended the sick body, while he held
His cloak's good web above him for a shield;
So cool he was to ward off every stone
And all the while care for that stricken one.

Then rose the fallen man, calm now and grave,
Looked, and saw battle bursting like a wave
That bursts, and knew that peril close at hand
Which now is come, and groaned. On every hand
We stood, and stoned and stoned, and ceased not. Aye,
'Twas then we heard that fearful battle-cry:
"Ho, Pylades, 'tis death! But let it be
A gallant death! Draw sword and follow me."

When those two swords came flashing, up the glen
Through the loose rocks we scattered back; but when
One band was flying, down by rocks and trees
Came others pelting: did they turn on these,
Back stole the first upon them, stone on stone.
'Twas past belief: of all those shots not one
Struck home. The goddess kept her fated prey
Perfect. Howbeit, at last we made our way
Right, left and round behind them on the sands,
And rushed, and beat the swords out of their hands,
So tired they scarce could stand. Then to the king
We bore them both, and he, not tarrying,
Sends them to thee, to touch with holy spray—
And then the blood-bowl!

                    I have heard thee pray,
Priestess, ere now for such a draft as this.
Aye, slay but these two chiefs to Artemis
And Hellas shall have paid thy debt, and know
What blood was spilt in Aulis long ago.

    Leader. I marvel that one mad, whoe'er he be,
Should sail from Hellas to the Friendless Sea.

    Iphigenia. 'Tis well. Let thy hand bring them, and mine own
Shall falter not till here God's will be done.

[274]

[*Exit* HERDSMAN.

O suffering heart, not fierce thou wast of old
To shipwrecked men. Nay, pities manifold
Held thee in fancy homeward, lest thy hand
At last should fall on one of thine own land.
But now, for visions that have turned to stone
My heart, to know Orestes sees the sun
No more, a cruel woman waits you here,
Whoe'er ye be, and one without a tear.

   'Tis true: I know by mine own evil will:
One long in pain, if things more suffering still
Fall to his hand, will hate them for his own
Torment. . . . And no great wind hath ever blown,
No ship from God hath passed the Clashing Gate,
To bring me Helen, who hath earned my hate,
And Menelaus, till I mocked their prayers
In this new Aulis, that is mine, not theirs:
Where Greek hands held me lifted, like a beast
For slaughter, and my throat bled. And the priest
My father! . . . Not one pang have I forgot.

  Ah me, the blind half-prisoned arms I shot
This way and that, to find his beard, his knees,
Groping and wondering: "Father, what are these
For bridal rites? My mother even now
Mid Argive women sings for me, whom thou . . .
What dost thou? She sings happy songs, and all
Is dance and sound of piping in the hall;
And here. . . . Is he a vampire, is he one
That fattens on the dead, thy Peleus' son—
Whose passion shaken like a torch before
My leaping chariot, lured me to this shore
To wed—"

        Ah me! And I had hid my face,
Burning, behind my veil. I would not press
Orestes to my arms . . . who now is slain! . . .
I would not kiss my sister's lips again,
For shame and fullness of the heart to meet
My bridegroom. All my kisses, all my sweet
Words were stored up and hid: I should come back
So soon to Argos!

And thou, too: alack,
Brother, if dead thou art, from what high things
Thy youth is outcast, and the pride of kings
Fallen!

And this the goddess deemeth good!
If ever mortal hand be dark with blood;
Nay, touch a new-made mother or one slain
In war, her ban is on him. 'Tis a stain
She driveth from her outer walls; and then
Herself doth drink this blood of slaughtered men?
Could ever Leto, she of the great King
Beloved, be mother to so gross a thing?
These tales be lies, false as those feastings wild
Of Tantalus and Gods that tore a child.
This land of murderers to its god hath given
Its own lust; evil dwelleth not in heaven.

[*She goes into the Temple.*

Chorus. Dark of the sea, dark of the sea,[4]   [*Strophe.*
    Gates of the warring water,
One, in the old time, conquered you,
A wingèd passion that burst the blue,
When the West was shut and the Dawn lay free
    To the pain of Inachus' daughter.

But who be these, from where the rushes blow
On pale Eurôtas, from pure Dirce's flow,
    That turn not neither falter,
Seeking Her land, where no man breaketh bread,
Her without pity, round whose virgin head
Blood on the pillars rusts from long ago,
    Blood on the ancient altar.

[*Antistrophe.*

A flash of the foam, a flash of the foam,
    A wave on the oarblade welling,
And out they passed to the heart of the blue:
A chariot shell that the wild winds drew.
Is it for passion of gold they come,
    Or pride to make great their dwelling?

For sweet is Hope, yea, to much mortal woe
So sweet that none may turn from it nor go,

Whom once the far voice calleth,
To wander through fierce peoples and the gleam
Of desolate seas, in every heart a dream:
And these she maketh empty die, and lo,
    To that man's hand she falleth.

                                    [*Strophe.*

    Through the Clashing Rocks they burst:
        They passed by the Cape unsleeping
    Of Phineus' sons accurst:
    They ran by the star-lit bay
        Upon magic surges sweeping,
    Where folk on the waves astray
    Have seen, through the gleaming grey,
    Ring behind ring, men say,
        The dance of the old Sea's daughters.

    The guiding oar abaft
        It rippled and it dinned,
    And now the west wind laughed
        And now the south-west wind;
    And the sail was full in flight,
    And they passed by the Island White:

    Birds, birds, everywhere,
    White as the foam, light as the air;
    And ghostly Achilles raceth there,
        Far in the Friendless Waters.

                                    [*Antistrophe.*

Ah, would that Leda's child . . .
    (So prayeth the priestess maiden)
From Troy, that she beguiled,
Hither were borne, to know
    What sin on her soul is laden!
Hair twisted, throat held low,
Head back for the blood to flow,
To die by the sword." . . . Ah no!
    One hope my soul yet hideth.

    A sail, a sail from Greece,
        Fearless to cross the sea,
                [277]

With ransom and with peace
   To my sick captivity.
O home, to see thee still,
And the old walls on the hill!
Dreams, dreams, gather to me!
Bear me on wings over the sea;
   O joy of the night, to slave and free,
      One good thing that abideth!

Leader.   But lo, the twain whom Thoas sends,
   Their arms in bondage graspèd sore;
   Strange offering this, to lay before
The Goddess! Hold your peace, O friends.

Onward, still onward, to this shrine
   They lead the first-fruits of the Greek.
   'Twas true, the tale he came to speak,
That watcher of the mountain kine.

O holy one, if it afford
   Thee joy, what these men bring to thee,
   Take thou their sacrifice, which we,
By law of Hellas, hold abhorred.

         [*Enter* ORESTES *and* PYLADES, *bound, and guarded by*
           TAURIANS. *Re-enter* IPHIGENIA.

Iphigenia. So be it.
My foremost care must be that nothing harms
The temple's holy rule.—Untie their arms.
That which is hallowed may no more be bound.
You, to the shrine within! Let all be found
As the law bids, and as we need this day.

         [ORESTES *and* PYLADES *are set free; some*
           ATTENDANTS *go into the Temple.*

Ah me!
What mother then was yours, O strangers, say,
And father? And your sister, if you have
A sister: both at once, so young and brave
To leave her brotherless! Who knows when heaven
May send that fortune? For to none is given
To know the coming nor the end of woe;

[278]

So dark is God, and to great darkness go
His paths, by blind chance mazèd from our ken.
   Whence are ye come, O most unhappy men?
From some far home, methinks, ye have found this shore
And far shall stay from home for evermore.

   Orestes. Why weepest thou, woman, to make worse the smart
Of that which needs must be, who'er thou art?
I count it not for gentleness, when one
Who means to slay, seeks first to make undone
By pity that sharp dread. Nor praise I him,
With hope long dead, who sheddeth tears to dim
The pain that grips him close. The evil so
Is doubled into twain. He doth but show
His feeble heart, and, as he must have died,
Dies.—Let ill fortune float upon her tide
And weep no more for us. What way this land
Worships its god we know and understand.

   Iphigenia. Say first . . . which is it men call Pylades?
   Orestes. 'Tis this man's name, if that will give thee ease.
   Iphigenia. From what walled town of Hellas cometh he?
   Orestes. Enough!—How would the knowledge profit thee?
   Iphigenia. Are ye two brethren of one mother born?
   Orestes. No, not in blood. In love we are brothers sworn.
   Iphigenia. Thou also hast a name: tell me thereof.
   Orestes. Call me Unfortunate. 'Tis name enough.
   Iphigenia. I asked not that. Let that with Fortune lie.
   Orestes. Fools cannot laugh at them that nameless die.
   Iphigenia. Why grudge me this? Hast thou such mighty
      fame?
   Orestes. My body, if thou wilt, but not my name.
   Iphigenia. Nor yet the land of Greece where thou wast bred?
   Orestes. What gain to have told it thee, when I am dead?
   Iphigenia. Nay: why shouldst thou deny so small a grace?
   Orestes. Know then, great Argos was my native place.
   Iphigenia. Stranger! The truth! . . . From Argos art thou
      come?
   Orestes. Mycenae, once a rich land, was my home.
   Iphigenia. 'Tis banishment that brings thee here—or what?
   Orestes. A kind of banishment, half forced, half sought.
   Iphigenia. Wouldst thou but tell me all I need of thee!

Orestes. 'Twere not much added to my misery.

Iphigenia. From Argos! . . . Oh, how sweet to see thee here!

Orestes. Enjoy it, then. To me 'tis sorry cheer.

Iphigenia. Thou knowest the name of Troy? Far doth it flit.

Orestes. Would God I had not; nay, nor dreamed of it.

Iphigenia. Men fable it is fallen beneath the sword?

Orestes. Fallen it is. Thou hast heard no idle word.

Iphigenia. Fallen! At last!—And Helen taken too?

Orestes. Aye; on an evil day for one I knew.

Iphigenia. Where is she? I too have some anger stored. . . .

Orestes. In Sparta! Once more happy with her lord!

Iphigenia. Oh, hated of all Greece, not only me!

Orestes. I too have tasted of her wizardry.

Iphigenia. And came the armies home, as the tales run?

Orestes. To answer that were many tales in one.

Iphigenia. Oh, give me this hour full! Thou wilt soon die.

Orestes. Ask, if such longing holds thee. I will try.

Iphigenia. A seer called Calchas! Did he ever come . . . ?

Orestes. Calchas is dead, as the news went at home.

Iphigenia. Good news, ye gods!—Odysseus, what of him?

Orestes. Not home yet, but still living, as men deem.

Iphigenia. Curse him! And may he see his home no more.

Orestes. Why curse him? All his house is stricken sore.

Iphigenia. How hath the Nereid's son, Achilles, sped?

Orestes. Small help his bridal brought him! He is dead.

Iphigenia. A false fierce bridal, so the sufferers tell!

Orestes. Who art thou, questioning of Greece so well?

Iphigenia. I was Greek. Evil caught me long ago.

Orestes. Small wonder, then, thou hast such wish to know.

Iphigenia. That war-lord, whom they call so high in bliss.

Orestes. None such is known to me. What name was his?

Iphigenia. They called him Agamemnon, Atreus' son.

Orestes. I know not. Cease.—My questioning is done.

Iphigenia. 'Twill be such joy to me! How fares he? Tell!

Orestes. Dead. And hath wrecked another's life as well.

Iphigenia. Dead? By what dreadful fortune? Woe is me!

Orestes. Why sighst thou? Had he any link with thee?

Iphigenia. I did but think of his old joy and pride.

Orestes. His own wife foully stabbed him, and he died.

Iphigenia. O God!
I pity her that slew . . . and him that slew.
   Orestes. Now cease thy questions. Add no word thereto.
   Iphigenia. But one word. Lives she still, that hapless wife?
   Orestes. No. Her own son, her first-born, took her life.
   Iphigenia. O shipwrecked house! What thought was in his
     brain?
   Orestes. Justice on her, to avenge his father slain.
   Iphigenia. Alas!
A bad false duty bravely hath he wrought.
   Orestes. Yet God, for all his duty, helps him not.
   Iphigenia. And not one branch of Atreus' tree lives on?
   Orestes. Electra lives, unmated and alone.
   Iphigenia. The child they slaughtered . . . is there word of
     her?
   Orestes. Why, no, save that she died in Aulis there.
   Iphigenia. Poor child! Poor father, too, who killed and
     lied!
   Orestes. For a bad woman's worthless sake she died.
   Iphigenia. The dead king's son, lives he in Argos still?
   Orestes. He lives, now here, now nowhere, bent with ill.
   Iphigenia. O dreams, light dreams, farewell! Ye too were
     lies.
   Orestes. Aye; the gods too, whom mortals deem so wise,
Are nothing clearer than some wingèd dream;
And all their ways, like man's ways, but a stream
Of turmoil. He who cares to suffer least,
Not blind, as fools are blinded, by a priest,
Goes straight . . . to what death, those who know him know.
   Leader. We too have kinsmen dear, but, being low,
None heedeth, live they still or live they not.
   Iphigenia (*with sudden impulse*). Listen! For I am fallen
     upon a thought,
Strangers, of some good use to you and me,
Both. And 'tis thus most good things come to be,
When different eyes hold the same way for fair.
   Stranger, if I can save thee, wilt thou bear
To Argos and the friends who loved my youth
Some word? There is a tablet which, in ruth
For me and mine ill works, a prisoner wrote,

Ta'en by the king in war. He knew 'twas not
My will that craved for blood, but One on high
Who holds it righteous her due prey shall die.
And since that day no Greek hath ever come
Whom I could save and send to Argos home
With prayer for help to any friend: but thou,
I think, dost loathe me not; and thou dost know
Mycenae and the names that fill my heart.
Help me! Be saved! Thou also hast thy part,
Thy life for one light letter. . . . (ORESTES *looks at* PYLADES.)
                                 For thy friend,
The law compelleth. He must bear the end
By Artemis ordained, apart from thee.

  Orestes. Strange woman, as thou biddest let it be,
Save one thing. 'Twere for me a heavy weight
Should this man die. 'Tis I and mine own fate
That steer our goings. He but sails with me
Because I suffer much. It must not be
That by his ruin I should 'scape mine own,
And win thy grace withal. 'Tis simply done.
Give him the tablet. He with faithful will
Shall all thy hest in Argolis fulfil.
And I . . . who cares may kill me. Vile is he
Who leaves a friend in peril and goes free
Himself. And, as it chances, this is one
Right dear to me; his life is as my own.

  Iphigenia. O royal heart! Surely from some great seed
This branch is born, that can so love indeed.
God grant the one yet living of my race
Be such as thou! For not quite brotherless
Am even I, save that I see him not,
Strangers. . . . Howbeit, thy pleasure shall be wrought.
This man shall bear the message, and thou go
To death. So greatly thou wilt have it so!

  Orestes. Where is the priest who does this cruelty?
  Iphigenia. 'Tis I. This altar's spell is over me.
  Orestes. A grievous office and unblest, O maid.
  Iphigenia. What dare I do? The law must be obeyed.
  Orestes. A girl to hold a sword and stab men dead!
  Iphigenia. I shall but sign the water on thy head.

[282]

Orestes. And who shall strike me, if I needs must ask?
Iphigenia. There be within these vaults who know their task.
Orestes. My grave, when they have finished their desire?
Iphigenia. A great gulf of the rock, and holy fire.
Orestes. Woe's me!
Would that my sister's hand could close mine eyes!
   Iphigenia. Alas, she dwelleth under distant skies,
Unhappy one, and vain is all thy prayer.
Yet, Oh, thou art from Argos: all of care
That can be, I will give and fail thee not.
Rich raiment to thy burial shall be brought,
And oil to cool thy pyre in golden floods,
And sweet that from a thousand mountain buds
The murmuring bee hath garnered, I will throw
To die with thee in fragrance. . . .

                    I must go
And seek the tablet from the Goddess' room
Within.—Oh, do not hate me for my doom!

    Watch them, ye servitors, but leave them free.

It may be, past all hoping, it may be,
My word shall sail to Argos, to his hand
Whom most I love. How joyous will he stand
To know, past hope, that here on the world's rim
His dead are living, and cry out for him!

                       [She goes into the Temple.

  Chorus. Alas, we pity thee; surely we pity thee: *[Strophe.*
Who art given over to the holy water,
    The drops that fall deadly as drops of blood.
Orestes. I weep not, ye Greek maidens: but farewell.
                       [Antistrophe.
Chorus. Aye, and rejoice with thee; surely rejoice with thee,
Thou happy rover from the place of slaughter;
    Thy foot shall stand again where thy father's stood.
Pylades. While he I love must die? 'Tis miserable.
Divers Women of the Chorus.
  A. Alas, the deathward faring of the lost!
  B. Woe, woe; thou too shalt move to misery.
  C. Which one shall suffer most?

D. My heart is torn by two words evenly,
  For thee should I most sorrow, or for thee?
Orestes. By heaven, is thy thought, Pylades, like mine?
Pylades. O friend, I cannot speak.—But what is thine?
Orestes. Who can the damsel be? How Greek her tone
Of question, all of Ilion overthrown,
And how the kings came back, the wizard flame
Of Calchas, and Achilles' mighty name,
And ill-starred Agamemnon. With a keen
Pity she spoke, and asked me of his queen
And children. . . . The strange woman comes from there
By race, an Argive maid.—What aileth her
With tablets, else, and questionings as though
Her own heart beat with Argos' joy or woe?
 Pylades. Thy speech is quicker, friend, else I had said
The same; though surely all men visited
By ships have heard the fall of the great kings.
But let that be: I think of other things. . . .
 Orestes. What? If thou hast need of me, let it be said.
 Pylades. I cannot live for shame if thou art dead.
I sailed together with thee; let us die
Together. What a coward slave were I,
Creeping through Argos and from glen to glen
Of wind-torn Phocian hills! And most of men—
For most are bad—will whisper how one day
I left my friend to die and made my way
Home. They will say I watched the sinking breath
Of thy great house and plotted for thy death
To wed thy sister, climb into thy throne. . . .
I dread, I loathe it.—Nay, all ways but one
Are shut. My last breath shall go forth with thine,
Thy bloody sword, thy gulf of fire be mine
Also. I love thee and I dread men's scorn.
 Orestes. Peace from such thoughts! My burden can be
  borne;
But where one pain sufficeth, double pain
I will not bear. Nay, all that scorn and stain
That fright thee, on mine own head worse would be
If I brought death on him who toiled for me.
It is no bitter thing for such an one

[284]

As God will have me be, at last to have done
With living. Thou art happy; thy house lies
At peace with God, unstainèd in men's eyes;
Mine is all evil fate and evil life. . . .
Nay, thou once safe, my sister for thy wife—
So we agreed—in sons of hers and thine
My name will live, nor Agamemnon's line
Be blurred for ever like an evil scroll.
Back! Rule thy land! Let life be in thy soul!
And when thou art come to Hellas, and the plain
Of Argos where the horsemen ride, again—
Give me thy hand!—I charge thee, let there be
Some death-mound and a graven stone for me.
My sister will go weep thereat, and shear
A tress or two. Say how I ended here,
Slain by a maid of Argolis, beside
God's altar, in mine own blood purified.

And fare thee well. I have no friend like thee
For truth and love, O boy that played with me,
And hunted on Greek hills, O thou on whom
Hath lain the hardest burden of my doom!
Farewell. The Prophet and the Lord of Lies
Hath done his worst. Far out from Grecian skies
With craft forethought he driveth me, to die
Where none may mark how ends his prophecy!
I trusted in his word. I gave him all
My heart. I slew my mother at his call;
For which things now he casts me here to die.

Pylades. Thy tomb shall fail thee not. Thy sister I
Will guard for ever. I, O stricken sore,
Who loved thee living and shall love thee more
Dead. But for all thou standest on the brink,
God's promise hath not yet destroyed thee. Think!
How oft, how oft the darkest hour of ill
Breaks brightest into dawn, if Fate but will!

Orestes. Enough. Nor god nor man can any more
Aid me. The woman standeth at the door.

[*Enter* IPHIGENIA *from the Temple.*

Iphigenia. Go ye within; and have all things of need
In order set for them that do the deed.

[285]

There wait my word.   [ATTENDANTS *go in*.
                      Ye strangers, here I hold
The many-lettered tablet, fold on fold.
Yet . . . one thing still. No man, once unafraid
And safe, remembereth all the vows he made
In fear of death. My heart misgiveth me,
Lest he who bears my tablet, once gone free,
Forget me here and set my charge at naught.

    Orestes. What wouldst thou, then? Thou hast some troubling thought.

    Iphigenia. His sworn oath let him give, to bear this same
Tablet to Argos, to the friend I name.

    Orestes. And if he give this oath, wilt thou swear too?

    Iphigenia. What should I swear to do or not to do?

    Orestes. Send him from Tauris safe and free from ill.

    Iphigenia. I promise. How else could he do my will?

    Orestes. The King will suffer this?

    Iphigenia.   Yes: I can bend
The King, and set upon his ship thy friend.

    Orestes. Choose then what oath is best, and he will swear.

    Iphigenia. (*to* PYLADES, *who has come up to her*). Say: "To
thy friend this tablet I will bear."

    Pylades (*taking the tablet*). Good. I will bear this tablet to
thy friend.

    Iphigenia. And I save thee beyond this kingdom's end.

    Pylades. What god dost thou invoke to witness this?

    Iphigenia. Her in whose house I labour, Artemis.

    Pylades. And I the Lord of Heaven, eternal Zeus.

    Iphigenia. And if thou fail me, or thine oath abuse . . . ?

    Pylades. May I see home no more. And thou, what then?

    Iphigenia. May this foot never tread Greek earth again.

    Pylades. But stay: there is one chance we have forgot.

    Iphigenia. A new oath can be sworn, if this serve not.

    Pylades. In one case set me free. Say I be crossed
With shipwreck, and, with ship and tablet lost
And all I bear, my life be saved alone:
Let not this oath be held a thing undone,
To curse me.

    Iphigenia. Nay, then, many ways are best
To many ends. The words thou carriest

Enrolled and hid beneath that tablet's rim,
I will repeat to thee, and thou to him
I look for. Safer so. If the scrip sail
Unhurt to Greece, itself will tell my tale
Unaided: if it drown in some wide sea,
Save but thyself, my words are saved with thee.

Pylades. For thy sake and for mine 'tis fairer so.
Now let me hear his name to whom I go
In Argolis, and how my words should run.

Iphigenia (*repeating the words by heart*). Say: "To Orestes,
    Agamemnon's son,
She that was slain in Aulis, dead to Greece
Yet quick, Iphigenia sendeth peace:"

Orestes. Iphigenia! Where? Back from the dead?

Iphigenia. 'Tis I. But speak not, lest thou break my thread.—
"Take me to Argos, brother, ere I die,
Back from the Friendless Peoples and the high
Altar of Her whose bloody rites I wreak."

Orestes (*aside*). Where am I, Pylades? How shall I speak?

Iphigenia. "Else one in grief forsaken shall, like shame,
Haunt thee."

Pylades (*aside*). Orestes!

Iphigenia. (*overhearing him*). Yes: that is the name.

Pylades. Ye Gods above!

Iphigenia.   Why callest thou on God
For words of mine?

Pylades.   'Tis nothing. 'Twas a road
My thoughts had turned. Speak on.—No need for us
To question; we shall hear things marvellous.

Iphigenia. Tell him that Artemis my soul did save,
I wot not how, and to the altar gave
A fawn instead; the which my father slew,
Not seeing, deeming that the sword he drew
Struck me. But she had borne me far away
And left me in this land.—I charge thee, say
So much. It all is written on the scroll.

Pylades. An easy charge thou layest on my soul,
A glad oath on thine own. I wait no more,
But here fulfil the service that I swore.
Orestes, take this tablet which I bear

To thine own hand, thy sister's messenger.

Orestes. I take it, but I reck not of its scrip
Nor message. Too much joy is at my lip.
Sister! Belovèd! Wildered though I be,
My arms believe not, yet they crave for thee.
Now, filled with wonder, give me my delight!

            [He goes to embrace her. She stands speechless.

Leader. Stranger, forbear! No living man hath right
To touch that robe. The Goddess were defiled!

Orestes. O Sister mine, O my dead father's child,
Agamemnon's child; take me and have no fear,
Beyond all dreams 'tis I thy brother here.

Iphigenia. My brother? Thou? . . . Peace! Mock at me
  no more.
Argos is bright with him and Nauplia's shore.

Orestes. Unhappy one! Thou hast no brother there.

Iphigenia. Orestes . . . thou? Whom Clytemnestra bare?

Orestes. To Atreus' firstborn son, thy sire and mine.

Iphigenia. Thou sayst it: Oh, give me some proof, some
  sign!

Orestes. What sign thou wilt. Ask anything from home.

Iphigenia. Nay, thou speak: 'tis from thee the sign should
  come.

Orestes. That will I.—First, old tales Electra told.
Thou knowest how Pelops' princes warred of old?

Iphigenia. I know: the Golden lamb that wrought their
  doom.

Orestes. Thine own hand wove that story on the loom. . . .

Iphigenia. How sweet! Thou movest near old memories.

Orestes. With a great Sun back beaten in the skies.

Iphigenia. Fine linen threads I used. The memories come.

Orestes. And mother gave thee shrift-water from home
For Aulis. . . .

Iphigenia.   I remember. Not so fair
A day did drink that water!

Orestes.   And thine hair
They brought us for thy dying gift, and gave
To mother.

Iphigenia. Yes: for record on the grave
I sent it, where this head should never lie.

Orestes. Another token, seen of mine own eye.
The ancient lance that leapt in Pelops' hand,
To win his bride, the virgin of the land,
And smite Oenomaus, in thy chamber hid. . . .
    Iphigenia (falling into his arms). Belovèd! Oh, no other,
      for indeed
                Belovèd art thou! In mine arms at last,
                    Orestes far away.
Orestes. And thou in mine, the evil dreaming past,
              Back from the dead this day!
  Yet through the joy tears, tears and sorrow loud
  Are o'er mine eyes and thine eyes, like a cloud.
Iphigenia. Is this the babe I knew,
           The little babe, light lifted like a bird?
           O heart of mine, too blest for any word,
              What shall I say or do?
           Beyond all wonders, beyond stories heard,
              This joy is here and true.

Orestes. Could we but stay thus joined for evermore!
Iphigenia. A joy is mine I may not understand,
      Friends, and a fear, lest sudden from my hand
          This dream will melt and soar
      Up to the fiery skies from whence it came.
      O Argos land, O hearth and holy flame
          That old Cyclôpes lit,
      I bless ye that he lives, that he is grown,
      A light and strength, my brother and mine own;
         I bless your name for it.

Orestes. One blood we are; so much is well. But Fate,
Sister, hath not yet made us fortunate.

Iphigenia. O most unfortunate! Did I not feel,
      Whose father, misery-hearted, at my bare
         Throat held the steel?

Orestes. Woe's me! Methinks even now I see thee there.

Iphigenia. No love-song of Achilles! Crafty arms
         Drew me to that cold sleep,
    And tears, blind tears amid the altar psalms
         And noise of them that weep—
  That was my cleansing!

[289]

Orestes.   My heart too doth bleed,
To think our father wrought so dire a deed.
   Iphigenia. My life hath known no father. Any road
                 To any end may run,
As god's will drives; else . . .
   Orestes.   Else, unhappy one,
Thyself had spilt this day thy brother's blood!
   Iphigenia. Ah God, my cruel deed! . . . 'Twas horrible.
       'Twas horrible. . . . O brother! Did my heart
          Endure it? . . . And things fell
      Right by so frail a chance; and here thou art.
           Bloody my hand had been,
           My heart heavy with sin.
          And now, what end cometh?
        Shall Chance yet comfort me,
         Finding a way for thee
        Back from the Friendless Strand,
          Back from the place of death—
        Ere yet the slayers come
        And thy blood sink in the sand—
        Home unto Argos, home? . . .
    Hard heart, so swift to slay,
    Is there to life no way? . . .
        No ship! . . . And how by land? . . .
          A rush of feet
       Out to the waste alone.
          Nay: 'twere to meet
    Death, amid tribes unknown
    And trackless ways of the waste. . . .
    Surely the sea were best.
    Back by the narrow bar
        To the Dark Blue Gate! . . .
       Ah God, too far, too far! . . .
        Desolate! Desolate!
What god or man, what unimagined flame,
    Can cleave this road where no road is, and bring
To us last wrecks of Agamemnon's name,
       Peace from long suffering?
   Leader. Lo, deeds of wonder and beyond surmise,
Not as tales told, but seen of mine own eyes.

Pylades. Men that have found the arms of those they love
Would fain long linger in the joy thereof.
But we, Orestes, have no respite yet
For tears or tenderness. Let us forget
All but the one word Freedom, calling us
To live, not die by altars barbarous.
Think not of joy in this great hour, nor lose
Fortune's first hold. Not thus do wise men use.

    Orestes. I think that Fortune watcheth o'er our lives,
Surer than we. But well said: he who strives
Will find his gods strive for him equally.

    Iphigenia. He shall not check us so, nor baffle me
Of this one word. How doth Electra move
Through life? Ye twain are all I have to love.

    Orestes. A wife and happy: this man hath her hand.

    Iphigenia. And what man's son is he, and of what land?

    Orestes. Son of King Strophios he is called of men.

    Iphigenia. Whom Atreus' daughter wed?—My kinsman then.

    Orestes. Our cousin, and my true and only friend.

    Iphigenia. He was not born, when I went to mine end.

    Orestes. No, Strophios had no child for many a year.

    Iphigenia. I give thee hail, husband of one so dear.

    Orestes. My more than kinsman, saviour in my need!

    Iphigenia. But mother. . . . Speak: how did ye dare that
      deed?

    Orestes. Our father's wrongs. . . . But let that story be.

    Iphigenia. And she to slay her king! What cause had she?

    Orestes. Forget her! . . . And no tale for thee it is.

    Iphigenia. So be it.—And thou art Lord of Argolis?

    Orestes. Our uncle rules. I walk an exile's ways.

    Iphigenia. Doth he so trample on our fallen days?

    Orestes. Nay: there be those that drive me, Shapes of Dread.

    Iphigenia. Ah!
That frenzy on the shore! 'Tis as they said. . . .

    Orestes. They saw me in mine hour. It needs must be.

    Iphigenia. 'Twas our dead mother's Furies hounding thee!

    Orestes. My mouth is bloody with the curb they ride.

    Iphigenia. What brought thee here beyond the Friendless
      Tide?

    Orestes. What leads me everywhere—Apollo's word.

[291]

Iphigenia. Seeking what end?—Or may the tale be heard?
Orestes. Nay, I can tell thee all. It needs must be
The whole tale of my days of misery.

When this sore evil that we speak not of
Lit on my hand, this way and that they drove
My body, till the God by diverse paths
Led me to Athens, that the nameless Wraths
Might bring me before judgement. For that land
A pure tribunal hath, where Ares' hand,
Red from an ancient stain, by Zeus was sent
For justice. Thither came I; and there went
God's hate before me, that at first no man
Would give me shelter. Then some few began
To pity, and set out for me aloof
One table. There I sate within their roof,
But without word they signed to me, as one
Apart, unspoken to, unlooked upon,
Lest touch of me should stain their meat and sup.
And every man in measure filled his cup
And gave me mine, and took their joy apart,
While I sat silent; for I had no heart
To upbraid the hosts that fed me. On I wrought
In my deep pain, feigning to mark them not.

And now, men say, mine evil days are made
A rite among them and the cups are laid
Apart for each. The rule abideth still.

Howbeit, when I was come to Ares' Hill
They gave me judgement. On one stone I stood,
On one she that was eldest of the brood
That hunted me so long. And many a word
Touching my mother's death was spoke and heard,
Till Phoebus rose to save me. Even lay
The votes of Death and Life; when, lo, a sway
Of Pallas' arm, and free at last I stood
From that death grapple. But the Shapes of Blood—
Some did accept the judgement, and of grace
Consent to make their house beneath that place
In darkness. Others still consented not,
But clove to me the more, like bloodhounds hot
On the dying; till to Phoebus' house once more

[292]

I crept, and cast me starving on the floor
Facing the Holy Place, and made my cry:
"Lord Phoebus, here I am come, and here will die,
Unless thou save me, as thou hast betrayed."
And, lo, from out that dark and golden shade
A voice: "Go, seek the Taurian citadel:
Seize there the carven Artemis that fell
From heaven, and stablish it on Attic soil.
So comes thy freedom."   [IPHIGENIA *shrinks.*
                      Sister, in this toil
Help us!—If once that image I may win
That day shall end my madness and my sin:
And thou, to Argos o'er the sundering foam
My many-oarèd barque shall bear thee home.
    O sister loved and lost, O pitying face,
Help my great peril; help our father's race.
For lost am I and perished all the powers
Of Pelops, save that heavenly thing be ours!
    Leader. Strange wrath of God hath fallen, like hot rain,
On Tantalus' house: he leadeth them through pain.
    Iphigenia. Long ere you came my heart hath yearned to be
In Argos, brother, and so near to thee:
But now—thy will is mine. To ease thy pain,
To lift our father's house to peace again,
And hate no more my murderers—aye, 'tis good.
Perchance to clean this hand that sought thy blood,
And save my people . . .
                  But the goddess' eyes,
How dream we to deceive them? Or what wise
Escape the King, when on his sight shall fall
The blank stone of the empty pedestal? . . .
I needs must die. . . . What better can I do?
    And yet, one chance there is: could I but go
Together with the image: couldst thou bear
Both on the leaping seas! The risk were fair.
But how?
           Nay, I must wait then and be slain:
Thou shalt walk free in Argolis again,
And all life smile on thee. . . . Dearest, we need
Not shrink from that. I shall by mine own deed

Have saved thee. And a man gone from the earth
Is wept for. Women are but little worth.

    Orestes. My mother, and then thou? It may not be.
This hand hath blood enough. I stand with thee
One-hearted here, be it for life or death,
And either bear thee, if God favoureth,
With me to Greece and home, or else lie here
Dead at thy side.—But mark me: if thou fear
Lest Artemis be wroth, how can that be?
Hath not her brother's self commanded me
To bear to Greece her image?—Oh, he knew
Her will! He knew that in this land we two
Must meet once more. All that so far hath past
Doth show his work. He will not at the last
Fail. We shall yet see Argos, thou and I.

    Iphigenia. To steal for thee the image, yet not die
Myself! 'Tis that we need. 'Tis that doth kill
My hope. Else. . . . Oh, God knows I have the will!

    Orestes. How if we slew your savage king?

    Iphigenia.   Ah, no:
He sheltered me, a stranger.

    Orestes.   Even so,
If it bring life for me and thee, the deed
May well be dared.

    Iphigenia.   I could not. . . . Nay; indeed
I thank thee for thy daring.

    Orestes.   Canst thou hide
My body in the shrine?

    Iphigenia.   There to abide
Till nightfall, and escape?

    Orestes.   Even so; the night
Is the safe time for robbers, as the light
For just men.

    Iphigenia.   There be sacred watchers there
Who needs must see us.

    Orestes.   Gods above! What prayer
Can help us then?

    Iphigenia.   I think I dimly see
One chance.

    Orestes.   What chance? Speak out thy fantasy.

[294]

Iphigenia. On thine affliction I would build my way.

Orestes.   Women have strange devices.

Iphigenia.   I would say
Thou com'st from Hellas with thy mother's blood
Upon thee.

Orestes.   Use my shame, if any good
Will follow.

Iphigenia.   Therefore, an offense most high
It were to slay thee to the goddess!

Orestes.   Why?
Though I half guess.

Iphigenia.   Thy body is unclean.—
Oh, I will fill them with the fear of sin!

Orestes. What help is that for the Image?

Iphigenia.   I will crave
To cleanse thee in the breaking of the wave.

Orestes. That leaves the goddess still inside her shrine,
And 'tis for her we sailed.

Iphigenia.   A touch of thine
Defiled her. She too must be purified.

Orestes. Where shall it be? Thou knowest where the tide
Sweeps up in a long channel?

Iphigenia.   Yes! And where
Your ship, I guess, lies moored.

Orestes.   Whose hand will bear—
Should it be thine?—the Image from her throne?

Iphigenia. No hand of man may touch it save mine own.

Orestes. And Pylades—what part hath he herein?

Iphigenia. The same as thine. He bears the self-same sin.

Orestes. How wilt thou work the plan—hid from the king
Or known?

Iphigenia.   To hide it were a hopeless thing. . . .
Oh, I will face him, make him yield to me.

Orestes. Well, fifty oars lie waiting on the sea.

Iphigenia. Aye, there comes thy work, till an end be made.

Orestes. Good. It needs only that these women aid
Our secret. Do thou speak with them, and find
Words of persuasion. Power is in the mind
Of woman to wake pity.—For the rest,
God knoweth: may it all end for the best!

Iphigenia. O women, you my comrades, in your eyes
I look to read my fate. In you it lies,
That either I find peace, or be cast down
To nothing, robbed forever of mine own—
Brother, and home, and sister pricelessly
Beloved.—Are we not women, you and I,
A broken race, to one another true,
And strong in our shared secrets? Help me through
This strait; keep hid the secret of our flight,
And share our peril! Honour shineth bright
On her whose lips are steadfast. . . . Heaven above!
Three souls, but one in fortune, one in love,
Thou seest us go—is it to death or home?
If home, then surely, surely, there shall come
Part of our joy to thee. I swear, I swear
To aid thee also home. . . .

> [*She goes to one after another, and presently
> kneels embracing the knees of the* LEADER.

                           I make my prayer
By that right hand; to thee, too, by that dear
Cheek; by thy knees; by all that is not here
Of things beloved, by mother, father, child—
Thou hadst a child!—How say ye? Have ye smiled
Or turned from me? For if ye turn away,
I and my brother are lost things this day.

    Leader. Be of good heart, sweet mistress. Only go
To happiness. No child of man shall know
From us thy secret. Hear me, Zeus on high!

    Iphigenia (*rising*). God bless you for that word, and fill
        your eye
With light!—   [*Turning to* ORESTES *and* PYLADES.
                  But now, to work! Go thou, and thou,
In to the deeper shrine. King Thoas now
Should soon be here to question if the price
Be yet paid of the strangers' sacrifice.

                      [ORESTES *and* PYLADES *go in.*
Thou Holy One, that on the shrouded sand
Of Aulis saved me from a father's hand
Blood-maddened, save me now, and save these twain.
Else shall Apollo's lips, through thy disdain,

[296]

Be no more true nor trusted in men's eyes.
Come from the friendless shore, the cruel skies,
Come back: what mak'st thou here, when o'er the sea
A clean and joyous land doth call for thee?

[*She follows the men into the Temple.*

[*Strophe.*

Chorus. Bird of the sea rocks,[5] of the bursting spray,
      O halcyon bird,
That wheelest crying, crying, on thy way;
Who knoweth grief can read the tale of thee:
One love long lost, one song for ever heard
      And wings that sweep the sea.

Sister, I too beside the sea complain,
      A bird that hath no wing.
Oh, for a kind Greek market-place again,
For Artemis that healeth woman's pain;
      Here I stand hungering.
Give me the little hill above the sea,
The palm of Delos fringèd delicately,
The young sweet laurel and the olive-tree
      Grey-leaved and glimmering;
O Isle of Leto, Isle of pain and love;
The Orbèd Water and the spell thereof;
Where still the Swan, minstrel of things to be,
      Doth serve the Muse and sing!

[*Antistrophe.*

Ah, the old tears, the old and blinding tears
      I gave God then,
When my town fell, and noise was in mine ears
Of crashing towers, and forth they guided me
Through spears and lifted oars and angry men
      Out to an unknown sea.
They bought my flesh with gold, and sore afraid
      I came to this dark East
To serve, in thrall to Agamemnon's maid,
This Huntress Artemis, to whom is paid
      The blood of no slain beast;
Yet all is bloody where I dwell, Ah me!

Envying, envying that misery
That through all life hath endured changelessly.
    For hard things borne from birth
Make iron of man's heart, and hurt the less.
'Tis change that paineth; and the bitterness
Of life's decay when joy hath ceased to be
    That makes dark all the earth.

[Strophe.

    Behold,
  Two score and ten there be
  Rowers that row for thee,
And a wild hill air, as if Pan were there,
  Shall sound on the Argive sea,
  Piping to set thee free.

  Or is it the stricken string
  Of Apollo's lyre doth sing
Joyously, as he guideth thee
  To Athens, the land of spring;
  While I wait wearying?

  Oh, the wind and the oar,
  When the great sail swells before,
With sheets astrain, like a horse on the rein;
  And on, through the race and roar,
  She feels for the farther shore.

[Antistrophe.

    Ah me,
  To rise upon wings and hold
  Straight on up the steeps of gold
Where the joyous Sun in fire doth run,
  Till the wings should faint and fold
  O'er the house that was mine of old:

  Or watch where the glade below
  With a marriage dance doth glow,
And a child will glide from her mother's side
  Out, out, where the dancers flow:
  As I did, long ago.

[298]

Oh, battles of gold and rare
Raiment and starrèd hair,
And bright veils crossed amid tresses tossed
In a dusk of dancing air!
O Youth and the days that were!

[*Enter* KING THOAS, *with Soldiers.*

Thoas. Where is the warden of this sacred gate,
The Greek woman? Is her work ended yet
With those two strangers? Do their bodies lie
Aflame now in the rock-cleft sanctuary?

Leader. Here is herself, O King, to give thee word.

[*Enter, from the Temple,* IPHIGENIA, *carrying the
Image on high.*

Thoas. How, child of Agamemnon! Hast thou stirred
From her eternal base, and to the sun
Bearest in thine own arms, the Holy One?

Iphigenia. Back Lord! No step beyond the pillared way.

Thoas. But how? Some rule is broken?

Iphigenia. I unsay
That word. Be all unspoken and unwrought!

Thoas. What means this greeting strange? Disclose thy
thought.

Iphigenia. Unclean the prey was that ye caught, O King.

Thoas. Who showed thee so? Thine own imagining?

Iphigenia. The Image stirred and shuddered from its seat.

Thoas. Itself? . . . Some shock of earthquake loosened it.

Iphigenia. Itself. And the eyes closed one breathing space.

Thoas. But why? For those two men's bloodguiltiness?

Iphigenia. That, nothing else. For, Oh, their guilt is sore.

Thoas. They killed some of my herdsmen on the shore?

Iphigenia. Their sin was brought from home, not gathered
here.

Thoas. What? I must know this.—Make thy story clear.

Iphigenia. (*She puts the Image down and moves nearer to
Thoas*). The men have slain their mother.

Thoas. God! And these
Be Greeks!

Iphigenia. They both are hunted out of Greece.

Thoas. For this thou has brought the Image to the sun?

Iphigenia. The fire of heaven can cleanse all malison.

[299]

Thoas. How didst thou first hear of their deed of shame?

Iphigenia. When the Image hid its eyes, I questioned them.

Thoas. Good. Greece hath taught thee many a subtle art.

Iphigenia. Ah, they too had sweet words to move my heart.

Thoas. Sweet words? How, did they bring some news of Greece?

Iphigenia. Orestes, my one brother, lives in peace.

Thoas. Surely! Good news to make thee spare their lives. . . .

Iphigenia. My father too in Argos lives and thrives.

Thoas. While thou didst think but of the goddess' laws!

Iphigenia. Do I not hate all Greeks? Have I not cause?

Thoas. Good cause. But now. . . . What service should be paid?

Iphigenia. The Law of long years needs must be obeyed.

Thoas. To work then, with thy sword and handwashing!

Iphigenia. First I must shrive them with some cleansing thing.

Thoas. What? Running water, or the sea's salt spray?

Iphigenia. The sea doth wash all the world's ills away.

Thoas. For sure. 'Twill make them cleaner for the knife.

Iphigenia. And my hand, too, cleaner for all my life.

Thoas. Well, the waves lap close by the temple floor.

Iphigenia. We need a secret place. I must do more.

Thoas. Some rite unseen? 'Tis well. Go where thou wilt.

Iphigenia. The Image likewise must be purged of guilt.

Thoas. The stain hath touched it of that mother's blood?

Iphigenia. I durst not move it else, from where it stood.

Thoas. How good thy godliness and forethought! Aye,
Small wonder all our people hold thee high.

Iphigenia. Dost know then what I fain would have?

Thoas. 'Tis thine to speak and it shall be.

Iphigenia. Put bondage on the strangers both. . . .

Thoas. Why bondage? Whither can they flee?

Iphigenia. Put not thy faith in any Greek.

Thoas (to Attendants). Ho, men! some thongs and fetters, go!

Iphigenia. Stay; let them lead the strangers here, outside the shrine. . . .

Thoas. It shall be so.

Iphigenia. And lay dark raiment on their heads. . . .

Thoas.   To veil them, lest the Sun should see.

Iphigenia. And lend me some of thine own spears.

Thoas.   This company shall go with thee.

Iphigenia. Next, send through all the city streets a herald.

Thoas.   Aye; and what to say?

Iphigenia. That no man living stir abroad.

Thoas.   The stain of blood might cross their way.

Iphigenia. Aye, sin like theirs doth spread contagion.

Thoas (to an Attendant). . . . . Forth, and publish my
  command. . . .

Iphigenia.   That none stir forth—nor look. . . .

Thoas.   Nor look.—How well thou carest for the land!

Iphigenia. For one whom I am bound to love.

Thoas.   Indeed, I think thou hat'st me not.

Iphigenia. And thou meanwhile, here at the temple, wait, O
  King, and. . . .

Thoas.   Wait for what?

Iphigenia. Purge all the shrine with fire.

Thoas.   'Twill all be clean before you come again.

Iphigenia. And while the strangers pass thee close, seeking
  the sea. . . .

Thoas.   What wouldst thou then?

Iphigenia. Put darkness on thine eyes.

Thoas.   Mine eyes might drink the evil of their crime?

Iphigenia. And, should I seem to stay too long. . . .

Thoas.   Too long? How shall I judge the time?

Iphigenia. Be not dismayed.

Thoas.   Perform thy rite all duly. We have time to spare.

Iphigenia. And God but grant this cleansing end as I desire!

Thoas.   I join thy prayer.

Iphigenia. The door doth open! See, they lead the strangers
  from the cell within,

And raiment holy and young lambs, whose blood shall shrive
  the blood of Sin.

And, lo, the light of sacred fires, and things of secret power,
  arrayed

By mine own hand to cleanse aright the strangers, to cleanse
  Leto's Maid.

                                    [*She takes up the Image again.*

There passeth here a holy thing: begone, I charge ye, from the
    road,
O whoso by these sacred gates may dwell, hand-consecrate to
    God,
What man hath marriage in his heart, what woman goeth great
    with child,
Begone and tremble from this road: fly swiftly, lest ye be
    defiled.—
O Queen and Virgin, Leto-born, have pity! Let me cleanse this
    stain,
And pray to thee where pray I would: a clean house shall be
    thine again,
And we at last win happiness.—Behold, I speak but as I dare;
The rest . . . Oh, God is wise, and thou, my Mistress, thou
    canst read my prayer.

> [*The procession passes out,* THOAS *and the by-
> standers veiled; Attendants in front, then*
> IPHIGENIA *with the Image, then veiled Sol-
> diers, then* ORESTES *and* PYLADES *bound,
> the bonds held by other veiled Soldiers fol-
> lowing them.* THOAS *goes into the Temple.*
> [*Strophe.*

Chorus. Oh, fair the fruits of Leto blow:
    A Virgin, one, with joyous bow,
    And one a Lord of flashing locks,
        Wise in the harp, Apollo:
    She bore them amid Delian rocks,
        Hid in a fruited hollow.

    But forth she fared from that low reef,
    Sea-cradle of her joy and grief.
    A crag she knew more near the skies
        And lit with wilder water,
    That leaps with joy of Dionyse:
        There brought she son and daughter.
    And there, behold, an ancient Snake,
    Wine-eyed, bronze-gleaming in the brake
    Of deep-leaved laurel, ruled the dell,
        Sent by old Earth from under

Strange caves to guard her oracle—
  A thing of fear and wonder.

Thou, Phoebus, still a new-born thing,
  Meet in thy mother's arms to lie,
Didst kill the Snake and crown thee king,
  In Pytho's land of prophecy:
Thine was the tripod and the chair
Of golden truth; and thronèd there,
Hard by the streams of Castaly,
  Beneath the untrodden portal
Of Earth's mid stone there flows from thee
  Wisdom for all things mortal.

                                       [*Antistrophe.*

He slew the Snake; he cast, men say,
Themis, the child of Earth, away
From Pytho and her hallowed stream;
  Then Earth, in dark derision,
Brought forth the Peoples of the Dream
  And all the tribes of Vision.

And men besought them; and from deep
Confusèd underworlds of sleep
They showed blind things that erst had been
And are and yet shall follow,
So did avenge that old Earth Queen
  Her child's wrong on Apollo.
Then swiftly flew that conquering one
To Zeus on high, and round the throne
Twining a small indignant hand,
Prayed him to send redeeming
To Pytho from that troublous band
  Sprung from the darks of dreaming.

Zeus laughed to see the babe, I trow,
So swift to claim his golden rite;
He laughed and bowed his head, in vow
To still those voices of the night.
And so from out the eyes of men
That dark dream-truth was lost again;

And Phoebus, thronèd where the throng
    Prays at the golden portal,
Again doth shed in sunlit song
    Hope unto all things mortal.

[*Enter a* MESSENGER, *running.*

Messenger. Ho, watchers of the fane! Ho, altar-guard,
Where is King Thoas gone? Undo the barred
Portals, and call the King! The King I seek.
    Leader. What tidings—if unbidden I may speak?
    Messenger. The strangers both are gone, and we beguiled,
By some dark plot of Agamemnon's child:
Fled from the land! And on a barque of Greece
They bear the heaven-sent shape of Artemis.
    Leader. Thy tale is past belief.—Go, swiftly on,
And find the King. He is but newly gone.
    Messenger. Where went he? He must know of what has
        passed!
    Leader. I know not where he went. But follow fast
And seek him. Thou wilt light on him ere long.
    Messenger. See there! The treason of a woman's tongue!
Ye all are in the plot, I warrant ye!
    Leader. Thy words are mad! What are the men to me? . . .
Go to the palace, go!
    Messenger (*seeing the great knocker on the Temple door*).
                           I will not stir
Till word be come by this good messenger
If Thoas be within these gates or no.—

[*Thundering at the door.*

Ho, loose the portals! Ye within! What ho!
Open, and tell our master one doth stand
Without here, with strange evil in his hand.

[*Enter* THOAS *from the Temple.*

Thoas. Who dares before this portal consecrate
Make uproar and lewd battering of the gate?
Thy noise hath broke the Altar's ancient peace.
    Messenger. Ye Gods! They swore to me—and bade me cease
My search—the King was gone. And all the while . . . . !
    Thoas. These women? How? What sought they by such
        guile?

[304]

Messenger. Of them hereafter!—Give me first thine ear
For greater things. The virgin minister
That served our altar, she hath fled from this
And stolen the dread Shape of Artemis,
With those two Greeks. The cleansing was a lie.
    Thoas. She fled?—What wild hope whispered her to fly?
    Messenger. The hope to save Orestes. Wonder on!
    Thoas. Orestes—how? Not Clytemnestra's son?
    Messenger. And our pledged altar-offering. 'Tis the same.
    Thoas. O marvel beyond marvel! By what name
More rich in wonder can I name thee right?
    Messenger. Give not thy mind to that. Let ear and sight
Be mine awhile; and when thou hast heard the whole
Devise how to best trap them ere the goal.
    Thoas. Aye, tell thy tale. Our Tauric seas stretch far,
Where no man may escape my wand of war.
    Messenger. Soon as we reached that headland of the sea,
Whereby Orestes' barque lay secretly,
We soldiers holding, by thine own commands,
The chain that bound the strangers, in our hands,
There Agamemnon's daughter made a sign,
Bidding us wait far off, for some divine
And secret fire of cleansing she must make.
We could but do her will. We saw her take
The chain in her own hands and walk behind.
Indeed thy servants bore a troubled mind,
O King, but how do else? So time went by.
Meanwhile to make it seem she wrought some high
Magic, she cried aloud: then came the long
Drone of some strange and necromantic song,
As though she toiled to cleanse that blood; and there
Sat we, that long time, waiting. Till a fear
O'ertook us, that the men might slip their chain
And strike the priestess down and plunge amain
For safety: yet the dread our eyes to fill
With sights unbidden held us, and we still
Sat silent. But at last all spoke as one,
Forbid or not forbid, to hasten on
And find them. On we went, and suddenly,
With oarage poised, like wings upon the sea,

An Argive ship we saw, her fifty men
All benched, and on the shore, with every chain
Cast off, our strangers, standing by the stern!
The prow was held by stay-poles: turn by turn
The anchor-cable rose; some men had strung
Long ropes into a ladder, which they swung
Over the side for those two Greeks to climb.

The plot was open, and we lost no time
But flew to seize the cables and the maid,
And through the stern dragged out the steering-blade,
To spoil her course, and shouted: "Ho, what way
Is this, to sail the seas and steal away
An holy image and its minister?
What man art thou, and what man's son, to bear
Our priestess from the land?" And clear thereon
He spoke: "Orestes, Agamemnon's son,
And brother to this maid, whom here in peace
I bear, my long lost sister, back to Greece."

We none the less clung fast to her, and strove
To drag her to thy judgement-seat. Thereof
Came trouble and bruised jaws. For neither they
Nor we had weapons with us. But the way
Hard-beaten fist and heel from those two men
Rained upon ribs and flank—again, again . . .
To touch was to fall gasping! Aye, they laid
Their mark on all of us, till back we fled
With bleeding crowns, and some with blinded eyes,
Up a rough bank of rock. There on the rise
We found good stones and stood, and fought again.

But archers then came out, and sent a rain
Of arrows from the poop, and drove us back.
And just then—for a wave came, long and black,
And swept them shoreward—lest the priestess' gown
Should feel the sea, Orestes stooping down
Caught her on his left shoulder: then one stride
Out through the sea, the ladder at the side
Was caught, and there amid the benches stood
The maid of Argos and the carven wood
Of heaven, the Image of God's daughter high.
And up from the mid galley rose a cry:

"For Greece! For Greece, O children of the shores
Of storm! Give way, and let her feel your oars;
Churn the long waves to foam. The prize is won,
The prize we followed, on and ever on,
Friendless beyond the blue Symplêgades."
    A roar of glad throats echoed down the breeze
And fifty oars struck, and away she flew.
And while the shelter lasted, she ran true
Full for the harbour-mouth; but ere she well
Reached it, the weather caught her, and the swell
Was strong. Then sudden in her teeth a squall
Drove the sail bellying back. The men withal
Worked with set teeth, kicking against the stream.
But back, still back, striving as in a dream,
She drifted. Then the damsel rose and prayed:
"O Child of Leto, save thy chosen maid
From this dark land to Hellas, and forgive
My theft this day, and let these brave men live.
Dost thou not love thy brother, Holy One?
What marvel if I also love mine own?"
    The sailors cried a paean to her prayers,
And set those brown and naked arms of theirs,
Half-mad with strain, quick swinging chime on chime
To the helmsman's shout. But vainly; all the time
Nearer and nearer rockward they were pressed.
One of our men was wading to his breast,
Some others roping a great grappling-hook,
While I sped hot-foot to the town, to look
For thee, my Prince, and tell thee what doth pass.
    Come with me, Lord. Bring manacles of brass
And bitter bonds. For now, unless the wave
Fall sudden calm, no mortal power can save
Orestes. There is One that rules the sea[6]
Who grieved for Troy and hates her enemy:
Poseidon's self will give into thine hand
And ours this dog, this troubler of the land—
The priestess, too, who, recking not what blood
Ran red in Aulis, hath betrayed her god!

Leader. Woe, woe! To fall in these men's hands again,
Mistress, and die, and see thy brother slain!

[307]

Thoas. Ho, all ye dwellers of my savage town
Set saddle on your steeds, and gallop down
To watch the heads, and gather what is cast
Alive from this Greek wreck. We shall make fast,
By God's help, the blasphemers.—Send a corps
Out in good boats a furlong from the shore;
So we shall either snare them on the seas
Or ride them down by land, and at our ease
Fling them down gulfs of rock, or pale them high
On stakes in the sun, to feed our birds and die.

Women: you knew this plot. Each one of you
Shall know, before the work I have to do
Is done, what torment is.—Enough. A clear
Task is afoot. I must not linger here.

> [*While* THOAS *is moving off, his men shouting
> and running before and behind him, there
> comes a sudden blasting light and thunder-
> roll, and* ATHENA *is seen in the air con-
> fronting them.*

Athena. Ho, whither now, so hot upon the prey,
King Thoas? It is I that bid thee stay,
Athena, child of Zeus. Turn back this flood
Of wrathful men, and get thee temperate blood.

Apollo's word and Fate's ordainèd path
Have led Orestes here, to escape the wrath
Of Them that Hate. To Argos he must bring
His sister's life, and guide that Holy Thing
Which fell from heaven, in mine own land to dwell.
So shall his pain have rest, and all be well.
Thou hast heard my speech, O King. No death from thee
May snare Orestes between rocks and sea:
Poseidon for my love doth make the sore
Waves gentle, and set free his labouring oar.

And thou, O far away—for, far or near
A goddess speaketh and thy heart must hear—
Go on thy ways, Orestes, bearing home
The Image and thy sister. When ye come
To god-built Athens, lo, a land there is
Half hid on Attica's last boundaries,

A little land, hard by Karystus' Rock,
But sacred. It is called by Attic folk
Halae. Build there a temple, and bestow
Therein thine Image, that the world may know
The tale of Tauris and of thee, cast out
From pole to pole of Greece, a blood-hound rout
Of ill thoughts driving thee. So through the whole
Of time to Artemis the Touropole
Shall men make hymns at Halae. And withal
Give them this law. At each high festival,
A sword, in record of thy death undone,
Shall touch a man's throat, and the red blood run—
One drop, for old religion's sake. In this
Shall live that old red rite of Artemis.

And thou, Iphigenia, by the stair
Of Brauron in the rocks, the Key shalt bear
Of Artemis. There shalt thou live and die,
And there have burial. And a gift shall lie
Above thy shrine, fair raiment undefiled
Left upon earth by mothers dead with child.

Ye last, O exiled women, true of heart
And faithful found, ye shall in peace depart,
Each to her home: behold Athena's will.

Orestes, long ago on Ares' Hill
I saved thee, when the votes of Death and Life
Lay equal: and henceforth, when men at strife
So stand, mid equal votes of Life and Death,
My law shall hold that Mercy conquereth.
Begone. Lead forth thy sister from this shore
In peace; and thou, Thoas, be wroth no more.
    Thoas. Most high Athena, he who bows not low
His head to God's word spoken, I scarce know
How such an one doth live. Orestes hath
Fled with mine Image hence. . . . I bear no wrath.
Nor yet against his sister. There is naught,
Methinks, of honour in a battle fought
'Gainst gods. The strength is theirs. Let those two fare

[309]

Forth to thy land and plant mine Image there.
I wish them well.

       These bondwomen no less
I will send free to Greece and happiness,
And stay my galleys' oars, and bid this brand
Be sheathed again, Goddess, at thy command.

    Athena. 'Tis well, O King. For that which needs must be
Holdeth the high gods as it holdeth thee.

Winds of the north, O winds that laugh and run,
Bear now to Athens Agamemnon's son:
Myself am with you, o'er long leagues of foam
Guiding my sister's hallowed Image home.

                    [She floats away.

   Chorus. Some Women.
      Go forth in bliss, O ye whose lot
      God shieldeth, that ye perish not!
   Others. O great in our dull world of clay,
      And great in heaven's undying gleam,
     Pallas, thy bidding we obey:
     And bless thee, for mine ears have heard
     The joy and wonder of a word
      Beyond my dream, beyond my dream.

EURIPIDES
MEDEA

⇒⇒⇒ ⇐⇐⇐

TRANSLATED
By
GILBERT MURRAY

CHARACTERS IN THE PLAY

MEDEA, *daughter of Aiêtês, King of Colchis.*

JASON, *chief of the Argonauts; nephew of Pelias, King of Iôlcos in Thessaly.*

CREON, *ruler of Corinth.*

AEGEUS, *King of Athens.*

NURSE *of Medea.*

TWO CHILDREN *of Jason and Medea.*

ATTENDANT *on the children.*

A MESSENGER.

CHORUS of Corinthian Women, with their LEADER.

Soldiers and Attendants.

The scene is laid in Corinth. The play was first acted when Pythodôrus was Archon, Olympiad 87, year 1 (B.C. 431). Euphorion was first, Sophocles second, Euripides third, with Medea, Philoctetes, Dictys, and the Harvesters, a Satyr-play.

ARGUMENT

Jason, son of Aeson, King of Iôlcos, in Thessaly, began his life in exile. His uncle Pelias had seized the kingdom, and Jason was borne away to the mountains by night and given to Chiron, the Centaur. When he reached manhood, he came down to Iôlcos to demand his throne. Pelias, cowed but loath to yield, promised to give up the kingdom if Jason would make his way to the unknown land of Colchis to secure the soul of his kinsman Phrixus and the Golden Fleece. Jason gathered the most daring heroes of all Hellas, built the first ship, Argo, and set to sea. When he reached the land of Aiêtês, king of the Colchians, all means failed. The Argonauts were surrounded and destruction seemed sure, when suddenly, unasked, Aiêtês' daughter Medea, an enchantress, fell in love with Jason. She slew for him her own sleepless serpent, who guarded the fleece, deceived her father, and secured both the fleece and the soul of Phrixus. Finally, when her brother, Absyrtus, plotted to kill Jason, she stabbed him dead and fled with Jason over the seas. Jason could not avoid taking Medea with him though of course, in fifth century Athens, no legal marriage was possible between a Greek and a barbarian from Colchis. Upon their return to Iôlcos, Pelias was still determined to keep the kingdom. Medea resolved to do her lover another act of service, persuaded Pelias that he could renew his youth, and in the process he died in agony. Medea and Jason had to fly for their lives, and directed their flight to Corinth where the ruler, now growing old, had an only daughter. Jason doubtless felt it necessary to free himself somehow from this wild beast of a woman who was ruining his life. He accepted the hand of the princess, and when Medea became violent, did not intervene to save her from exile.

MEDEA

The Scene represents the front of MEDEA'S *House in Corinth.
A road to the right leads towards the royal castle, one on the
left to the harbour. The* NURSE *is discovered alone.*

Nurse. Would God no Argo e'er had winged the seas
To Colchis through the blue Symplêgades:[1]
No shaft of riven pine in Pêlion's glen[2]
Shaped that first oar-blade in the hands of men
Valiant, who won, to save King Pelias' vow,
The fleece All-golden! Never then, I trow,
Mine own princess, her spirit wounded sore
With love of Jason, to the encastled shore
Had sailed of old Iôlcos: never wrought
The daughters of King Pelias, knowing not,
To spill their father's life: nor fled in fear,
Hunted for that fierce sin, to Corinth here
With Jason and her babes. This folk at need
Stood friend to her, and she in word and deed
Served alway Jason. Surely this doth bind,
Through all ill days, the hurts of humankind,
When man and woman in one music move.

But now, the world is angry, and true love
Sick as with poison. Jason doth forsake
My mistress and his own two sons, to make
His couch in a king's chamber. He must wed:[3]
Wed with this Creon's child, who now is head
And chief of Corinth. Wherefore sore betrayed
Medea calleth up the oath they made,
They two, and wakes the claspèd hands again,
The troth surpassing speech, and cries amain
On God in heaven to mark the end, and how
Jason hath paid his debt.

           All fasting now
And cold, her body yielded up to pain,
Her days a waste of weeping, she hath lain,
Since first she knew that he was false. Her eyes

Are lifted not; and all her visage lies
In the dust. If friends will speak, she hears no more
Than some dead rock or wave that beats the shore:
Only the white throat in a sudden shame
May writhe, and all alone she moans the name
Of father, and land, and home, forsook that day
For this man's sake, who casteth her away.
Not to be quite shut out from home . . . alas,
She knoweth now how rare a thing that was!
Methinks she hath a dread, not joy, to see
Her children near. 'Tis this that maketh me
Most tremble, lest she do I know not what.
Her heart is no light thing, and useth not
To brook much wrong. I know that woman, aye,
And dread her! Will she creep alone to die
Bleeding in that old room, where still is laid
Lord Jason's bed? She hath for that a blade
Made keen. Or slay the bridegroom and the king,
And win herself God knows what direr thing?
'Tis a fell spirit. Few, I ween, shall stir
Her hate unscathed, or lightly humble her.

  Ha! 'Tis the children from their games again,
Rested and gay; and all their mother's pain
Forgotten! Young lives ever turn from gloom!

            [*The* CHILDREN *and their* ATTENDANT *come in.*
  Attendant. Thou ancient treasure of my lady's room,
What mak'st thou here before the gates alone,
And alway turning on thy lips some moan
Of old mischances? Will our mistress be
Content, this long time to be left by thee?
  Nurse. Grey guard of Jason's children, a good thrall
Hath his own grief, if any hurt befall
His master's. Aye, it holds one's heart! . . . Meseems
I have strayed out so deep in evil dreams,
I longed to rest me here alone, and cry
Medea's wrongs to this still Earth and Sky.
  Attendant. How? Are the tears yet running in her eyes?
  Nurse. 'Twere good to be like thee! . . . Her sorrow lies
Scarce wakened yet, not half its perils wrought.
  Attendant. Mad spirit! . . . if a man may speak his thought

Of masters mad.—And nothing in her ears
Hath sounded yet of her last cause for tears!

> [*He moves towards the house, but the* NURSE
> *checks him.*

  Nurse. What cause, old man? . . . Nay, grudge me not one
  word.
  Attendant. 'Tis nothing. Best forget what thou hast heard.
  Nurse. Nay, housemate, by thy beard! Hold it not hid
From me. . . . I will keep silence if thou bid.
  Attendant. I heard an old man talking, where he sate
At draughts in the sun, beside the fountain gate,
And never thought of me, there standing still
Beside him. And he said 'twas Creon's will,
Being lord of all this land, that she be sent,
And with her her two sons, to banishment.
Maybe 'tis all false. For myself, I know
No further, and I would it were not so.
  Nurse. Jason will never bear it—his own sons
Banished,—however hot his anger runs
Against their mother!
  Attendant.   Old love burneth low
When new love wakes, men say. He is not now
Husband nor father here, nor any kin.
  Nurse. But this is ruin! New waves breaking in
To wreck us, ere we are righted from the old!
  Attendant. Well, hold thy peace. Our mistress will be told
All in good time. Speak thou no word hereof.
  Nurse. My babes! What think ye of your father's love?
God curse him not, he is my master still:
But, oh, to them that loved him, 'tis an ill
Friend. . . .
  Attendant. And what man on earth is different? How?
Hast thou lived all these years, and learned but now
That every man more loveth his own head
Than other men's? He dreameth of the bed
Of this new bride, and thinks not of his sons.
  Nurse. Go: run into the house, my little ones:
All will end happily! . . . Keep them apart:
Let not their mother meet them while her heart
Is darkened. Yester night I saw a flame

[315]

Stand in her eye, as though she hated them,
And would I know not what. For sure her wrath
Will never turn nor slumber, till she hath . . .
Go: and if some must suffer, may it be
Not we who love her, but some enemy!

   Voice (*within*). Oh shame and pain: O woe is me!
      Would I could die in my misery!

            [*The* CHILDREN *and the* ATTENDANT *go in.*

  Nurse. Ah, children, hark! She moves again
     Her frozen heart, her sleeping wrath.
     In, quick! And never cross her path,
    Nor rouse that dark eye in its pain;

    That fell sea-spirit, and the dire
     Spring of a will untaught, unbowed.
     Quick, now!—Methinks this weeping cloud
    Hath in its heart some thunder-fire,

    Slow gathering, that must flash ere long.
     I know not how, for ill or well,
     It turns, this uncontrollable
    Tempestuous spirit, blind with wrong.

  Voice (*within*). Have I not suffered? Doth it call
    No tears? . . . Ha, ye beside the wall
    Unfathered children, God hate you
    As I am hated, and him, too,
     That gat you, and this house and all!

  Nurse. For pity! What have they to do,
     Babes, with their father's sin? Why call
     Thy curse on these? . . . Ah, children, all
    These days my bosom bleeds for you.

    Rude are the wills of princes: yea,
     Prevailing alway, seldom crossed,
     On fitful winds their moods are tossed:
    'Tis best men tread the equal way.

    Aye, not with glory but with peace
     May the long summers find me crowned:
     For gentleness—her very sound
    Is magic, and her usages

All wholesome: but the fiercely great
  Hath little music on his road,
  And falleth, when the hand of God
Shall move, most deep and desolate.

> [*During the last words the* LEADER *of the*
> *Chorus has entered. Other women fol-*
> *low her.*

Leader. I heard a voice and a moan,
    A voice of the eastern seas:
    Hath she found not yet her ease?
      Speak, O agèd one.
    For I stood afar at the gate,
      And there came from within a cry,
    And wailing desolate.
      Ah, no more joy have I,
      For the griefs this house doth see,
    And the love it hath wrought in me.

Nurse. There is no house! 'Tis gone. The lord
    Seeketh a prouder bed: and she
  Wastes in her chamber, nor one word
    Will hear of care or charity.

Voice (within). O Zeus, O Earth, O Light,
    Will the fire not stab my brain?
    What profiteth living? Oh,
    Shall I not lift the slow
    Yoke, and let Life go,
  As a beast out in the night,
    To lie, and be rid of pain?

Chorus (Some Women). A. "O Zeus, O Earth, O Light:"
    The cry of a bride forlorn
    Heard ye, and wailing born
      Of lost delight?

    B. Why weariest thou this day,
      Wild heart, for the bed abhorrèd,
    The cold bed in the clay?
    Death cometh though no man pray,
      Ungarlanded, un-adorèd.
        Call him not thou.

  C. If another's arms be now
     Where thine have been,
     On his head be the sin:
   Rend not thy brow!

  D. All that thou sufferest,
     God seeth: Oh, not so sore
   Waste nor weep for the breast
    That was thine of yore.

Voice (within). Virgin of Righteousness,
   Virgin of hallowed Troth,
   Ye marked me when with an oath
   I bound him; mark no less
   That oath's end. Give me to see
   Him and his bride, who sought
   My grief when I wronged her not,
   Broken in misery,
   And all her house. . . . O God,
   My mother's home, and the dim
   Shore that I left for him,
   And the voice of my brother's blood. . . .

Nurse. Oh, wild words! Did ye hear her cry
   To them that guard man's faith forsworn,
   Themis and Zeus? . . . This wrath new-born
  Shall make mad workings ere it die.

Chorus. (Other Women). A. Would she but come to seek
   Our faces, that love her well,
   And take to her heart the spell
    Of words that speak?

  B. Alas for the heavy hate
    And anger that burneth ever!
   Would it but now abate,
   Ah God, I love her yet.
    And surely my love's endeavour
    Shall fail not here.

[318]

C. Go: from that chamber drear
  Forth to the day
Lead her, and say, Oh, say
  That we love her dear.

D. Go, lest her hand be hard
    On the innocent: Ah, let be!
  For her grief moves hitherward,
    Like an angry sea.

Nurse. That will I: though what words of mine
Or love shall move her? Let them lie
With the old lost labours! . . . Yet her eye—
Know ye the eyes of the wild kine,

The lion flash that guards their brood?
  So looks she now if any thrall
  Speak comfort, or draw near at all
My mistress in her evil mood.

                    [*The* NURSE *goes into the house.*

Chorus. (*A Woman*). Alas, the bold blithe bards of old
  That all for joy their music made,
For feasts and dancing manifold,
  That Life might listen and be glad.

But all the darkness and the wrong,
  Quick deaths and dim heart-aching things,
Would no man ease them with a song
  Or music of a thousand strings?

Then song had served us in our need.
  What profit, o'er the banquet's swell
That lingering cry that none may heed?
  The feast hath filled them: all is well!

Others. I heard a song, but it comes no more.
  Where the tears ran over:
A keen cry but tired, tired:
A woman's cry for her heart's desired,
  For a traitor's kiss and a lost lover.
But a prayer, methinks, yet riseth sore

　　　To God, to Faith, God's ancient daughter—
　　The Faith that over sundering seas
　　Drew her to Hellas, and the breeze
　　Of midnight shivered, and the door
　　　Closed of the salt unsounded water.

　　　　　　　[*During the last words* MEDEA *has come
　　　　　　　　out from the house.*

　Medea.　Women of Corinth, I am come to show
My face, lest ye despise me. For I know
Some heads stand high and fail not, even at night
Alone—far less like this, in all men's sight:
And we, who study not our wayfarings
But feel and cry—Oh we are drifting things,
And evil! For what truth is in men's eyes,
Which search no heart, but in a flash despise
A strange face, shuddering back from one that ne'er
Hath wronged them? . . . Sure, far-comers anywhere,
I know, must bow them and be gentle. Nay,
A Greek himself men praise not, who alway
Should seek his own will recking not. . . . But I—
This thing undreamed of, sudden from on high,
Hath sapped my soul: I dazzle where I stand,
The cup of all life shattered in my hand,
Longing to die—O friends! He, even he,
Whom to know well was all the world to me,
The man I loved, hath proved most evil.—Oh,
Of all things upon earth that bleed and grow,
A herb most bruised is woman. We must pay
Our store of gold, hoarded for that one day,
To buy us some man's love; and lo, they bring
A master of our flesh! There comes the sting
Of the whole shame. And then the jeopardy,
For good or ill, what shall that master be;
Reject she cannot: and if he but stays
His suit, 'tis shame on all that woman's days.
So thrown amid new laws, new places, why,
'Tis magic she must have, or prophecy—
Home never taught her that—how best to guide
Toward peace this thing that sleepeth at her side.
And she who, labouring long, shall find some way

[320]

Whereby her lord may bear with her, nor fray
His yoke too fiercely, blessèd is the breath
That woman draws! Else, let her pray for death.
Her lord, if he be wearied of the face
Withindoors, gets him forth; some merrier place
Will ease his heart: but she waits on, her whole
Vision enchainèd on a single soul.
And then, forsooth, 'tis they that face the call
Of war, while we sit sheltered, hid from all
Peril!—False mocking! Sooner would I stand
Three times to face their battles, shield in hand,
Than bear one child.

                  But peace! There cannot be
Ever the same tale told of thee and me.
Thou hast this city, and thy father's home,
And joy of friends, and hope in days to come:
But I, being cityless, am cast aside
By him that wedded me, a savage bride
Won in far seas and left—no mother near,
No brother, not one kinsman anywhere
For harbour in this storm. Therefore of thee
I ask one thing. If chance yet ope to me
Some path, if even now my hand can win
Strength to requite this Jason for his sin,
Betray me not! Oh, in all things but this,
I know how full of fears a woman is,
And faint at need, and shrinking from the light
Of battle: but once spoil her of her right
In man's love, and there moves, I warn thee well,
No bloodier spirit between heaven and hell.

    Leader. I will betray thee not. It is but just,
Thou smite him.—And that weeping in the dust
And stormy tears, how should I blame them? . . . Stay:
'Tis Creon, lord of Corinth, makes his way
Hither, and bears, methinks, some word of weight.

          [*Enter from the right* CREON, *the King, with armed*
            Attendants.

    Creon. Thou woman sullen-eyed and hot with hate
Against thy lord, Medea, I here command
That thou and thy two children from this land

Go forth to banishment. Make no delay:
Seeing ourselves, the King, are come this day
To see our charge fulfilled; nor shall again
Look homeward ere we have led thy children twain
And thee beyond our realm's last boundary.

 Medea. Lost! Lost!
Mine haters at the helm with sail flung free
Pursuing; and for us no beach nor shore
In the endless waters! . . . Yet, though stricken sore,
I still will ask thee, for what crime, what thing
Unlawful, wilt thou cast me out, O King?

 Creon. What crime? I fear thee, woman—little need
To cloak my reasons—lest thou work some deed
Of darkness on my child. And in that fear
Reasons enough have part. Thou comest here
A wise-woman confessed, and full of lore
In unknown ways of evil. Thou art sore
In heart, being parted from thy lover's arms.
And more, thou hast made menace . . . so the alarms
But now have reached mine ear . . . on bride and groom,
And him who gave the bride, to work thy doom
Of vengeance. Which, ere yet it be too late,
I sweep aside. I choose to earn thine hate
Of set will now, not palter with the mood
Of mercy, and hereafter weep in blood.

 Medea. 'Tis not the first nor second time, O King,
That fame hath hurt me, and come nigh to bring
My ruin. . . . How can any man, whose eyes
Are wholesome, seek to rear his children wise[4]
Beyond men's wont? Much helplessness in arts
Of common life, and in their townsmen's hearts
Envy deep-set . . . so much their learning brings!
Come unto fools with knowledge of new things,
They deem it vanity, not knowledge. Aye,
And men that erst for wisdom were held high,
Feel thee a thorn to fret them, privily
Held higher than they. So hath it been with me.
A wise-woman I am; and for that sin
To divers ill names men would pen me in;
A seed of strife; an eastern dreamer; one

[322]

Of brand not theirs; one hard to play upon . . .
Ah, I am not so wondrous wise!—And now,
To thee, I am terrible! What fearest thou?
What dire deed? Do I tread so proud a path—
Fear me not thou!—that I should brave the wrath
Of princes? Thou: what hast thou ever done
To wrong me? Granted thine own child to one
Whom thy soul chose.—Ah, *him* out of my heart
I hate; but thou, meseems, hast done thy part
Not ill. And for thine houses' happiness
I hold no grudge. Go: marry, and God bless
Your issues. Only suffer me to rest
Somewhere within this land. Though sore oppressed,
I will be still, knowing mine own defeat.

   Creon. Thy words be gentle: but I fear me yet
Lest even now there creep some wickedness
Deep hid within thee. And for that the less
I trust thee now than ere these words began.
A woman quick of wrath, aye, or a man,
Is easier watching than the cold and still.

   Up, straight, and find thy road! Mock not my will
With words. This doom is passed beyond recall;
Nor all thy crafts shall help thee, being withal
My manifest foe, to linger at my side.

   Medea (*suddenly throwing herself down and clinging to
     Creon*). Oh, by thy knees! By that new-wedded bride . . .

   Creon. 'Tis waste of words. Thou shalt not weaken me.

   Medea. Wilt hunt me? Spurn me when I kneel to thee?

   Creon. 'Tis mine own house that kneels to me, not thou.

   Medea. Home, my lost home, how I desire thee now!

   Creon. And I mine, and my child, beyond all things.

   Medea. O Loves of man, what curse is on your wings!

   Creon. Blessing or curse, 'tis as their chances flow.

   Medea. Remember, Zeus, the cause of all this woe!

   Creon. Oh, rid me of my pains! Up, get thee gone!

   Medea. What would I with thy pains? I have mine own.

   Creon. Up: or, 'fore God, my soldiers here shall fling . . .

   Medea. Not that! Not that! . . . I do but pray, O
   King . . .

   Creon. Thou wilt not? I must face the harsher task?

Medea. I accept mine exile. 'Tis not that I ask.

Creon. Why then so wild? Why clinging to mine hand?

Medea (*rising*). For one day only leave me in thy land
At peace, to find some counsel, ere the strain
Of exile fall, some comfort for these twain,
Mine innocents; since others take no thought,
It seems, to save the babes that they begot.

Ah! Thou wilt pity them! Thou also art
A father: thou hast somewhere still a heart
That feels. . . . I reck not of myself: 'tis they
That break me, fallen upon so dire a day.

Creon. Mine is no tyrant's mood. Aye, many a time
Ere this my tenderness hath marred the chime
Of wisest counsels. And I know that now
I do mere folly. But so be it! Thou
Shalt have this grace . . . But this I warn thee clear,
If once the morrow's sunlight find thee here
Within my borders, thee or child of thine,
Thou diest! . . . Of this judgement not a line
Shall waver nor abate. So linger on,
If thou needs must, till the next risen sun;
No further. . . . In one day there scarce can be
Those perils wrought whose dread yet haunteth me.

[*Exit* CREON *with his suite.*

Chorus. O woman, woman of sorrow,
    Where wilt thou turn and flee?
What town shall be thine to-morrow,
    What land of all lands that be,
    What door of a strange man's home?
    Yea, God hath hunted thee,
    Medea, forth to the foam
      Of a trackless sea.

Medea. Defeat on every side; what else?—But Oh,
Not here the end is: think it not! I know
For bride and groom one battle yet untried,
And goodly pains for him that gave the bride.

Dost dream I would have grovelled to this man,
Save that I won mine end, and shaped my plan
For merry deeds? My lips had never deigned
Speak word with him: my flesh been never stained

With touching. . . . Fool, Oh, triple fool!   It lay
So plain for him to kill my whole essay
By exile swift: and, lo, he sets me free
This one long day: wherein mine haters three
Shall lie here dead, the father and the bride
And husband—mine, not hers!   Oh, I have tried
So many thoughts of murder to my turn,
I know not which best likes me.   Shall I burn
Their house with fire?   Or stealing past unseen
To Jason's bed—I have a blade made keen
For that—stab, breast to breast, that wedded pair?
Good, but for one thing.   When I am taken there,
And killed, they will laugh loud who hate me. . . .
                                                              Nay,

I love the old way best, the simple way
Of poison, where we too are strong as men.
Ah me!
And they being dead—what place shall hold me then?
What friend shall rise, with land inviolate
And trusty doors, to shelter from their hate
This flesh? . . . None anywhere! . . . A little more
I needs must wait: and, if there ope some door
Of refuge, some strong tower to shield me, good:
In craft and darkness I will hunt this blood.
Else, if mine hour be come and no hope nigh,
Then sword in hand, full-willed and sure to die,
I yet will live to slay them.   I will wend
Man-like, their road of daring to the end.
    So help me She who of all Gods hath been
The best to me, of all my chosen queen
And helpmate, Hecatê, who dwells apart,
The flame of flame, in my fire's inmost heart:
For all their strength, they shall not stab my soul
And laugh thereafter!   Dark and full of dole
Their bridal feast shall be, most dark the day
They joined their hands, and hunted me away.
    Awake thee now, Medea!   Whatso plot
Thou hast, or cunning, strive and falter not.
On to the peril-point!   Now comes the strain
Of daring.   Shall they trample thee again?

How?   And with Hellas laughing o'er thy fall
While this thief's daughter weds, and weds withal
Jason? . . . A true king was thy father, yea,
And born of the ancient Sun! . . . Thou know'st the way;
And God hath made thee woman, things most vain
For help, but wondrous in the paths of pain.

[MEDEA *goes into the House.*

Chorus.   Back streams the wave on the ever-running river:
   Life, life is changed and the laws of it o'ertrod.
Man shall be the slave, the affrighted, the low-liver!
      Man hath forgotten God.
And woman, yea, woman, shall be terrible in story:
   The tales too, meseemeth, shall be other than of yore.
For a fear there is that cometh out of Woman, and a glory,
   And the hard hating voices shall encompass her no more!

The old bards shall cease, and their memory that lingers
   Of frail brides and faithless, shall be shrivelled as with fire.
For they loved us not, nor knew us: and our lips were dumb, our
      fingers
         Could wake not the secret of the lyre.

Else, else, O God the Singer, I had sung amid their rages
   A long tale of Man and his deeds for good and ill.
But the old World knoweth—'tis the speech of all his ages—
   Man's wrong and ours: he knoweth and is still.

Some Women.   Forth from thy father's home
         Thou camest, O heart of fire,
   To the Dark Blue Rocks, to the clashing foam,
         To the seas of thy desire:

      Till the Dark Blue Bar was crossed;
            And, lo, by an alien river
      Standing, thy lover lost,
            Void-armed for ever,

      Forth yet again, O lowest
         Of landless women, a ranger
      Of desolate ways, thou goest,
            From the walls of the stranger.

[326]

Others. And the great Oath waxeth weak;
    And Ruth, as a thing outstriven,
Is fled, fled, from the shores of the Greek,
Away on the winds of heaven.

Dark is the house afar,
    Where an old king called thee daughter;
All that was once thy star
    In stormy water,

Dark: and, lo, in the nearer
    House that was sworn to love thee,
Another, queenlier, dearer,
    Is thronèd above thee.

              [*Enter from the right* JASON.

Jason. Oft have I seen, in other days than these,
How a dark temper maketh maladies
No friend can heal. 'Twas easy to have kept
Both land and home. It needed but to accept
Unstrivingly the pleasure of our lords.
But thou, for mere delight in stormy words,
Wilt lose all! . . . Now thy speech provokes not me.
Rail on. Of all mankind let Jason be
Most evil; none shall check thee. But for these
Dark threats cast out against the majesties
Of Corinth, count as veriest gain thy path
Of exile. I myself, when princely wrath
Was hot against thee, strove with all good will
To appease the wrath, and wished to keep thee still
Beside me. But thy mouth would never stay
From vanity, blaspheming night and day
Our masters. Therefore thou shalt fly the land.
    Yet, even so, I will not hold my hand
From succouring mine own people. Here am I
To help thee, woman, pondering heedfully
Thy new state. For I would not have thee flung
Provisionless away—aye, and the young
Children as well; nor lacking aught that will
Of mine can bring thee. Many a lesser ill
Hangs on the heels of exile. . . . Aye, and though

[327]

Thou hate me, dream not that my heart can know
Or fashion aught of angry will to thee.

    Medea. Evil, most evil! . . . since thou grantest me
That comfort, the worst weapon left me now
To smite a coward. . . . Thou comest to me, thou,
Mine enemy! (*Turning to the* CHORUS) Oh, say, how call ye
    this,
To face, and smile, the comrade whom his kiss
Betrayed? Scorn? Insult? Courage? None of these:
'Tis but of all man's inward sicknesses
The vilest, that he knoweth not of shame
Nor pity! Yet I praise him that he came . . .
To me it shall bring comfort, once to clear
My heart on thee, and thou shalt wince to hear.

    I will begin with that, 'twixt me and thee,
That first befell. I saved thee. I saved thee—
Let thine own Greeks be witness, every one
That sailed on Argo—saved thee, sent alone
To yoke with yokes the bulls of fiery breath,[5]
And sow that Acre of the Lords of Death;
And mine own ancient Serpent, who did keep
The Golden Fleece, the eyes that knew not sleep,
And shining coils, him also did I smite
Dead for thy sake, and lifted up the light
That bade thee live. Myself, uncounsellèd,
Stole forth from father and from home, and fled
Where dark Iôlcos under Pelion lies,
With thee—Oh, single-hearted more than wise!
I murdered Pelias, yea, in agony,
By his own daughters' hands, for sake of thee;
I swept their house like War.—And hast thou then
Accepted all—O evil yet again!—
And cast me off and taken thee for bride
Another? And with children at thy side!
One could forgive a childless man. But no:
I have borne thee children . . .

                     Is sworn faith so low
And weak a thing? I understand it not.
Are the old gods dead? Are the old laws forgot,
And new laws made? Since not my passioning,

But thine own heart, doth cry thee for a thing
Forsworn.

> [*She catches sight of her own hand which she
> has thrown out to denounce him.*

Poor, poor right hand of mine, whom he
Did cling to, and these knees, so cravingly,
We are unclean, thou and I; we have caught the stain
Of bad men's flesh . . . and dreamed our dreams in vain.

Thou comest to befriend me? Give me, then,
Thy counsel. 'Tis not that I dream again
For good from thee: but, questioned, thou wilt show
The viler. Say: now whither shall I go?
Back to my father? Him I did betray,
And all his land, when we two fled away.
To those poor Peliad maids? For them 'twere good
To take me in, who spilled their father's blood. . . .
Aye, so my whole life stands! There were at home
Who loved me well: to them I am become
A curse. And the first friends who sheltered me,[6]
Whom most I should have spared, to pleasure thee
I have turned to foes. Oh, therefore hast thou laid
My crown upon me, blest of many a maid
In Hellas, now I have won what all did crave,
Thee, the world-wondered lover and the brave;
Who this day looks and sees me banished, thrown
Away with these two babes, all, all, alone . . .
Oh, merry mocking when the lamps are red:
"Where go the bridegroom's babes to beg their bread
In exile, and the woman who gave all
To save him?"

O great God, shall gold withal
Bear thy clear mark, to sift the base and fine,
And o'er man's living visage runs no sign
To show the lie within, ere all too late?

Leader. Dire and beyond all healing is the hate
When hearts that loved are turned to enmity.

Jason. In speech at least, meseemeth, I must be
Not evil; but, as some old pilot goes
Furled to his sail's last edge, when danger blows
Too fiery, run before the wind and swell,

Woman, of thy loud storms.—And thus I tell
My tale. Since thou wilt build so wondrous high
Thy deeds of service in my jeopardy,
To all my crew and quest I know but one
Saviour, of Gods or mortals one alone,
The Cyprian. Oh, thou hast both brain and wit,
Yet underneath . . . nay, all the tale of it
Were graceless telling; how sheer love, a fire
Of poison-shafts, compelled thee with desire
To save me. But enough. I will not score
That count too close. 'Twas good help: and therefor
I give thee thanks, howe'er the help was wrought.
Howbeit, in my deliverance, thou hast got
Far more than given. A good Greek land hath been
Thy lasting home, not barbary. Thou hast seen
Our ordered life, and justice, and the long
Still grasp of law not changing with the strong
Man's pleasure. Then, all Hellas far and near
Hath learned thy wisdom, and in every ear
Thy fame is. Had thy days run by unseen
On that last edge of the world, where then had been
The story of great Medea? Thou and I . . .
What worth to us were treasures heapèd high
In rich kings' rooms; what worth a voice of gold
More sweet than ever rang from Orpheus old,
Unless our deeds have glory?

                              Speak I so,
Touching the Quest I wrought, thyself did throw
The challenge down. Next for thy cavilling
Of wrath at mine alliance with a king,
Here thou shalt see I both was wise, and free
From touch of passion, and a friend to thee
Most potent, and my children . . . Nay, be still!
   When first I stood in Corinth, clogged with ill
From many a desperate mischance, what bliss
Could I that day have dreamed of, like to this,
To wed with a king's daughter, I exiled
And beggared? Not—what makes thy passion wild—
From loathing of thy bed; not over-fraught
With love for this new bride; not that I sought

[330]

To upbuild mine house with offspring: 'tis enough,
What thou hast borne: I make no word thereof:
But, first and greatest, that we all might dwell
In a fair house and want not, knowing well
That poor men have no friends, but far and near
Shunning and silence.   Next, I sought to rear
Our sons in nurture worthy of my race,
And, raising brethren to them, in one place
Join both my houses, and be all from now
Prince-like and happy.   What more need hast thou
Of children? And for me, it serves my star
To link in strength the children that now are
With those that shall be.

       Have I counselled ill?
Not thine own self would say it, couldst thou still
One hour thy jealous flesh.—'Tis ever so!
Who looks for more in women?   When the flow
Of love runs plain, why, all the world is fair:
But, once there fall some ill chance anywhere
To baulk that thirst, down in swift hate are trod
Men's dearest aims and noblest.   Would to God
We mortals by some other seed could raise
Our fruits, and no blind women block our ways!
Then had there been no curse to wreck mankind.

 Leader.   Lord Jason, very subtly hast thou twined
Thy speech: but yet, though all athwart thy will
I speak, this is not well thou dost, but ill,
Betraying her who loved thee and was true.

 Medea.   Surely I have my thoughts, and not a few
Have held me strange.   To me it seemeth, when
A crafty tongue is given to evil men
'Tis like to wreck, not help them.   Their own brain
Tempts them with lies to dare and dare again,
Till . . . no man hath enough of subtlety.
As thou—be not so seeming-fair to me
Nor deft of speech.   One word will make thee fall.
Wert thou not false, 'twas thine to tell me all,
And charge me help thy marriage path, as I
Did love thee; not befool me with a lie.

 Jason.   An easy task had that been!   Aye, and thou

[331]

A loving aid, who canst not, even now,
Still that loud heart that surges like the tide!

Medea. That moved thee not. Thine old barbarian bride,
The queen out of the east who loved thee sore,
She grew grey-haired, she served thy pride no more.

Jason. Now understand for once! The girl to me
Is nothing, in this web of sovranty
I hold. I do but seek to save, even yet,
Thee: and for brethren to our sons beget
Young kings, to prosper all our lives again.

Medea. God shelter me from prosperous days of pain,
And wealth that maketh wounds about my heart.

Jason. Wilt change that prayer, and choose a wiser part?
Pray not to hold true sense for pain, nor rate
Thyself unhappy, being too fortunate.

Medea. Aye, mock me; thou hast where to lay thine head,
But I go naked to mine exile.

Jason.   Tread
Thine own path! Thou hast made it all to be.

Medea. How? By seducing and forsaking thee?

Jason. By those vile curses on the royal halls
Let loose. . . .

Medea.   On thy house also, as chance falls,
I am a living curse.

Jason.   Oh, peace! Enough
Of these vain wars: I will no more thereof.
If thou wilt take from all that I possess
Aid for these babes and thine own helplessness
Of exile, speak thy bidding. Here I stand
Full-willed to succour thee with stintless hand,
And send my signet to old friends that dwell
On foreign shores, who will entreat thee well.
Refuse, and thou shalt do a deed most vain.
But cast thy rage away, and thou shalt gain
Much, and lose little for thine anger's sake.

Medea. I will not seek thy friends. I will not take
Thy givings. Give them not. Fruits of a stem
Unholy bring no blessing after them.

Jason. Now God in heaven be witness, all my heart
Is willing, in all ways, to do its part

For thee and for thy babes. But nothing good
Can please thee. In sheer savageness of mood
Thou drivest from thee every friend. Wherefore
I warrant thee, thy pains shall be the more.

[He goes slowly away.

Medea. Go: thou art weary for the new delight
Thou wooest, so long tarrying out of sight
Of her sweet chamber. Go, fulfil thy pride,
O bridegroom! For it may be, such a bride
Shall wait thee,—yea, God heareth me in this—
As thine own heart shall sicken ere it kiss.

Chorus. Alas, the Love that falleth like a flood,
     Strong-winged and transitory:
  Why praise ye him? What beareth he of good
     To man, or glory?
  Yet Love there is that moves in gentleness,
  Heart-filling, sweetest of all powers that bless.
  Loose not on me, O Holder of man's heart,
     Thy golden quiver,
  Nor steep in poison of desire the dart
     That heals not ever.

The pent hate of the word that cavilleth,
     The strife that hath no fill,
Where once was fondness; and the mad heart's breath
     For strange love panting still:
O Cyprian, cast me not on these; but sift,
Keen-eyed, of love the good and evil gift.
Make Innocence my friend, God's fairest star,
     Yea, and abate not
The rare sweet beat of bosoms without war,
     That love, and hate not.

Others. Home of my heart, land of my own,
     Cast me not, nay, for pity,
  Out on my ways, helpless, alone,
  Where the feet fail in the mire and stone,
     A woman without a city.
  Ah, not that! Better the end:
     The green grave cover me rather,
  If a break must come in the days I know,

[333]

And the skies be changed and the earth below;
For the weariest road that man may wend
　　Is forth from the home of his father.

Lo, we have seen: 'tis not a song
　　Sung, nor learned of another.
For whom hast thou in thy direst wrong
For comfort?　Never a city strong
　　To hide thee, never a brother.
Ah, but the man—cursed be he,
　　Cursèd beyond recover,
Who openeth, shattering, seal by seal,
A friend's clean heart, then turns his heel,
Deaf unto love: never in me
　　Friend shall he know nor lover.

> [*While Medea is waiting downcast, seated
> upon her door-step, there passes from the
> left a traveller with followers. As he
> catches sight of Medea he stops.*

Aegeus.　Have joy, Medea!　'Tis the homeliest
Word that old friends can greet with, and the best.
　Medea (*looking up, surprised*).　Oh, joy on thee, too, Aegeus,
　　gentle king
Of Athens!—But whence com'st thou journeying?
　Aegeus.　From Delphi now and the old encaverned stair. . . .
　Medea.　Where Earth's heart speaks in song?　What mad'st
　　thou there?
　Aegeus.　Prayed heaven for children—the same search alway.
　Medea.　Children?　Ah God!　Art childless to this day?
　Aegeus.　So God hath willed.　Childless and desolate.
　Medea.　What word did Phœbus speak, to change thy fate?
　Aegeus.　Riddles, too hard for mortal man to read.
　Medea.　Which I may hear?
　Aegeus.　　　　　　　　　　Assuredly: they need
A rarer wit.
　Medea.　　　　　　　How said he?
　Aegeus.　　　　　　　　　　　　Not to spill
Life's wine, nor seek for more. . . .
　Medea.　　　　　　　　　　　Until?

[334]

Aegeus.   Until
I tread the hearth-stone of my sires of yore.

Medea. And what should bring thee here, by Creon's shore?

Aegeus. One Pittheus know'st thou, high lord of Trozên?

Medea. Aye, Pelops' son, a man most pure of sin.

Aegeus. Him I would ask, touching Apollo's will.

Medea. Much use in God's ways hath he, and much skill.

Aegeus. And, long years back he was my battle-friend,
The truest e'er man had.

Medea.   Well, may God send
Good hap to thee, and grant all thy desire.

Aegeus. But thou . . . ? Thy frame is wasted, and the fire
Dead in thine eyes.

Medea.   Aegeus, my husband is
The falsest man in the world.

Aegeus.   What word is this?
Say clearly what thus makes thy visage dim?

Medea. He is false to me, who never injured him.

Aegeus. What hath he done? Show all, that I may see.

Medea. Ta'en him a wife; a wife, set over me
To rule his house.

Aegeus.   He hath not dared to do,
Jason, a thing so shameful?

Medea.   Aye, 'tis true:
And those he loved of yore have no place now.

Aegeus. Some passion sweepeth him? Or is it thou
He turns from?

Medea.   Passion, passion to betray
His dearest!

Aegeus.   Shame be his, so fallen away
From honour!

Medea.   Passion to be near a throne,
A king's heir!

Aegeus.   How, who gives the bride? Say on.

Medea. Creon, who o'er all Corinth standeth chief.

Aegeus. Woman, thou hast indeed much cause for grief.

Medea. 'Tis ruin.—And they have cast me out as well.

Aegeus. Who? 'Tis a new wrong this, and terrible.

Medea. Creon the king, from every land and shore. . . .

Aegeus. And Jason suffers him? Oh, 'tis too sore!

[335]

Medea. He loveth to bear bravely ills like these!
But, Aegeus, by thy beard, oh, by thy knees,
I pray thee, and I give me for thine own,
Thy suppliant, pity me! Oh, pity one
So miserable. Thou never wilt stand there
And see me cast out friendless to despair.
Give me a home in Athens . . . by the fire
Of thine own hearth! Oh, so may thy desire
Of children be fulfilled of God, and thou
Die happy! . . . Thou canst know not; even **now**
Thy prize is won! I, I will make of thee
A childless man no more. The seed shall be,
I swear it, sown. Such magic herbs I know.

    Aegeus. Woman, indeed my heart goes forth **to show**
This help to thee, first for religion's sake,
Then for thy promised hope, to heal my ache
Of childlessness. 'Tis this hath made mine whole
Life as a shadow, and starved out my soul.
But thus it stands with me. Once make thy way
To Attic earth, I, as in law I may,
Will keep thee and befriend. But in this land,
Where Creon rules, I may not raise my hand
To shelter thee. Move of thine own essay
To seek my house, there thou shalt alway stay,
Inviolate, never to be seized again.
But come thyself from Corinth. I would fain
Even in foreign eyes be alway just.

    Medea. Tis well. Give me an oath wherein to trust
And all that man could ask thou hast granted me.

    Aegeus. Dost trust me not? Or what thing troubleth thee?

    Medea. I trust thee. But so many, far and near,
Do hate me—all King Pelias' house, and here
Creon. Once bound by oaths and sanctities
Thou canst not yield me up for such as these
To drag from Athens. But a spoken word,
No more, to bind thee, which no God hath heard . . .
The embassies, methinks, would come and go:
They all are friends to thee. . . . Ah me, I know
Thou wilt not list to me! So weak am I,
And they full-filled with gold and majesty.

Aegeus. Methinks 'tis a far foresight, this thine oath.
Still, if thou so wilt have it, nothing loath
Am I to serve thee. Mine own hand is so
The stronger, if I have this plea to show
Thy persecutors: and for thee withal
The bond more sure.—On what God shall I call?

Medea. Swear by the Earth thou treadest, by the Sun,
Sire of my sires, and all the gods as one. . . .

Aegeus. To do what thing or not do? Make all plain.

Medea. Never thyself to cast me out again.
Nor let another, whatsoe'er his plea,
Take me, while thou yet livest and art free.

Aegeus. Never: so hear me, Earth, and the great star
Of daylight, and all other gods that are!

Medea. 'Tis well: and if thou falter from thy vow . . . ?

Aegeus. God's judgement on the godless break my brow!

Medea. Go! Go thy ways rejoicing.—All is bright
And clear before me. Go: and ere the night
Myself will follow, when the deed is done
I purpose, and the end I thirst for won.

                    [Aegeus and his train depart.

Chorus. Farewell: and Maia's guiding Son
      Back lead thee to thy hearth and fire,
      Aegeus; and all the long desire
    That wasteth thee, at last be won:
    Our eyes have seen thee as thou art,
    A gentle and a righteous heart.

Medea. God, and God's Justice, and ye blinding Skies!
At last the victory dawneth! Yea, mine eyes
See, and my foot is on the mountain's brow.
Mine enemies! Mine enemies, oh, now
Atonement cometh! Here at my worst hour
A friend is found, a very port of power
To save my shipwreck. Here will I make fast
Mine anchor, and escape them at the last
In Athens' wallèd hill.—But ere the end
'Tis meet I show thee all my counsel, friend:
Take it, no tale to make men laugh withal!
    Straightway to Jason I will send some thrall
To entreat him to my presence. Comes he here,

Then with soft reasons will I feed his ear,
How his will now is my will, how all things
Are well, touching this marriage-bed of kings
For which I am betrayed—all wise and rare
And profitable! Yet will I make one prayer,
That my two children be no more exiled
But stay. . . . Oh, not that I would leave a child
Here upon angry shores till those have laughed
Who hate me: 'tis that I will slay by craft
The king's daughter. With gifts they shall be sent,
Gifts to the bride to spare their banishment,
Fine robings and a carcanet of gold.
Which raiment let her once but take, and fold
About her, a foul death that girl shall die
And all who touch her in her agony.
Such poison shall they drink, my robe and wreath!

    Howbeit, of that no more. I gnash my teeth
Thinking on what a path my feet must tread
Thereafter. I shall lay those children dead—
Mine, whom no hand shall steal from me away!
Then, leaving Jason childless, and the day
As night above him, I will go my road
To exile, flying, flying from the blood
Of these my best-beloved, and having wrought
All horror, so but one thing reach me not,
The laugh of them that hate us.

                              Let it come!
What profits life to me? I have no home,
No country now, nor shield from any wrong.
That was my evil hour, when down the long
Halls of my father out I stole, my will
Chained by a Greek man's voice, who still, oh, still,
If God yet live, shall all requited be.
For never child of mine shall Jason see
Hereafter living, never child beget
From his new bride, who this day, desolate
Even as she made me desolate, shall die
Shrieking amid my poisons. . . . Names have I
Among your folk? One light? One weak of hand?
An eastern dreamer?—Nay, but with the brand

Of strange suns burnt, my hate, by God above,
A perilous thing, and passing sweet my love!
For these it is that make life glorious.

    Leader. Since thou hast bared thy fell intent to us
I, loving thee, and helping in their need
Man's laws, adjure thee, dream not of this deed!

    Medea. There is no other way.—I pardon thee
Thy littleness, who art not wronged like me.

    Leader. Thou canst not kill the fruit thy body bore!

    Medea. Yes: if the man I hate be pained the more.

    Leader. And thou made miserable, most miserable?

    Medea. Oh, let it come! All words of good or ill
Are wasted now.

            [*She claps her hands: the Nurse comes out from
              the house.*

                          Ho, woman; get thee gone
And lead lord Jason hither. . . . There is none
Like thee, to work me these high services.
But speak no word of what my purpose is,
As thou art faithful, thou, and bold to try
All succours, and a woman even as I!

                          [*The Nurse departs.*

    Chorus. The sons of Erechtheus, the olden,
        Whom high gods planted of yore
    In an old land of heaven upholden,
        A proud land untrodden of war:
    They are hungered, and, lo, their desire
        With wisdom is fed as with meat:
    In their skies is a shining of fire,
        A joy in the fall of their feet:
    And thither, with manifold dowers,
        From the North, from the hills, from the morn,
    The Muses did gather their powers,
        That a child of the Nine should be born;
    And Harmony, sown as the flowers,
        Grew gold in the acres of corn.

    And Cephîsus, the fair-flowing river—
        The Cyprian dipping her hand
    Hath drawn of his dew, and the shiver

Of her touch is as joy in the land.
For her breathing in fragrance is written,
    And in music her path as she goes,
And the cloud of her hair, it is litten
    With stars of the wind-woven rose.
So fareth she ever and ever,
    And forth of her bosom is blown,
As dews on the winds of the river,
    An hunger of passions unknown,
Strong Loves of all godlike endeavour,
    Whom Wisdom shall throne on her throne.

Some Women. But Cephîsus the fair-flowing,
    Will he bear thee on his shore?
        Shall the land that succours all, succour thee,
    Who art foul among thy kind,
    With the tears of children blind?
Dost thou see the red gash growing,
    Thine own burden dost thou see?
        Every side, Every way,
    Lo, we kneel to thee and pray:
        By thy knees, by thy soul, O woman wild!
    One at least thou canst not slay,
        Not thy child!
Others. Hast thou ice that thou shalt bind it
    To thy breast, and make thee dead
        To thy children, to thine own spirit's pain?
    When the hand knows what it dares,
    When thine eyes look into theirs,
Shalt thou keep by tears unblinded
    Thy dividing of the slain?
        These be deeds not for thee:
    These be things that cannot be!
        Thy babes—though thine hardihood be fell,
    When they cling about thy knee,
        'Twill be well!

                                            [*Enter* JASON.

Jason. I answer to thy call. Though full of hate
Thou be, I yet will not so far abate
My kindness for thee, nor refuse mine ear.
Say in what new desire thou hast called me here.

Medea. Jason, I pray thee, for my words but now
Spoken, forgive me. My bad moods. . . . Oh, thou
At least wilt strive to bear with them! There be
Many old deeds of love 'twixt me and thee.
Lo, I have reasoned with myself apart
And chidden: "Why must I be mad, O heart
Of mine: and raging against one whose word
Is wisdom: making me a thing abhorred
To them that rule the land, and to mine own
Husband, who doth but that which, being done,
Will help us all—to wed a queen, and get
Young kings for brethren to my sons? And yet
I rage alone, and cannot quit my rage—
What aileth me?—when God sends harbourage
So simple? Have I not my children? Know
I not we are but exiles, and must go
Beggared and friendless else?" Thought upon thought
So pressed me, till I knew myself full-fraught
With bitterness of heart and blinded eyes.
So now—I give thee thanks: and hold thee wise
To have caught this anchor for our aid. The fool
Was I; who should have been thy friend, thy tool;
Gone wooing with thee, stood at thy bed-side
Serving, and welcomed duteously thy bride.
But, as we are, we are—I will not say
Mere evil—women! Why must thou to-day
Turn strange, and make thee like some evil thing,
Childish, to meet my childish passioning?
See, I surrender: and confess that then
I had bad thoughts, but now have turned again
And found my wiser mind.   *[She claps her hands.*
                         Ho, children! Run
Quickly! Come hither, out into the sun,
         *[The Children come from the house, followed
          by their Attendant.*
And greet your father. Welcome him with us,
And throw quite, quite away, as mother does,
Your anger against one so dear. Our peace
Is made, and all the old bad war shall cease
For ever.—Go, and take his hand. . . .

EURIPIDES

[*As the Children go to Jason, she suddenly bursts
into tears. The Children quickly return to her:
she recovers herself, smiling amid her tears.*

Ah me,

I am full of hidden horrors! . . . Shall it be
A long time more, my children, that ye live
To reach to me those dear, dear arms? . . . Forgive!
I am so ready with my tears to-day,
And full of dread. . . . I sought to smooth away
The long strife with your father, and, lo, now
I have all drowned with tears this little brow!

[*She wipes the child's face.*

Leader. O'er mine eyes too there stealeth a pale tear:
Let the evil rest, O God, let it rest here!
Jason. Woman, indeed I praise thee now, nor say
Ill of thine other hour. 'Tis nature's way,
A woman needs must stir herself to wrath,
When work of marriage by so strange a path
Crosseth her lord. But thou, thine heart doth wend
The happier road. Thou hast seen, ere quite the end,
What choice must needs be stronger: which to do
Shows a wise-minded woman. . . . And for you,
Children, your father never has forgot
Your needs. If God but help him, he hath wrought
A strong deliverance for your weakness. Yea,
I think you, with your brethren, yet one day
Shall be the mightiest voices in this land.
Do you grow tall and strong. Your father's hand
Guideth all else, and whatso power divine
Hath alway helped him. . . . Ah, may it be mine
To see you yet in manhood, stern of brow,
Strong-armed, set high o'er those that hate me. . . .

How?

Woman, thy face is turned. Thy cheek is swept
With pallor of strange tears. Dost not accept
Gladly and of good will my benisons?
Medea. 'Tis nothing. Thinking of these little ones. . . .
Jason. Take heart, then. I will guard them from all ill.
Medea. I do take heart. Thy word I never will

[342]

Mistrust. Alas, a woman's bosom bears
But woman's courage, a thing born for tears.
   Jason. What ails thee?—All too sore thou weepest there.
   Medea. I was their mother! When I heard thy prayer
Of long life for them, there swept over me
A horror, wondering how these things shall be.
   But for the matter of my need that thou
Should speak with me, part I have said, and now
Will finish.—Seeing it is the king's behest
To cast me out from Corinth . . . aye, and best,
Far best, for me—I know it—not to stay
Longer to trouble thee and those who sway
The realm, being held to all their house a foe. . . .
Behold, I spread my sails, and meekly go
To exile. But our children. . . . Could this land
Be still their home awhile: could thine own hand
But guide their boyhood. . . . Seek the king, and pray
His pity, that he bid thy children stay!
   Jason. He is hard to move. Yet surely 'twere well done.
   Medea. Bid her—for thy sake, for a daughter's boon. . . .
   Jason. Well thought! Her I can fashion to my mind.
   Medea. Surely. She is a woman like her kind. . . .
Yet I will aid thee in thy labour; I
Will send her gifts, the fairest gifts that lie
In the hands of men, things of the days of old,
Fine robings and a carcanet of gold,
By the boys' hands.—Go, quick, some handmaiden,
And fetch the raiment.   [*A handmaid goes into the house.*
               Ah, her cup shall then
Be filled indeed! What more should woman crave,
Being wed with thee, the bravest of the brave,
And girt with raiment which of old the sire
Of all my house, the Sun, gave, steeped in fire,
To his own fiery race?

     [*The handmaid has returned bearing the Gifts.*

              Come, children, lift
With heed these caskets. Bear them as your gift
To her, being bride and princess and of right
Blessed!—I think she will not hold them light.

[343]

Jason. Fond woman, why wilt empty thus thine hand
Of treasure? Doth King Creon's castle stand
In stint of raiment, or in stint of gold?
Keep these, and make no gift. For if she hold
Jason of any worth at all, I swear
Chattels like these will not weigh more with her.

Medea. Ah, chide me not! 'Tis written, gifts persuade
The gods in heaven; and gold is stronger made
Than words innumerable to bend men's ways.
Fortune is hers. God maketh great her days:
Young and a crownèd queen! And banishment
For those two babes. . . . I would not gold were spent,
But life's blood, ere that come.

                          My children, go
Forth into those rich halls, and, bowing low,
Beseech your father's bride, whom I obey,
Ye be not, of her mercy, cast away
Exiled: and give the caskets—above all
Mark this!—to none but her, to hold withal
And keep. . . . Go quick! And let your mother know
Soon the good tidings that she longs for. . . . Go!

           [*She goes quickly into the house. Jason and the
                Children with their Attendant depart.*

Chorus. Now I have no hope more of the children's living;
   No hope more. They are gone forth unto death.
The bride, she taketh the poison of their giving:
   She taketh the bounden gold and openeth;
And the crown, the crown, she lifteth about her brow,
Where the light brown curls are clustering. No hope now!
O sweet and cloudy gleam of the garments golden!
   The robe, it hath clasped her breast and the crown her head.
Then, then, she decketh the bride, as a bride of olden
   Story, that goeth pale to the kiss of the dead.
For the ring hath closed, and the portion of death is there;
And she flieth not, but perisheth unaware.

Some Women. O bridegroom, bridegroom of the kiss so
       cold,
Art thou wed with princes, art thou girt with gold,
          Who know'st not, suing
          For thy child's undoing,

And, on her thou lovest, for a doom untold?
How art thou fallen from thy place of old!
  Others. O Mother, Mother, what hast thou to reap,
When the harvest cometh, between wake and sleep?
            For a heart unslaken,
            For a troth forsaken,
Lo, babes that call thee from a bloody deep:
And thy love returns not. Get thee forth and weep!

> [*Enter the Attendant with the two Children:
> Medea comes out from the house.*

  Attendant. Mistress, these children from their banishment
Are spared. The royal bride hath mildly bent
Her hand to accept thy gifts, and all is now
Peace for the children.—Ha, why standest thou
Confounded, when good fortune draweth near?
  Medea. Ah God!
  Attendant. This chimes not with the news I bear.
  Medea. O God, have mercy!
  Attendant. Is some word of wrath
Here hidden that I knew not of? And hath
My hope to give thee joy so cheated me?
  Medea. Thou givest what thou givest: I blame not thee.
  Attendant. Thy brows are all o'ercast: thine eyes are
    filled. . . .
  Medea. For bitter need, Old Man! The gods have willed,
And my own evil mind, that this should come.
  Attendant. Take heart! Thy sons one day will bring thee
    home.
  Medea. Home? . . . I have others to send home. Woe's me!
  Attendant. Be patient. Many a mother before thee
Hath parted from her children. We poor things
Of men must needs endure what fortune brings.
  Medea. I will endure.—Go thou within, and lay
All ready that my sons may need to-day.

> [*The Attendant goes into the House.*

O children, children mine: and you have found
A land and home, where, leaving me discrowned
And desolate, forever you will stay,
Motherless children! And I go my way
To other lands, an exile, ere you bring

Your fruits home, ere I see you prospering
Or know your brides, or deck the bridal bed,
All flowers, and lift your torches overhead.

　Oh, cursèd be mine own hard heart! 'Twas all
In vain, then, that I reared you up, so tall
And fair; in vain I bore you, and was torn
With those long pitiless pains, when you were born.
Ah, wondrous hopes my poor heart had in you,
How you would tend me in mine age, and do
The shroud about me with your own dear hands,
When I lay cold, blessèd in all the lands
That knew us. And that gentle thought is dead!
You go, and I live on, to eat the bread
Of long years, to myself most full of pain.
And never your dear eyes, never again,
Shall see your mother, far away being thrown
To other shapes of life. . . . My babes, my own,
Why gaze ye so?—What is it that ye see?—
And laugh with that last laughter? . . . Woe is me,
What shall I do?
　　　　　　　　　Women, my strength is gone,
Gone like a dream, since once I looked upon
Those shining faces. . . . I can do it not.
Good-bye to all the thoughts that burned so hot
Aforetime! I will take and hide them far,
Far, from men's eyes. Why should I seek a war
So blind: by these babes' wounds to sting again
Their father's heart, and win myself a pain
Twice deeper? Never, never! I forget
Henceforward all I laboured for.
　　　　　　　　　　　　　And yet,
What is it with me? Would I be a thing
Mocked at, and leave mine enemies to sting
Unsmitten? It must be. O coward heart,
Ever to harbour such soft words!—Depart
Out of my sight, ye twain.　　　　[*The Children go in.*
　　　　　　　　　　　And they whose eyes
Shall hold it sin to share my sacrifice,
On their heads be it! My hand shall swerve not now.
　Ah, Ah, thou Wrath within me! Do not thou,

Do not. . . . Down, down, thou tortured thing, and spare
My children! They will dwell with us, aye, there
Far off, and give thee peace.

                             Too late, too late!
By all Hell's living agonies of hate,
They shall not take my little ones alive
To make their mock with! Howsoe'er I strive
The thing is doomed; it shall not escape now
From being. Aye, the crown is on the brow,
And the robe girt, and in the robe that high
Queen dying.

                  I know all. Yet . . . seeing that I
Must go so long a journey, and these twain
A longer yet and darker, I would fain
Speak with them, ere I go.

             [A handmaid brings the Children out again.

                        Come, children; stand
A little from me. There. Reach out your hand,
Your right hand—so—to mother: and good-bye!

        [She kept them hitherto at arm's length: but at
             the touch of their hands, her resolution breaks
             down, and she gathers them passionately
             into her arms.

Oh, darling hand! Oh, darling mouth, and eye,
And royal mien, and bright brave faces clear,
May you be blessèd, but not here! What here
Was yours, your father stole. . . . Ah God, the glow
Of cheek on cheek, the tender touch; and Oh,
Sweet scent of childhood. . . . Go! Go! . . . Am I
    blind? . . .
Mine eyes can see not, when I look to find
Their places. I am broken by the wings
Of evil. . . . Yea, I know to what bad things
I go, but louder than all thought doth cry
Anger, which maketh man's worst misery.

             [She follows the Children into the house.
  Chorus. My thoughts have roamed a cloudy land,
        And heard a fierier music fall
        Than woman's heart should stir withal:
        And yet some Muse majestical,

Unknown, hath hold of woman's hand
Seeking for Wisdom—not in all:
A feeble seed, a scattered band,
Thou yet shalt find in lonely places,
Not dead amongst us, nor our faces
Turned alway from the Muses' call.
And thus my thought would speak: that she
Who ne'er hath borne a child nor known
Is nearer to felicity:
Unlit she goeth and alone,
With little understanding what
A child's touch means of joy or woe,
And many toils she beareth not.
But they within whose garden fair
That gentle plant hath blown, they go
Deep-written all their days with care—
To rear the children, to make fast
Their hold, to win them wealth; and then
Much darkness, if the seed at last
Bear fruit in good or evil men!
And one thing at the end of all
Abideth, that which all men dread:
The wealth is won, the limbs are bred
To manhood, and the heart withal
Honest: and, lo, where Fortune smiled,
Some change, and what hath fallen? Hark!
'Tis death slow winging to the dark,
And in his arms what was thy child.
What therefore doth it bring of gain
To man, whose cup stood full before,
That God should send this one thing more
Of hunger and of dread, a door
Set wide to every wind of pain?

[*Medea comes out alone from the house.*

Medea. Friends, this long hour I wait on Fortune's eyes,
And strain my senses in a hot surmise
What passeth on that hill.—Ha! even now
There comes . . . 'tis one of Jason's men, I trow.
His wild-perturbèd breath doth warrant me
The tidings of some strange calamity.

[348]

[*Enter* MESSENGER.

Messenger. O dire and ghastly deed! Get thee away,
Medea! Fly! Nor let behind thee stay
One chariot's wing, one keel that sweeps the seas. . . .

Medea. And what hath chanced, to cause such flights as
these?

Messenger. The maiden princess lieth—and her sire,
The king—both murdered by thy poison-fire.

Medea. Most happy tiding! Which thy name prefers
Henceforth among my friends and well-wishers.

Messenger. What say'st thou? Woman, is thy mind within
Clear, and not raving? Thou art found in sin
Most bloody wrought against the king's high head,
And laughest at the tale, and hast no dread?

Medea. I have words also that could answer well
Thy word. But take thine ease, good friend, and tell,
How died they? Hath it been a very foul
Death, prithee? That were comfort to my soul.

Messenger. When thy two children, hand in hand entwined,
Came with their father, and passed on to find
The new-made bridal rooms, Oh, we were glad,
We thralls, who ever loved thee well, and had
Grief in thy grief. And straight there passed a word
From ear to ear, that thou and thy false lord
Had poured peace offering upon wrath foregone.
A right glad welcome gave we them, and one
Kissed the small hand, and one the shining hair:
Myself, for very joy, I followed where
The women's rooms are. There our mistress . . . she
Whom now we name so . . . thinking not to see
Thy little pair, with glad and eager brow
Sate waiting Jason. Then she saw, and slow
Shrouded her eyes, and backward turned again,
Sick that thy children should come near her. Then
Thy husband quick went forward, to entreat
The young maid's fitful wrath. "Thou wilt not meet
Love's coming with unkindness? Nay, refrain
Thy suddenness, and turn thy face again,
Holding as friends all that to me are dear,
Thine husband. And accept these robes they bear

[349]

As gifts: and beg thy father to unmake
His doom of exile on them—for my sake."
When once she saw the raiment, she could still
Her joy no more, but gave him all his will.
And almost ere the father and the two
Children were gone from out the room, she drew
The flowerèd garments forth, and sate her down
To her arraying: bound the golden crown
Through her long curls, and in a mirror fair
Arranged their separate clusters, smiling there
At the dead self[7] that faced her. Then aside
She pushed her seat, and paced those chambers wide
Alone, her white foot poising delicately—
So passing joyful in those gifts was she!—
And many a time would pause, straight-limbed, and wheel
Her head to watch the long fold to her heel
Sweeping. And then came something strange. Her cheek
Seemed pale, and back with crooked steps and weak
Groping of arms she walked, and scarcely found
Her old seat, that she fell not to the ground.

    Among the handmaids was a woman old
And grey, who deemed, I think, that Pan had hold
Upon her, or some spirit, and raised a keen
Awakening shout; till through her lips was seen
A white foam crawling, and her eyeballs back
Twisted, and all her face dead pale for lack
Of life: and while that old dame called, the cry
Turned strangely to its opposite,[8] to die
Sobbing. Oh, swiftly then one woman flew
To seek her father's rooms, one for the new
Bridegroom, to tell the tale. And all the place
Was loud with hurrying feet.

               So long a space
As a swift walker on a measured way
Would pace a furlong's course in, there she lay
Speechless, with veilèd lids. Then wide her eyes
She oped, and wildly, as she strove to rise,
Shrieked: for two diverse waves upon her rolled
Of stabbing death. The carcanet of gold
That gripped her brow was molten in a dire

And wondrous river of devouring fire.
And those fine robes, the gift thy children gave—
God's mercy!—everywhere did lap and lave
The delicate flesh; till up she sprang, and fled,
A fiery pillar, shaking locks and head
This way and that, seeking to cast the crown
Somewhere away. But like a thing nailed down
The burning gold held fast the anadem,
And through her locks, the more she scattered them,
Came fire the fiercer, till to earth she fell
A thing—save to her sire—scarce nameable,
And strove no more. That cheek of royal mien,
Where was it—or the place where eyes had been?
Only from crown and temples came faint blood
Shot through with fire. The very flesh, it stood
Out from the bones, as from a wounded pine
The gum starts, where those gnawing poisons fine
Bit in the dark—a ghastly sight! And touch
The dead we durst not. We had seen too much.

  But that poor father, knowing not, had sped,
Swift to his daughter's room, and there the dead
Lay at his feet. He knelt, and groaning low,
Folded her in his arms, and kissed her: "Oh,
Unhappy child, what thing unnatural hath
So hideously undone thee? Or what wrath
Of gods, to make this old grey sepulchre
Childless of thee? Would God but lay me there
To die with thee, my daughter!" So he cried.
But after, when he stayed from tears, and tried
To uplift his old bent frame, lo, in the folds
Of those fine robes it held, as ivy holds
Strangling among young laurel boughs. Oh, then
A ghastly struggle came! Again, again,
Up on his knee he writhed; but that dead breast
Clung still to his: till, wild, like one possessed,
He dragged himself half free; and, lo, the live
Flesh parted; and he laid him down to strive
No more with death, but perish; for the deep
Had risen above his soul. And there they sleep,
At last, the old proud father and the bride,

Even as his tears had craved it, side by side.
　　For thee—Oh, no word more! Thyself will **know**
How best to baffle vengeance. . . . Long ago
I looked upon man's days, and found a grey
Shadow. And this thing more I surely say,
That those of all men who are counted wise,
Strong wits, devisers of great policies,
Do pay the bitterest toll. Since life began,
Hath there in God's eye stood one happy man?
Fair days roll on, and bear more gifts or less
Of fortune, but to no man happiness.

　　　　　　　　　　　　　　　　[*Exit* MESSENGER.

　　Chorus. Some Women. Wrath upon wrath, meseems, this
　　　　day shall fall
From God on Jason! He hath earned it all.
　　Other Women. O miserable maiden, all my heart
Is torn for thee, so sudden to depart
From thy king's chambers and the light above
To darkness, all for sake of Jason's love!
　　Medea. Women, my mind is clear. I go to slay
My children with all speed, and then, away
From hence; not wait yet longer till they stand
Beneath another and an angrier hand
To die. Yea, howsoe'er I shield them, die
They must. And, seeing that they must, 'tis I
Shall slay them, I their mother, touched of none
Beside. Oh, up and get thine armour on,
My heart! Why longer tarry we to win
Our crown of dire inevitable sin?
Take up thy sword, O poor right hand of mine,
Thy sword: then onward to the thin-drawn line
Where life turns agony. Let there be naught
Of softness now: and keep thee from that thought,
'Born of thy flesh,' 'thine own belovèd.' Now,
For one brief day, forget thy children: thou
Shalt weep hereafter. Though thou slay them, yet
Sweet were they. . . . I am sore unfortunate.

　　　　　　　　　　　　　　　　[*She goes into the house.*

Chorus. Some Women. O Earth, our mother; and thou
      All-seër, arrowy crown
  Of Sunlight, manward now
    Look down, Oh, look down!
  Look upon one accurst,
    Ere yet in blood she twine
    Red hands—blood that is thine!
  O Sun, save her first!
  She is thy daughter still,
    Of thine own golden line;
  Save her! Or shall man spill
    The life divine?
Give peace, O Fire that diest not! Send thy spell
  To stay her yet, to lift her afar, afar—
A torture-changèd spirit, a voice of Hell
  Wrought of old wrongs and war!
Others. Alas for the mother's pain
    Wasted! Alas the dear
  Life that was born in vain!
    Woman, what mak'st thou here,
  Thou from beyond the Gate
  Where dim Symplêgades
  Clash in the dark blue seas,
  The shores where death doth wait?
  Why hast thou taken on thee,
    To make us desolate,
  This anger of misery
    And guilt of hate?
For fierce are the smitings back of blood once shed
  Where love hath been: God's wrath upon them that kill,
And an anguished earth, and the wonder of the dead
  Haunting as music still. . . .

                      [A cry is heard within.

A Woman. Hark! Did ye hear? Heard ye the children's cry?
Another. O miserable woman! O abhorred!
A Child within. What shall I do? What is it? Keep me fast
  From mother!
The Other Child. I know nothing. Brother! Oh,
  I think she means to kill us.

[353]

A Woman. Let me go!

        I will—Help! Help!—and save them at the last.

A Child. Yes, in God's name! Help quickly ere we die!

The Other Child. She has almost caught me now. She has a sword.

        [*Many of the Women are now beating at the barred door to get in. Others are standing apart.*

Women at the door. Thou stone, thou thing of iron! Wilt verily

      Spill with thine hand that life, the vintage stored

        Of thine own agony?

The Other Women. A Mother slew her babes in days of yore,[9]

      One, only one, from dawn to eventide,

        Ino, god-maddened, whom the Queen of Heaven

          Set frenzied, flying to the dark: and she

          Cast her for sorrow to the wide salt sea,

        Forth from those rooms of murder unforgiven,

      Wild-footed from a white crag of the shore,

      And clasping still her children twain, she died.

      O Love of Woman, charged with sorrow sore,

        What hast thou wrought upon us? What beside

        Resteth to tremble for?

        [*Enter hurriedly Jason and Attendants.*

Jason. Ye women by this doorway clustering

Speak, is the doer of the ghastly thing

Yet here, or fled? What hopeth she of flight?

Shall the deep yawn to shield her? Shall the height

Send wings, and hide her in the vaulted sky

To work red murder on her lords, and fly

Unrecompensed? But let her go! My care

Is but to save my children, not for her.

Let them she wronged requite her as they may.

I care not. 'Tis my sons I must some way

Save, ere the kinsmen of the dead can win

From them the payment of their mother's sin.

    Leader. Unhappy man, indeed thou knowest not

What dark place thou art come to! Else, God wot,

Jason, no word like these could fall from thee.

    Jason. What is it?—Ha! The woman would kill me?

Leader. Thy sons are dead, slain by their mother's hand.
Jason. How? Not the children. . . . I scarce understand. . . .
O God, thou hast broken me!
Leader.   Think of those twain
As things once fair, that ne'er shall bloom again.
   Jason. Where did she murder them? In that old room?
   Leader. Open, and thou shalt see thy children's doom.
   Jason. Ho, thralls! Unloose me yonder bars! Make more
Of speed! Wrench out the jointing of the door.
And show my two-edged curse, the children dead,
The woman. . . . Oh, this sword upon her head. . . .

> [*While the Attendants are still battering at the
> door Medea appears on the roof, standing
> on a chariot of winged Dragons, in which
> are the children's bodies.*

   Medea. What make ye at my gates? Why batter ye
With brazen bars, seeking the dead and me
Who slew them? Peace! . . . And thou, if aught of mine
Thou needest, speak, though never touch of thine
Shall scathe me more. Out of his firmament
My fathers' father, the high Sun, hath sent
This, that shall save me from mine enemies' rage.
   Jason. Thou living hate! Thou wife in every age
Abhorrèd, blood-red mother, who didst kill
My sons, and make me as the dead: and still
Canst take the sunshine to thine eyes, and smell
The green earth, reeking from thy deed of hell;
I curse thee! Now, Oh, now mine eyes can see,
That then were blinded, when from savagery
Of eastern chambers, from a cruel land,
To Greece and home I gathered in mine hand
Thee, thou incarnate curse: one that betrayed
Her home, her father, her . . . Oh, God hath laid
Thy sins on me!—I knew, I knew, there lay
A brother murdered on thy hearth that day
When thy first footstep fell on Argo's hull. . . .
Argo, my own, my swift and beautiful!
   That was her first beginning. Then a wife
I made her in my house. She bore to life

Children: and now for love, for chambering
And men's arms, she hath murdered them! A thing
Not one of all the maids of Greece, not one,
Had dreamed of; whom I spurned, and for mine own
Chose thee, a bride of hate to me and death,
Tigress, not woman, beast of wilder breath
Than Skylla shrieking o'er the Tuscan sea.
Enough! No scorn of mine can reach to thee,
Such iron is o'er thine eyes. Out from my road,
Thou crime-begetter, blind with children's blood!
And let me weep alone the bitter tide
That sweepeth Jason's days, no gentle bride
To speak with more, no child to look upon
Whom once I reared . . . all, all for ever gone!

    Medea. An easy answer had I to this swell
Of speech, but Zeus our father knoweth well,
All I for thee have wrought, and thou for me.
So let it rest. This thing was not to be,
That thou shouldst live a merry life, my bed
Forgotten and my heart uncomforted,
Thou nor thy princess: nor the king that planned
Thy marriage drive Medea from his land,
And suffer not. Call me what thing thou please,
Tigress or Skylla from the Tuscan seas:
My claws have gripped thine hearth, and all things shine.

    Jason. Thou too hast grief. Thy pain is fierce as mine.
    Medea. I love the pain, so thou shalt laugh no more.
    Jason. Oh, what a womb of sin my children bore!
    Medea. Sons, did ye perish for your father's shame?
    Jason. How? It was not my hand that murdered them.
    Medea. 'Twas thy false wooings, 'twas thy trampling pride.
    Jason. Thou hast said it! For thy lust of love they died.
    Medea. And love to women a slight thing should be?
    Jason. To women pure!—All thy vile life to thee!
    Medea. Think of thy torment. They are dead, they are dead!
    Jason. No: quick, great God; quick curses round thy head!
    Medea. The Gods know who began this work of woe.
    Jason. Thy heart and all its loathliness they know.
    Medea. Loathe on. . . . But, Oh, thy voice. It hurts me sore.
    Jason. Aye, and thine me. Wouldst hear me then no more?

Medea. How? Show me but the way. 'Tis this I crave.

Jason. Give me the dead to weep, and make their grave.

Medea. Never! Myself will lay them in a still
Green sepulchre, where Hera by the Hill
Hath precinct holy, that no angry men
May break their graves and cast them forth again
To evil. So I lay on all this shore
Of Corinth a high feast for evermore
And rite, to purge them yearly of the stain
Of this poor blood. And I, to Pallas' plain
I go, to dwell beside Pandion's son,
Aegeus.—For thee, behold, death draweth on,
Evil and lonely, like thine heart: the hands
Of thine old Argo,[10] rotting where she stands,
Shall smite thine head in twain, and bitter be
To the last end thy memories of me.

    [*She rises on the chariot and is slowly borne away.*

Jason. May They that hear the weeping child
  Blast thee, and They that walk in blood!

Medea. Thy broken vows, thy friends beguiled
  Have shut for thee the ears of God.

Jason. Go, thou art wet with children's tears!

Medea. Go thou, and lay thy bride to sleep.

Jason. Childless, I go, to weep and weep.

Medea. Not yet! Age cometh and long years.

Jason. My sons, mine own!

Medea.   Not thine, but mine . . .

Jason. . . Who slew them!

Medea.   Yes: to torture thee.

Jason. Once let me kiss their lips, once twine
  Mine arms and touch. . . . Ah, woe is me!

Medea. Wouldst love them and entreat? But now
  They were as nothing.

Jason.   At the last,
  O God, to touch that tender brow!

Medea. Thy words upon the wind are cast.

Jason. Thou, Zeus, wilt hear me. All is said
  For naught. I am but spurned away
  And trampled by this tigress, red
  With children's blood. Yet, come what may,

[357]

So far as thou hast granted, yea,
   So far as yet my strength may stand,
I weep upon these dead, and say
   Their last farewell, and raise my hand
To all the daemons of the air
   In witness of these things; how she
   Who slew them, will not suffer me
To gather up my babes, nor bear
To earth their bodies; whom, O stone
Of women, would I ne'er had known
   Nor gotten, to be slain by thee!

           [*He casts himself upon the earth.*

Chorus. Great treasure halls hath Zeus in heaven,
   From whence to man strange dooms be given,
      Past hope or fear.
And the end men looked for cometh not,
And a path is there where no man thought:
      So hath it fallen here.

ARISTOPHANES
THE FROGS

>>> <<<

TRANSLATED
By
JOHN HOOKHAM FRERE

CHARACTERS IN THE PLAY

BACCHUS, *god of wine.*
XANTHIAS, *slave to Bacchus.*
HERCULES, *son of Zeus by Alcmeda.*
CHARON, *the ferryman on the Styx.*
AEACUS, *King of Aegina, a Greek demi-god.*
EURIPIDES, *the tragic poet,* 480–406 B. C.
ASCHYLUS, *the tragic poet,* 495–406 B. C.
PLUTO, *King of Hades.*
Two Women, keepers of an Eating-House in Hades.
Servant Maid to Proserpine, Queen of Hades.
CHORUS *of Frogs.*
CHORUS *of Votaries.*

ARGUMENT

BACCHUS, the patron of the stage, in despair at the decline of the dramatic art (which had lately been deprived of its best tragic authors, Sophocles and Euripides), determines to descend the infernal regions with the intention of procuring the release of Euripides. He appears accordingly, equipped for the expedition, with the lion's skin and club (in imitation of Hercules, whose success in a similar adventure has encouraged him to the attempt); he still retains, however, his usual effeminate costume, which forms a contrast with these heroic attributes. Xanthias, his slave (like Silenus, the mythologic attendant of Bacchus), is mounted upon an ass; but, in conformity with the practice of other human slaves when attending their mortal masters upon an earthly journey, he carries a certain pole upon his shoulder, at the ends of which the various packages, necessary for his master's accommodation, are suspended in equilibrio. The first scene (which, if it had not been the first, might perhaps have been omitted) contains a censure of the gross taste of the audience (suitable to the character of Bacchus as patron of the stage) with allusions to some contemporary rival authors, who submitted to court the applause of the vulgar by mere buffoonery.—The argument between Bacchus and Xanthias, at the end of this scene, probably contains some temporary allusion now unknown, but is obviously, and in the first place, a humorous exemplification of the philosophical, verbal sophisms, not, in all probability, new, even then, but which were then, for the first time, introduced in Athens, and which may be traced from thence to the schoolmen of the Middle Ages. Xanthias carries the bundles *passivè* et *formaliter*, the ass carries them *activè* et *materialiter*.

THE FROGS

Xanthias.   Master, shall I begin with the usual jokes
That the audience always laugh at?
Bacchus.   If you please;
Any joke you please except 'being overburthen'd.'
Don't use it yet—We've time enough before us.
Xanthias.   Well, something else that's comical and clever?
Bacchus.   I forbid being 'overpress'd and overburthen'd.'
Xanthias.   Well, but the drollest joke of all—?
Bacchus.   Remember
There's one thing I protest against—
Xanthias.   What's that?
Bacchus.   Why, shifting off your load to the other shoulder,
And fidgeting and complaining of the gripes.
Xanthias.   What then do you mean to say, that I must not say
That I'm ready to befoul myself?
Bacchus (*peremptorily*).   By no means—
Except when I take an emetic.
Xanthias (*in a sullen, muttering tone, as if resentful of hard
      usage*).   What's the use, then,
Of my being burthen'd here with all these bundles,
If I'm to be deprived of the common jokes
That Phrynichus, and Lycis, and Ameipsias
Allow the servants always in their comedies,
Without exception, when they carry bundles?
Bacchus.   Pray, leave them off—for those ingenious sallies
Have such an effect upon my health and spirits
That I feel grown old and dull when I get home.
Xanthias (*as before, or with a sort of half-mutinous whine*).
It's hard for me to suffer in my limbs,
To be overburthen'd and debarr'd from joking.
Bacchus.   Well, this is monstrous, quite, and insupportable!
Such insolence in a servant!   When your master
Is going afoot and has provided you
With a beast to carry ye.
Xanthias.   What! do I carry nothing?
Bacchus.   You're carried yourself.

[361]

Xanthias. But I carry bundles, don't I?

Bacchus. But the beast bears all the bundles that you carry.

Xanthias. Not those that I carry myself—'tis I that carry 'em.

Bacchus. You're carried yourself, I tell ye.

Xanthias. I can't explain it,
But I feel it in my shoulders plainly enough.

Bacchus. Well, if the beast don't help you, take and try;
Change places with the ass and carry him.

Xanthias (*in a tone of mere disgust*).
Oh, dear! I wish I had gone for a volunteer,
And left you to yourself. I wish I had.

Bacchus. Dismount, you rascal! Here, we're at the house
Where Hercules lives.—Holloh, there! who's within there.

> [BACCHUS *kicks outrageously at the door.*

Hercules. Who's there? (He has bang'd at the door, whoever he is,
With the kick of a centaur.) What's the matter, there?

Bacchus (*aside*). Ha! Xanthias!

Xanthias. What?

Bacchus (*aside*). Did ye mind how he was frighten'd?

Xanthias. I suppose he was afraid you were going mad.

Hercules (*aside*). By Jove! I shall laugh outright; I'm
ready to burst.
I shall laugh, in spite of myself, upon my life.

> [HERCULES *shifts about, and turns aside to disguise
> his laughter: this apparent shyness confirms
> BACCHUS in the opinion of his own ascendancy,
> which he manifests accordingly.*

Bacchus (*with a tone of protection*).
Come hither, friend.—What ails ye? Step this way;
I want to speak to ye.

Hercules (*with a good-humoured but unsuccessful endeavour
to suppress laughter, or to conceal it. Suppose
him, for instance, speaking with his hand before
his mouth.*) But I can't help laughing,
To see the lion's skin with a saffron robe,
And the club with the women's sandals—altogether—
What's the meaning of it all? Have you been abroad?

Bacchus. I've been aboard—in the Fleet—with Cleisthenes.

[362]

Hercules (*sharply and ironically*). You fought—?

Bacchus (*briskly and sillily*). Yes, that we did—we gain'd
    a victory;

And we sunk the enemies' ships—thirteen of 'em.

    Hercules. 'So you woke at last and found it was a dream?'

    Bacchus. But aboard the fleet, as I pursued my studies,

I read the tragedy of Andromeda[1];

And then such a vehement passion struck my heart,

You can't imagine.

    Hercules.   A small one, I suppose,

My little fellow—a moderate little passion?

    Bacchus (*ironically: the irony of imbecility*).

It's just as small as Molon[2] is—that's all—

Molon the wrestler, I mean—as small as he is—

    Hercules. Well, what was it like? what kind of thing? what
        was it?

    Bacchus (*meaning to be very serious and interesting*).

No, friend, you must not laugh; it's past a joke;

It's quite a serious feeling—quite distressing;

I suffer from it—

    Hercules (*bluntly*). Well, explain. What was it?

    Bacchus. I can't declare it at once; but I'll explain it

Theatrically and enigmatically:

        (*With a buffoonish assumption of tragic gesture
          and emphasis*).

Were you ever seized with a sudden passionate longing

For a mess of porridge?

    Hercules.   Often enough, if that's all.

    Bacchus. Shall I state the matter to you plainly at once;

Or put it circumlocutorily?[3]

    Hercules. Not about the porridge. I understand your in-
        stance.

    Bacchus. Such is the passion that possesses me

For poor Euripides, that's dead and gone;

And it's all in vain people trying to persuade me

From going after him.

    Hercules.   What, to the shades below?

    Bacchus. Yes, to the shades below, or the shades beneath
        'em.

[363]

To the undermost shades of all. I'm quite determined.

    Hercules. But what's your object?

    Bacchus (*with a ridiculous imitation of tragical action and emphasis*).   Why, my object is

That I want a clever poet—'for the good,

The gracious and the good, are dead and gone;

The worthless and the weak are left alive'.[4]

    Hercules. Is not Iophon a good one?—He's alive, sure?

    Bacchus. If he's a good one, he's our only good one;

But it's a question; I'm in doubt about him.

    Hercules. There's Sophocles; he's older than Euripides—

If you'd go so far for 'em, you'd best bring him.

    Bacchus. No; first I'll try what Iophon[5] can do,

Without his father, Sophocles, to assist him.

—Besides, Euripides is a clever rascal;

A sharp, contriving rogue that will make a shift

To desert and steal away with me; the other

Is an easy-minded soul, and always was.

    Hercules. Where's Agathon[6]?

    Bacchus.   He's gone and left me too,

Regretted by his friends; a worthy poet—

    Hercules. Gone! Where, poor soul?

    Bacchus.   To the banquets of the blest!

    Hercules. But then you've Xenocles[7]—

    Bacchus.   Yes! a plague upon him!

    Hercules. Pythangelus[8] too—

    Xanthias.   But nobody thinks of me;

Standing all this while with the bundles on my shoulder.

    Hercules. But have not you other young ingenious youths

That are fit to out-talk Euripides ten times over;

To the amount of a thousand, at least, all writing tragedy—?

    Bacchus. They're good for nothing—'Warblers of the Grove'—

—'Little, foolish, fluttering things'—poor puny wretches,

That dawdle and dangle about with the tragic muse;

Incapable of any serious meaning—

—There's not one hearty poet amongst them all

That's fit to risk an adventurous valiant phrase.

    Hercules. How—'hearty'? What do you mean by 'valiant phrases'?

Bacchus (*the puzzle of a person who is called upon for a definition*). I mean a . . . kind . . . of a . . . doubtful, bold expression
To talk about . . . 'The viewless foot of Time'—
     (*Tragic emphasis in the quotations*[9]).
And . . . 'Jupiter's Secret Chamber in the Skies'—
And about . . . a person's soul . . . not being perjured
When . . . the tongue . . . forswears itself . . . in spite of the soul.

  Hercules. Do you like that kind of stuff?
  Bacchus.   I'm crazy after it.
  Hercules. Why, sure, it's trash and rubbish—Don't you think so?
  Bacchus. 'Men's fancies are their own—Let mine alone'—
  Hercules. But, in fact, it seems to me quite bad—rank nonsense.
  Bacchus. You'll tell me next what I ought to like for supper.
  Xanthias. But nobody thinks of me here, with the bundles.
  Bacchus (*with a careless, easy, voluble, dégagé style*).
But now to the business that I came upon—
     (*Upon a footing of equality,—the tone of a person who is dispatching business off-hand, with readiness and unconcern.*)

(With the apparel that you see—the same as yours)
To obtain a direction from you to your friends
(To apply to them—in case of anything—
If anything should occur), the acquaintances
That received you there—(the time you went before
—For the business about Cerberus[10])—if you'd give me
Their names and their directions, and communicate
Any information relative to the country,
The roads,—the streets,—the bridges, and the brothels,
The wharves,—the public walks,—the public houses,
The fountains,—aqueducts,—and inns, and taverns,
And lodgings,—free from bugs and fleas, if possible,
If you know any such—
  Xanthias.   But nobody thinks of me.
  Hercules. What a notion! You! will you risk it? are ye mad?

Bacchus (*meaning to be very serious and manly*). I beseech
    you say no more—no more of that,
But inform me briefly and plainly about my journey:
The shortest road and the most convenient one.

Hercules (*with a tone of easy, indolent, deliberate banter*).
Well,—which shall I tell ye first, now?—Let me see now—
There's a good convenient road by the Rope and Noose;
The Hanging Road.

    Bacchus.   No; that's too close and stifling.

    Hercules. Then, there's an easy, fair, well-beaten track,
As you go by the Pestle and Mortar—

    Bacchus.   What, the Hemlock?

    Hercules. To be sure—

    Bacchus.   That's much too cold—it will never do.
They tell me it strikes a chill to the legs and feet.

    Hercules. Should you like a speedy, rapid, downhill road?

    Bacchus. Indeed I should, for I'm a sorry traveller.

    Hercules. Go to the Keramicus then.

    Bacchus.   What then?

    Hercules. Get up to the very top of the tower.

    Bacchus.   What then?

    Hercules. Stand there and watch when the Race of the
    Torch[11] begins;
And mind when you hear the people cry '*Start! Start!*'
Then start at once with 'em.

    Bacchus.   Me? Start? Where from?

    Hercules. From the top of the tower to the bottom.

    Bacchus.   No, not I.
It's enough to dash my brains out! I'll not go
Such a road upon any account.

    Hercules.   Well, which way then?

    Bacchus. The way you went yourself.

    Hercules.   But it's a long one,
For first you come to a monstrous bottomless lake.

    Bacchus. And what must I do to pass?

    Hercules.   You'll find a boat there;
A little tiny boat, as big as that,
And an old man that ferries you over in it,
Receiving twopence as the usual fee.

    Bacchus. Ah! the same twopence[12] governs everything

Wherever it goes.—I wonder how it managed
To find its way there?

Hercules. Theseus introduced it.
Next you'll meet serpents, and wild beasts, and monsters,
(*Suddenly, and with a shout in Bacchus' ear*) Horrific to
behold!

Bacchus (*starting a little*). Don't try to fright me;
You'll not succeed, I promise you.—I'm determined.

Hercules. Then there's an abyss of mire and floating filth,
In which the damn'd lie wallowing and overwhelm'd;
The unjust, the cruel, and the inhospitable;
And the barbarous bilking Cullies that withhold
The price of intercourse with fraud and wrong;
The incestuous, and the parricides, and the robbers;
The perjurers, and assassins, and the wretches
That wilfully and presumptuously transcribe
Extracts and trash from Morsimus's plays.

Bacchus. And, by Jove! Kinesias with his Pyrrhic dancers
Ought to be there—they're worse, or quite as bad.

Hercules. But after this your sense will be saluted
With a gentle breathing sound of flutes and voices,
And a beautiful spreading light like ours on earth,
And myrtle glades and happy choirs among,
Of women and men with rapid applause and mirth.

Bacchus. And who are all those folks?

Hercules. The Initiated.[13]

Xanthias (*gives indications of restiveness, as if ready to
throw down his bundles*).
I won't stand here like a mule in a procession
Any longer with these packages and bundles.

Hercules (*hastily, in a civil hurry, as when you shake a man
by the hand, and shove him out of the room, and give him
your best wishes and advice all at once*).
They'll tell you everything you want to know,
For they're establish'd close upon the road,
By the corner of Pluto's house—so fare you well;
Farewell, my little fellow. [*Exit.*

Bacchus (*pettishly*). I wish you better.
(*to* XANTHIAS) You, sirrah, take your bundles up again.

Xanthias. What, before I put them down?

Bacchus.   Yes! now this moment.

Xanthias. Nah! don't insist; there's plenty of people going
As corpses with the convenience of a carriage;
They'd take it for a trifle gladly enough.

Bacchus. But if we meet with nobody?

Xanthias.   Then I'll take 'em.

Bacchus. Come, come, that's fairly spoken, and in good time;
For there they're carrying a corpse out to be buried.

[*A funeral, with a corpse on an open bier, crosses the stage.*
—Holloh! you, there—you Deadman—can't you hear?
Would you take any bundles to hell with ye, my good fellow?

Deadman. What are they?

Bacchus.   These.

Deadman.   Then I must have two drachmas.

Bacchus. I can't—you must take less.

Deadman (peremptorily).   Bearers, move on.

Bacchus. No, stop! we shall settle between us—you're so
      hasty.

Deadman. It's no use arguing; I must have two drachmas.

Bacchus (emphatically and significantly). Ninepence!

Deadman. I'd best be alive again at that rate.   [*Exit.*

Bacchus. Fine airs the fellow gives himself—a rascal!
I'll have him punish'd, I vow, for overcharging.

Xanthias. Best give him a good beating: give me the bundles,
I'll carry 'em.

Bacchus. You're a good, true-hearted fellow;
And a willing servant.—Let's move on to the ferry.

[*They proceed to the Styx where
                they find* CHARON *in his boat.*

Charon. Hoy! Bear a hand, there—Heave ashore.

Bacchus.   What's this?

Xanthias. The lake it is—the place he told us of.
By Jove! and there's the boat—and here's old Charon.

Bacchus. Well, Charon!—Welcome, Charon!—Welcome
      kindly!

Charon. Who wants the ferryman? Anybody waiting
To remove from the sorrows of life? A passage, anybody?
To Lethe's Wharf?—to Cerberus's Reach?
To Tartarus?—to Taenarus?—to Perdition?

Bacchus. Yes, I.

Charon.   Get in then.

Bacchus (*hesitatingly*). Tell me, where are you going?
To Perdition really—?

Charon (*not sarcastically, but civilly, in the way of business*).   Yes, to oblige you, I will
With all my heart—Step in there.

Bacchus.   Have a care!
Take care, good Charon!—Charon, have a care!

                        [BACCHUS *gets into the boat.*

Come, Xanthias, come!

Charon.   I take no slaves aboard
Except they've volunteer'd for the naval victory.[14]

Xanthias. I could not—I was suffering with sore eyes.

Charon. You must trudge away then, round by the end of the
   lake there.

Xanthias. And whereabouts shall I wait?

Charon.   At the Stone of Repentance,
By the Slough of Despond beyond the Tribulations;
You understand me?

Xanthias.   Yes, I understand you;
A lucky, promising direction, truly.

Charon (*to* BACCHUS). Sit down at the oar—Come quick, if
   there's more coming!

(*To* BACCHUS *again*). Holloh! what's that you're doing?

          [BACCHUS *is seated in a buffoonish attitude on the
               side of the boat where the oar was fastened.*

Bacchus.   What you told me.
I'm sitting at the oar.

Charon.   Sit *there,* I tell you,
You Fatguts; that's your place.

Bacchus (*changes his place*).   Well, so I do.

Charon. Now ply your hands and arms.

Bacchus (*makes a silly motion with his arms*). Well, so I do.

Charon. You'd best leave off your fooling. Take to the oar,
And pull away.

Bacchus.   But how shall I contrive?
I've never served on board—I'm only a landsman;
I'm quite unused to it—

Charon.   We can manage it.
As soon as you begin you shall have some music

[369]

That will teach you to keep time.

Bacchus.   What music's that?

Charon. A chorus of Frogs—uncommon musical Frogs.

Bacchus. Well, give me the word and the time.

Charon.   Whooh up, up; whooh up, up.

Chorus of Frogs. Brekeke-kesh, koash, koash,
> Shall the Choral Quiristers of the Marsh[15]
> Be censured and rejected as hoarse and harsh;
>> And their Chromatic essays
>> Deprived of praise?
> No, let us raise afresh
> Our obstreperous Brekeke-kesh;
> The customary croak and cry
>> Of the creatures
>> At the theatres,
> In their yearly revelry.
> Brekeke-kesh, koash, koash.

Bacchus (*rowing in great misery*).
>> How I'm maul'd,
>> How I'm gall'd;
> Worn and mangled to a mash—
> They there go! '*Koash, koash*'!

Frogs. Brekeke-kesh, koash, koash.

Bacchus. Oh, beshrew,
>> All your crew;
> You don't consider how I smart.

Frogs.   Now, for a sample of the Art!
> Brekeke-kesh, koash, koash.

Bacchus. I wish you hang'd with all my heart.
> —Have you nothing else to say?
> '*Brekeke-kesh, koash*' all day!

Frogs.   We've a right,
> We've a right;
> And we croak at ye for spite.
> We've a right,
> We've a right;
> Day and night,
> Day and night;
> Night and day,
> Still to creak and croak away.

Phoebus and every Grace
Admire and approve of the croaking race;
And the egregious guttural notes
That are gargled and warbled in their lyrical throats.

    In reproof
    Of your scorn
    Mighty Pan
    Nods his horn;
    Beating time
    To the rime
    With his hoof,
    With his hoof.
    Persisting in our plan,
    We proceed as we began,
    Breke-kesh, Breke-kesh,
    Kooash, kooash.

Bacchus. Oh, the Frogs, consume and rot 'em,
    I've a blister on my bottom.
    Hold your tongues, you tuneful creatures.

Frogs.   Cease with your profane entreaties
    All in vain for ever striving:
      Silence is against our natures.
    With the vernal heat reviving,
      Our aquatic crew repair
    From their periodic sleep,
    In the dark and chilly deep,
    To the cheerful upper air;
    Then we frolic here and there
    All amidst the meadows fair;
    Shady plants of asphodel,
    Are the lodges where we dwell;
    Chanting in the leafy bowers
    All the livelong summer hours,
    Till the sudden gusty showers
    Send us headlong, helter skelter,
    To the pool to seek for shelter;
    Meagre, eager, leaping, lunging,
    From the sedgy wharfage plunging
    To the tranquil depth below,
    There we muster all a-row;

[371]

Where, secure from toil and trouble,
With a tuneful hubble-bubble,
Our symphonious accents flow.
Brekeke-kesh, koash, koash.

Bacchus. I forbid you to proceed.

Frogs. That would be severe indeed;
Arbitrary, bold, and rash—
Brekeke-kesh, koash, koash.

Bacchus. I command you to desist—
Oh, my back, there! oh, my wrist!
What a twist!
What a sprain!

Frogs. Once again—
We renew the tuneful strain.
Brekeke-kesh, koash, koash.

Bacchus. I disdain—(Hang the pain!)
All your nonsense, noise, and trash.
Oh, my blister! Oh, my sprain!

Frogs. Brekeke-kesh, koash, koash.
Friends and Frogs, we must display
All our powers of voice to-day;
Suffer not this stranger here,
With fastidious foreign ear,
To confound us and abash.
Brekeke-kesh, koash, koash.

Bacchus. Well, my spirit is not broke,
If it's only for the joke,
I'll outdo you with a croak.
Here it goes—(*very loud*) 'Koash, koash'.

Frogs. Now for a glorious croaking crash,

(*Still louder.*)

Brekeke-kesh, koash, koash.

Bacchus (*splashing with his oar*).
I'll disperse you with a splash.

Frogs. Brekeke-kesh, koash, koash.

Bacchus. I'll subdue
Your rebellious, noisy crew—
—Have amongst you there, slap-dash.

[*Strikes at them.*

Frogs.   Brekeke-kesh, koash, koash.
          We defy your oar and you.
Charon. Hold! We're ashore just—shift your oar. Get out.
—Now pay for your fare.
Bacchus.   There—there it is—the twopence.

      [CHARON *returns.* BACCHUS, *finding himself*
        alone and in a strange place, begins to call out.

Bacchus. Hoh, Xanthias! Xanthias, I say! Where's Xanthias?
Xanthias. A-hoy!
Bacchus.   Come here.
Xanthias.   I'm glad to see you, master.
Bacchus. What's that before us there?
Xanthias.   The mire and darkness.
Bacchus. Do you see the villains and the perjurers
That he told us of?
    Xanthias.   Yes, plain enough, don't you?
Bacchus. Ah! now I see them, indeed, quite plain—and now
    too.   [*Turning to the audience.*
Well, what shall we do next?
    Xanthias.   We'd best move forward;
For here's the place that Hercules there inform'd us
Was haunted by these monsters.
    Bacchus.   Oh, confound him!
He vapour'd and talk'd at random to deter me
From venturing.—He's amazingly conceited
And jealous of other people, is Hercules;
He reckon'd I should rival him, and, in fact
(Since I've come here so far), I should rather like
To meet with an adventure in some shape.
    Xanthias. By Jove! and I think I hear a kind of a noise.
Bacchus. Where? where?
Xanthias.   There, just behind us.
Bacchus.   Go behind, then.
Xanthias. There!—it's before us now.—There!
Bacchus.   Go before, then.
Xanthias. Ah! now I see it—a monstrous beast indeed!
Bacchus. What kind?
Xanthias.   A dreadful kind—all kinds at once.
It changes and transforms itself about

[373]

To a mule and an ox,—and now to a beautiful creature;
A woman!

    Bacchus. Where? where is she? Let me seize her.

    Xanthias. But now she's turn'd to a mastiff all of a sudden.

    Bacchus. It's the Weird hag![16] the Vampyre!

    Xanthias (collectedly).   Like enough.
She's all of a blaze of fire about the mouth.

    Bacchus (with great trepidation).
Has she got the brazen foot?

    Xanthias (with cool despair).   Yes, there it is—
By Jove!—and the cloven hoof to the other leg,
Distinct enough—that's she!

    Bacchus.   But what shall I do?

    Xanthias. And I, too?

    [BACCHUS *runs to the front of the stage, where there was
        a seat of honour appropriated to the priest of* BACCHUS.

    Bacchus.   Save me, Priest, protect and save me,
That we may drink and be jolly together hereafter.

    Xanthias. We're ruin'd, Master Hercules.

    Bacchus.   Don't call me so, I beg:
Don't mention my name, good friend, upon any account.

    Xanthias. Well, BACCHUS, then!

    Bacchus.   That's worse, ten thousand times.

    [BACCHUS *remains hiding his face before the seat of the
        priest—in the meantime affairs take a more favourable
        turn.

    Xanthias (cheerfully). Come, master, move along—Come,
    come this way.

    Bacchus (without looking round). What's happen'd?

    Xanthias.   Why, we're prosperous and victorious;
The storm of fear and danger has subsided,
And (as the actor said the other day)
'Has only left a gentle *qualm* behind.'
The Vampyre's vanished.

    Bacchus.   Has she? upon your oath?

    Xanthias. By Jove! she has.

    Bacchus.   No, swear again.

    Xanthias.   By Jove!

    Bacchus. Is she, by Jupiter?

    Xanthias.   By Jupiter!

Bacchus. Oh dear! what a fright I was in with the very sight
   of her:
It turn'd me sick and pale—but see, the priest here!
He has colour'd up quite with the same alarm.
What has brought me to this pass?—It must be Jupiter
With his *'Chamber in the skies,'* and the *'Foot of Time.'*

> [*A flute sounds.* BACCHUS *remains absorbed and
> inattentive to the objects about him.*

Xanthias. Holloh, you!
Bacchus.   What?
Xanthias   Why, did you not hear?
Bacchus.   Why, what?
Xanthias. The sound of a flute.
Bacchus (*recollecting himself*). Indeed! And there's a smell
   too;
A pretty mystical ceremonious smell
Of torches. We'll watch here, and keep quite quiet.
Chorus of Votaries (*Shouting and Singing*).
>   Iacchus! Iacchus! Ho!
>   Iacchus! Iacchus! Ho!

Xanthias. There, Master, there they are, the Initiated;
All sporting about as he told us we should find 'em.
They're singing in praise of Bacchus like Diagoras.[17]
Bacchus. Indeed, and so they are; but we'll keep quiet
Till we make them out a little more distinctly.
Chorus. Mighty Bacchus! Holy Power!
>   Hither at the wonted hour
>   Come away,
>   Come away,
>   With the wanton holiday,
>   Where the revel uproar leads
>   To the mystic holy meads,
>   Where the frolic votaries fly, ⎫
>   With a tipsy shout and cry; ⎬
>   Flourishing the Thyrsus high, ⎭
>   Flinging forth, alert and airy,
>   To the sacred old vagary,
>   The tumultuous dance and song,
>   Sacred from the vulgar throng;
>   Mystic orgies, that are known

>   To the votaries alone—
>   To the mystic chorus solely—
>   Secret—unreveal'd and holy.

Xanthias. Oh glorious virgin, daughter of the goddess!
What a scent of roasted griskin reach'd my senses.

Bacchus. Keep quiet—and watch for a chance of a piece of
the haslets.

Chorus. Raise the fiery torches high.

>   Bacchus is approaching nigh,
>   Like the planet of the morn,
>   Breaking with the hoary dawn,
>   On the dark solemnity—
>   There they flash upon the sight; ⎫
>   All the plain is blazing bright, ⎬
>   Flush'd and overflown with light: ⎭
>   Age has cast his years away, ⎫
>   And the cares of many a day, ⎬
>   Sporting to the lively lay— ⎭
>   Mighty Bacchus! march and lead
>   (Torch in hand toward the mead)
>   Thy devoted humble Chorus,
>   Mighty Bacchus—move before us!

Semichorus. Keep silence—keep peace—and let all the pro-
fane
From our holy solemnity duly refrain;
Whose souls unenlighten'd by taste, are obscure;
Whose poetical notions are dark and impure;
>   Whose theatrical conscience
>   Is sullied by nonsense;
Who never were train'd by the mighty Cratinus[18]
In mystical orgies poetic and vinous;
Who delight in buffooning and jests out of season;
Who promote the designs of oppression and treason;
Who foster sedition, and strife, and debate;
All traitors, in short, to the stage and the state;
Who surrender a fort, or in private, export
To places and harbours of hostile resort,
Clandestine consignments of cables and pitch;
In the way that Thorycion grew to be rich
From a scoundrelly dirty collector of tribute;

All such we reject and severely prohibit:
All statesmen retrenching the fees and the salaries
Of theatrical bards, in revenge for the railleries,
And jests, and lampoons, of this holy solemnity,
Profanely pursuing their personal enmity,
For having been flouted, and scoff'd and scorn'd,
All such are admonish'd and heartily warn'd;

  We warn them once,
  We warn them twice,
  We warn and admonish—we warn them thrice,

To conform to the law,
To retire and withdraw;
While the Chorus again with the formal saw
(Fix'd and assign'd to the festive day)
Move to the measure and march away.

 Semichorus. March! march! lead forth,
    Lead forth manfully,
    March in order all;
    Bustling, hustling, justling,
     As it may befall;
    Flocking, shouting, laughing,
    Mocking, flouting, quaffing,
     One and all;
    All have had a belly-full
    Of breakfast brave and plentiful;
     Therefore
     Evermore
    With your voices and your bodies
    Serve the goddess,
     And raise
     Songs of praise;
    She shall save the country still,
    And save it against the traitor's will;
     So she says.

 Semichorus. Now let us raise, in a different strain,
The praise of the goddess the giver of grain;
Imploring her favour
With other behaviour,
In measures more sober, submissive, and graver.

[377]

Semichorus. Ceres, holy patroness,
　　　　　Condescend to mark and bless,
　　　　　With benevolent regard,
　　　　　Both the Chorus and the Bard;
　　　　　Grant them for the present day
　　　　　Many things to sing and say,
　　　　　Follies intermix'd with sense;
　　　　　Folly, but without offence.
　　　　　Grant them with the present play
　　　　　To bear the prize of verse away.

Semichorus. Now call again, and with a different measure,
　　　　　The power, mirth, and pleasure,
　　　　　The florid, active Bacchus, bright and gay,
　　　　　To journey forth and join us on the way.

Semichorus. O Bacchus, attend! the customary patron
　　　　　Of every lively lay;
　　　　　Go forth without delay
　　　　　Thy wonted annual way,
　　　　　To meet the ceremonious holy matron:
　　　　　　Her grave procession gracing,
　　　　　　Thine airy footsteps tracing
　　　　　With unlaborious, light, celestial motion
　　　　　And here at thy devotion
　　　　　　Behold thy faithful choir
　　　　　　In pitiful attire;
　　　　　All overworn and ragged,
　　　　　This jerkin old and jagged,
　　　　　These buskins torn and burst,
　　　　　　Though sufferers in the fray,
　　　　　May serve us at the worst
　　　　　　To sport throughout the day;
　　　　　And there within the shades
　　　　　I spy some lovely maids;
　　　　　With whom we romp'd and revell'd,
　　　　　Dismantled and dishevell'd;
　　　　　With their bosoms open,
　　　　　With whom we might be coping.

Xanthias. 　Well, I was always hearty,
　　　　　Disposed to mirth and ease,
　　　　　I'm ready to join the party.

Bacchus. And I will, if you please.

* * *

Some verses follow, which are sung by the Chorus, and in which some of the characters of the state are lampooned; they are not capable of translation, but are introduced appropriately, as the Bacchic and Eleusinian processions, which are here represented, were accompanied by a great licence of abuse and ribaldry.

* * *

Bacchus (to the Chorus).

Prithee, my good fellows,
Would you please to tell us
Which is Pluto's door,
I'm an utter stranger,
Never here before.

Chorus.   Friend, you're out of danger,
You need not seek it far;
There it stands before ye,
Before ye, where you are.

Bacchus. Take up your bundles, Xanthias.

Xanthias.   Hang all bundles;
A bundle has no end, and these have none.

[*Exeunt* BACCHUS *and* XANTHIAS.

Semichorus. Now we go to dance and sing
In the consecrated shades;
Round the secret holy ring,
With the matrons and the maids,
Thither I must haste to bring
The mysterious early light;   ⎫
Which must witness every rite ⎬
Of the joyous happy night.   ⎭

Semichorus. Let us hasten—let us fly—
Where the lovely meadows lie;
Where the living waters flow;
Where the roses bloom and blow.
Heirs of Immortality,
Segregated, safe and pure,
Easy, sorrowless, secure;
Since our earthly course is run,
We behold a brighter sun.

[379]

Holy lives—a holy vow—
Such rewards await them now.

Scene. The Gate of Pluto's Palace.

[*Enter* BACCHUS *and* XANTHIAS.

Bacchus (*going up to the door with considerable hesitation*).
Well, how must I knock at the door now? Can't ye tell me?
How do the native inhabitants knock at doors?

Xanthias. Pah; don't stand fooling there; but smite it smartly,
With the very spirit and air of Hercules.

Bacchus. Holloh!

Aeacus (*from within, the voice of a royal and internal porter*).   Who's there?

Bacchus (*with forced voice*). 'Tis I, the valiant Hercules!

Aeacus (*coming out*). Thou brutal, abominable, detestable,
Vile, villainous, infamous, nefarious scoundrel!
—How durst thou, villain as thou wert, to seize
Our watch-dog, Cerberus, whom I kept and tended,
Hurrying him off, half-strangled in your grasp?
—But now, be sure we have you safe and fast,
Miscreant and villain!—Thee, the Stygian cliffs,
With stern adamantine durance, and the rocks
Of inaccessible Acheron, red with gore,
Environ and beleaguer; and the watch,
And swift pursuit of the hideous hounds of hell;
And the horrible Hydra, with her hundred heads,
Whose furious ravening fangs shall rend and tear thee;
Wrenching thy vitals forth, with the heart and midriff;
While inexpressible Tartesian monsters,
And grim Tithrasian Gorgons, toss and scatter,
With clattering claws, thine intertwined intestines.
To them, with instant summons, I repair,
Moving in hasty march with steps of speed.

[AEACUS *departs with a tremendous tragical exit,
and* BACCHUS *falls to the ground in a fright.*

Xanthias. Holloh, you! What's the matter there—?

Bacchus.   Oh dear,
I've had an accident.

Xanthias.   Poh! poh! jump up!

[380]

Come! you ridiculous simpleton! don't lie there,
The people will see you.

 Bacchus.   Indeed I'm sick at heart, lah!
  (*Here a few lines are omitted.*)

 Xanthias. Was there ever in heaven or earth such a coward?
 Bacchus.   Me?
A coward! Did not I show my presence of mind—
And call for a sponge and water in a moment?
Would a coward have done that?

 Xanthias.   What else would he do?
 Bacchus. He'd have lain there stinking like a nasty coward;
But I jump'd up at once, like a lusty wrestler,
And look'd about, and wiped myself, withal.

 Xanthias. Most manfully done!

 Bacchus.   By Jove, and I think it was;
But tell me, weren't you frighten'd with that speech?
—Such horrible expressions!

 Xanthias (*cooly, but with conscious and intentional cool-*
  ness).   No, not I;
I took no notice—

 Bacchus.   Well, I'll tell you what,
Since you're such a valiant-spirited kind of fellow,
Do you be *Me*—with the club and the lion-skin,
Now you're in this courageous temper of mind;
And I'll go take my turn and carry the bundles.

 Xanthias. Well—give us hold—I must humour you, forsooth;
Make haste, (*he changes his dress*), and now behold the Xanth-
  ian Hercules,
And mind if I don't display more heart and spirit.

 Bacchus. Indeed, and you look the character completely,
Like that heroic Melitensian hangdog—
Come, now for my bundles. I must mind my bundles.

   [*Enter* PROSERPINE'S SERVANT MAID (*a kind of Dame*
    Quickly), *who immediately addresses* XANTHIAS.

 Servant Maid. Dear Hercules. Well, you're come at last.
  Come in,
For the goddess, as soon as she heard of it, set to work
Baking peck loaves, and frying stacks of pancakes,
And making messes of frumenty; there's an ox

Besides, she has roasted whole, with a relishing stuffing,
If you'll only just step in this way.

Xanthias (*with dignity and reserve*). I thank you,
I'm equally obliged.

  Servant Maid.   No, no, by Jupiter!
We must not let you off, indeed. There's wild fowl,
And sweetmeats for the dessert, and the best of wine;
Only walk in.

  Xanthias (*as before*). I thank you. You'll excuse me.

  Servant Maid. No, no, we can't excuse you, indeed we can't;
There are dancing and singing girls besides.

  Xanthias (*with dissembled emotion*). What! dancers?

  Servant Maid. Yes, that there are; the sweetest, charmingest
    things
That ever you saw—and there's the cook this moment
Is dishing up the dinner.

  Xanthias (*with an air of lofty condescension*). Go before
   then,
And tell the girls—those singing girls you mention'd—
To prepare for my approach in person presently.
(*To Bacchus.*) You, sirrah! follow behind me with the
  bundles.

  Bacchus. Holloh, you! what, do you take the thing in earnest,
Because, for a joke, I drest you up like Hercules?

      [XANTHIAS *continues to gesticulate as* HERCULES.

Come, don't stand fooling, Xanthias. You'll provoke me.
There, carry the bundles, sirrah, when I bid you.

  Xanthias (*relapsing at once into his natural air*).
Why, sure, do you mean to take the things away
That you gave me yourself of your own accord this instant?

  Bacchus. I never mean a thing; I do it at once.
Let go of the lion's skin directly, I tell you.

  Xanthias (*resigning his heroical insignia with a tragical air
   and tone*). To you, just gods, I make my last appeal,
Bear witness!

  Bacchus. What! the gods?—do you think they mind you?
How could you take it in your head, I wonder;
Such a foolish fancy for a fellow like you,
A mortal and a slave, to pass for Hercules?

Xanthias. There. Take them.—There—you may have them—
but, please God,
You may come to want my help some time or other.
  Chorus. Dexterous and wily wits
        Find their own advantage ever;
     For the wind where'er it sits,
        Leaves a berth secure and clever
    To the ready navigator,
    That foresees and knows the nature
    Of the wind and weather's drift;
    And betimes can turn and shift
    To the shelter'd easy side;
    'Tis a practice proved and tried,
    Not to wear a formal face;
    Fix'd in attitude and place,
    Like an image on its base;
    'Tis the custom of the seas,
    Which, as all the world agrees,
    Justifies Theramenes.[19]
Bacchus. How ridiculous and strange;
      What a monstrous proposition,
   That I should condescend to change
      My dress, my name, and my condition,
   To follow Xanthias, and behave
   Like a mortal and a slave;
   To be set to watch outside
   While he wallow'd in his pride,
   Tumbling on a purple bed;
   While I waited with submission,
   To receive a broken head;
   Or be kick'd upon suspicion
   Of impertinence and peeping
   At the joys that he was reaping.

             [*Enter Two* WOMEN, *Sutlers or*
                Keepers of an Eating-House.
  First Woman. What, Platana! Goody Platana! there! that's
he,
The fellow that robs and cheats poor victuallers;
That came to our house and eat those nineteen loaves.
  Second Woman. Aye, sure enough, that's he, the very man.

Xanthias (*tauntingly to* BACCHUS). There's mischief in the
    wind for somebody!

First Woman. —And a dozen and a half of cutlets and fried
    chops,

At a penny halfpenny a-piece—

    Xanthias (*significantly*). There are pains and penalties im-
    pending—

First Woman. —And all the garlic: such a quantity
    As he swallow'd—

Bacchus (*delivers this speech with Herculean dignity, after
    his fashion; having hitherto remained silent upon the same
    principle*).   Woman, you're beside yourself;

You talk you know not what—

    Second Woman.   No, no! you reckon'd

I should not know you again with them there buskins.[20]

    First Woman. —Good lack! and there was all that fish
    besides.

Indeed—with the pickle, and all—and the good green cheese

That he gorged at once, with the rind, and the rush-baskets;

And then, when I call'd for payment, he look'd fierce,

And stared at me in the face, and grinn'd, and roar'd—

    Xanthias. Just like him! That's the way wherever he goes.

    First Woman. —And snatch'd his sword out and behaved
    like mad.

    Xanthias. Poor souls! you suffer'd sadly!

    First Woman.   Yes, indeed;

And then we both ran off with the fright and terror,

And scrambled into the loft beneath the roof;

And he took up two rugs and stole them off.

    Xanthias. Just like him again—but something must be done.

Go call me Cleon, he's my advocate.

    Second Woman. And Hyperbolus, if you meet him send
    him here.

He's mine, and we'll demolish him, I warrant.

    First Woman (*going close up to* BACCHUS *in the true ter-
    magant attitude of rage and defiance, with the arms
    akimbo, and a neck and chin thrust out*).

How I should like to strike those ugly teeth out

With a good big stone, you ravenous greedy villain!

You gormandizing villain! that I should—

Yes, that I should; your wicked ugly fangs
That have eaten up my substance, and devour'd me.
  Bacchus. And I could toss you into the public pit
With the malefactor's carcases; that I could,
With pleasure and satisfaction; that I could.
  First Woman. And I should like to rip that gullet out
With a reaping hook that swallow'd all my tripe,
And liver and lights—but I'll fetch Cleon here,
And he shall summon him. He shall settle him,
And have it out of him this very day.

> [*Exeunt* FIRST and SECOND WOMAN.

  Bacchus (*in a pretended soliloquy*). I love poor Xanthias
    dearly, that I do;
I wish I might be hang'd else.
  Xanthias.   Yes, I know—
I know your meaning—No; no more of that,
I won't act Hercules—
  Bacchus.   Now pray, don't say so,
My little Xanthias.
  Xanthias.   How should I be Hercules?
A mortal and a slave, a fellow like me?—
  Bacchus. I know you're angry, and you've a right to be angry;
And if you beat me for it I'd not complain;
But if ever I strip you again, from this time forward,
I wish I may be utterly confounded,
With my wife, my children, and my family,
And the blear-eyed Archedemus[21] into the bargain.
  Xanthias. I agree then, on that oath, and those conditions.

> [XANTHIAS *equips himself with*
>   *the club and lion's skin, and*
>   BACCHUS *resumes his bundles.*

  Chorus (*addressing* XANTHIAS).
      Now that you revive and flourish
        In your old attire again,
      You must rouse afresh and nourish
        Thoughts of an heroic strain;
      That exalt and raise the figure,
      And assume a fire and vigour;
      And an attitude and air
      Suited to the garb you wear;

> With a brow severely bent,
> Like the god you represent.
>> But beware,
>> Have a care!
> If you blunder or betray
> Any weakness any way;
> Weakness of the heart or brain,
> We shall see you once again
> Trudging in the former track,
> With the bundles at your back.

Xanthias (*in reply to the Chorus*).

> Friends, I thank you for your care;
> Your advice was good and fair;
> Corresponding in its tone
> With reflections of my own.
> —Though I clearly comprehend
> All the upshot and the end,
> (That if any good comes of it,
> Any pleasure, any profit—
> He, my master, will recede
> From the terms that were agreed,)
> You shall see me, notwithstanding,
> Stern, intrepid, and commanding.
> Now's the time!—For there's a noise!
> Now for figure, look, and voice!

> [AEACUS *enters again as a vulgar
> executioner of the law, with suit-
> able understrappers in attendance.*

Aeacus. Arrest me, there, that fellow that stole my dog.
There!—Pinion him!—Quick!

Bacchus (*tauntingly to* XANTHIAS). There's somebody in a scrape.

Xanthias (*in a menacing attitude*). Keep off, and be hang'd.

Aeacus. Oh, hoh! do you mean to fight for it?
Here! Pardokas, and Skeblias, and the rest of ye,
Make up to the rogue, and settle him.—Come, be quick.

> [*A scuffle ensues, in which* XANTHIAS *succeeds in oblig-
> ing* AEACUS' *runners to keep their distance.*

Bacchus (*mortified at* XANTHIAS' *prowess*).

Well, is not this quite monstrous and outrageous,

[386]

To steal a dog, and then to make an assault
In justification of it?

    Xanthias (*triumphantly and ironically*). Quite outrageous!

    Aeacus (*gravely, and dissembling his mortification*). An
      aggravated case!

    Xanthias (*with candour and gallantry*). Well, now—by
      Jupiter,

May I die, but I never saw this place before—
Nor ever stole the amount of a farthing from you:
Nor a hair of your dog's tail.—But you shall see now,
I'll settle all this business nobly and fairly,
—This slave of mine—you may take and torture him;
And if you make out anything against me,
You may take and put me to death for aught I care.

    Aeacus (*in an obliging tone, softened into deference and
      civility by the liberality of* XANTHIAS' *proposal*).

But which way would you please to have him tortured?

    Xanthias (*with a gentlemanly spirit of accommodation*).

In your own way—with . . . the lash—with . . . knots and
    screws,
With . . . the common usual customary tortures.
With the rack—with . . . the water-torture . . . any way—
With fire and vinegar—all sort of ways.
(*After a very slight pause.*) There's only one thing
    I should warn you of:
I must not have him treated like a child,
To be whipp'd with fennel, or with lettuce leaves.

    Aeacus. That's fair—and if so be . . . he's maim'd or crip-
      pled
In any respect—the valy[22] shall be paid you.

    Xanthias. Oh no!—by no means! not to me!—by no means!
You must not mention it!—Take him to the torture.

    Aeacus. It had better be here, and under your own eye.
(*To* BACCHUS.) Come you—put down your bundles and make
    ready.
And mind—Let me hear no lies!

    Bacchus.   I'll tell you what:
I'd advise people not to torture me;
I give you notice—I'm a deity.

[387]

So mind now—you'll have nobody to blame
But your own self—

    Aeacus.   What's that you're saying there?

    Bacchus. Why, that I'm Bacchus, Jupiter's own son:
That fellow there's a slave.   [*Pointing to* Xanthias.

    Aeacus (*to* Xanthias). Do ye hear?

    Xanthias.   I hear him—
A reason the more to give him a good beating;
If he's immortal he need never mind it.

    Bacchus. Why should not you be beat as well as I then,
If you're immortal, as you say you are?

    Xanthias. Agreed—and him, the first that you see flinching,
Or seeming to mind it at all, you may set him down
For an impostor and no real deity.

    Aeacus (*to* Xanthias *with warmth and cordiality*).
Ah, you're a worthy gentleman, I'll be bound for't;
You're all for the truth and the proof. Come—Strip there both
      o' ye.

    Xanthias. But how can ye put us to the question fairly,
Upon equal terms?

    Aeacus (*in the tone of a person proposing a convenient, agreeable arrangement*). Oh, easily enough,
Conveniently enough—a lash a piece,
Each in your turn: you can have 'em one by one.

    Xanthias. That's right. (*Putting himself in an attitude to receive the blow*). Now mind if ye see me flinch or swerve.

    Aeacus (*strikes him, but without producing any expression of pain*). I've struck.

    Xanthias.   Not you!

    Aeacus.   Why it seems as if I had not.
I'll smite this other fellow. (*Strikes* Bacchus.)

    Bacchus (*pretending not to feel*). When will you do it?
                           [Bacchus *receives a blow.*

                *   *   *

    Bacchus. Oh dear! (*and immediately subjoins*) Companions
    of my youthful years.

    Xanthias (*to* Aeacus). Did ye hear? he made an outcry.

    Aeacus.   What was that?

    Bacchus. A favourite passage from Archilochus.
                            [Xanthias *receives a blow.*

Xanthias. O Jupiter (*and subjoins*) that on the Idaean height;
   (*and contends that he has been repeating the first line of
   a well-known hymn*).

* * *

Aeacus (*at length giving the matter up*). Well, after all my
   pains, I'm quite at a loss
To discover which is the true, real deity.
By the Holy Goddess—I'm completely puzzled;
I must take you before Proserpine and Pluto;
Being gods themselves they're likeliest to know.
   Bacchus. Why, that's a lucky thought. I only wish
It had happen'd to occur before you beat us.
   Chorus. Muse, attend our solemn summons
      And survey the assembled commons,
      Congregated as they sit,
      An enormous mass of wit,
      —Full of genius, taste, and fire,
      Jealous pride, and critic ire—
      Cleophon[23] among the rest
      (Like the swallow from her nest,
      A familiar foreign bird),
      Chatters loud and will be heard
      (With the accent and the grace
      Which he brought with him from Thrace);
      But we fear the tuneful strain
      Will be turn'd to grief and pain;
      He must sing a dirge perforce
      When his trial takes its course;
      We shall hear him moan and wail,
      Like the plaintive nightingale.

[*Epirrhema.*

It behoves the sacred Chorus, and of right to them belongs,
To suggest the best advice   in their addresses and their songs.
In performance of our office,   we present with all humility
A proposal for removing   groundless fears and disability.
First, that all that were inveigled   into Phrynichus's treason,
Should be suffer'd and received   by rules of evidence and
   reason
To clear their conduct—Secondly,   that none of our Athenian
   race

[389]

Should live suspected and subjected   to loss of franchise and
    disgrace,
Feeling it a grievous scandal   when a single naval fight
Renders foreigners and slaves   partakers of the city's right:
—Not that we condemn the measure;   we conceived it wisely
    done,
As a just and timely measure,   and the first and only one:
—But your kinsman and your comrades,   those with whom
    you fought and bore
Danger, hardship, and fatigue,   or with their fathers long
    before,
Struggling on the land and ocean,   labouring with the spear
    and oar,
—These we think, as they profess   repentance for their past
    behaviour,
Might, by your exalted wisdoms,   be received to grace and
    favour.
Better it would be, believe us,   casting off revenge and pride,
To receive as friends and kinsmen   all that combat on our side
Into full and equal franchise: on the other hand we fear,
If your hearts are fill'd with fancies,   haughty, captious, and
    severe;
While the shock of instant danger   threatens shipwreck to the
    state,
Such resolves will be lamented   and repented of too late.

       If the Muse foresees at all
       What in future will befall
       Dirty Cleigenes the small—
       He, the sovereign of the bath,
       Will not long escape from scath;
       But must perish by and by,
       With his potash and his lye;
       With his realm and dynasty,
       His terraqueous scouring ball,
       And his washes, one and all;
       Therefore he can never cease
       To declaim against a peace.[24]

                             [Antepirrhema.

Often times have we reflected   on a similar abuse,
In the choice of men for office,   and of coins for common use;

For your old and standard pieces,   valued, and approved, and
    tried,
Here among the Grecian nations,   and in all the world beside;
Recognized in every realm   for trusty stamp and pure assay,
Are rejected and abandon'd   for the trash of yesterday;
For a vile, adulterate issue,   drossy, counterfeit, and base,
Which the traffic of the city   passes current in their place!
And the men that stood for office,   noted for acknowledged
    worth,
And for manly deeds of honour,   and for honourable birth;
Train'd in exercise and art,   in sacred dances and in song,
All are ousted and supplanted   by a base ignoble throng;
Paltry stamp and vulgar mettle   raise them to command and
    place,
Brazen counterfeit pretenders,   scoundrels of a scoundrel race;
Whom the state in former ages   scarce would have allow'd to
    stand,
At the sacrifice of outcasts,   as the scape-goats of the land.
—Time it is—and long has been,   renouncing all your follies
    past,
To recur to sterling merit   and intrinsic worth at last.
—If we rise, we rise with honour;   if we fall, it must be so!
—But there was an ancient saying,   which we all have heard
    and know,
That the wise, in dangerous cases,   have esteem'd it safe and
    good
To receive a slight chastisement   from *a wand of noble wood.*

        Scene. XANTHIAS *and* AEACUS.

Aeacus. By Jupiter! but he's a gentleman,
That master of yours.
   Xanthias.   A gentleman! To be sure he is;
Why, he does nothing else but wench and drink.
   Aeacus. His never striking you when you took his name—
Outfacing him and contradicting him!—
   Xanthias. It might have been worse for him if he had.
   Aeacus. Well, that's well spoken, like a true-bred slave.
It's just the sort of language I delight in.
   Xanthias. You love excuses?
   Aeacus.   Yes; but I prefer
Cursing my master quietly in private.

            [391]

Xanthias. Mischief you're fond of?

Aeacus.   Very fond indeed.

Xanthias. What think ye of muttering as you leave the room
After a beating?

Aeacus.   Why, that's pleasant too.

Xanthias. By Jove, is it! But listening at the door
To hear their secrets?

Aeacus.   Oh, there's nothing like it.

Xanthias. And then the reporting them in the neighbourhood.

Aeacus. That's beyond everything.—That's quite ecstatic.

Xanthias. Well, give me your hand. And, there, take mine—
and buss me.

And there again—and now for Jupiter's sake!—
(For he's the patron of our cuffs and beatings)
Do tell me what's that noise of people quarrelling
And abusing one another there within?

Aeacus. Aeschylus and Euripides, only!

Xanthias.   Heh?—?—?

Aeacus. Why, there's a desperate business has broke out
Among these here dead people;—quite a tumult.

Xanthias. As how?

Aeacus. First, there's a custom we have establish'd
In favour of professors of the arts.
When any one, the first in his own line,
Comes down amongst us here, he stands entitled
To privilege and precedence, with a seat[25]
At Pluto's royal board.

Xanthias.   I understand you.

Aeacus. So he maintains it, till there comes a better
Of the same sort, and then resigns it up.

Xanthias. But why should Aeschylus be disturb'd at this?

Aeacus. He held the seat for tragedy, as the master
In that profession.

Xanthias.   ·   Well, and who's there now?

Aeacus. He kept it till Euripides appear'd;
But he collected audiences about him,
And flourish'd, and exhibited, and harangued
Before the thieves, and housebreakers, and rogues,
Cut-purses, cheats, and vagabonds, and villains,

[392]

That make the mass of population there; (*pointing to the audience*)
And they—being quite transported, and delighted
With his equivocations and evasions,
His subtleties and niceties and quibbles—
In short—they raised an uproar, and declared him
Arch-poet, by a general acclamation.
And he with this grew proud and confident,
And laid a claim to the seat where Aeschylus sat.

  Xanthias. And did not he get pelted for his pains?

  Aeacus (*with the dry concise importance of superior local information*). Why, no—The mob call'd out, and it was carried,
To have a public trial of skill between them.

  Xanthias. You mean the mob of scoundrels that you mention'd?

  Aeacus. Scoundrels indeed! Aye, scoundrels without number.

  Xanthias. But Aeschylus must have had good friends and hearty?

  Aeacus. Yes; but good men are scarce both here and elsewhere.

  Xanthias. Well, what has Pluto settled to be done?

  Aeacus. To have an examination and a trial
In public.

  Xanthias.   But how comes it?—Sophocles?—
Why does not he put forth his claim amongst them?

  Aeacus. No, no!—He's not the kind of man—not he!
I tell ye; the first moment that he came,
He went up to Aeschylus and saluted him
And kiss'd his cheek and took his hand quite kindly;
And Aeschylus edged a little from his seat
To give him room; so now the story goes
(At least I had it from Cleidemides[26]),
He means to attend there as a stander-by,
Proposing to take up the conqueror;
If Aeschylus gets the better, well and good,
He gives up his pretensions—but if not,
He'll stand a trial, he says, against Euripides.

  Xanthias. There'll be strange doings.

  Aeacus.   That there will—and shortly

—Here—in this place—strange things, I promise you;
A kind of thing that no man could have thought of;
Why, you'll see poetry weigh'd out and measured.

   Xanthias. What, will they bring their tragedies to the steel-
     yards?

   Aeacus. Yes, will they—with their rules and compasses
They'll measure, and examine, and compare,
And bring their plummets, and their lines and levels,
To take the bearings—for Euripides
Says that he'll make a survey, word by word.

   Xanthias. Aeschylus takes the thing to heart, I doubt.

   Aeacus. He bent his brows and pored upon the ground;
I saw him.

   Xanthias.   Well, but who decides the business?

   Aeacus. Why, there the difficulty lies—for judges,
True learned judges, are grown scarce, and Aeschylus
Objected to the Athenians absolutely.

   Xanthias. Considering them as rogues and villains mostly.

   Aeacus. As being ignorant and empty generally;
And in their judgement of the stage particularly.
In fine, they've fix'd upon that master of yours,
As having had some practice in the business.
But we must wait within—for when our masters
Are warm and eager, stripes and blows ensue.

   Chorus. The full-mouth'd master of the tragic choir,
     We shall behold him foam with rage and ire;
     —Confronting in the list
     His eager, shrewd, sharp-tooth'd antagonist.
     Then will his visual orbs be wildly whirl'd
     And huge invectives will be hurl'd.
       Superb and supercilious,
       Atrocious, atrabilious,
     With furious gesture and with lips of foam,
     And lion crest unconscious of the comb;
     Erect with rage—his brow's impending gloom
     O'ershadowing his dark eyes' terrific blaze.
       The opponent, dexterous and wary,
       Will fend and parry:
     While masses of conglomerated phrase,
       Enormous, ponderous, and pedantic,

With indignation frantic,
  And strength and force gigantic,
    Are desperately sped
    At his devoted head—
Then in different style
The touchstone and the file,
And subtleties of art
In turn will play their part;
Analysis and rule,
And every modern tool;
With critic scratch and scribble,
And nice invidious nibble;
Contending for the important choice,
A vast expenditure of human voice!

Scene. EURIPIDES, BACCHUS, AESCHYLUS.

Euripides. Don't give me your advice, I claim the seat
As being the better and superior artist.
  Bacchus. What, Aeschylus, don't you speak? you hear his
    language.
  Euripides. He's mustering up a grand commanding visage
A silent attitude—the common trick
That he begins with in his tragedies.
  Bacchus. Come, have a care, my friend—You'll say too much.
  Euripides. I know the man of old—I've scrutinized
And shown him long ago for what he is,
A rude unbridled tongue, a haughty spirit;
Proud, arrogant, and insolently pompous;
Rough, clownish, boisterous, and overbearing.
  Aeschylus. Say'st thou me so? Thou bastard of the earth,
With thy patch'd robes and rags of sentiment
Raked from the streets and stitch'd and tack'd together!
Thou mumping, whining, beggarly hypocrite!
But you shall pay for it.
  Bacchus (*in addressing Aeschylus attempts to speak in more
    elevated style*). There now, Aeschylus,
You grow too warm. Restrain your ireful mood.
  Aeschylus. Yes; but I'll seize that sturdy beggar first,
And search and strip him bare of his pretensions.

Bacchus. Quick! Quick! A sacrifice to the winds—Make
    ready;
The storm of rage is gathering. Bring a victim.
  Aeschylus. —A wretch that has corrupted everything;
Our music with his melodies from Crete;
Our morals with incestuous tragedies.
  Bacchus. Dear, worthy Aeschylus, contain yourself,
And as for you, Euripides, move off
This instant, if you're wise; I give you warning.
Or else, with one of his big thumping phrases
You'll get your brains dash'd out, and all your notions
And sentiments and matter mash'd to pieces.
—And thee, most noble Aeschylus (*as above*), I beseech
With mild demeanour calm and affable
To hear and answer.—For it ill beseems
Illustrious bards to scold like market-women.
But you roar out and bellow like a furnace.
  Euripides (*in the tone of a town-blackguard working himself
    up for a quarrel*).
I'm up to it. I'm resolv'd, and here I stand
Ready and steady—take what course you will;
Let him be first to speak, or else let me.
I'll match my plots and characters against him;
My sentiments and language, and what not:
Aye! and my music too, my Meleager,
My Aeolus and my Telephus and all.
  Bacchus. Well, Aeschylus,—determine. What say you?
  Aeschylus (*speaks in a tone of grave manly despondency*).
I wish the place of trial had been elsewhere,
I stand at disadvantage here.
  Bacchus.   As how?
  Aeschylus. Because my poems live on earth above,
And his died with him, and descended here,
And are at hand as ready witnesses;
But you decide the matter: I submit.
  Bacchus (*with official pertness and importance*).
Come—let them bring me fire and frankincense,
That I may offer vows and make oblations
For an ingenious critical conclusion
To this same elegant and clever trial—

(*To the Chorus*). And you too,—sing me a hymn there.
—To the Muses.

Chorus. To the Heavenly Nine we petition,
Ye, that on earth or in air   are for ever kindly protecting
  the vagaries of learned ambition,
And at your ease from above   our sense and folly directing,
  (or poetical contests inspecting,
Deign to behold for a while   as a scene of amusing attention,
  all the struggles of style and invention,)
Aid, and assist, and attend,   and afford to the furious authors
  your refined and enlighten'd suggestions;
Grant them ability—force and agility, quick recollections,
  and address in their answers and questions,
Pithy replies, with a word to the wise, and pulling and hauling,
  with inordinate uproar and bawling,
Driving and drawing, like carpenters sawing, their dramas
  asunder:
                 With suspended sense and wonder,
                 All are waiting and attending
                 On the conflict now depending!

Bacchus. Come, say your prayers, you two before the trial.
                               [AESCHYLUS *offers incense.*

Aeschylus. O Ceres, nourisher of my soul, maintain me
A worthy follower of thy mysteries.[27]

Bacchus (*to* EURIPIDES). There, you there, make your offering.

Euripides.   Well, I will;
But I direct myself to other deities.

Bacchus. Heh, what? Your own? Some new ones?

Euripides.   Most assuredly!

Bacchus. Well! Pray away, then—to your own new deities.
                               [EURIPIDES *offers incense.*

Euripides. Thou foodful Air, the nurse of all my notions;
And ye, the organic powers of sense and speech,
And keen refined olfactory discernment,
Assist my present search for faults and errors.

Chorus. Here beside you, here are we,
                 Eager all to hear and see
                 This abstruse and mighty battle
                 Of profound and learned prattle.

[397]

    —But, as it appears to me,
    Thus the course of it will be;
    He, the junior and appellant,
    Will advance as the assailant.
    Aiming shrewd satiric darts
    At his rival's noble parts;
    And with sallies sharp and keen
    Try to wound him in the spleen,
    While the veteran rends and raises
    Rifted, rough, uprooted phrases,
    Wielded like a threshing staff
    Scattering the dust and chaff.

  Bacchus. Come, now begin, dispute away, but first I give you notice
That every phrase in your discourse must be refined, avoiding
Vulgar absurd comparisons, and awkward silly joking.

  Euripides. At the first outset, I forbear to state my own pretensions;
Hereafter I shall mention them, when his have been refuted;
After I shall have fairly shown, how he befool'd and cheated
The rustic audience that he found, which Phrynichus[28] bequeathed him.
He planted first upon the stage a figure veil'd and muffled,
An Achilles or a Niobe, that never show'd their faces;
But kept a tragic attitude, without a word to utter.

  Bacchus. No more they did: 'tis very true.

  Euripides.   —In the meanwhile the Chorus
Strung on ten strophes right-an-end, but they remain'd in silence.

  Bacchus. I liked that silence well enough, as well, perhaps, or better
Than those new talking characters—

  Euripides.   That's from your want of judgement,
Believe me.

  Bacchus. Why, perhaps it is; but what was his intention?

  Euripides. Why, mere conceit and insolence; to keep the people waiting
Till Niobe should deign to speak, to drive his drama forward.

  Bacchus. O what a rascal. Now I see the tricks he used to play me.

       [To AESCHYLUS, *who is showing signs of indigna-*
        tion by various contortions.

What makes you writhe and wince about?—

    Euripides.   Because he feels my censures.

Then having dragg'd and drawl'd along, half-way to the
    conclusion,
He foisted in a dozen words of noisy boisterous accent,
With lofty plumes and shaggy brows, mere bugbears of the
    language,
That no man ever heard before.—

    Aeschylus.   Alas! alas!

    Bacchus (to AESCHYLUS).   Have done there!

    Euripides. He never used a simple word.

    Bacchus (to AESCHYLUS). Don't grind your teeth so
    strangely.

    Euripides. But 'Bulwarks and Scamanders' and 'Hippogrifs
    and Gorgons.'
'On burnish'd shields emboss'd in brass'; bloody, remorseless
    phrases
Which nobody could understand.

    Bacchus.   Well, I confess, for my part,
I used to keep awake at night, with guesses and conjectures
To think what kind of foreign bird he meant by griffin-horses.

    Aeschylus. A figure on the heads of ships; you goose, you
    must have seen them.

    Bacchus. Well, from the likeness, I declare, I took it for
    Eruxis.[29]

    Euripides. So! Figures from the heads of ships are fit
    for tragic diction.

    Aeschylus. Well then—thou paltry wretch, explain. What
    were your own devices?

    Euripides. Not stories about flying-stags, like yours, and
    griffin-horses;
Nor terms nor images derived from tapestry Persian hangings.
When I received the Muse from you I found her puff'd and
    pamper'd
With pompous sentences and terms, a cumbrous huge virago.
My first attention was applied to make her look genteelly;

And bring her to a slighter shape   by dint of lighter diet:

I fed her with plain household phrase,   and cool familiar salad,

With water-gruel episode,   with sentimental jelly,

With moral mincemeat; till at length   I brought her into compass;

Cephisophon, who was my cook,   contrived to make them relish.

I kept my plots distinct and clear, and, to prevent confusion,

My leading characters rehearsed   their pedigrees for prologues.

    Aeschylus. 'Twas well, at least, that you forbore   to quote your own extraction.

    Euripides. From the first opening of the scene,   all persons were in action;

The master spoke, the slave replied,   the women, young and old ones,

All had their equal share of talk—

    Aeschylus.   Come, then, stand forth and tell us,

What forfeit less than death is due for such an innovation?

    Euripides. I did it upon principle,   from democratic motives.

    Bacchus. Take care, my friend—upon that ground   your footing is but ticklish.

    Euripides. I taught these youths to speechify.

    Aeschylus.   I say so too.—Moreover

I say that—for the public good—you ought to have been hang'd first.

    Euripides. The rules and forms of rhetoric,—the laws of composition,

To prate—to state—and in debate   to meet a question fairly:

At a dead lift to turn and shift—to make a nice distinction.

    Aeschylus. I grant it all—I make it all—my ground of accusation.

    Euripides. The whole in cases and concerns   occurring and recurring

At every turn and every day domestic and familiar,

So that the audience, one and all,   from personal experience,

Were competent to judge the piece,   and form a fair opinion

Whether my scenes and sentiments   agreed with truth and nature.

I never took them by surprise   to storm their understandings,
With Memnons and Tydides's   and idle rattle-trappings
Of battle-steeds and clattering shields   to scare them from their
    senses;
But for a test (perhaps the best) our pupils and adherents
May be distinguish'd instantly   by person and behaviour;
His are Phormisius the rough,   Meganetes the gloomy,
Hobgoblin-headed,   trumpet-mouth'd,   grim-visaged,   ugly-
    bearded;
But mine are Cleitophon the smooth,—Theramenes the gentle.

   Bacchus. Theramenes—a clever hand, a universal genius,
I never found him at a loss   in all the turns of party
To change his watchword at a word or at a moment's warning.

   Euripides. Thus it was that I began,
With a nicer, neater plan;
Teaching men to look about,
Both within doors and without;
To direct their own affairs,
And their house and household wares;
Marking everything amiss—
'Where is that? and—What is this?
This is broken—that is gone,'
'Tis the modern style and tone.

   Bacchus. Yes, by Jove—and at their homes
Nowadays each master comes,
Of a sudden bolting in
With an uproar and a din;
Rating all the servants round,
'If it's lost, it must be found.
Why was all the garlic wasted?
There, that honey has been tasted:
And these olives pilfer'd here.
Where's the pot we bought last year?
What's become of all the fish?
Which of you has broke the dish?'
Thus it is, but heretofore,
The moment that they cross'd the door,
They sat them down to doze and snore.

   Chorus. 'Noble Achilles!   you see the disaster,
'The shame and affront, and an enemy nigh!'[30]

Oh! bethink thee, mighty master,
  Think betimes of your reply;
Yet beware, lest anger force
Your hasty chariot from the course;
Grievous charges have been heard,
With many a sharp and bitter word,
Notwithstanding, mighty chief,
Let Prudence fold her cautious reef
In your anger's swelling sail;
By degrees you may prevail,
But beware of your behaviour
Till the wind is in your favour:
Now for your answer, illustrious architect,
Founder of lofty theatrical lays!
Patron in chief of our tragical trumperies!
  Open the floodgate of figure and phrase!
  Aeschylus. My spirit is kindled with anger and shame,
To so base a competitor forced to reply,
But I needs must retort, or the wretch will report
That he left me refuted and foil'd in debate;
Tell me then, What are the principal merits
Entitling a poet to praise and renown?
  Euripides. The improvement of morals, the progress of
    mind,
When a poet, by skill and invention,
Can render his audience virtuous and wise.
  Aeschylus. But if you, by neglect or intention,
Have done the reverse, and from brave honest spirits
Depraved, and have left them degraded and base,
Tell me, what punishment ought you to suffer?
  Bacchus. Death, to be sure!—Take that answer from me.
  Aeschylus. Observe then, and mark, what our citizens were,
When first from my care they were trusted to you;
Not scoundrel informers, or paltry buffoons,
Evading the services due to the state;
But with hearts all on fire, for adventure and war,
Distinguish'd for hardiness, stature, and strength,
Breathing forth nothing but lances and darts,
Arms, and equipment, and battle array,
Bucklers, and shields, and habergeons, and hauberks,

[402]

Helmets, and plumes, and heroic attire.

Bacchus.   There he goes, hammering on with his helmets,
He'll be the death of me one of these days.

Euripides.   But how did you manage to make 'em so manly,
What was the method, the means that you took?

Bacchus.   Speak, Aeschylus, speak, and behave yourself
    better,
And don't in your rage stand so silent and stern.

Aeschylus.   A drama, brimful with heroical spirit.

Euripides.   What did you call it?

Aeschylus.   'The Chiefs against Thebes,'
That inspired each spectator with martial ambition,
Courage, and ardour, and prowess, and pride.

Bacchus.   But you did very wrong to encourage the Thebans.
Indeed, you deserve to be punish'd, you do,
For the Thebans are grown to be capital soldiers,
You've done us a mischief by that very thing.

Aeschylus.   The fault was your own, if you took other
    courses;
The lesson I taught was directed to you:
Then I gave you the glorious theme of 'the Persians',
Replete with sublime patriotical strains,
The record and example of noble achievement,
The delight of the city, the pride of the stage.

Bacchus.   I rejoiced, I confess, when the tidings were carried
To old King Darius, so long dead and buried,
And the chorus in concert kept wringing their hands,
Weeping and wailing, and crying, Alas!

Aeschylus.   Such is the duty, the task of a poet,
Fulfilling in honour his office and trust.
Look to traditional history—look
To antiquity, primitive, early, remote:
See there, what a blessing illustrious poets
Conferr'd on mankind, in the centuries past,
Orpheus instructed mankind in religion,
Reclaim'd them from bloodshed and barbarous rites:
Musaeus deliver'd the doctrine of medicine,
And warnings prophetic for ages to come:
Next came old Hesiod, teaching us husbandry,
Ploughing, and sowing, and rural affairs,

[403]

Rural economy, rural astronomy,
Homely morality, labour, and thrift:
Homer himself, our adorable Homer,
What was his title to praise and renown?
What, but the worth of the lessons he taught us,
Discipline, arms, and equipment of war?

Bacchus. Yes, but Pantacles[31] was never the wiser;
For in the procession he ought to have led,
When his helmet was tied, he kept puzzling, and tried
To fasten the crest on the crown of his head.

Aeschylus. But other brave warriors and noble commanders
Were train'd in his lessons to valour and skill;
Such was the noble heroical Lamachus;
Others besides were instructed by him;
And I, from his fragments ordaining a banquet,
Furnish'd and deck'd with majestical phrase,
Brought forward the models of ancient achievement,
Teucer, Patroclus, and chiefs of antiquity;
Raising and rousing Athenian hearts,
When the signal of onset was blown in their ear,
With a similar ardour to dare and to do;
But I never allow'd of your lewd Sthenoboeas,
Or filthy, detestable Phaedra—not I—
Indeed, I should doubt if my drama throughout
Exhibit an instance of woman in love.

Euripides. No, you were too stern for an amorous turn,
For Venus and Cupid too stern and too stupid.

Aeschylus. May they leave me at rest, and with peace in my breast,
And infest and pursue your kindred and you,
With the very same blow that despatch'd you below.[32]

Bacchus. That was well enough said; with the life that he led,
He himself in the end got a wound from a friend.

Euripides. But what, after all, is the horrible mischief?
My poor Sthenoboeas, what harm have they done?

Aeschylus. The example is follow'd, the practice has gain'd,
And women of family, fortune, and worth,
Bewilder'd with shame in a passionate fury,
Have poison'd themselves for Bellerophon's sake.[33]

Euripides. But at least you'll allow that I never invented it,
Phaedra's affair was a matter of fact.

Aeschylus. A fact, with a vengeance! but horrible facts
Should be buried in silence, not bruited abroad,
Nor brought forth on the stage, nor emblazon'd in poetry.
Children and boys have a teacher assign'd them—
The bard is a master for manhood and youth,
Bound to instruct them in virtue and truth,
Beholden and bound.

Euripides.   But is virtue a sound?
Can any mysterious virtue be found
In bombastical, huge, hyperbolical phrase?

Aeschylus. Thou dirty, calamitous wretch, recollect
That exalted ideas of fancy require
To be clothed in a suitable vesture of phrase;
And that heroes and gods may be fairly supposed
Discoursing in words of a mightier import,
More lofty by far than the children of man;
As the pomp of apparel assign'd to their persons,
Produced on the stage and presented to view,
Surpasses in dignity, splendour, and lustre
Our popular garb and domestic attire,
A practice which nature and reason allow,
But which you disannull'd and rejected.

Euripides.   As how?

Aeschylus. When you brought forth your kings, in a villainous fashion,
In patches and rags, as a claim for compassion.

Euripides. And this is a grave misdemeanour, forsooth!

Aeschylus. It has taught an example of sordid untruth:
For the rich of the city, that ought to equip,
And to serve with, a ship, are appealing to pity,
Pretending distress—with an overworn dress.

Bacchus. By Jove, so they do; with a waistcoat brand new,
Worn closely within, warm and new for the skin;
And if they escape in this beggarly shape,
You'll meet 'em at market, I warrant 'em all,
Buying the best at the fishmonger's stall.

Aeschylus. He has taught every soul to sophisticate truth;
And debauch'd all the bodies and minds of the youth;

Leaving them morbid, and pallid, and spare;
And the places of exercise vacant and bare:—
The disorder has spread to the fleet and the crew;
The service is ruin'd, and ruin'd by you—
With prate and debate in a mutinous state;
Whereas, in my day, 'twas a different way;
Nothing they said, nor knew nothing to say,
But to call for their porridge, and cry, 'Pull away'.

    Bacchus. Yes—yes, they knew this,
How to stink in the teeth
Of the rower beneath;
And befoul their own comrades,
And pillage ashore;
But now they forget the command of the oar:—
Prating and splashing,
Discussing and dashing,
They steer here and there,
With their eyes in the air,
Hither and thither,
Nobody knows whither.

    Aeschylus. Can the reprobate mark in the course he has run,
One crime unattempted, a mischief undone?
With his horrible passions, of sisters and brothers,
And sons-in-law, tempted by villainous mothers,
And temples defiled with a bastardly birth,
And women, divested of honour or worth,
That talk about life 'as a death upon earth';
And sophistical frauds and rhetorical bawds;
Till now the whole state is infested with tribes
Of scriveners and scribblers, and rascally scribes—
All practice of masculine vigour and pride,
Our wrestling and running, are all laid aside,
And we see that the city can hardly provide
For the Feast of the Founder, a racer of force
To carry the torch and accomplish a course.

    Bacchus. Well, I laugh'd till I cried
The last festival tide,
At the fellow that ran,—
'Twas a heavy fat man,
And he panted and hobbled,

[406]

And stumbled and wabbled,
And the pottery people about the gate,
Seeing him hurried, and tired, and late,
Stood to receive him in open rank,
Helping him on with a hearty spank
Over the shoulder and over the flank,
The flank, the loin, the back, the shoulders,
With shouts of applause from all beholders;
While he ran on with a filthy fright,
Puffing his link to keep it alight.

   Chorus. Ere the prize is lost and won
      Mighty doings will be done.
      Now then—(though to judge aright
      Is difficult, when force and might
      Are opposed with ready slight,
      When the Champion that is cast
      Tumbles uppermost at last)
      —Since you meet in equal match,
      Argue, contradict and scratch,
      Scuffle, and abuse and bite,
      Tear and fight,
      With all your wits and all your might,
      —Fear not for a want of sense
      Or judgement in your audience,
      That defect has been removed;
      They're prodigiously improved,
      Disciplined, alert and smart,
      Drill'd and exercised in art:
      Each has got a little book,
      In the which they read and look,
      Doing all their best endeavour
      To be critical and clever;
      Thus their own ingenious natures,
        Aided and improved by learning,
      Will provide you with spectators
        Shrewd, attentive, and discerning.

* * *

The altercation which follows, turning upon a question of verbal criticism, is incapable of an exact translation. The attack with its answer occupies about forty-five lines in the original; Euripides begins it, saying that his opponent is incorrect in his use of words, and offers to prove it from those parts of his tragedies which were usually the most carefully composed (the opening speeches, or prologues as they were called).—He then calls upon Aeschylus to repeat the first lines from the tragedy of Orestes; in this tragedy Orestes is represented as having returned secretly to Argos, standing at the tomb of his father, and invoking Mercury,—not the vulgar patron of thieves and pedlars and spies, but that more awful deity, the terrestrial Hermes, the guardian of the dead, and inspector general of the infernal regions, the care of which had been delegated to him by the paternal authority of Jupiter.

The obscurity and ambiguity of the original may be represented by the following lines,

Terrestrial Hermes with supreme espial,
Inspector of that old paternal realm,
Aid and assist me now, your suppliant,
Revisiting and returning to my country!

This is variously misinterpreted. The 'espial' is supposed to refer to the treason practised against Agamemnon,—the 'paternal realm' to be that of Argos; and the last line is objected to as containing a tautology;—Aeschylus defends himself by the explanation of his meaning, which has been already given, and in answer to the last objection contends that for an exile to 'revisit' his country and to 'return' to it is not the same thing: to which Euripides replies:

Euripides. It is not justly express'd, since he return'd Clandestinely without authority.

Bacchus. That's well remark'd; but I don't comprehend it.

Euripides (*tauntingly and coolly*). Proceed—Continue!

Bacchus (*jealous of his authority*). Yes, you must continue, Aeschylus, I command you to continue.

(*To* EURIPIDES.) And you, keep a look-out and mark his blunders.

Aeschylus. 'From his sepulchral mound I call my father To listen and hear'—

Euripides.   There's a tautology!
'To listen and hear'—

Bacchus.   Why, don't you see, you ruffian!

[408]

It's a dead man he's calling to—Three times
We call[34] to 'em, but they can't be made to hear.

Aeschylus. And you: your prologues, of what kind were
they?

Euripides. I'll show ye; and if you'll point out a tautology,
Or a single word clapp'd in to botch a verse—
That's all!—I'll give you leave to spit upon me.

Bacchus (*with an absurd air of patience and resignation*).
Well, I can't help myself; I'm bound to attend.
Begin then with these same fine-spoken prologues.

Euripides. 'Oedipus was at first a happy man.' . .

Aeschylus. Not he, by Jove!—but born to misery;
Predicted and predestined by an oracle
Before his birth to murder his own father!
—Could he have been 'at first a happy man'?

Euripides. . . . 'But afterwards became a wretched mortal.'

Aeschylus. By no means! he continued to be wretched,
Born wretched, and exposed as soon as born
Upon a potsherd in a winter's night;
Brought up a foundling with disabled feet;
Then married—a young man to an aged woman,
That proved to be his mother—whereupon
He tore his eyes out.

Bacchus. To complete his happiness,
He ought to have served at sea with Erasinides.

*Aeschylus then attacks Euripides for the monotony of his
metre, and the continued recurrence of a pause on the fifth
syllable, which he ridicules by a burlesque addition subjoined
to all the verses in which this cadence is detected. The point
and humour of this supplementary phrase is not explained to us
by the ancient scholiasts, nor has the industry of modern com-
mentators enabled them to detect it. Euripides repeats the first
lines of several of his tragedies, but falls perpetually upon the
same pause, and is met at every turn with the absurd sup-
plement, till Bacchus calls out to him—*

Bacchus. There!—that's enough—now come to music, can't
ye?

Euripides. I mean it; I shall now proceed to expose him
As a bad composer, awkward, uninventive,

Repeating the same strain perpetually.—
    Chorus. I stand in wonder and perplext
        To think of what will follow next.
        Will he dare to criticize
        The noble bard, that did devise
        Our oldest, boldest harmonies,
        Whose mighty music we revere?
        Much I marvel, much I fear.—
    Euripides. Mighty fine music, truly! I'll give ye a sample;
It's every inch cut out to the same pattern.
    Bacchus. I'll mark—I've pick'd these pebbles up for
    counters.
    Euripides. Noble Achilles! Forth to the rescue!
        Forth to the rescue with ready support!
        Hasten and go,
        There is havoc and woe,
        Hasty defeat,
        And a bloody retreat,
        Confusion and rout,
        And the terrible shout
        Of a conquering foe,
        Tribulation and woe!
    Bacchus. Whoh hoh there! we've had woes enough, I reckon;
Therefore I'll go to wash away my woe
In a warm bath.
    Euripides.   No, do pray wait an instant,
And let me give you first another strain,
Transferr'd to the stage from music to the lyre.
    Bacchus. Proceed then—only give us no more woes.
    Euripides. The supremacy, sceptre, and haughty command
Of the Grecian land—with a flatto-flatto-flatto-thrat—
And the ravenous sphinx, with her horrible brood,
Thirsting for blood—with a flatto-flatto-flatto-thrat,
And armies equipp'd for a vengeful assault,
For Paris's fault—with a flatto-flatto-flatto-thrat.
    Bacchus. What herb is that same flatto-thrat? some simple,
I guess, you met with in the field of Marathon:
—But such a tune as this! you must have learnt it
From fellows hauling buckets at the well.
    Aeschylus. Such were the strains I purified and brought

To just perfection—taught by Phrynichus,
Not copying him, but culling other flowers
From those fair meadows which the Muses love—
—But he filches and begs, adapts and borrows
Snatches of tunes from minstrels in the street,
Strumpets and vagabonds—the lullabys
Of nurses and old women—jigs and ballads—
I'll give ye a proof—Bring me a lyre here, somebody.
What signifies a lyre? the castanets
Will suit him better—Bring the castanets,
With Euripides's Muse to snap her fingers
In cadence to her master's compositions.

    Bacchus. This Muse, I take it, is a Lesbian Muse.[35]
    Aeschylus. Gentle halcyons, ye that lave
           Your snowy plume,
       Sporting on the summer wave;
           Ye too that around the room,
    On the rafters of the roof
    Strain aloft your airy woof;
    Ye spiders, spiders ever spinning,
    Never ending, still beginning—
    Where the dolphin loves to follow,
    Weltering in the surge's hollow,
    Dear to Neptune and Apollo;
    By the seamen understood
    Ominous of harm or good;
    In capricious, eager sallies,
    Chasing, racing round the galleys.

*What follows is not very intelligible; it should seem that
Aeschylus beats the measure of the music which he ridicules.
He says, 'Do you see this foot?' or (as the scholiast explains
it) 'this rhythm?' to which Bacchus answers, 'I see it—'*

    Aeschylus. Well now. Do you see this?
    Bacchus.   I see it—
    Aeschylus (to his antagonist). Such is your music. I shall
    now proceed
       To give a specimen of your monodies[36]—
*The Burlesque which follows admits of a tolerably close
translation.*

O dreary shades of night!
What phantoms of affright
Have scared my troubled sense
With saucer eyes immense;
And huge horrific paws
With bloody claws!
Ye maidens haste, and bring
From the fair spring
A bucket of fresh water; whose clear stream
May purify me from this dreadful dream:
But oh! my dream is out
Ye maidens search about!
O mighty powers of mercy, can it be;
That Glyke, Glyke, she,
(My friend and civil neighbour heretofore),
Has robb'd my henroost of its feather'd store?
With the dawn I was beginning,
Spinning, spinning, spinning, spinning,
Unconscious of the meditated crime;
Meaning to sell my yarn at market-time.
Now tears alone are left me,
My neighbour hath bereft me,
Of all—of all—of all—all but a tear!
Since he, my faithful trusty chanticleer
Is flown—is flown!—is gone—is gone!
—But, O ye nymphs of sacred Ida, bring
Torches and bows, with arrows on the string;
And search around
All the suspected ground:
And thou, fair huntress of the sky;
Deign to attend, descending from on high—
—While Hecate, with her tremendous torch,
Even from the topmost garret to the porch
Explores the premises with search exact,
To find the thief and ascertain the fact—
Bacchus. Come, no more songs!
   Aeschylus.   I've had enough of 'em;
For my part, I shall bring him to the balance,
As a true test of our poetic merit,
To prove the weight of our respective verses.

Bacchus. Well then, so be it—if it must be so,
That I'm to stand here like a cheesemonger
Retailing poetry with a pair of scales.

> [*A huge pair of scales are here discovered on the stage.*

Chorus. Curious eager wits pursue
Strange devices quaint and new,
Like the scene you witness here,
Unaccountable and queer;
I myself, if merely told it,
If I did not here behold it,
Should have deem'd it utter folly,
Craziness and nonsense wholly.

Bacchus. Move up; stand close to the balance!
Euripides.   Here are we—
Bacchus. Take hold now, and each of you repeat a verse,
And don't leave go before I call to you!
Euripides. We're ready.
Bacchus.   Now, then, each repeat a verse.
Euripides.   'I wish that Argo with her woven wings.'[37]
Aeschylus. 'O streams of Sperchius, and ye pastured
plains.'[38]
Bacchus. Let go!—See now—this scale outweighs that other
Very considerably—
Euripides.   How did it happen?
Bacchus. He slipp'd a river in, like the wool-jobbers,
To moisten his metre—but your line was light,
A thing with wings—ready to fly away.
Euripides. Let him try once again then, and take hold.
Bacchus. Take hold once more.
Euripides.   We're ready.
Bacchus.   Now repeat.
Euripides. 'Speech is the temple and altar of persuasion.'[39]
Aeschylus. 'Death is a God that loves no sacrifice.'[40]
Bacchus. Let go!—See there again! This scale sinks down;
No wonder that it should, with Death put into it,
The heaviest of all calamities.
Euripides. But I put in persuasion finely express'd
In the best terms.

[413]

Bacchus.   Perhaps so; but persuasion
Is soft and light and silly—Think of something
That's heavy and huge, to outweigh him, something solid.
        Euripides. Let's see—Where have I got it? Something solid?
        Bacchus. 'Achilles has thrown twice—Twice a deuce—
             ace!'[41]
Come now, one trial more; this is the last.
        Euripides.   'He grasp'd a mighty mace of massy weight.'[42]
        Aeschylus. 'Cars upon cars, and corpses heap'd pell-mell.'[43]
        Bacchus. He has nick'd you again—
        Euripides.   Why so? What has he done?
        Bacchus. He has heap'd ye up cars and corpses, such a load
As twenty Egyptian labourers could not carry—
        Aeschylus. Come, no more single lines—let him bring all,
His wife, his children, his Cephisophon,
His books[44] and everything, himself to boot—
I'll counterpoise them with a couple of lines.
        Bacchus. Well, they're both friends of mine—I shan't decide
To get myself ill-will from either party;
One of them seems extraordinary clever,
And the other suits my taste particularly.
        Pluto. Won't you decide then, and conclude the business?
        Bacchus. Suppose then I decide; what then?
        Pluto.   Then take him
Away with you, whichever you prefer,
As a present for your pains in coming down here.
        Bacchus. Heaven bless ye—Well—let's see now—Can't ye
             advise me?
This is the case—I'm come in search of a poet—
        Pluto. With what design?
        Bacchus.   With this design; to see
The City again restored to peace and wealth,
Exhibiting tragedies in a proper style.
—Therefore whichever gives the best advice
On public matters I shall take him with me.
—First then of Alcibiades, what think ye?
The City is in hard labour with the question.
        Euripides. What are her sentiments towards him?
        Bacchus.   What?
'She loves and she detests and longs to have him.'[45]

[414]

But tell me, both of you, your own opinions.

[EURIPIDES *and* AESCHYLUS *speak each
in his own tragical style.*

Euripides. I hate the man that in his country's service
Is slow, but ready and quick to work her harm;
Unserviceable except to serve himself.

Bacchus. Well said, by Jove!—Now you—Give us a sentence.

Aeschylus. 'Tis rash and idle policy to foster
A lion's whelp within the city walls,
But when he's rear'd and grown you must indulge him.

Bacchus. By Jove then, I'm quite puzzled; one of them
Has answer'd clearly, and the other sensibly:
But give us both of ye one more opinion;
—What means are left of safety for the state?

Euripides. To tack Kinesias like a pair of wings
To Cleocritus's shoulders, and despatch them
From a precipice to sail across the seas.

Bacchus. It seems a joke; but there's some sense in it.

Euripides. . . . Then being both equipp'd with little cruets
They might co-operate in a naval action,
By sprinkling vinegar in the enemies' eyes.
—But I can tell you and will.

Bacchus.   Speak, and explain then—

Euripides. If we mistrust where present trust is placed,
Trusting in what was heretofore mistrusted—

Bacchus. How! What? I'm at a loss—Speak it again
Not quite so learnedly—more plainly and simply.

Euripides. If we withdraw the confidence we placed
In these our present statesmen, and transfer it
To those whom we mistrusted heretofore,
This seems I think our fairest chance for safety:
If with our present counsellors we fail,
Then with their opposites we might succeed.

Bacchus. That's capitally said, my Palamedes!
My politician! was it all your own?
Your own invention?

Euripides.   All except the cruets;
That was a notion of Cephisophon's.

Bacchus (*to* AESCHYLUS). Now you—What say you?

[415]

Aeschylus.   Inform me about the city—
What kind of persons has she placed in office?
Does she promote the worthiest?

Bacchus.   No, not she,
She can't abide 'em.

Aeschylus.   Rogues then she prefers?

Bacchus. Not altogether, she makes use of 'em
Perforce as it were.

Aeschylus.   Then who can hope to save
A state so wayward and perverse, that finds
No sort of habit fitted for her wear?
Drugget or superfine, nothing will suit her!

Bacchus. Do think a little how she can be saved.

Aeschylus. Not here; when I return there, I shall speak.

Bacchus. No, do pray send some good advice before you.

Aeschylus. When they regard their lands as enemy's ground,
Their enemy's possessions as their own,
Their seamen and the fleet their only safeguard,
Their sole resource hardship and poverty,
And resolute endurance in distress—

Bacchus. That's well,—but juries eat up everything,
And we shall lose our supper if we stay.

Pluto. Decide then—

Bacchus.   You'll decide for your own selves,
I'll make a choice according to my fancy.

Euripides. Remember, then, your oath to your poor friend;
And, as you swore and promised, rescue me.

Bacchus. 'It was my tongue that swore'[46]—I fix on Aeschylus.

Euripides. O wretch! what have you done?

Bacchus.   Me? done? What should I?
Voted for Aeschylus to be sure—Why not?

Euripides. And after such a villainous act, you dare
To view me face to face—Art not ashamed?

Bacchus. Why shame, in point of fact, is nothing real:
Shame is the apprehension of a vision
Reflected from the surface of opinion—
—The opinion of the public—They must judge.

Euripides. O cruel!—Will you abandon me to death?

Bacchus. Why perhaps death is life, and life is death,
And victuals and drink an illusion of the senses;

[416]

For what is Death but an eternal sleep?
And does not Life consist of sleeping and eating?
   Pluto. Now, Bacchus, you'll come here with us within.
   Bacchus (*a little startled and alarmed*). What for?
   Pluto.   To be received and entertain'd
With a feast before you go.
   Bacchus.   That's well imagined,
With all my heart—I've not the least objection.
   Chorus. Happy is the man possessing
        The superior holy blessing
        Of a judgement and a taste
        Accurate, refined and chaste;
        As it plainly doth appear
        In the scene presented here;
        Where the noble worthy Bard
        Meets with a deserved reward,
        Suffer'd to depart in peace
        Freely with a full release,
        To revisit once again
        His kindred and his countrymen—
           Hence moreover
           You discover,
        That to sit with Socrates,
        In a dream of learned ease;
        Quibbling, counter-quibbling, prating,
        Argufying and debating
        With the metaphysic sect,
        Daily sinking in neglect,
        Growing careless, incorrect,
        While the practice and the rules
        Of the true poetic Schools
        Are renounced or slighted wholly,
        Is a madness and a folly.
   Pluto. Go forth with good wishes and hearty good-will,
And salute the good people on Pallas's hill;
Let them hear and admire father Aeschylus still
In his office of old which again he must fill:
—You must guide and direct them,
Instruct and correct them,
With a lesson in verse,

For you'll find them much worse;
Greater fools than before, and their folly much more,
And more numerous far than the blockheads of yore—
And give Cleophon this,
And bid him not miss,
But be sure to attend
To the summons I send:
To Nicomachus too,
And the rest of the crew
That devise and invent
  New taxes and tribute,
Are summonses sent,
  Which you'll mind to distribute.
Bid them come to their graves,
Or, like runaway slaves,
If they linger and fail,
We shall drag them to jail;
Down here in the dark
With a brand and a mark.

  Aeschylus. I shall do as you say;
But the while I'm away,
Let the seat that I held
Be by Sophocles fill'd,
As deservedly reckon'd
My pupil and second
In learning and merit
And tragical spirit—
And take special care;
Keep that reprobate there
Far aloof from the Chair;
Let him never sit in it
An hour or a minute,
By chance or design
To profane what was mine.

  Pluto. Bring forward the torches!—The Chorus shall wait
And attend on the Poet in triumph and state
With a thundering chant of majestical tone
To wish him farewell, with a tune of his own.

  Chorus. Now may the powers of the earth give a safe and
    speedy departure

To the Bard at his second birth, with a prosperous happy
    revival;
And may the city, fatigued with wars and long revolution,
At length be brought to return to just and wise resolutions;
Long in peace to remain—Let restless Cleophon hasten
Far from amongst us here—since wars are his only diversion,
Thrace, his native land, will afford him wars in abundance.

ARISTOPHANES
PLUTUS, THE GOD OF RICHES

≫≫⋘⋘

TRANSLATED
By
SIR D. K. SANDFORD D.C.L.

CHARACTERS IN THE PLAY

CHREMYLUS.
CARION, *his Slave.*
PLUTUS.
Chorus of Husbandmen.
BLEPSIDEMUS.
Poverty.
The Wife of CHREMYLUS.

A Good Man.
An Informer.
An Old Woman.
A Youth.
HERMES.
Priest of Jove.

The play was first performed in 388 B. C.

ARGUMENT

"A very pretty allegory, which is wrought into a play by Aristophanes the Greek comedian. It seems originally designed as a satire upon the rich, though, in some parts of it, it is a kind of comparison between wealth and poverty. . . . .

"This allegory instructed the Athenians in two points; first, as it vindicated the conduct of Providence in its ordinary distributions of wealth; and, in the next place, as it showed the great tendency of riches to corrupt the morals of those who possess them."—ADDISON, *Spec. No.* 464.

PLUTUS, THE GOD OF RICHES

SCENE.—*A street in Athens.*
CHREMYLUS *and* CARION *following* PLUTUS, *who is blind.*

Carion. How hard a hap, O Jove, and all ye gods,
Bondman to be of a half-witted master!
For let the slave give counsel e'er so precious,
An please it not his lord to take it—mark me,
Your slave perforce shall have his share of—basting:
Since of his carcase not the owner, but,
By Fortune's grace, the buyer has disposal.
Well,
E'en let it pass! But Delphi's obscure god,
Who from the golden tripod, where he haunts,
Breathes verse oracular, of right I charge,
That being leech, and seer, they say, and sage,
Bile-mad he's sent my master from him. Lo!
He dogs a blind man's heels—a blind old beggar's—
O huge reverse of what beseems! 'Tis we,
We that have eyes should lead the eyeless—but
He goes behind, and me to boot compels—
And all for one says not so much as—boh!
Now then I'll hold no longer:—master mine,
Why, in the name of wonder, tell me, why
We follow thus, or I will plague thee rarely.
Beat me thou durst not, while I wear the laurel.[1]

Chremylus. No! But I'll doff thy laurel, an thou tease me,
So shalt thou smart the more.

Carion.   Pooh, pooh! I rest not
Till thou reveal me who this knave may be.
Of kindness 'tis I ask it—all of kindness.

Chremylus. Well, thou shalt hear; for of my household slaves
I rate thee, after all, the truest—rascal.
I—the good man and pious that thou know'st me—
Still poor have been, and bare of means.

Carion.   No doubt on't!

Chremylus. All else were rich—church-robbers, orators,
Informers, reprobates—

[423]

Carion.   I'll take thy word for't.

Chremylus. So to the god I went a-questioning.
Not for my miserable self—I thought
My days already spent, my quiver empty—
But for my son and sole inheritor,
To ask if he should mend his ways—
Should turn dare-devil, common cheat, mere vileness,
Since such, methought, was now the road to riches.

Carion. And what did Phoebus from his chaplets—bounce?

Chremylus. Attend. Distinctly thus the god gave answer:
Whom on my exit first I should encounter,
From him he bade me part no more, but win him
To make his home with me.

Carion.   And, prithee, whom
Was it thy luck to light on?

Chremylus.   This man here.

Carion. What then—O numskull!—what! thou apprehend'st
    not
His godship's meaning! Why, he tells thee plainly,
Young Hopeful must adopt our country's fashions.

Chremylus. How dost thou so conclude?

Carion.   Conclude? Why,
    Phœbus
Thinks even the blind can see how passing good
It is to play the thorough rogue in these times.

Chremylus. Impossible! It cannot be the oracle
Should point at this, but something loftier. Now,
Would but our man give token of his quality,
And why he came with us, and what in quest of,
We'd riddle the response I warrant thee!

Carion. Come then, be smart! your name at once, old gentle-
    man—
Or else you know what follows. Come, out with it.

Plutus. I tell thee—go be hang'd!

Carion.   D'ye understand, sir?
What name was that?

Chremylus.   To thee, not me, he says it:
Since doltishly and rudely thou dost question him.—
But—if a gentleman's address delight thee—
To *me* make known—

[424]

Plutus.   Go hang thyself for company!

Carion. There, sir, take man and omen too, and welcome!

Chremylus. How now?

Now, by great Ceres, thou shalt 'scape no longer.

Speak, dog, or doglike I will use thee—speak—

Plutus. Be off, my friends—both one and t'other.

Chremylus.   Off?

A likely tale!

Carion.   Well, I declare, good master,

My plan's the best, and to his cost he'll find so.

I'll set him on a certain crag, and—leave him.

Away go I—down he—his neck—

Chremylus.   Up with him!

Despatch!

Plutus.   O mercy, mercy!

Chremylus.   Won't you speak, then?

Plutus. But should ye learn whom ye have hold of—ah!

Ye'll work me harm—ye'll never let me go.

Chremylus. Nay, by the gods, we will though—if thou ask it.

Plutus. First, then, unhand me.

Chremylus.   See! thou art unhanded.

Plutus. Now, ope your ears and hear! For, will I nill I,

Declare I must, it seems, what I was minded

To hide for aye. I am—yes—I am—PLUTUS.

Chremylus. Plutus—O villain! Plutus, and conceal it!

Carion. You Plutus!—you!—in such a beggar's pickle!

Chremylus. O Phoebus! O Apollo! Gods and demons!

O Jove! What say'st thou? He himself?

Plutus.   E'en so.

Chremylus. His very self?

Plutus.   His self of selves.

Chremylus.   Whence, then,

So filthy com'st thou?

Plutus.   From Patrocles's,[2]

Who ne'er, since his first birth-day, washed himself.

Chremylus. But this misfortune—how befell it?—speak!

Plutus. Jove dealt the blow in envy to mankind.

For I, a stripling yet, would oft-times threaten

That to the good, and wise, and chaste alone,

My steps should bend; and so with stroke of blindness

[425]

Jove seal'd my sight, that it should not discern them.
Such malice doth he bear to virtuous men!

Chremylus. And yet, but for the virtuous and the just,
Where were this Jove?

Plutus. I grant it.

Chremylus. Go to now—
Mightst thou once more have all thine eyes about thee,
Wouldst henceforth shun the bad?

Plutus. For ever shun them.

Chremylus. And to the good resort?

Plutus. None else, I promise thee.
I've seen them not, this many a year.

Chremylus. No wonder!
Nor I, whose eyes were open.

Plutus. Now let me pass, ye know my story.

Chremylus. Pass!
Not we, by Jove, we'll stick the closer to thee.

Plutus. There, there, I warn'd thee. Said I not 'twas sure
Ye'd work me harm?

Chremylus. Nay, nay, be thou entreated!
Desert me not. Search where thou pleasest—
Long as thou wilt—thou'lt find no better man.
By Jupiter I stand alone—none like me!

Plutus. So say they all—but let them once
Lay hold on me and fill their money-bags,
They change their note, and beat the world for villainy.

Chremylus. 'Tis true—too true—yet all are not so graceless.

Plutus. Not all—but one and all.

Carion. The saucy varlet!

Chremylus. But for thyself—just to make plain what good
Awaits thy tarrying here—a moment's patience—
I look—I look—with heaven's assistance, mark me,
To make thee rid of this infirmity,
And give thee back thine eye-sight.

Plutus. Pray, excuse me;
Not for the world!

Chremylus. How's that?

Carion. By very nature
This fellow was just made for kicks and cuffs!

Plutus. Jove—well I know—did he but hear their madness,
Would grind me into powder.
 Chremylus.   What does he now,
That lets thee grope and stumble up and down?
 Plutus. I know not—but most mortally I fear him.
 Chremylus. Is't possible? O lily-livered thing,
Scum of celestial spirits, think'st thou Jove,
His empire and his thunders, worth three obols,
Hadst thou a moment's space thine eyes again?
 Plutus. Avaunt, blasphemer, rave not thus!
 Chremylus.   Be easy!
I will demonstrate thee more mighty far
Than Jove.
 Plutus. *Me thou* demonstrate!
 Chremylus.   Yes, by heavens!
For, look you now, through whom hath Jove the crown?
 Carion. Through—money; 'cause his purse is longest.
 Chremylus.   Well:
And where gets Jove the money?
 Carion.   From our friend here.
 Chremylus. Through whom do altars blaze? Is't not through
   Plutus?
 Carion. Lord, sir, they make no secret on't in praying.
 Chremylus. Then is not he the cause? And could he fail
Lightly to end it, were he minded so?
 Plutus. As how?
 Chremylus.   Because no mortal more would offer
Nor ox, nor cake—not they—nor earthly thing,
Thou not consenting.
 Plutus.   How?
 Chremylus.   Still *how?* How could they?
How will they buy, forsooth, if you're not there
To tell the money down? So, were Jove restive,
His power you'd soon extinguish—single-handed.
 Plutus. Say'st thou through *me* they worship him?
 Chremylus.   Through
  THEE.
And, by Jove's self, if aught of bright or fair
Or lovely bless mankind, through thee it flows.
The world, and all therein, bow down to riches.

Carion. I—I MYSELF—for a little paltry coin
Am servitor:—'tis all for want of riches.
    Chremylus. Then there's the dames of Corinth, as they say,
If a poor suitor try to tempt them—O
They turn him a deaf ear—but let a rich one,
And straight to him they turn—whate'er he pleases.
    Carion. Yes; and our youths, they say, will do as much
For love—not of the lovers but their purses.
    Chremylus. Fye! not our gentle youths:—our base ones may.
No money do the gentle ask.
    Carion.   What then?
    Chremylus. One—a good horse; and one—a pack to hunt
    with.
    Carion. Ay, that's their modesty!—Blushing to ask outright
For gold, what pretty names they salve it o'er with!
    Chremylus. All arts, all crafts, all man's inventions
Are born of thee. One sets him down
And shapes me certain gear of leather; one
The anvil plies; and one the joiner's tools;
One casts the gold he has of thee; another
Cleans clothes; another—steals them; bent on thee
The burglar breaks stone-walls; one washes hides;
One tans, and one cries leeks; for lack of thee
The trapp'd adulterer feels a husband's vengeance.
    Plutus. Wretch that I was—all this escap'd me!
    Carion.   What!
Is't not through him the great king plumes himself?
Through him the Assembly holds its sessions? What!
Dost thou not man our galleys? Tell me that.
At Corinth feeds not he our noble—hirelings?
And shall not Pamphilus for him be trounc'd?
And Belonopoles too with Pamphilus?
Is't not through him Agyrrhius vents his wind,
Philepsius his—stories? Was it not
Through him we sent the swart Egyptians succour?
For what but him does Lais love Philonides?
Timotheus' tower——[3]
    Chremylus.   Crush thee, eternal prater!
But O, my Plutus, what is *not* thy doing?
For thou most only universal cause

Of good and evil art, be sure.

    Carion.   In war

That party ever wins, whose sinking scale

This gentleman is pleas'd to perch on.

    Plutus.   I!

Poor I—unbacked—do all these things ye speak of!

    Chremylus. Yes, and, by Jupiter, ten thousand more:

So that no living wight had e'er his fill

Of thee. Of all besides there may be surfeit:

Of love,

    Carion. Of loaves,

    Chremylus.   Of songs,

    Carion.   Of sugar-comfits;

    Chremylus. Of honour,

    Carion.   Cheese-cakes,

    Chremylus.   Martial glory,

    Carion.   Figs;

    Chremylus. Ambition,

    Carion.   Flummery,

    Chremylus.   Command,

    Carion.   Pease-porridge.

    Chremylus. But thee! No mortal e'er was sated of thee.

Say he has thirteen talents,

Three, three to boot he craves he pines to grapple:

That total rounded, lo! his mark is forty—

Or life, he swears, no more is worth the living.

    Plutus. Ye talk it well at least, methinks;—

One thing yet gives me pause.

    Chremylus.   Announce it.

    Plutus.   How

Of all this power ye say I have, I e'er

Shall lord and master be?

    Chremylus.   By Jove thou shalt:

And yet all say—as *thou* hast said—that Plutus

Is cowardliest of creatures.

    Plutus.   Slander, slander!

A burglar's calumny! He stole one day,

And could not—stole into the house, ye mark me—

And could not steal—aught out of it—all fast!

And so he call'd my caution cowardice.

Chremylus. Vex not thyself about it; be
But bold and zealous for thine own behoof,
I'll make thee see more sharp than Lynceus.
    Plutus. And how shalt thou—a mortal—so prevail?
    Chremylus. Tut, man, there's hope—such utterance Phoebus
      gave
While Delphian laurels shook to hear him.
    Plutus.   Phoebus!
Thou canst not mean that Phoebus knows it?
    Chremylus.   Yea.
    Plutus. Beware!
    Chremylus.   Waste thou no thought upon it, friend!
For I, be certain sure, although I die for't,
Myself will bear thee through.
    Carion.   With *me* to help thee—
    Chremylus. And many a prompt ally—good souls, whose
      goodness
Could never keep their pots a-boiling.
    Plutus.   Pshaw!
Sorry confederates!
    Chremylus. Not if they get their pockets lined afresh—
But you there—haste, skip, vanish!
    Carion.   Speak your errand.
    Chremylus. Summon our fellow-husbandmen, perchance
A-field you'll find them, sweating at their tasks,
That hurrying hither, each may have his due
With us in just partition of this Plutus.
    Carion. I'm gone—but soft—this little steak of mine—⁴
Within there—some one give it safe conveyance. [*Exit* CARION.

    Chremylus. Trust me with that: away!
But O, great Plutus, mightiest of deities,
Do thou pass in with me. Behold the house,
The which thou must, ere time be a day older,
Cram full of wealth—by fair means or by foul ones.
    Plutus. Now, by the powers above, I am ever loath
To tread a stranger's floor, exceeding loath:
Ne'er yet to me did good come of it.
For say I made some thrifty soul my host,
Straight under ground he earth'd me, fathom-deep;
Then came a friend, an honest, worthy friend,

Seeking some petty pelting coin to borrow,
O—on his oath he never saw my face!
Or did I share some brain-sick spendthrift's quarters,
To dice and harlots thrown, out of his doors
Stark-naked was I kick'd in less than no time.
   Chremylus. Ay, for as yet
Thou ne'er hast tried one reasonable man.
But I—I know not how—a way of mine—
Have ever had this turn. In saving, none
Shall e'er out-save me; nor out-spend in spending
At seasons meet. But in—I long to show thee
To my good wife, and only son, whom dearest
I cherish—after thee.
   Plutus.   I do believe thee.
   Chremylus. For why with *thee* dissemble!   [*Exeunt.*
         The Open Country. CARION.

   Carion. O ye that here for a many a year, our trusty friends
    and neighbours,
Have had your share of master's fare—leek-broth and country
    labours,
Come stir your stumps and scour along—no room for shilly-
    shally—
But now's the very nick of time to make with us a rally.
   Chorus. And dost not see how eagerly we tramp it and we
    trudge it,
As fast as poor old fellows, sure, with tottering knees can budge
    it?
But bless my heart, you'd have me start to race with thee—un-
    knowing
For what, forsooth, this master rare of thine has set me going!
   Carion. And don't I roar, this hour and more? 'Tis thou art
    hard of hearing—
How master says that better days for all of you appearing—
Cold hearths shall turn to fires that burn, and churlish times to
    cheering?
   Chorus. What's this you tell—and how befell the burden of
    your story?
   Carion. Why, master's come, and brings us home a lodger—
    old and hoary:
He's bent and bow'd; he's scar'd and cow'd; he's toothless,
    foul, and tatter'd,

And scarce, I trow, the parts below are left him quite unbatter'd.

Chorus. Thou glad'st my ear! once more to hear this golden news it itches:

Our neighbour then's at home again, and brings a heap of riches.

Carion. A heap of—woes that age bestows, sore bones and empty breeches.

Chorus. And think'st thou so to come and go—to mock me and to flout me

Unscath'd, while I a staff can ply, and lay it well about me?

Carion. And think ye me a rogue to be so false and eke so graceless,

That every word my lips have pour'd must rotten be and baseless?

Chorus. O curse the knave, how sour and grave!—but hark, thy shins are bawling

Halloo, halloo!—and stocks and chains is that for which they're calling.

Carion. Thy lot's[5] decreed—in burial-weed must thine awards be spoken:

What! still withstand! when Charon's hand is holding out thy token?

Chorus. O burst thy skin, thou devil's kin! so apt to cheat and scold, sir,

To flout me and to scout me, and to leave it still untold, sir,

For what this summons-sending lord of thine has made so bold, sir;

Yet hasten we, though labour-spent and loath to lose a minute—

And reckless tread o'er many a bed with dainty onions in it!

Carion. The glorious tale no more I'll veil:—'tis PLUTUS' self we hold, boys,

In master's train he troops amain, to glut us all with gold, boys!

Chorus. What! one and all such luck befall!—to turn to peace and plenty?

Carion. An if ye please, to Midases:—if asses' ears content ye.

Chorus. How glad I am, and mad I am, and keen I am for dancing it!

Such news as this, if true it is, will set our feet a-prancing it.

Carion. Then on, my boys, I'll share your joys—sing derry, hey down derry—
With Cyclop's-step,[6] with rub-a-dub, I'll caper it so merry!
So whisk it, frisk it, jolly flock,[7] with bleatings shake the air, O!

> And sound the lambkin's, kidling's strain,
> Till startled echo *baa* again,

And cock your tails like stinking goats, and goat-like ye shall fare, O!

Chorus. Then bleating we Cyclopian thee—sing derry, hey down derry—
Will catch full soon and change thy tune to doleful notes for merry!
With shepherd's scrip and dewy herbs, and reeling ripe and randy, O,

> You lead your fleecy company,
> Or careless snore with fast-shut eye,

Then up we take a huge burnt stake, and twist it out so handy, O![8]

Carion. Then Circe next, the drugs who mix'd, shall teach to me the knack o' them,
That gull'd with ease—Philonides[9] at Corinth, and a pack o' them:

> *We're swine*, thought they, nor dreaded it

To make a meal of kneaded dung, and she it was that kneaded it:

> I'll beat the sorc'ress—beat her hollow—
> And you in full cry, grunt—grunting with joy,
> Follow, piglings, follow!

Chorus. And say'st thou so! for vengeance ho! thou men-befouling Circe,
With dung to mix, and magic tricks that place 'em at your mercy—

> We'll make a sport of banging thee,

And then as wise Ulysses did[10] by nether parts uphanging thee,

> We'll bung with dirt thy nose's hollow,
> Till you squeak in a tone Aristyllus[11] might own,
> Follow, piglings, follow!

Carion. Away, away, a truce with play! no more of fun and laughter!

    Now turn ye back to t'other shape,
    While I with covert steps escape,
    Of bread and meat a tiny meal
    From master's larder-stores to—steal;
And that discuss'd, methinks I must—attend to business after.
              [*Exit* CARION.

  Before the house of CHREMYLUS. CHREMYLUS, CHORUS.
  Chremylus. To give good den, good townsmen,
Is now a stale and musty salutation:
But I do *kiss your hands,* that zealously,
Eager and most unloiterer-like ye come.
See then ye still stand by me: show yourselves
True patrons and preservers of the god.
  Chorus. Fear not: I'll wear
Such looks—thou'lt think a very Mars beside thee
'Twere strange were we, who for three obols push
And jostle i' th' Assembly—were *we* to let
The actual MONEY-GOD be wrested from us!
  Chremylus. 'Tis he—I'll swear to it—'tis Blepsidemus
That comes towards us. Ay, he has got some wind
Of our affair, his pace bewrays it.
        [*Enter* BLEPSIDEMUS (*soliloquizing*).
  Blepsidemus. Did they say Chremylus!
How can it be—whence—by what contrivance—
Has *he* grown rich at once? I'll not believe it.
Yet thus at least says rumour:—so help me, Hercules,
There's not a barber's shop but has the story,
That all at once the fellow's rich. Again
'Tis strange—'tis passing strange—that in the moment
Of luck he begs his friends to visit him—
That's not the mode with us!
  Chremylus. Out it shall come, by heavens! Yes, Blepsidemus,
Things go more smooth to-day than yesterday—
And thou shalt share;—we hold thee one of us.
  Blepsidemus. Nay but—is't true? Art really, truly rich?
  Chremylus. Shall be, at least—right suddenly—God willing.
There is—there is some—danger in the business.
  Blepsidemus. What kind?
  Chremylus.   Why such as—

Blepsidemus   Quick, whate'er you say.

Chremylus. Such as—with luck—makes men of us for ever.
But, should we fail, 'tis utter ruination.

Blepsidemus. Ha!
It has an ugly air—this load upon thee—
It likes me not; for thus, too hurriedly
To wax so over-rich—and then to tremble—
Looks something else than honest.

Chremylus.   Else than honest!

Blepsidemus.   Suppose, now—just suppose—thou com'st
    from yonder,
With gold or silver from the sacred treasure
Which thou hast—filch'd; and peradventure now
Repenting—

Chremylus. Phoebus shield me! no, by Jupiter!

Blepsidemus.   No nonsense, friend! I know the whole.

Chremylus.   Suspect not
Of *me* such deed as this.

Blepsidemus.   Alas, alas!
That honesty should clean forgotten be,
And all be slaves of greed and gain!

Chremylus.   By Ceres,
Thine upper story seems a little damag'd.

Blepsidemus. How chang'd a man from all his whilom ways!

Chremylus. Stark mad—by heaven above!—the fellow
    foams.

Blepsidemus. His very eye unfixed!—See how it wanders!
Sure mark of guilt!

Chremylus.   Croak on, I understand thee;
Thou deem'st me thief, and fain wouldst be partaker.

Blepsidemus. Partaker would I be? Of *what* partaker?

Chremylus. It is not as thou deem'st, but—

Blepsidemus. What? Hast not filched but—forced?

Chremylus.   The devil's in thee.

Blepsidemus. A breach of trust then?

Chremylus.   No.

Blepsidemus.   O Hercules!
Where must one turn one's self? No truth from thee!

Chremylus. You charge at random, ere you learn my story.

Blepsidemus. Come friend, I'm ready, for a very trifle

[435]

To compromise this case before 'tis public,
Stopping the pleaders' mouths with certain—pieces.

    Chremylus. Yes! like a kind—good friend—you'll under-
take

To spend three minæ and charge me—a dozen.

    Blepsidemus. I see—I see—one to the Bema[12] wending,
Suppliant to sit with customary bough—
His wife, his children near;—no eye shall know them
From the Heraclidae drawn by Pamphilus.[13]

    Chremylus. Not so, thou sorry devil, but the worthy—
None else—shrewd fellows—wise and sober fellows—
Will I make full of riches.

    Blepsidemus.   What?

Hast stol'n so monstrous much?

    Chremylus.   Beshrew my heart!

Thou wilt destroy—

    Blepsidemus.   Thou wilt thyself destroy.

    Chremylus. Never; for, hark ye, rogue—I've hold of—
    PLUTUS.

    Blepsidemus. You—Plutus—you! What Plutus?

    Chremylus.   The divine one.

    Blepsidemus. And where?

    Chremylus.   Here.

    Blepsidemus.   Where?

    Chremylus.   With me.

    Blepsidemus.   With thee?

    Chremylus.   Precisely.

    Blepsidemus. O, you be hanged! Plutus with *thee*?

    Chremylus.   I swear it.

    Blepsidemus. Say'st true?

    Chremylus.   Most true?

    Blepsidemus.   By Vesta?

    Chremylus.   Yea, by Neptune.

    Blepsidemus. The ocean Neptune?

    Chremylus. And if there be another—by that other.

    Blepsidemus. What? And not send him round to us—thy
friends!

    Chremylus. Not yet are matters come to this.

    Blepsidemus.   Not yet!

Not come to sharing?

Chremylus.   No: for first—
Blepsidemus.   What first?
Chremylus. We two must give back sight—
Blepsidemus.   Give sight? To whom?
Chremylus. To Plutus—by some one device or other.
Blepsidemus. So then, he's really blind?
Chremylus.   He is, by Heaven.
Blepsidemus. No wonder that he never came to me!
Chremylus.   But now—so please the gods—he'll make
amends.
Blepsidemus. Come then—a leech! a leech!—shouldst not
have fetched one?
Chremylus. What leech has Athens now? They're gone
together,
The art and its rewards—no fee no physic!
Blepsidemus. Let's see.
Chremylus.   There's none.
Blepsidemus.   Thou'rt right, i' faith.
Chremylus.   Not one.
But listen, I was thinking
To lay him down at Aesculapius' shrine.
That were the way—
Blepsidemus.   Far best, by all the powers!
Away—delay not—something do, and quickly.
Chremylus. I go.
Blepsidemus.   But haste!
Chremylus.   Why, I *am* hasting.

                                   [*Enter* POVERTY.

Poverty.   STOP!—
O ye hot bloods! Ye moon-struck mannikins!
That dare such lawless, rash, and impious deed—
Where, where so fast? I charge ye stop—
Blepsidemus.   O Hercules!
Poverty. Wretches, a wretched end I'll make of you.
Your venture—yes, your venture is a rare one,
Unbrook'd, unventured yet by god or mortal:
So that your doom is fix'd.
Chremylus.   And who art thou?
Thy chops look blue—

Blepsidemus. Perhaps some fury from the tragic boards:
Truly her air's a little touch'd and tragic.

Chremylus. But where's her torch?

Blepsidemus.   No torch! Then let her howl for't.

Poverty. And whom suppose ye me?

Chremylus.   Some paltry hostess,
Or market wife mayhap: else would'st thou not
Have bawl'd so loud at us for nothing.

Poverty.   Nothing!
Have ye not done me deadliest injury,
Plotting from this whole land to banish me?

Chremylus. Why, hast thou not the Barathrum[14] to go to?
But—who thou art behoved thee answer—quick!

Poverty. One that this day
Will ample vengeance take on both your heads
For striving thus to blot me from your city—

Blepsidemus. Sure now 'tis just my neighbour, the old tap-
    stress,
That's always cheating with her half-pint measures.

Poverty. One that for many a year with both has mated—
POVERTY.

Blepsidemus. King Apollo! Gods of heaven!
Where *can* one flee?

Chremylus. You there—what now? Thou coward reptile,
    thou—
Not stand thy ground!

Blepsidemus.   Ne'er dream of it.

Chremylus.   Not stand!
What we—two men—to run, and from a woman!

Blepsidemus. But she is POVERTY, thou rogue, than whom
No creature more pernicious e'er was gender'd.

Chremylus. Stand, I beseech thee, stand.

Blepsidemus.   Not I, by Jupiter!

Chremylus. Nay, do but listen: of all unheard-of things
Ours were the biggest folly, if the god
We thus forsook, and fled this filthy hag,
Nor tried to fight it out.

Blepsidemus. Fight! With what arms—what backing—how
    made bold?
What breast-plate, and what buckler,

Does she—infernal witch—not bring to—pawn?

Chremylus. Cheer up:
Ours, certes, is the very god to turn
Round on her turns, and show her feats defeated.

Poverty. What! grumble too! ye sinks, ye offal, will ye?
Caught in the fact, and dare to mutter!

Chremylus. What have we done, thou doom'd one? Wherefore com'st thou
Hither to rail, unwrong'd of us?

Poverty. Unwrong'd?
Patience, ye gods! Unwrong'd? Is't nothing, think ye,
No wrong to me—essaying thus to give
Sight back to Plutus?

Chremylus. Where's the wrong to thee,
If good we so achieve for all mankind?

Poverty. The good—the mighty good—that ye can compass?

Chremylus. The good?
Imprimis, having thrust thee forth of Greece—

Poverty. ME forth of Greece? And O, what huger mischief
Could your curst frenzy work the race of man?

Chremylus. Why, if we purpos'd so, and slept upon it.

Poverty. Now, on this very point I first address me
To reckon with you: if I prove myself
Sole source of all your blessings; that through me
Ye live and breathe:—if not,
Do your joint pleasure on me.

Chremylus. Loathliest hag,
Dar'st thou to teach such things?

Poverty. Dare thou to learn them!
Right readily I'll show thee all astray,
If 'tis the good thou think'st to endow with riches.

Blepsidemus. Cudgels and collars, help me to requite her!

Poverty. No need to bawl and bluster ere thou hear.

Blepsidemus. And who'd not bawl and call *ohon! ohon!*
At words like these?

Poverty. Whoe'er has brains in noddle.

Chremylus. Name then the damages—how much to lay at—
If thou be cast.

Poverty. At what thou pleasest.

[439]

Chremylus.   Good.

Poverty. The same must ye disburse in t'other issue.

Blepsidemus. Dost think a score of—hangings—were
   enough?

Chremylus. For her:—for us a pair or so may serve.

Poverty. About it then—away!—or who hereafter

Shall law or justice plead?

Chorus. Now clear your wit—the time is fit—and deal her
   blow for blow,

In the contest keen of the wordy war no weakness must ye know.

Chremylus. And plain it is to all I wis—there's none will
   say me nay—

That virtue fair and honesty should carry still the day,

And the rabble rout of godless men be worsted in the fray.

To compass aim, so worthy fame, our bosoms long have glow'd,

And scarce at last have chanc'd upon a right and royal road:

If Plutus' sight be burnish'd bright, and dark no more he rove,

Where the wise and pure his steps allure, their mansions he will
   love;

And straight eschew the impious crew, and of the righteous rear

A race around, with riches crown'd, the holy gods to fear;

And where's the man for brother men can better lot espy?

Blepsidemus. There's none can do't, I'm witness to't, a fig
   for her reply!

Chremylus. For mark as now the fates ordain the life of
   man to run,

'Tis bedlam hurl'd upon the world—'tis hell beneath the sun:

The base that gather'd gold by crime, they flaunt in gallant trim,

The good, they spend with thee their time, and pine with famine
   grim,

While sorrow brews their cup of tears, and fills it to the brim.

Blepsidemus. But Plutus once to sight restor'd, and master
   of the field,

Then doubled see the joys of man, and all his wrongs repeal'd!

Poverty. Ye dotard twain, whose addled brain no law of
   reason rules,

Joint-fellows in the maudlin band of drivellers and fools!

Had ye your silly hearts' desire, what benefit to you,

Though Plutus saw and portion'd fair his heritage anew?

For who would then of mortal men to handicrafts apply,

Or cumber more his head with lore of science stern and high?
And who would forge, or frame a wheel, or stately vessel plan,
Or clout a shoe, or bake a tile, or tailor it, or tan?
Or break with ploughs the face of earth and reap the yellow
    grain,
When all in ease and idle mirth might laugh at toil and pain?
    Chremylus. Thou senseless jade, each toil and trade your
        tongue has rattled o'er,
Our servitors will take in hand and labour as of yore.
    Poverty. And how obtain this servile train?
    Chremylus.   For money.
    Poverty.   Who will sell,
When rich himself with stores of pelf?
    Chremylus.   Dark Thessaly may tell:—
'Tis there the slaver's trade is rife, that deals in human ware.
    Poverty. But who will lead the slaver's life, the slaver's for-
        feit dare,
When, thanks to thee, his wealth is free, and comes without a
    care?
So arm thee fast with spade and plough, to dig, and drudge, and
    groan,
With burthen heavier far than now—
    Chremylus.   The burthen be thine own!
    Poverty. Nor bed shalt thou repose upon—for bed there will
    not be,
Nor rug be wrought in coming times of blest equality:—
Nor sprinkle oils of rich perfume on happy bridal day;
Nor broider'd work from cunning loom of thousand hues dis-
    play;
And where's the good of golden store, if these be reft away?
But all ye want 'tis mine to grant—and lavish the supply—
For mistress like I set me down the base mechanic by,
And force for need and lack of bread his daily task to try.
    Chremylus. What precious grant is thine to vaunt but
    blisters on the skin
From bagnio fires,[15] and starving brats, and scolding grannums'
    din?
And the swarm of lice, and gnats, and fleas what lips can ever
    sum,
That buzz about the tortur'd head with sleep-dispelling hum,

While *"up and work, or lie and starve"* they trumpet as they
    come?
And rags for robes thou givest us; and for the bed of down
A lair of rushes stuffed with—bugs, to lie and—wake upon;
For carpet gay, a rotten mat; for pillow under head,
A thumping stone to prop the crown; and mallow-shoots for
    bread,
O dainty treat!—for barley-brose, the meagre cabbage leaves;
And for a seat, a broken jar our weary weight receives;
For bolting-trough a barrel-side, with cracks to make it fine,
How rich and rare these blessings are!—and all the merit thine!

    Poverty. Thou gib'st not me—'tis BEGGARY thou pommellest
      with scorn.

    Chremylus. And deem'd we not thy sister come, when beg-
      gary was born?

    Poverty. Yes—ye that Dionysus hold of Thrasybulus
      strain:—[16]

But sunder'd still our lots have been, and sunder'd shall remain.
The beggar he—as drawn by thee—that still on nothing lives;
The poor man's share is frugal care, and all that labour gives,
A modest store—nor less nor more, than reason's choice allowed.

    Chremylus. O rest his soul—the happy dole by Poverty
      avow'd!—

To pinch and grieve, and toil and leave—no money for a shroud.

    Poverty. With your jesting and your jeering, and your fleer-
      ing rail away—

Nor dream I boast a nobler host than Plutus can array!—
Ay! nobler far in mood and make:—the gouty go to him,
Huge tuns of men, with baggy guts and dropsy-swollen limb;
To me the tight, the merry wasps, the terrors of the foe.

    Chremylus. That wasp-like waist by famine brac'd, thy
      nursing cares bestow!

    Poverty. And virtue meek and modesty with me are fast
      allied,

While the lawless hand and the ruthless brand are seen on
    Plutus' side.

    Chremylus. O modest trick!—a purse to pick, or neighbour's
      house invade.

    Blepsidemus. Most modest sure! for modest worth has ever
      lov'd—the shade.

Poverty. Then mark your fiery orators, the people's *honest* friends,

When poor they stand for their father-land, and patriotic ends;
But fatten'd once on civic jobs, they plead another cause,
'Tis *down with tumult-stirring mobs* and *up with gagging laws!*

    Chremylus. Thou hitt'st 'em fair, old beldame there—all venom as thou art—

Yet plume not thou thyself, nor hope unpunish'd to depart:
Fine lesson this thou teachest!—not *money makes the man*—
But poverty thou preachest—

    Poverty.   Confute it, if you can!

In vain you flap and flutter—[17]

    Chremylus.   From *you* the hearer flees.

    Poverty. Because the words I utter are virtue's homilies.

So see the son his father shun, who counsels him to good;
For late and slow by man below the right is understood.

    Chremylus. Then Jove, it seems, unwisely deems, and foolish things commends,

For wealth beside himself he keeps—

    Blepsidemus.   And *her* to us he sends.

    Poverty. Dull-sighted pair, whose minds are blear with film of other times,

Great Jove is poor—and proof full sure shall fortify my rhymes:

Behold when Greece together throngs each fifth revolving year,
And in his own Olympic lists the combatants appear,
A herald's breath—an olive wreath—is all the victor's prize;
Gold were the meed, had Jove indeed a treasure in the skies.

    Chremylus. 'Tis thus he proves how dear his cash, how close he keeps his gains,

He binds the victor's brow with trash, the money he retains.

    Poverty. Thy ribald tongue a fouler wrong than want upon him puts—

That not for need but dirty greed his money-bag he shuts.

    Chremylus. Jove strike thee down—but first a crown of olive-twigs bestow!

    Poverty. To dare disown from me alone all earthly blessings flow!

    Chremylus. Of Hecate ask the question—let her decision tell,

If riches or if hunger should bear away the bell.
To her, she says, the jolly rich a monthly feast[18] afford,
But ere 'tis set the harpy poor have swept it from the board.

    But curse thee—rot! No more upbraid us
      With groan or sign;
    Persuasion's self shall not persuade us.

Poverty.   "Town of Argos hear his cry!"[19]

Chremylus. On Pauson[20] call, thy messmate true!

Poverty.   Unhappy-happy me!

Chremylus. Go feed the crows that wait for you!

Poverty.   Ah wither, whither flee?

Chremylus. To whipping-post; nor linger more!—
    Thy steps are slack.

Poverty.   Yet soon will ye my loss deplore,
    And woo me, woo me back!

Chremylus. Return thou then!—now, ruin seize thee—
    Be mine the riches that displease thee—
    And thou—go rave and roar to ease thee!
           [*Exit* POVERTY.

Blepsidemus. Wealth and wealthy joys for me!
    With wife and babes to revel free—
    And sleek returning from the bath,
    On handicraftsmen in my path
    And Poverty that lags behind
    To break my jest and break my—wind!

Chremylus. There—she is gone at last—the scurvy jade!
And now let me and thee at once lead off
Our god to bed in Aesculapius' temple.

 Blepsidemus. Ay, bustle, neighbour, bustle—sharp's the
  word!
Lest fresh disturbers mar our opening plot.

 Chremylus. What, Carion! Slave, I say—out with the
  blankets!
And Plutus' self bring forth, with due observance,
And all besides you've furnished for the nonce. [*Exeunt.*

   Before the house of CHREMYLUS. CARION, CHORUS.
 Carion. Hilloa there!
Ye grey beards, oft on Theseus' days,[21] spoon-cramm'd
With broth good store, to bread in sparest scraps,

How happy now, how blest of favouring fortune!
Both ye, and all that take an honest turn.

    Chorus. Sweet sir, thy news? What have thy friends to
      boast of?

'Tis something rare thou seem'st to bring for tidings.

    Carion. The master, boys, has prosper'd gloriously,
Or rather Plutus' self: instead of blind,
His eyes are clear—clean'd out, and fairly—whiten'd,
A kindly leech in Aesculapius finding.

    Chorus.   O lucky day!
                  Hurra! Huzza!

    Carion. Like it or not, rejoicing-time is come.

    Chorus.   Great Aesculapius, sons never fail thee;
          Star of the human race, loud will we hail thee!

                        [Enter WIFE OF CHREMYLUS.

    Wife. What meant that shout? Is't news, good news, it tells?
O I have pin'd for it, and sat within,
Longing to greet this home-returning varlet.

    Carion. Quick, mistress, quick; some wine there, that with
      me

Thou too may'st taste a drop—thou lov'st it dearly;   *[Aside.*
For all rich blessings in a lump I bring thee.

    Wife. And where—where are they?

    Carion.   Soon in words thou'lt know them.

    Wife. Thy words then—haste, have done.

    Carion.   Attend.

The whole affair will I from foot to head[22]——

    Wife. To head! Beware! *To* head nor *on* head neither!

    Carion. What! not this joyful business?

    Wife.   *Business,* quotha?

Affair? No—none of your *affairs* for me!

    Carion. Soon as we reach'd the god,
Guiding a man, most miserable then,
Most happy now, if happy man there be;
First to the salt sea sand we led him down,
And there we—duck'd him.

    Wife.   Happy he, by Jupiter!
A poor old fellow, duck'd in the cold brine.

    Carion. Thence to the sanctuary hied we; and
When on the altar cakes and corn-oblations

Were dedicate—to Vulcan's flame a wafer—
We laid our Plutus down, as meet it was,
While each of us fell to, to patch a bed up.
  Wife. And were there other suitors to the god?
  Carion. Why, one was Neoclides, blind is he,
Yet our best eyes he will out-aim at—thieving;
And many a one besides, with all diseases
Laden;—but when the beadle gave
The word to sleep, the lamps extinguishing,
And strictly charged *"if any hear a noise,*
Mute let him be"—we squatted round in order.
Well:
Sleep could I not, but me a certain pot
Of porridge hugely struck; 'twas lying there
Some small space distant from an old wife's head,
Towards which I felt a wondrous motion draw me;—
So, venturing a peep, I spy the priest
Our offerings—scones and figs—snatching away
From off the holy table; after this,
Round every altar, one by one, he grop'd
If any where a single cake were left;
Then these he *bless'd*—into a sort of satchel.
So, thinking 'twas a deed of vast devotion,
Bent on the pot of porridge, up get I.
  Wife. Wretch! Fear'st thou not the god?
  Carion.   By the gods, I did,
Lest he should get before me to the pot,
Garlands and all;—his priest had tutor'd me.
Mean while old grannum,
When once her ear had caught the stir I made,
Was stealing out her hand—so, hissing high,
With teeth I seized it, like a puff-cheek snake;
But she incontinent her hand pluck'd back,
And lay all quiet, cuddled in a heap,
Fizzling for fear—ugh! worse than any pole-cat.
Then gobbled I my bellyful of porridge,
And so—well stuff'd—turn'd in to snooze a little.
  Wife. But say—the god—approach'd he not?
  Carion.   Not yet.
So, after this—O such a merry trick

I play'd! As he drew near, a rousing blast
I let—my guts, d'ye see, were almost bursting.
   Wife. And sure for this he straight abhorr'd thee.
   Carion.   No.
But there was Madam Jaso,[23] in his train,
Did blush a bit, and Panacea turn'd,
Holding her nose; for, 'faith, I vent no incense.
   Wife. But he himself?
   Carion.   Car'd not, 'icod, not he.
   Wife. A clownish god thou mak'st of him.
   Carion.   A clown!
No; but an ordure-taster.[24]
   Wife.   Out upon thee!
   Carion. When this was past, forthwith I muffled up,
Cowering with dread; but he, most doctor-like,
Perform'd his rounds, inspecting case by case.
Then placed a lad beside him his stone mortar,
Pestle, and chest.
   Wife.   Stone, too?[25]
   Carion.   No, not the chest.
   Wife. And thou—thou gallows-bird—how could'st thou see,
Who say'st thy head was hid?
   Carion.   Through this bald jerkin;
Windows it had, and not a few, by Jupiter.
For Neoclides first he took in hand
To pound a cataplasm—throwing in
Three heads of Tenian garlic; these he bruised,
Commixing in the mortar benjamin
And mastic; drenching all with Sphettian vinegar,
He plaster'd o'er his eyelids, inside out,
To give him greater torment;—squalling, bawling,
The wretch sprung up to flee; then laugh'd the god,
And cried, "Now sit ye down beplaster'd there,
And take thine oath I keep thee from the sessions!"
   Wife. O what a patriot and a prudent god!
   Carion. He next sat down by Plutus;
And handled first his head; then with a cloth
Of linen, clean and napless, wiped the eyelids
Quite round and round; then Panacea
Wrapp'd in a purple petticoat his head,

[447]

And all his face; then Aesculapius whistled—
With that out darted from the shrine two serpents
Of most prodigious size.
  Wife.   Merciful heavens!

 Carion. And these, smooth gliding underneath the petticoat,
Lick'd with their tongues—so seem'd to me—his eyelids.
And, ere you'd toss me off ten half-pint bumpers,
Plutus—O mistress!—up rose Plutus SEEING.
Loud clapp'd I then both hands for ecstacy,
And fell to wakening master; but the god
Vanish'd into the temple, self and serpents.
Then those that couch'd beside him—canst thou guess
How they *did* fondle Plutus, and all night
Slept not, but watch'd till morning glimmer'd through?
While I was lauding lustily the god,
That in a twinkling he gave sight to Plutus,
And Neoclides blinded worse than ever.

 Wife. What marvellous power is thine, O sovereign lord!
But tell me where is Plutus?

 Carion.   This way coming.
But there were crowds about him, infinite great.
For such as heretofore had decent morals,
And lean subsistence—these were greeting him,
And locking hand in hand for very transport.
But such as wealthy were, with means o'erflowing,
And gain'd by no unquestionable arts—
O theirs were knitted brows and clouded faces!
The rest were tripping, chaplet-crown'd, behind him,
With laugh and jubilant cry; the old men's slipper
Clatter'd, with modulated steps advancing.
Halloo then! one and all, with one accord,
Dance ye and jump ye—hands round—cut and shuffle.
For none henceforth shall meet ye on the threshold
With *"harkye, friend, there's nothing in the meal tub!"*

 Wife. So help me, Hecate, I will garland thee,
For these fair tidings, with a wreath of—pan-loaves.
Such news thou bringst!

 Carion.   About it instantly!
The company's already at the door.

Wife. Nay, let me hurry in and fetch some sweetmeats,
To welcome these new-purchased—eyes—slave-fashion.[26]
    Carion. And I to meet them fly.

                      [Exeunt. Enter PLUTUS *and* CHREMYLUS.

    Plutus. Thy beams, bright Sol! prostrate I first adore,
Next great Minerva's world-renowned city,
And Cecrops' total bounds that harbour'd me,
O how I blush for past calamities!
The men—the men—that I unconscious dealt with!
And these, the worthy of my fellowship,
All-ignorant avoided, luckless me!
'Twas foully done—both that and this—most foully.
But treading now reverted paths, I'll show
To all of mortal mould, in coming times,
Unwilling with the bad I held communion.
    Chremylus. Off to the crows, I say. Why, what a pest,
These friends that sprout so fast when days are sunny!
They rub, scrub, crush one's shins;[27] so dear one's grown,
Each must needs find some vent for his affection.
Who miss'd *God save ye* to me? What a throng
Of reverend seniors squeezed me at the market!

                    [Re-enter WIFE OF CHREMYLUS.

    Wife. All hail!
Thou paragon of men—and thou—and thou too.
Come now—so custom rules it—let me scatter
These sweetmeat offerings on thee.
    Plutus.   Prithee, no.
For entering thy house on a first visit,
And with recover'd eyesight, it were meet
Not *out* but *in* to take an offering.
    Wife. What, not accept my sweatmeats!
    Plutus.   Well; within then,
Beside your hearth, as best observance rules.
So, too, we 'scape turmoil and trickery.
Our poet would it misbecome to fling
Dried figs and comfits to the lookers on,
Thus to extort a laugh.[28]
    Wife.   Right, right; for see
There's Dexinicus yonder, up and ready
To scramble for the figs.   *[Exeunt.*

Before the House of Chremylus.

Carion, O it is sweet, my friends, when things go merrily,
To roll in wealth, cost free, without a venture.
Here's a whole heap of luxuries come bouncing
Whack! right into the house—and all unsinn'd for!
Full is our bread-bin now of white wheat flour,
Our casks of red aroma-scented wine;
There's not a trunk nor box, but gold and silver
Heave up the coin-burst lid—you'd gape to see it.
The well runs out with oil, the cruets teem
With nard, the loft with figs; pot, pan, and pipkin
Are turn'd to shining brass; the rotten trenchers,
That stunk of fish they held, are solid silver;
Kitchen and kitchen gear are ivory;
And we—the gentlemen-domestics—there
At odds and evens play with sterling staters;
So dainty grown, that not those rasping stones
But onion-shaws we use for our occasions.
And now high sacrifice the master holds
Within; wreath-crown'd, swine, goat, and ram he offers.
But me—the smoke has driven me forth; I could
Stand it no more; my eyes so smarted with it.

[*Enter a* GOOD MAN *with his Slave.*

Good Man.　Come on, my lad, come on, that to the god
We may repair.

[*Enter* CHREMYLUS.

Chremylus.　　　　　Hey day! whom have we here?
Good Man.　A man, once wretched, prosperous now.
Chremylus.　　　　　　　　　　　　　　Just so;
Clearly, methinks, one of the honest folk.
Good Man.　Most true.
Chremylus.　　　　　What may'st thou want then?
Good Man.　　　　　　　　　　　　　　To the god
I come, the source to me of mighty blessings.
For, mark my tale—
I from my sire a fair inheritance
Receiving, hence my needy friends I aided.
Trust me, I thought it prudent policy.
　Chremylus.　And so thy money shortly fail'd thee.

Good Man.   Very.

Chremylus. And so you wax'd right miserable.

Good Man.   Very.

And yet, methought, those in their need so long
I heap'd with kindnesses, were steadfast friends,
Steadfast and staunch when I might need—but they
Turn'd them aside, nor seem'd to see me more.

Chremylus. And laugh'd thee loud to scorn, I know it.

Good Man.   Very.

For 'twas a drought of—dishes, that destroy'd me.

Chremylus. But now not so.

Good Man.   And therefore to the god

Here am I fitly come, my vows to pay.

Chremylus. But this bald cloak—what's this, pray, *to the god*,[29]

Thy foot-boy brings?

Good Man.   To offer to the god.

Chremylus. What, was't in this thou wert initiated?

Good Man. No; but in this for thirteen years I—shiver'd.

Chremylus. And these pantofles?

Good Man.   Winter'd with me too.

Chremylus. These, too, thou bring'st to offer?

Good Man.   Yes, by Jove.

Chremylus. A proper pair of offerings *to the god!*

[*Enter an* INFORMER *with his Witness.*

Informer. Woe's me! woe's me!
Me miserable! undone, undone for ever!
Thrice wretched—four times wretched—five times wretched—
Twelve times—ten thousand times—ohon! ohon!
With so robust a devil my fate is dash'd![30]

Chremylus. Phoebus protect us! Gracious deities!
Why, what the mischief has this fellow met with?

Informer. Now, is it hard or no,
To see one's substance gone—stock, rock, and block—
Through this confounded god? But he shall pay for't;
Blind—blind again—if law be left in Athens.

Good Man. Oho! methinks I smell the matter out.
Here comes a knave, in a bad way, no doubt on't;
And of bad stamp to boot, I warrant ye.

Chremylus. Bad way! *fair* way for him—the road to ruin.

Informer. Where, where is he that promis'd all unholpen,
To make us rich at once—each mother's son—
If he but saw afresh? Here's some of us
He has beggar'd past example.

Chremylus.   Say'st thou so?
Whom has he handled thus?

Informer.   ME; me, I tell thee;
Here as I stand.

Chremylus. So, so; a rogue—a burglar?

Informer. No, villain, no! 'Tis ye—stark naught ye are—
'Tis ye—none other—robb'd me of my money.

Carion. Now, Ceres bless us, how the Informer goes it,
So fierce and famine-like—a wolfish hunger!

Informer. To court with ye—to court—no time to dally—
That stretched upon the wheel of torture there,
Thou may'st confess thy villainy.

Carion.   You be hang'd!

Good Man. O, by preserving Jove, a glorious god
To all of Greekish blood our god will be,
That brings to end as vile these vile informers.

Informer. Confusion!
Thou too must laugh—as their *accomplice*—thou!
Whence came this mantle else, so spruce and trim?
But yesterday thy thread-bare cloak I noted.

Good Man. I heed thee not; behold this charmed ring!
Mine own; bought from Eudamus for a drachma.

Chremylus. Alas, no charm for an informer's bite!

Informer. What insolence is this? Ye scoff, ye rail,
And have not answer'd yet what make ye here?
'Tis for no good ye come.

Chremylus.   No good of thine.

Informer. No; for at cost of mine ye think to revel.

Chremylus. O that to prove it true, thyself and witness
Might both asunder burst—but not with eating!

Informer. Will ye deny? Within, ye cursed scoundrels,
Such roasts there are, such loads of fish in slices!
Uhu, uhu, uhu, uhu, uhu.   [*Sniffling.*

Chremylus. Wretch, snuff'st thou aught?

Good Man.   Cold air, mayhap,

[452]

In such a rascal suit of rags attir'd.

Informer. Shall this be borne? Jove, and ye powers above,
That *these* should scoff at ME! O how it galls
Thus to endure—the good—the patriot.

Chremylus. You!
The *patriot* and the *good!*

Informer. Ay, none to match me.

Chremylus. Come now, an answer to my question.

Informer. What?

Chremylus. Dost work a farm?

Informer. Dost take me for stark mad?

Chremylus. A merchant then?

Informer. Can seem so on occasions.[31]

Chremylus. What then, hast learnt a trade?

Informer. Not I, by Jupiter.

Chremylus. Why, how didst live, or whence, without a
calling?

Informer. Live? Of all state affairs Intendant I,
And private business.

Chremylus. You! For what?

Informer. I choose it.

Chremylus. False thief, how art thou good then,
Mixing and meddling where it nought concerns thee?

Informer. Concerns me nought, old gull! Concerns it not,
Far as I may, to benefit my city?

Chremylus. So, so—to meddle is to benefit?

Informer. Yes, the establish'd laws to succour—yes,
If rogues offend, to hold them to the forfeit.

Chremylus. And does the state not crowd her bench with
judges
Express for this?

Informer. But who must play the accuser?

Chremylus. Whoever will.

Informer. Ergo, that man am I.
So that on me devolve the state's affairs.

Chremylus. Now, by the powers, she hath a rare protector!
But would'st thou not incline, meddling no more,
To live a life of ease?

Informer. A sheep's existence!
No occupation left to stir the soul.

Chremylus. What then, thou'lt not reform?

Informer.   Not if you'd give me
Plutus himself, and the benzoin of Battus.[32]

Chremylus. Down with thy cloak.

Carion.   *You*, sirrah, *you* he speaks to.

Chremylus. Off with thy shoes.

Carion.   'Tis *you*, still *you* he means.

Informer. Come on and take them then; come on, I say,
Whoever will.

Carion. Ergo, that man am I.   [*Witness runs out.*

Informer. Help! robbery! help! I'm stripp'd in open day.

Carion. Yes; for thou claim'st to live on stranger's business.

Informer. Thou seest the act; I hold thee witness to it.

Chremylus. Witness! he's vanish'd: witness, quotha!

Informer.   Woe!
Caught and alone!

Carion.   Now thou wilt clamour, wilt thou?

Informer. Woe's me again!

Carion.   Hand me the thread-bare cloak here,
To gird this base informing rogue withal.

Good Man. Nay now, already 'tis devote to Plutus.

Carion. And where, I pray thee, shall it hang more fitly
Than round a caitiff's limbs—a plund'ring bandit's?
Plutus 'twere meet to deck in costly garments.

Good Man. But these pantofles—

Carion.   To his forehead these,
Wild-olive-like, incontinent I'll nail.

Informer. I'm off; for well I know myself the weaker
'Gainst odds like these; yet, grant me but a partner,
Ay, though a fig-tree block—your potent god
This day I'd bring to justice and his doom;
For that alone, unbacked, democracy
He plots to end—a traitor manifest—
Council nor people to his side persuading.

Good Man. Hark! as in gorgeous panoply of mine
Adorn'd thou struttest, to the bath with thee!
There as head-man take station next the fire;
That post was mine of yore.

Chremylus.   Nay, but the bath-man
Straight out of doors will haul him by the scrotum;

One glance will show the stamp of scoundrel on him.
For us—let's in; the god expects thy vows.   [*Exeunt.*

Before the House of CHREMYLUS. *An* OLD WOMAN.
Old Woman. A word, beseech you, dear old gentlemen;
Is't true we've reach'd the house of this new god,
Or are we off the road and quite astray?
                                        [*Enter* CHREMYLUS.
Chremylus. Believe me, now, you're at the very doors,
My buxom lass:—so prettily you ask it.
Old Woman. And must I call for some one from within?
Chremylus. Nay, here I am myself, come forth already.
Let's hear thy purpose rather.
Old Woman. Dear sir, kind sir—a tale of grief and wrong:
For from the hour this god began to see,
He has made for me my life unliveable.
Chremylus. What's this? Mayhap thou wert *Informeress*
Among the dames?
Old Woman.   Marry come up, not I.
Chremylus. Thy lot, perchance, turn'd out no drinking-
  ticket.[33]
Old Woman. You jeer: but me—I itch—I burn—I die.
Chremylus. Thine itch—thine itch? Let's hear—as short as
  may be.
Old Woman. Hear, then:—a certain darling youth I had:
Grant he was poor—but O, a proper youth!
Comely and shapely—so obliging too—
If any little services I wanted,
He'd do them for me orderly and featly:
And me in these same things he found complying.
Chremylus. And what he suits he press'd the warmest, eh?
Old Woman. But few: for his respect was quite prodigious.
He'd ask, perhaps, some twenty silver drachms
For a new coat—some eight or ten for slippers:—
"Buy," he would say, "a little shift for sisters,
A cloakey for mamma—poor soul—'gainst winter:"
Or beg of wheat some half-a-dozen bushels.
Chremylus. By my troth, not much—as thou hast told the
  story—
'Tis plain he stood in mighty awe of thee.

[455]

Old Woman. And then observe, "not out of greediness
I ask," quoth he, "but love, that wearing still
Thy coat—thy colours—I may think of thee."

Chremylus. Unhappy man! how desperately smitten!

Old Woman. But now—wouldst credit it?—the rogue **no**
more
Holds the same mind: he's quite another creature.
For when I sent to him this cheesecake here,
And those—the other sweetmeats on the platter—
And hinted, too, he might expect a visit
Against the afternoon——

Chremylus.　　　　　　What did he? Say,

Old Woman. Did? Sent 'em back—this tart into the bar-
gain—
On these plain terms—that I should call no longer!
And sent besides this message by the bearer,
"Once the Milesians were a potent people."[34]

Chremylus. I'faith no blockhead was the boy;—
When rich, pease-porridge charms no more his palate:
Till then he took whatever came, and thankful.

Old Woman. Yes, and till then, each blessed day—O
Gemini!—
Still was he come—come—coming to my gate.

Chremylus. To carry thee out?[35]

Old Woman.　　　　　　　　To carry! No—to listen
An he might hear my voice——

Chremylus.　　　　　　　　Say *"sweet, here's for thee."*

Old Woman. And if he saw me vex'd at aught—my stars!—
My duckling and *my doveling,* would he whisper.

Chremylus. Then, too, mayhap, would beg for *slipper-money.*

Old Woman. And once, as at the greater mysteries
I rode my car—because one gaz'd upon me—
Bless you! the livelong day my bones paid for it.—
So mortal jealous was the stripling of me.

Chremylus. Just so:—he lik'd, I guess, to—eat alone.

Old Woman. And then my hands, he vow'd, were matchless
fair.—

Chremylus. Oft as they told him down *some twenty drachms.*

Old Woman. And sweet, he'd say, the fragrance of my
skin.—

Chremylus. Right, right, by Jove—when Thasian wine you
    pour'd—

Old Woman. And eyes I had, so soft and beautiful.—

Chremylus. No clumsy rogue was this: full well he knew
To sweat a rutting beldame's ready cash.

Old Woman. Here, then, dear sir, the god unfairly deals—
Your god, that boasts himself the wrong'd one's righter.

Chremylus. How shall he serve thee! Speak, and it is done.

Old Woman. Sure 'tis but fair to force
Him whom I help'd to lend me help in turn:
Or not one glimpse of good the wretch should see.

Chremylus. Nay—clear'd he not each night his scores with
    thee?

Old Woman. Ah! but he swore he'd never, never leave me,
Long as I liv'd.

Chremylus. True—as you liv'd: but now
You live, he thinks, no more.

Old Woman. 'Tis sorrow's doing—
I own I've pin'd away.

Chremylus. Or *rotted* rather.

Old Woman. See, you might draw me through a ring.

Chremylus. A ring!
An 'twere a barley-boulter's.

Old Woman. Well, as I live, here comes the very youth
I've been a-telling thee the tantrums of:
He seems on revel bound.

Chremylus. No question;—lo,
Fillets and flambeau bearing, on he trips it.

                                            [*Enter* YOUTH.

Youth. I kiss your hands.

Old Woman. *Kiss,* says he? *Kiss?*

Youth. Old sweetheart,
How grey thou'rt grown, and all at once, by Jingo.

Old Woman. Wretch that I am! The buffets I must bear!

Chremylus. 'Tis long, belike, since last he saw thee.

Old Woman. Long!
When 'twas but yesterday, thou monster, thou.

Chremylus. Then trust me, friend, his is no common case:—
Fuddled, it seems, he sees the sharper for it.

Old Woman. No: but 'tis always such a saucy rogue!

Youth. O thou sea-Neptune,[36] and ye senior gods,
How seam'd with ruts and wrinkles are her chops!

Old Woman. Ah! O! Ah!
Hold not your torch to me.

Chremylus. Well thought of, old 'un:
For should one single spark but catch her,
Off, like a wool-clad olive-branch,[37] she blazes!

Youth. What say you now?—We have not met for ages—
A little sport?—

Old Woman. O you audacious!—Where!

Youth. Here—nuts in hand.

Old Woman. What sport's he driving at?

Youth. How many—teeth hast thou?[38]

Chremylus. A guess—a guess—
A guess for me!—Some three, mayhap, or four.

Youth. Pay down:—she has but one, and that's a grinder.

Old Woman. Vilest of men, thy wits have left thee: what,
Before such crowds to make a wash-pot of me!

Youth. 'Faith, no bad turn—to wash thee out, pot-fashion.

Chremylus. Fie on't not so: she's now made up for sale,
Right huckster's trim—but only wash the paint off—
Lord, how the tatters of her face would show!

Old Woman. Old as you are, your sense is wondrous scanty.

Youth. He tempts thee, sure—the rogue!—and thinks the
    while
Those daring hands escape my jealous eye.

Old Woman. So help me, Venus, not a hand on me
He lays, you brute.

Chremylus. So help me, Hecate, no:
Else were I mad. But come, my boy, this lass
Thou must not loathe.

Youth. What, me? I love to frenzy.

Chremylus. And yet she 'plains of thee.

Youth. She 'plains! As how?

Chremylus. O, a proud peat you are, she says, and tell her
Once the Milesians were a potent people.

Youth. Well, I'll not fight with thee about her.—

Chremylus. No!
Your why and wherefore?

Youth. Reverence for thine years:—

[458]

There breathes no other wight I'd yield her to.
And now, take off the *lass,* and joy be with thee!
    Chremylus. I see, I see your drift: you mean no more
To herd with her.
    Old Woman.   And who will brook the traitor?
    Youth. I've not a word for one so rak'd and riddled
By full ten thousand, *plus* three thousand—years.
    Chremylus. Yet, since you deign'd to quaff the wine—you
    take me?—
'Twere fair to suck the dregs.
    Youth. Ugh! but these dregs—they are so stale and rancid.
    Chremylus. A strainer cures all that—
    Youth.   In, in, I say:
These garlands to the god I fain would offer.
    Old Woman. And I—I do remember me—I too
Have a word to say to him.
    Youth.   Then go not I.
    Chremylus. Tut, man, cheer up! She shall not ravish thee.
    Youth. A gracious promise:—for enough in conscience
I've pitch'd that weather-beaten hulk already.
    Old Woman. Ay, march away:—I'll not be far behind thee.
    Chremylus. O, sov'reign Jove! how fast and firm the beldame
Cleaves like a limpet to her stripling flame!   [*Exeunt.*

Before the House of CHREMYLUS.

HERMES *knocks at the door, and hides.*[39]

    Carion (*coming out*). Who knocks the door there, ho? Why,
    what could this be?
No one, it seems: and so the little wicket
Makes all this hullabaloo, forsooth, for nothing.
    Hermes (*showing himself*). You there, I say,
You, Carion, stop!
    Carion.   What, fellow, was it thee
That bang'd so lustily against the door?
    Hermes. No:—I but thought on't—thou hast sav'd the trouble.
But *presto,* post away and call thy master,
And furthermore, the mistress and her brats;
And furthermore, the slaves, and eke the mastiff,
And furthermore, thyself—the pig—

Carion.   Nay, tell me,
What *is* all this?
Hermes.   'Tis Jove, you rogue, is minded
Hashing you up into one hotch-potch mess,
To send you, great and small, to pot together.
Carion.   Heralds like this shall get the tongue[40]—cut out.
But why, an please you, does he plan such fare
For us?
Hermes. Because you've done—a deed without a name:
Since first this Plutus' eyes were op'd again,
Nor frankincense, nor laurel bough, nor cake,
Nor victim, nor one other thing one mortal
Offers to us—the gods.
Carion.   Nor will for ever:
Such wretched care ye took of us heretofore.
Hermes. Well: for the rest I'm somewhat less concern'd,
But I myself am perishing—am pounded.
Carion. Shrewd fellow![41]
Hermes.   Up till now, among the tapstresses,
I far'd not ill o' mornings; winecake—honey—
Dried figs—and all that's meet for Hermes' palate:
But now, cross-legg'd, I mope for grief and hunger.
Carion. And serves ye right, too—many a time and oft,
For all their gifts—you left them in the lurch.
Hermes. O me! the cake—
The monthly cheese-cake[42] kneaded once for me!
Carion.   Thou crav'st the lost and callest out in vain.[43]
Hermes. And O the ham—that I was wont devour!
Carion. Ham! Ply your ham in dancing on a bottle.[44]
Hermes. The tripes—the trolly-bags—I guzzled hot!
Carion. The tripes—the gripes!—I guess the tripes torment
    thee.
Hermes. And O the jolly jorum—half and half!
Carion. Come, take a swig of this, and off with thee.
Hermes. Ah! wouldst thou do thy friend a little favour!
Carion. Well: if it lie within my power—command me.
Hermes. Wouldst thou but fetch a well-fir'd loaf or two—
And add a whacking lump of that same meat
You're offering up within!—

[460]

Carion. Impossible!
No fetching forth allow'd.

Hermes. Yet when your lord's stray articles you pilfer'd,
I always help'd to hide, and sav'd your bacon.

Carion. Just on condition you should share—you thief!
You never miss'd your cake on such occasions.

Hermes. Nor *you* to gobble it down before I touch'd it.

Carion. So: for no equal share of stripes had you,
When master caught me in a peccadillo.

Hermes. Think not of past offence, now Phyle's taken:[45]
But O—by all the gods—for an inmate take me.

Carion. Why, wilt thou leave the gods, and quarter here?

Hermes. You're better off, I trow.

Carion. What then?
Desert! Is that a handsome trick to play them?

Hermes. 'Tis still one's country, where one prospers well.[46]

Carion. And say we took thee in—how couldst thou serve us?

Hermes. Beside your door establish me as TURNKEY.[47]

Carion. Turnkey! we want no *turns* of thine, I promise thee.

Hermes. As TRADER, then.

Carion. Nay, we are rich, and so
What need have we to keep a pedlar-Hermes.

Hermes. DECEIVER, then.

Carion. Deceiver? Cheat? Ne'er dream on't—
No room for cheating now, but honest practice.

Hermes. Well, then, as GUIDE.

Carion. Our god's regain'd his twinklers,
So we have business for a guide no longer.

Hermes. I have it—REVEL-MASTER let me be then—
What canst thou say to that?
For sure with Plutus' pomp it best agrees
To hold high games of music and gymnastics.

Carion. What luck to have good store of *aliases!*
See now—this knave will earn his bite and sup.
Ay, ay—'tis not for nought our judging varlets
Would fain be written down with many letters.[48]

Hermes. On these terms, then, I've leave to enter?

Carion. Yes:
And hark ye, sirrah, find the cistern out,

[461]

And wash me, with thy proper hands, these guts;
So shalt thou straightway figure off as SCULLION.

[*Exit* HERMES. *Enter* PRIEST OF JOVE.

 Priest. Who'll tell me where is Chremylus?
 Chremylus (*entering*).   **Good fellow,**
What is the matter?
 Priest.   What, but ruination?
For since your Plutus 'gan to see, I die
Of downright famine—not a crumb to eat—
I—the arch-priest of GUARDIAN JOVE.
 Chremylus.   Ye Powers!
What *can* the cause be?
 Priest.   Not a sacrifice
Comes our way any longer.
 Chremylus.   Wherefore so?
 Priest. 'Cause they're all rich. And yet, in good old times,
When they had nought—some home-returning merchant
Would bring thanks-offering for safety; or
Some one had bilk'd the law—or splendid rites
Were held by some magnifico, and I
The priest was sure to be invited: but
No victims now—not one—no visitors—
Except the thousands that come there to—ease them.
 Chremylus. And hast not lawful share of their—oblations?
 Priest. So to this Jove—this Guardian—this Preserver—
I think to bid good by, and mess with you.
 Chremylus. Cheer up, man; all shall yet go well with thee.
Preserving Jove is *here*[49]—alive and kicking—
Come of his own accord.
 Priest.   O glorious news!
 Chremylus. Ay! And we soon shall set—stop but an instant—
Our Plutus, where of yore he sate in state,
On sleepless watch behind Minerva's temple.—[50]
Lights from within there!—Take the torches, friend,
And marshal on the god.
 Priest.   No question of it:—
Thus must I do.
 Chremylus.   And some one call Plutus.

[*The Procession comes out from the House.*

 Old Woman (*coming out*). And what of me?

Chremylus. Look here, these pots,[51]
    with which
We consecrate the god, mount on thy noddle,
And bear them gravely: flower'd petticoat
Thou of thyself hast don'd.
    Old Woman. But– what I came for?
    Chremylus. Nay, thou shalt have thy will—
This evening the young fellow shall be with thee.
    Old Woman. Well, then—O Lud!—if you will pledge his
      coming—
I'll bear your pots.
    Carion. Were never pots before
In such a case:—in *those* the scum's a-top,
In *these* a scum—a very scum's at bottom!
    Chorus. Delay, delay no longer, then: the jolly pomp's
      before us—
Make way, make way—and form again, to follow them in
      Chorus!

                        [*Exeunt Omnes.*

BIBLIOGRAPHY

A Brief List of Useful Books

(The list includes a number of prose translations; other books listed, as Allen's, contain bibliographies.)

AESCHYLUS.—With an English Translation by Herbert Weir Smyth. 2 vols. New York, G. P. Putnam's Sons, 1922 (Loeb Classical Library)

AESCHYLUS.—*Plays*, translated by Walter Headlam and C. E. S. Headlam. London, George Bell and Sons, 1909 (Bohn's Classical Library)

ALLEN, JAMES TURNEY.—*The Stage Antiquities of the Greeks and Romans and Their Influence.* New York, Longmans, Green and Company, 1927 (*Our Debt to Greece and Rome*, No. 28)

ARISTOPHANES.—With the English Translation of Benjamin Bickley Rogers. 3 vols. New York, G. P. Putnam's Sons, 1924 (Loeb Classical Library)

ARISTOTLE.—*On the Art of Poetry;* a Revised Text, with Critical Introduction, Translation, and Commentary, by Ingram Bywater. Oxford, At The Clarendon Press, 1909

ARISTOTLE.—*On the Art of Poetry;* an Amplified Version . . . for Students of English, by Lane Cooper. Boston, 1913; New York, Harcourt, Brace and Company

BIEBER, MARGARETE.—*Die Denkmaler zum Theaterwesen im Altertum.* Berlin, De Gruyter, 1920 (with 142 illustrations in the text, and 109 tabular illustrations)

COOPER, LANE.—*An Aristotelian Theory of Comedy* (etc.). New York, Harcourt, Brace and Company, 1922

CROISET, ALFRED AND MAURICE.—*An Abridged History of Greek Literature,* translated by George F. Heffelbower. New York, The Macmillan Company, 1904

CROISET, ALFRED AND MAURICE.—*Histoire de la Littérature Grecque.* Vol. 3 by Maurice Croiset. Paris, Fontemoing, 1914

EURIPIDES.—*The Plays* . . . translated into English Prose . . . by Edward P. Coleridge. 2 vols. London, George Bell and Sons, 1891 (Bohn's Classical Library)

FLICKINGER, ROY C.—*The Greek Theater and Its Drama.* Chicago, University of Chicago Press, 1926

HAIGH, A. E.—*The Attic Theatre.* Third edition . . . by A. W. Pickard-Cambridge. Oxford, At The Clarendon Press, 1907

HAIGH, A. E.—*The Tragic Drama of the Greeks.* Oxford, At The Clarendon Press, 1896

MENANDER.—*The Principal Fragments,* with an English Translation by Francis G. Allison. New York, G. P. Putnam's Sons, 1921 (Loeb Classical Library)

PICKARD-CAMBRIDGE, A. W.—*Dithyramb, Tragedy, and Comedy.* Oxford, At The Clarendon Press, 1927

SOPHOCLES.—*The Ichneutae* ('Trackers'), with . . . a Translation into English (etc.) by Richard Johnson Walker. London, Burns and Oates, 1919

SOPHOCLES.—*The Tragedies,* translated into English Prose by Sir Richard C. Jebb. Cambridge, At The University Press, 1904 (the translations are taken from Jebb's edition of Sophocles; this also should be consulted)

NOTES

The Notes to the Plays translated by Gilbert Murray have been selected and abridged from the translator's original notes by Professor H. B. Densmore of the University of Washington.

OEDIPUS, KING OF THEBES

1. *Dry Ash of Ismênus.* Divination by burnt offerings was practised at an altar of Apollo by the river Ismênus in Thebes.

2. *Who were they?* This momentary doubt of Oedipus, who of course regarded himself as the son of Polybus, King of Corinth, is explained later.

3. *Thebes is my country.* It must be remembered that to the Chorus Creon is a real Theban, Oedipus a stranger from Corinth.

4. *Crossing of three ways.* Cross roads always had dark associations. This particular spot was well known to tradition and is still pointed out.

ANTIGONE

1. *The burden of our race.* The woes that fell upon the royal house of Thebes on account of the curse that Pelops had laid upon Laïus, the father of Oedipus. Hence Oedipus unwittingly killed his father and married his mother, Jocasta.

2. *The prince.* Creon, Jocasta's brother, who had become king of Thebes on the death of the sons of Oedipus.

3. *Two brothers.* Eteocles and Polynices, the two sons of Oedipus, who slew each other, when the Argive host that came to restore Polynices made its unsuccessful assault upon the seven gates of Thebes.

4. *The Serpent.* This monster was killed by Cadmus, the founder of Thebes, and the warriors that sprung from its teeth were the ancestors of the Thebans. So it represents the Theban army.

5. *Thrice-poured.* Libations of milk, wine and honey.

6. *Labdacid race.* The race of Labdacus, the father of Laïus. What the Chorus means is that there is no cessation from woes to the race of Labdacus; on each generation are they accumulated.

7. *That stranger.* Niobe: her children were killed by Apollo and Artemis, and she was turned into stone. On Mount Sipylus near Smyrna was a rock, which from a distance looked like a woman weeping, and was supposed by the Greeks to be the stone image into which Niobe was transformed.

8. *A bride ill-starred.* Polynices married the daughter of Adrastus, king of Argos, who therefore consented to lead an Argive army against Thebes.

9. *Persephone.* Proserpine, wife of Hades.

10. *Danaë.* The mother of Perseus, imprisoned in a brazen tower because it had been foretold that she would have a son who would kill her father.

11. *The dark rock-portals.* The small rocky islands which divide the Bosporus from the Euxine Sea. They were called Cyaneae (dark blue) on account of their colour, and are famous in the story of the Argo.

12. *That fierce stepdame.* Eidothea, who became the wife of Phineus after he had put away Cleopatra. She put out with a shuttle the eyes of

the two sons of Phineus, who was himself punished by the Gods with blindness.

13. *She.* Cleopatra, whose mother Oreithyia was daughter of Erechtheus. Cleopatra's father was Boreas, the North-wind.

14. *That hear and hear me not.* Present and absent.

15. *Semele.* The mother of Bacchus was the daughter of Cadmus, the founder of Thebes.

16. *Thyiad troop.* The Thyiades were female votaries of Bacchus, his attendant nymphs.

17. *Amphion.* Niobe's husband, who, with his brother Zethus, built the Theban wall.

18. *Hecate.* Goddess of the lower world, sometimes identified with Artemis: she haunted the places where roads meet, and so is sometimes called Trioditis. She is invoked with Pluto as representing the Deities of the nether world.

19. *Megareus.* This was a son of Creon, who had already perished.

AGAMEMNON

The chief characters in this and in the two following plays belong to one family, as is shown by the two genealogies:—

I.

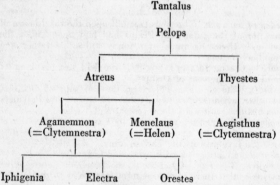

(Asso, a sister of Agamemnon, name variously given, married Strophios, and was the mother of Pylades.)

II.

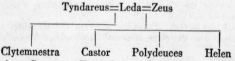

1. *Winds from Strymon.* From the great river gorge of Thrace, NNE.

2. *Artemis.* Her name was terrible, because of its suggestion. She demanded the sacrifice of Agamemnon's Daughter, Iphigenia. (See Euripides' two plays, *Iphigenia in Tauris* and *Iphigenia in Aulis.*)

3. *This Heart of Argos, this frail Tower.* Themselves.

4. This break in the action, covering a space of several days, was first pointed out by Dr. Walter Headlam.

5. *Pythian Lord.* Apollo is often a sinister figure in tragedy. Here it is a shock to the Herald to come suddenly on the god who was the chief enemy of the Greeks at Troy.

6. *"One there was of old."* Asklepios, the physician, restored Hippoly-tus to life, and Zeus blasted him for so oversetting the laws of nature.

7. *Alcmena's son.* Heracles was made a slave to Omphale, Queen of Lydia.

8. *That wingèd voice.* Procne (or Philoméla) was an Attic princess who, in fury against her Thracian husband, Têreus, killed their child Itys, or Itylus, and was changed into a nightingale, to weep for him for ever.

9. *Aegisthus.* At last the name is mentioned which has been in the mind of every one!—Chryseïs was a prisoner of war, daughter of Chryses, priest of Apollo. Agamemnon was made to surrender her to her father, and from this arose his quarrel with Achilles, which is the subject of the Iliad.

10. *Daemon.* The Genius or guardian spirit of the house has in this House become a Wrath, an 'Alastor' or 'Driver Astray'.

11. *Pleisthenes.* He may be identical with Pelops. See genealogy.

THE CHOËPHOROE

1. *Inachos.* The river of Argos. So Achilles on reaching manhood cut off his long hair as a gift to the River Spercheios.

2. *The House hath healing.* The House itself can cure bloodshed by bloodshed, sin by vengeance.

3. *What power the Daemon hath which guardeth thee.* The word Daemon has no connotation of evil in classical Greek.

4. *One Below.* Agamemnon.

5. *Chorus.* The sense of this chorus is often difficult and the text apparently corrupt, especially the end. "There are many terrible things, but none so terrible as a woman's passion; for instance, Althaea, daughter of Thestios, who slew her son Meleager; or Skylla of Megara who betrayed her father Nisos; or the Lemnian women, who slew their husbands; and, after all have we not an example here in Clytemnestra?"

6. Again the sense is difficult and the text extremely uncertain. The chorus pray in the name of their innocence and Agamemnon's long service to Zeus for pity; to the Gods of the Possessions of the House (Latin "penates," sometimes grouped together as Zeus Ktêsios) to help in the cleansing and rebuilding of the House; to Apollo of the Cavern of Delphi, the God of Light, to help the House to light out of darkness; to Hermes, the God of craft and secrecy, to help in a plot for the right. The battle will be a battle of liberation from tyrants.

7. Orestes should think of his duty to his father and forget all else. As Perseus when killing the Gorgon turned his eyes away lest her face should freeze him to stone, so let Orestes, when he meets his mother, veil his eyes and smite.

THE EUMENIDES

1. The scene is conceived as different in different parts of the play, but probably no actual change was made. A stage with the usual "House" background, representing a Temple or Castle, with a round orchestra (dancing floor) on a lower level in front, will suit all the needs of the action. A statue of Athena in place of the Omphalos Altar will turn the "House" from the Temple of Apollo at Delphi to that of Athena in

Athens. A semi-circle of seats, or something similar, will symbolize the Areopagus.

2. Literally: "Loxias is the forthshower (*prophêtês*) of Zeus the Father": Loxias is the special title of Phoebus Apollo as prophet: the line is important for the understanding of the play.

3. The City of Pallas is Athens, her Rock the Acropolis.

4. *Hermes.* He is not present, but is invoked as the regular Guide of the Wanderer. "Zeus pitieth," etc.: this is the essential doctrine of the play.

5. *The Ghost.* The Ghost is a Dream, and vanishes as the Furies wake.

6. Apollo speaks here, not as "forthshower of Zeus," but in his own person as a Hellenic God, hating this lust for punishment which the Furies show.

7. Athena comes from Sigeum in the neighbourhood of Troy, which in the time of Aeschylus had long been part of the Athenian Empire. Tradition said that it had been given by the Greek army to the "Sons of Theseus" (the Athenians) for their services in the Trojan War.

8. The Trial Scene, though curious, is perhaps below the level of the rest of the play. The interest lies in the foundation of the Court of the Areopagus, as a tribunal superseding the blood-feud, the ordeal by oath, and all the rigid and unreasoning practices of primitive justice, by a justice which can understand and therefore sympathize.

9. An Argive alliance was traditional in Athens.

10. *Your secret chambers.* Amid the limestone rocks of the Areopagus was a chasm through which rose a spring of dark water. It was held to be a way to the Underworld. It also led to the seat of these goddesses, called generally Semnai (Venerable) or Eumenides (Kindly Ones) because their real name, Erinyes, was rather too awful for common use.

ELECTRA

For the chief characters in this play and in the *Iphigenia in Tauris* see the genealogical tables in the notes to the *Agamemnon*.

1. *Son of his father's foe.* Both foe and brother. Atreus and Thyestes became enemies after the theft of the Golden Lamb.

2. *Thy brethren even now.* Castor and Polydeuces, who were received into the stars after their death.

3. *God's horsemen, stars without a stain.* Castor and Polydeuces were sons of Zeus and Leda, brothers of Helen, and half-brothers of Clytemnestra, whose father was the mortal Tyndareus. They lived as knights without reproach, and afterwards became stars and demigods.

4. *Cast his child away.* The Greek fleet assembled for Troy was held by contrary winds at Aulis, in the Straits of Euboea, and the whole expedition was in danger of breaking up. The prophets demanded a human sacrifice, and Agamemnon gave his own daughter, Iphigenia. He induced Clytemnestra to send her to him, by the pretext that Achilles had asked for her in marriage.

5. *The giants' cloud-capt ring.* The great walls of Mycenae, built by the Cyclôpes.

6. *Scourge thee as a burning wheel.* At certain feasts a big wheel soaked in some inflammable resin or tar was set fire to and rolled down a mountain.

7. *Kêres.* The death-spirits that flutter over our heads, as Homer says, "innumerable, whom no man can fly nor hide from."

NOTES

IPHIGENIA IN TAURIS

1. Oenomaüs, King of Elis, offered his daughter and his kingdom to any man who should beat him in a chariot race; those who failed he slew. Pelops challenged him and won the race through a trick of his servant, Myrtilus, who treacherously took the linchpins out of Oenomaüs' chariot. Oenomaüs was thrown out and killed; Pelops took the kingdom, but in remorse or indignation threw Myrtilus into the sea.

2. The land of Tauris is conceived as being beyond the Symplêgades, or, as here, as being the country of the Symplêgades.

3. *The dark and wheeling coursers.* Those of Pelops. The cry of one betrayed: Myrtilus, when he was thrown into the sea.

4. *Dark of the sea.* The Dark-Blue of the Symplêgades is meant. Sometimes it is only the *Argo* that has ever passed through them; here it is only Io, daughter of Inachus, loved by Zeus and hunted by the gadfly, then by the usurping Pelias.

5. *Bird of the sea rocks.* A wonderful lyric, as spoken by these exiles waiting on the shore. In their craving for home the island of Delos becomes the symbol for all that is Greek. Delos, the birthplace of Apollo and of a kinder Artemis than that which they now serve, was the meeting-place of all the Ionians. The palm-tree, the laurel, the olive, and the Orbed Lake of Delos were all celebrated in ritual poetry. The singing Swan is not a myth; it is a migratory swan, with a bell-like cry, which comes in the winter down from South Russia to Greece.

6. *There is One who rules the sea.* Poseidon, the sea god, was traditionally a friend of Troy.

MEDEA

1. *To Colchis through the blue Symplêgades.* The Symplêgades ("Clashing") or Kuaneai ("Dark blue") were two rocks in the sea which used to clash together and crush anything that was between them. They stood above the north end of the Bosphorus and formed the Gate to the Axeinos Pontos, or "Stranger-less Sea," where all Greeks were murdered. At the farthest eastern end of that sea was the land of Colchis.

2. *Pêlion.* The great mountain in Thessaly. Iôlcos, a little kingdom between Pêlion and the sea, ruled originally by Aeson, Jason's father, then by the usurping Pëlias.

3. *Wed.* Medea was not legally married to Jason, and could not be, though in common parlance he is sometimes called her husband. Inter-marriage between the subjects of two separate states was not possible in antiquity without a special treaty. And naturally there was no such treaty with Colchis.

4. *Wise beyond men's wont.* Medea was a "wise woman" which in her time meant much the same as a witch or enchantress. She did really know more than other women; but most of this extra knowledge consisted —or was supposed to consist—either in lore of poisons and charms, or in useless learning and speculation.

5. *Bulls of Fiery breath.* Among the tasks set him by Aiêtês, Jason had to yoke two fire-breathing bulls, and plough with them a certain Field of Ares, sow the field with dragon's teeth, and reap a harvest of earth-born or giant warriors which sprang from the seed. When all this was done, there remained the ancient serpent coiled round the tree where the Golden Fleece was hanging.

6. *The first friends who sheltered me.* The kindred of Pëlias.

7. *Dead self.* The reflection in the glass, often regarded as ominous or uncanny in some way.

8. *The cry turned strangely to its opposite.* The notion was that an evil spirit could be scared away by loud cheerful shouts—*ololugae.* But while this old woman is making an ololugê, she sees that the trouble is graver than she thought, and the cheerful cry turns into a wail.

9. *A mother slew her babes in days of yore.* Ino, wife of Athamas, King of Thebes, nursed the infant Dionysus. For this Hera punished her with madness.

10. *The hands of thine old Argo.* Jason, left friendless and avoided by his kind, went back to live with his old ship, now rotting on the shore. While he was sleeping under it, a beam of wood fell upon him and broke his head.

THE FROGS

1. *Andromeda.* A play of Euripides.

2. *Molon.* Remarkable for his bulk and stature.

3. A ridicule of the circuitous preambles to confidential communications in tragedy.

4. Quotation from Euripides.

5. *Iophon.* A tragic poet, the son of Sophocles, and supposed to have been assisted by him in the composition of his tragedies.

6. *Agathon.* A tragic poet, a young man of wealth and of refined habits, who had lately died at the Court of Archelaus, whither he had retired from Athens.

7. *Xenocles.* One of the theatric family of Carcinus, the constant butts of Aristophanes' humour.

8. *Pythangelus.* An obscure writer of tragedies.

9. A confused, vulgarized recollection of Euripides. The 1st citation is from Aeschylus, the 2nd from Sophocles, the 3rd from Euripides.

10. *Cerberus.* Hercules was employed by Eurystheus to drag us the three-headed dog, Cerberus from the gates of Hell.

11. *Race of the Torch.* A sacred race in honour of Minerva, Vulcan, and Prometheus. The runners carried a lighted torch.

12. *Twopence.* The salary of the poorer citizens, who sat as jurymen, and who were in fact the arbiters of the lives and fortunes of their subjects and fellow-citizens.

13. *The Initiated.* Those who had been initiated in the mysteries of Ceres and Bacchus.

14. *Naval victory.* The victory of Arginusae, where the slaves who were enlisted fought for the first time.

15. *Choral Quiristers of the Marsh.* The theatre of Bacchus in the marsh. Anti-Lyrical caricature.

16. *The Weird Hag.* Empusa, a fabulous hag, known only in the mythology of Athenian nursery.

17. *Diagoras.* Ironical allusion to Diagoras, a dithyrambic poet, and consequently a composer of hymns in praise of Bacchus; banished from Athens, and proscribed on a charge of Atheism.

18. *Cratinus.* Doubly a votary of Bacchus, as a dramatic poet, and a hard drinker.

19. *Theramenes.* The political versatility of Theramenes is noticed in a subsequent passage, in the altercation between Aeschylus and Euripides. The naval allusion may be supposed to refer to his conduct towards his colleagues in command, after the battle of Arginusae.

20. *Buskins.* Peculiar to Bacchus; the woman mistaking him for Hercules considers them as an attempt at disguise.

21. *Archedemus.* Seems to have been a meddling foreigner; his want of claim to the character of citizen is noticed by Aristophanes and in a fragment of Eupolis.

22. *Valy.* Value, the vulgar pronunciation is given.

23. *Cleophon.* One of the chief demagogues in the then ruined and degraded democracy. He was put to death in a popular tumult.

24. Parody from a tragic chorus predicting the downfall of some reigning family. Cleigenes, one of the obscure demagogues of the time, not mentioned by the Scholiast.

25. *A seat.* A seat at the public table in the Prytaneum was the reward of superior merit and services in Athens.

26. *Cleidemides.* The favourite actor of Sophocles.

27. *Thy mysteries.* The first idea of tragedy was derived from the scenic exhibitions in the mysteries of *Ceres,* where they formed a part of the initiatory rites.

28. *Phrynichus.* The earliest tragic poet whose dramas were in any degree esteemed among the ancients.

29. *Eruxis.* Eminent for ugliness.

30. From Aeschylus' tragedy of *The Myrmidons,* which opened with the death of Patroclus and the defeat of the Greeks.

31. *Pantacles.* Of Pantacles nothing is known but that he was laughed at for his awkwardness by the comic poets; probably an *absent man,* not a usual character among the Athenians.

32. *Despatch'd you below.* Euripides' death is said to have been hastened by his wife's misconduct.

33. *Belerophon's sake.* In a tragedy of Euripides, now lost, Sthenoboea poisons herself for love of Bellerophon.

34. *Three times we call.* The custom at funerals of invoking the dead by name three times.

35. *Lesbian Muse.* The Lesbian women were of very bad fame.

36. *Monodies.* Verses sung by a single actor unaccompanied by the chorus. The burlesque turns upon the faults of Euripides' style, the false sublime—the vulgar pathetic; and impertinent supplications for divine assistance.

37. The first line of the *Medea* still existing.

38. From the *Philoctetes,* now lost.

39. From the *Antigone,* now lost.

40. From the *Niobe,* now lost.

41. *Twice a deuce ace.* That is, Euripides (for Achilles) has failed twice.

42. From the *Meleager,* now lost.

43. From a play called *Glaucus Potnicus.*

44. Euripides was a collector of books. Cephisophon was the chief actor in Euripides' tragedies, and partly, it was said, the author of some of them.

45. From a verse of one of the tragedies of Ion of Chios.

46. A line in the *Hippolytus* which had given great offence. Here and in what follows, Bacchus pays Euripides in his own philosophic coin vulgarized after his own (Bacchus') fashion.

PLUTUS, THE GOD OF RICHES

1. *The laurel.* The insignia of a sacro-sanct messenger returning from the oracle.

2. *Patrocles.* A rich niggard who adopted *Spartan* manners.

3. *Timotheus' tower.* The *rich* Timotheus had built himself a splendid castle. But Carion is interrupted when about to say so.

4. *Little steak of mine.* A *portion* brought from the sacrifice at Delphi.

5. *Thy lot.* The judges, or jurymen (*dicasts*), at Athens, were distributed among the several courts by *lot*, and received a staff as the *token* of their office.

6. *Cyclop's-step.* So was named a *dance* which set forth the love of Polyphemus for the sea-nymph Galatea. Our "derry, hey down derry," is substituted for the similar "*threttanello*" of the original.

7. *Jolly flock.* When Carion assumes the Cyclops, he treats the chorus as the *flock* of Polyphemus.

8. *A la* Ulysses.

9. Carion means:—"I will turn you into swine as the *Corinthian* Circe (*i. e.* the courtesan Lais) did Philonides (mentioned before) and his cater cousins." The allusion to the Homeric Circe is obvious.

10. *As wise Ulysses did.* To Melancthius. Od. xxii. 175.

11. *Aristyllus.* "This Aristyllus was a poet, who added to many other vices that of obscenity; for which reason Aristophanes gives him here this nasty entertainment. When he spoke, he screwed up his mouth, either through affectation, or natural impediment, and snorted out his words through his nose: so that, says Erasmus, he imitated the sound of a pig."—Fielding.

12. *The Bemo.* Here *the tribunal of justice.*

13. *Drawn by Pamphilus.* A picture of Alcmena and the children of Hercules as *supplicants.*

14. *Barathrum.* The *execution pit* of Athens.

15. *Bagnio fires.* A common resort of the poor in cold weather. See Defoe's *Memoirs of Colonel Jack* for a similar picture of a beggar's life in London in the olden times.

16. *That confound* Dionysius the Tyrant *with* Thrasybulus the Patriot.

17. Like an unfledged bird—unable to fly.

18. *A monthly feast.* Offered to her statues at the places where three ways met:—but soon carried off by the poor.

19. A line made up of words from Euripides.—Argos was poor.

20. *Pauson.* A very poor painter.

21. *Theseus' days.* On the eighth of each month the poor were entertained in honour of Theseus, but at small cost, and chiefly on *spoon meat.*

22. *From foot to head.* An ominous phraseology, which alarms the old lady's superstition, and is meant by Carion to do so.

23. *Madam Jaso.* Jaso and Panacea (*Doctoress* and *Cure-all*), daughters of Aesculapius. Doubtless they had fair representatives in the temple.

24. *Ordure-taster. More Medicorum.*

25. *She tries to catch him tripping.* But Carion is too sharp for her.

26. *Slave-fashion.* As a *new purchased slave* was greeted on coming to his master's house.

27. *Crush one's shins.* As flatterers were wont to do to the rich; rubbing their shin bones as the Squire in "Count Fathom" has *his back scratched.*

NOTES

28. A common trick of poets in those days.
29. *To the god.* Chremylus, a wag in his way, plays on the Good Man's repetitions of this phrase.
30. *Dash'd.* Like water dashed with strong wine.
31. *Can seem so on occasions.* Merchants were exempted from military service.
32. *The benzoin of Battus.* Battus founded Cyrene, famous for its benzoin.
33. *Drinking-ticket.* Another allusion to the distribution of *dicasts* by lot.
34. A proverbial expression to denote reverses of fortune; drawn from the fate of Miletus.
35. *To carry thee out?* For *burial,* to wit.
36. *O thou sea-Neptune. Referential swearing*: Neptune was an *ancient* deity.
37. *A wool-clad olive-branch.* The Athenians used to hang a branch of this kind above their doors, to keep off famine and pestilence. It hung a year before it was renewed, and was, therefore, sufficiently dry and combustible by the end of the twelvemonth.
38. *How many—teeth hast thou?* Instead of—*"How many nuts have I? —odd or even?"*
39. *Hermes knocks and hides.* To make it appear that the door had rattled of itself, at the approach of his godship.
40. The victim's tongue was devoted to Hermes. But Carion uses an ambiguous phrase, by way of threat.
41. To care only for himself.
42. *Monthly cheese-cake.* On the 4th day of each month.
43. The announcement from heaven to Hercules, when he called for his lost Hylas.
44. A well-oiled *skin bottle.* It was one of their bacchanal games to jump, barefooted, on such a bottle; and he who kept his footing, won the prize.
45. As Thrasybulus proclaimed an amnesty after the re-establishment of the republic, which followed his seizure of Phyle. Hence the proverb.
46. Quoted probably from Euripides.
47. The poet plays upon the various attributes of Hermes.
48. Another hit at the *allotment* of dicasts.
49. In the person of Plutus.
50. *Minerva's temple.* Where the public treasury was.
51. Pots of pulse, &c.